Authority, Authorship and Aristocratic Identity
in Seventeenth-Century England

Rulers & Elites

Comparative Studies in Governance

Series Editor

Jeroen Duindam (*Leiden University*)

Editorial Board

VOLUME 9

The titles published in this series are listed at *brill.com/rule*

Authority, Authorship and Aristocratic Identity in Seventeenth-Century England

William Cavendish, 1st Duke of Newcastle, and his Political, Social and Cultural Connections

Edited by

Peter Edwards and Elspeth Graham

BRILL

LEIDEN | BOSTON

Cover illustration: William Cavendish, 1st Duke of Newcastle, by Daniel Mytens the Younger, c. 1624. Oil on Canvas.

Library of Congress Cataloging-in-Publication Data

Names: Edwards, Peter (Peter Roger), editor. | Graham, Elspeth, 1953– editor.
Title: Authority, authorship and aristocratic identity in seventeenth-century
    England : William Cavendish, 1st Duke of Newcastle, and his political,
    social and cultural connections / edited by Peter Edwards and Elspeth Graham.
Description: Leiden ; Boston : Brill, 2016. | Series: Rulers & elites:
    comparative studies in governance, ISSN 2211-4610 ; volume 9 | Papers
    based on those presented at a conference on the life and career of William
    Cavendish, 1st Duke of Newcastle, held at Bolsover Castle in Derbyshire on
    14–15 April, 2012. | Includes bibliographical references and index.
Identifiers: LCCN 2016034680 (print) | LCCN 2016035032 (ebook) | ISBN
    9789004326200 (hardback : alk. paper) | ISBN 9789004326217 (E-book)
Subjects: LCSH: Newcastle, William Cavendish, Duke of, 1592–1676—Congresses.
    | Authors, English—17th century—Biography—Congresses. |
    Nobility—England—History—17th century—Biography—Congresses. |
    Aristocracy (Social class)—England—History—17th
    century—Biography—Congresses. | Power (Social
    sciences)—England—History—17th century—Congresses.
Classification: LCC PR3605.N4 Z55 2016 (print) | LCC PR3605.N4 (ebook) | DDC
    941.06/2092—dc23
LC record available at https://lccn.loc.gov/2016034680

Typeface for the Latin, Greek, and Cyrillic scripts: "Brill". See and download: brill.com/brill-typeface.

ISSN 2211-4610
ISBN 978-90-04-32620-0 (hardback)
ISBN 978-90-04-32621-7 (e-book)

Printed by Printforce, the Netherlands

Contents

Acknowledgements   IX
Notes on the Editors   X
List of Illustrations   XI
List of Abbreviations   XIV
Notes on the Contributors   XV

Introduction: Authority, Authorship and Aristocratic Identity in
Seventeenth Century England: William Cavendish, 1st Duke of
Newcastle, and his Political, Social and Cultural Connections   1
   Peter Edwards and Elspeth Graham

PART I
Aristocratic Identity

1   Setting the Scenes: The Pre-Civil War Building Works of William
   Cavendish in Context   41
    Adrian Woodhouse

2   Whimsy and Medieval Romance in the Life and Writing of
   William Cavendish   60
    James Fitzmaurice

3   'An After-Game of Reputation': Systems of Representation, William
   Cavendish and the Battle of Marston Moor   83
    Elspeth Graham

4   The Concealed Fancies and Cavendish Identity   111
    Lisa Hopkins

5   Flogging a Dead Horse?: Margaret Cavendish and the Pursuit
   of Authority   129
    Alison Findlay

PART 2
Politics and Authority

6   Courtly Rivalry: The Context for William Cavendish's
       Equestrian Buildings   151
       Malcolm Airs

7   William Cavendish, Galileo, Hobbes and the
       Mechanical Philosophy   173
       Timothy Raylor

8   The Role of Honour in the Life of William Cavendish and the
       Philosophy of Thomas Hobbes   196
       Lisa T. Sarasohn

9   William Cavendish as a Military Commander   216
       Andrew Hopper

10   The Double Edged Sword: William Cavendish's Political
       Career 1644–1660   237
       Madeline Dewhurst

PART 3
Horsemanship, Authority and Identity

11   'The Epitome of Horsemanship': William Cavendish's Method
       'Anatomized'   259
       Elaine Walker

12   Embodying *'Bonne Homme à Cheval'*: William Cavendish and the
       Politics of the Centaur   281
       Monica Mattfeld

13   'Manèging' to Survive: Horsemanship and the Rehabilitation of the
       Exiled William Cavendish, Marquis of Newcastle   300
       Peter Edwards

14   William Cavendish: Riding School and Race Track   317
      Richard Nash

15   William Cavendish's Horsemanship Treatises and
      Cultural Capital   331
      Karen Raber

      Index   353

Acknowledgements

This collection developed, in part, out of a conference on the life and career of William Cavendish, 1st Duke of Newcastle, held at Bolsover Castle in Derbyshire on 14–15 April 2012. We should like to thank English Heritage for their collaboration in the event, and for their generous help and hospitality. We are also grateful to Liverpool John Moores University for their contribution to the funding of the conference. Phillip Rothwell filmed and photographed the event and we are enormously grateful for all of his work in producing images and for his support. Indiana University's Office of International Programs and College of Arts and Humanities also provided funding which helped defray research and travel costs.

The editors of, and contributors to, this volume are also extremely grateful to the staff at a number of record offices and libraries, particularly those in the Department of Manuscripts and Special Collections at the University of Nottingham; at Nottinghamshire Archives Office; and in the Manuscript Room and the Reproductions Department of the British Library, who deserve special mention for the efficient way they handled requests for documents and copies. We would also like to acknowledge the help with rare books and manuscripts given by Amanda Bernstein and Jacky Hodgson in the University of Sheffield Special Collections Department.

We are especially grateful to Elaine Walker, one of the contributors to this volume, for making available her copyrighted images of all the plates published in *La Méthode Nouvelle et Invention Extraordinaire de Dresser les Chevaux*, the 1658 version of William Cavendish's manual on horsemanship. The Department of Manuscripts and Special Collections at the University of Nottingham kindly allowed us to publish images in their possession, as did Alexandra Sitwell and Mike Thrift. Warsop Parish Council kindly gave us permission to photograph and reproduce an image of the memorial panel to John Rolleston in St Peter and St Paul parish church, Church Warsop.

Among the individuals who commented on an essay, provided information or helped its production in other ways were Timothy Ashplant, Andrew Hiscock, Lisa Jardine, Donna Landry, Stephen May, Emma Rees, Tom Rutter, Matt Steggle, Crosby Stevens, Colin Teevan and Tom Willard, as well as members of the Margaret Cavendish Society and scholars who attended the early modern conference on War Reporting and Reportage at Bangor in 2012. We are grateful to them all.

Notes on the Editors

Peter Edwards

is Professor Emeritus in Early Modern Social and Economic History at the University of Roehampton and has written extensively on the multi-functional role of horses in pre-modern society. His publications include *The horse trade of Tudor and Stuart England* (Cambridge: 1988/reprinted 2004); *Horse and man in early modern England* (London: 2007) and with Elspeth Graham (eds.) *The horse as cultural icon: the real and the symbolic horse in the early modern world* (Leiden: 2011). He is currently writing a book on William Cavendish, 1st. Earl of Devonshire and his horses. Essays include "Nature bridled: the treatment and training of horses in early modern England", in Brantz D. (ed.), *Beastly Natures* (Charlottesville: 2010); "Image and reality: human perceptions of horses in early modern England", in Edwards & Graham, *The horse as cultural icon*; "Horses and élite identity in early modern England: the case of Sir Richard Newdigate II of Arbury Hall (Warwickshire)", in Cuneo P. (ed.), *Animals and early modern identity* (Farnham, 2014); "The tale of a horse: the Levinz Colt 1721–1729", in Cockram S. & Wells A., (eds.), *Interspecies interactions: human and animal in the early modern world* (London, forthcoming) and "Visiting London for business and pleasure in the years 1599–1623: on the road with William Cavendish, 1st Earl of Devonshire", in Stobart J. (ed.), *Travel and the British country house: cultures, critiques and consumption in the long eighteenth century* (Manchester, forthcoming).

Elspeth Graham

is Professor of Early-Modern Literature at Liverpool John Moores University. She has written on early-modern women's writing, nonconformist writing and animal/human relationships. With Peter Edwards, she co-edited *The Horse as Cultural Icon: The Real and the Symbolic Horse in the Early Modern World.* Her recent work is concerned with networks of people involved in early-modern play cultures—especially the aristocratic, urban and theatrical groups associated with the Elizabethan Playhouse in Prescot of the 1590s. She also works in the field of the medical humanities.

List of Illustrations

1   Frontispiece of William Cavendish, *La Méthode Nouvelle et Invention Extraordinaire de Dresser Les Chevaux* (Antwerp 1658). All illustrations from the book are reproduced by kind permission of Dr Elaine Walker, one of the contributors to this volume   7

2   Portrait of William Cavendish: original artist unknown (English School), Oil on Canvas, 8.9 × 4.4 cm. Reproduced by kind permission of the Department of Manuscripts and Special Collections, University of Nottingham: Accession Number Ne4 2/31   8

3   The Warsop Parochial Church Council kindly gave us permission to photograph and reproduce an image of the memorial panel to John Rolleston in St Peter and St Paul, Church Warsop. Copyright Elspeth Graham   23

4   Payments to household servants showing their place in the household through conventions of naming and salaries. Captain Mazin (Cavendish's Master of the Horse), Mr Andrew Layton and Mr John Lutton. Reproduced by kind permission of the Department of Manuscripts and Special Commissions, University of Nottingham, ref. no. Portland Collection, Pw1/670   25

1.1   1650s ink sketch of Bolsover Castle from the west by an unknown hand and adapted by Abraham van Diepenbecke to create his best-known image of William Cavendish, "Monsieur le Marquis à cheval". Note that the sketch, although executed to virtually the same dimensions as those adopted by Diepenbecke for his large pencil and chalk drawings, only showed half of the state apartment. This most probably reflected the despoilation of the southern half by the Castle's asset-stripping Parliamentary owner in the early 1650s. Reproduced by kind permission of Alexandra Sitwell   56

2.1   Detail of the vaulted ceiling in the hall of the Little Castle at Bolsover. Copyright James Fitzmaurice   61

2.2   Man urinating. Private Collection   68

3.1   "La Bataille Gagnée". From William Cavendish, *La Méthode Nouvelle*, plate 1. Copyright Elaine Walker   101

3.2   Stonework winged horses in Bolsover's Pillar Parlour. Copyright Elspeth Graham   103

3.3   Cavendish riding Pegasus. From William Cavendish, *La Méthode Nouvelle*, plate 4. Copyright Elaine Walker   104

3.4   Cavendish riding in a coach drawn by centaurs receives the homage of his horses. From William Cavendish, *La Méthode Nouvelle*, plate 3. Copyright Elaine Walker   105

3.5   Bolsover Castle's Stool Closet looking onto the Venus Fountain. Copyright Elspeth Graham   106

6.1   The stable courtyard at Osterley from the south showing the rebuilt eastern tower and the added central doorcase and clock turret. Copyright Malcolm Airs   154

6.2   Interior of the stable at Dunster Castle with heel posts and hanging bales. Copyright Malcolm Airs   156

6.3   The stable range at Blickling Hall flanking the approach to the entrance of the house. Copyright Malcolm Airs   157

6.4   Stalls arcade at Shapwick Manor. Copyright Malcolm Airs   158

6.5   Audley End stable and coach house with added projecting viewing bays. Copyright Malcolm Airs   160

6.6   Holland House stable and coach house. Reconstructed west elevation with the coach house to the left and the stable to the right of the central entrance. Reproduced by kind permission of Mike Thrift   161

6.7   Holland House stable. Engraving of the internal elevation of the stalls from Isaac Ware, *Designs of Inigo Jones and Others*   162

6.8   Wolfeton riding house. Copyright Malcolm Airs   167

6.9   Bolsover stable and riding house. Copyright Malcolm Airs   169

6.10 Welbeck stable. From William Cavendish, *La Méthode Nouvelle*, plate 9. Copyright Elaine Walker   170

8.1   "La Bataille Gagnée". From William Cavendish, *La Méthode Nouvelle*, plate 1. Copyright Elaine Walker   211

8.2   Horses worshipping Cavendish. From William Cavendish, *La Méthode Nouvelle*, plate 3. Copyright Elaine Walker   212

11.1 The Perfect Horseman. From William Cavendish, La Méthode Nouvelle, plate 14. All images in this chapter are copyright Elaine Walker   270

11.2 Using the cavesson to develop suppleness in the horse. From William Cavendish, *La Méthode Nouvelle*, plate 15   272

11.3 Detail of plate 15, showing rotation of the rider's wrist   272

11.4 Progression away from the circle: one exercise at the trot and 'galop'. From William Cavendish, *La Méthode Nouvelle*, plate 16   274

11.5 Directing the horse using the rider's weight and body alignment. From William Cavendish, *La Méthode Nouvelle*, plate 17   275

11.6 Cavendish uses his body position to put the horse on the haunches. From William Cavendish, *La Méthode Nouvelle*, plate 20   276

11.7   Detail of plate 20, showing use of rider's focus to influence the horse's centre of balance   276

12.1   Cavendish riding Pegasus. From William Cavendish, *La Méthode Nouvelle*, plate 4. Copyright Elaine Walker   291

List of Abbreviations

BL   British Library.
CSPD   Calendar of State Papers Domestic.
EEBO   Early English Books Online.
HMC   Historical Manuscripts Commission.
The Horse as Cultural Icon   Edwards P. – Enenkel K.A.E. – Graham E. (eds.),
            *The Horse as Cultural Icon: the Real and the Symbolic Horse in the
            Early Modern World* (Leiden: 2012)
Cavendish M., Life of William Cavendish   Cavendish, Margaret, *The life of the
            thrice noble, high and puissant Prince William Cavendishe, Duke,
            Marquess and Earl of Newcastle* (London, A.Maxwell: 1667)
Firth, ed., Life of William Cavendish   Cavendish Margaret, Duchess of
            Newcastle, *The Life of William Cavendish, Duke of Newcastle*, (ed.)
            Firth C.H., (London, (1906)
NA   Nottinghamshire Archives.
"Newcastle's advice to Charles II"   Slaughter T.P. (ed.), *Ideology and Politics on
            the Eve of Restoration: Newcastle's Advice to Charles II*, The American
            Philosophical Society (1984).
NUL   Nottingham University Library, Manuscripts and Special Collections.
ODNB   The Oxford Dictionary of National Biography (Oxford: 2004).
RIBA   Royal Institute of British Architects.
TNA   The National Archives.

As William Cavendish's manuals are extensively cited in this volume, references will be inserted in the text, indicating date of publication and page number. Apart from Adrian Woodhouse's and Elaine Walker's essays, all references to the 1658 manual, *La Méthode Nouvelle et Invention Extraordinaire de Dresser les Chevaux* (Antwerp, Jacques van Meurs : 1658), are taken from a modern facsimile of John Brindley's English translation of 1743, entitled A *General System of Horsemanship*. Contributors have used either the one published by Trafalgar Square Publishing (North Pomfret, Vermont) or that of J.A. Allen & Co. Ltd. (London: 2000), indicated by the letter 'L' or 'V' after the date, 1743.

Notes on the Contributors

Malcolm Airs
is Emeritus Professor of Conservation and the Historic Environment at Oxford University and a past President of the Society of Architectural Historians of Great Britain. He has published extensively on the architectural history of the early modern period.

Madeline Dewhurst
completed an AHRC funded doctoral thesis on Margaret and William Cavendish, at the Centre for Editing Lives and Letters, Queen Mary College, University of London, under the supervision of Lisa Jardine, in 2009. Her interdisciplinary thesis re-contextualizes this historically unique pair by placing them within their cultural, political and familial framework during the period 1648–1660. This period of English history and literature is an on-going area of interest and research. Madeline has also expanded her research area into seventeenth and eighteenth century medical history, completing a research project on eighteenth century surgery for Touchpaper Television, funded by a Wellcome Trust award. Academic publications include "True Relations: piecing together a family divided by war", *Lives & Letters: a journal for early modern archival research*, vol. 2, no. 1, (Summer 2010). 'True Relations' analyses the relationships between William Cavendish and his children through an examination of their letters during the Interregnum.

Alison Findlay
is Professor of Renaissance Drama (Lancaster University). Her books include *Illegitimate Power* (1994), *A Feminist Perspective on Renaissance Drama* (1999), *Women in Shakespeare* (2010). She co-edited *Twelfth Night: A Critical Reader* (2014) and is now co-editing *Shakespeare and Greece*, both for Arden. Alison's work on early women's drama, including that of the Cavendish women, has appeared in filmed versions, a co-authored book, *Women and Dramatic Production 1550–1700* (2000) and a monograph, *Playing Spaces in Early Women's Drama* (2006). She is currently editing Lady Mary Wroth's *Love's Victory* for Revels Plays.

James Fitzmaurice
is Emeritus Professor of English at Northern Arizona University and Honorary Research Fellow at the University of Sheffield. He has published on various seventeenth century writers including Aphra Behn, Thomas Carew, Margaret

Cavendish, Ben Jonson, Dorothy Osborne, William Shakespeare and Jane Barker. He has edited the letters of Margaret Cavendish for Broadview Press. These days he is active as an organizer of the Othello's Island Conference that takes place in Cyprus each spring, manages the International Margaret Cavendish Society Facebook page, and blogs at margaretcavendish.net. Twitter: @JamesFitzmauri1.

Lisa Hopkins

is Professor of English and head of the Graduate School at Sheffield Hallam University. She is a co-editor of *Shakespeare*, the journal of the British Shakespeare Association, of the Arden Early Modern Drama Guides, and of Arden Studies in Early Modern Drama. She has published extensively on Renaissance drama, principally Marlowe, Shakespeare and Ford, and runs a series of day events on the Literary Cultures of the Cavendish Family (https://blogs.shu.ac.uk/cavendish/).

Andy Hopper

is Senior Lecturer in the Centre for English Local History at the University of Leicester. He is best known for his two monographs *'Black Tom': Sir Thomas Fairfax and the English Revolution* (Manchester: Manchester University Press, 2007) and *Turncoats and Renegadoes: Changing Sides in the English Civil Wars* (Oxford: 2012). He has also produced several edited volumes pertinent to this collection, including "The Papers of the Hothams, Governors of Hull during the Civil War", *Camden Society*, 5th series, 39 (2011), and alongside Richard Cust, "Cases in the High Court of Chivalry, 1634–1640", *Publications of the Harleian Society*, new series, 18 (2006). He is currently researching widowhood and bereavement during the Civil Wars and is guest curator of the 'Battle-Scarred' exhibition at the National Civil War Centre.

Monica Mattfeld

is an adjunct professor at the University of Northern British Columbia where she lectures on animal studies, the history of gender and eighteenth-century literature and history. Her first book, *Performing Horse-Men: Eighteenth-Century Horsemanship and English Masculinity*, which is forthcoming from Penn State University Press, examines human-animal relationships and their influence on performances of gender during the seventeenth and eighteenth centuries. Having written on the influence and impact of performing animals in the eighteenth-century theatre, Monica's current research focuses on the animals and humans in the early English circus, especially Astley's

Amphitheatre. She is specifically interested in the late eighteenth- and early nineteenth-century craze for equestrian extravaganzas, or hippodramas, and in the material culture of horse-human relationships in British history.

Richard Nash

is Professor of English at Indiana University, Bloomington, and author of several books and articles on eighteenth-century culture and the history of horse-racing, including most recently (with co-authors David Oldrey and Tim Cox) *The Heath and The Horse: A history of racing and art on Newmarket heath* (London, 2015).

Karen Raber

is Professor of English at the University of Mississippi, and editor of Routledge's series, Perspectives on the Non-Human in Literature and Culture. She has written extensively on early modern gender and women writers, ecostudies, animal studies and other topics. Her most recent monograph, *Animal Bodies, Renaissance Culture*, appeared in 2013. Current projects include *Shakespeare and Posthumanist Theory* and *A Dictionary of Shakespeare and Animals*, both forthcoming from Arden Press, as well as a monograph, *Animals at the Table: Making Meat in the Early Modern World.*

Timothy Raylor

is Professor of English at Carleton College, Minnesota. He is author of *Cavaliers, Clubs, and Literary Culture: Sir John Mennes, James Smith, and the Order of the Fancy* (1994); of *The Essex House Masque of 1621: Viscount Doncaster and the Jacobean Masque* (2000); and editor of "The Cavendish Circle," a special issue of *The Seventeenth Century* (1994). He is currently working, with Stephen Clucas, on an edition of *De Corpore* and its related manuscripts for The Clarendon Edition of the Works of Thomas Hobbes.

Lisa Sarasohn

is Professor Emerita from Oregon State University where she spent 34 years teaching medieval, Renaissance and early modern European history. She has published two books: *Gassendi's Ethics: Freedom in a Mechanistic Universe* (Ithaca, NY: 1996) and *The Natural Philosophy of Margaret Cavendish: Reason and Fancy during the Scientific Revolution* (Baltimore: 2010). Articles on Thomas Hobbes and William Cavendish have appeared in *Isis* (1999), *History of Political Thought* (2000), *History of Science* (2004), and *English Studies* (2001). Her current project is a cultural history of vermin—fleas, lice, bed bugs, and rats.

Elaine Walker

is a writer of non-fiction, fiction and poetry and a consultant on the horse in cultural history (elaine-walker.com). She lectures in English Literature and Creative Writing. Her doctoral thesis on Newcastle's horsemanship manuals is published as '*To Amaze the People with Pleasure and Delight*' (2010; new edition 2015). Other titles include a novel, *The Horses* (2010; new edition 2016), *Horse* (2008), which was chosen by the Kalima Project, and *The Horse* (2014), as well as *Teaching Creative Writing: Practical Approaches* (2012).

Adrian Woodhouse

is an independent architectural and garden historian. He has specialised in the 16th/17th century Smithson dynasty of mason-architects since revealing their origins in Westmorland in *Country Life* in 1991. While his iconoclastic book on John Smithson awaits publication he has recently completed an HLF-funded report on the history of the mid-17th century terraced gardens of Staveley Hall in north-east Derbyshire.

Introduction: Authority, Authorship and Aristocratic Identity in Seventeenth Century England: William Cavendish, 1st Duke of Newcastle, and his Political, Social and Cultural Connections

The lives of William Cavendish, first duke of Newcastle, and his family including, centrally, his second wife, Margaret Cavendish, are intimately bound up with the overarching story of seventeenth-century England: the violently negotiated changes in structures of power that constituted the Civil Wars, and the ensuing Commonwealth and Restoration of the monarchy. Not only were their life trajectories shaped by their participation, as committed royalists, in the major events of the century and the fortunes of Charles I and Charles II, but their sensibilities and world views both contributed to, and were inflected by, the evolving cultures of the loyalist Stuart Courts, both at home in England and, during the 1640s and 50s, in exile in continental Europe. Although in recent years there has been a growing interest in royalist history and cultural production,[1] it is perhaps still true to say, repeating Conrad Russell's words from 1991, that 'English Royalists are the real peculiarity we should be attempting to explain' in relation to the cataclysmic events and profound political,

---

1 Among studies on English Royalism in the past twenty years, see, for instance: Atherton I. – Sanders J. (eds.), *The 1630s: Interdisciplinary Essays on Culture and Politics in the Caroline Era* (Manchester: 2013 edn.); Barrett J., *Cavaliers: the Royalist Army at War 1642–1646* (Stroud: 2000); Chalmers H., *Royalist Women Writers 1650–1689* (Oxford: 2004); de Groot J., *Royalist Identities* (Basingstoke: 2004); Hutton R., *The Royalist War Effort, 1642–1646* (London: 2nd edition 1999); McElligott J. – Smith D.L. (eds.), *Royalists and Royalism during the English Civil Wars* (Cambridge: 2007); Milton A., *Laudian and Royalist Polemic in Seventeenth-Century England: The Career and Writings of Peter Heylyn* (Manchester: 2014); Newman P., *The Old Service: Royalist Regimental Colonels and the Civil War, 1642–46* (Manchester: 1993); Newman, P., "The King's Servants: Conscience, Principle and Sacrifice in Armed Royalism", in Morrill J. – Slack P. – Woolf D., (eds.) *Public Duty and Private Conscience in Seventeenth-Century England: Essays Presented to G.E. Aylmer* (Oxford: 1993); Russell C., *The Fall of the British Monarchies, 1637–1642* (Oxford: 1991); Smith D., *Constitutional Royalism and the Search for Settlement, c.1640–1649* (Cambridge: 1994); Raylor T., *Cavaliers, Clubs and Literary Culture: Sir John Mennes, James Smith and the Order of the Fancy* (Newark, London & New York: 1994); Smith G., *Royalist Agents, Conspirators and Spies* (London: 2011); Sommerville J.P., *Royalists & Patriots: politics and ideology in England 1603–1640* (Harlow: 1999) Spencer C., *Prince Rupert: The Last Cavalier* (London: 2007); Wilcher R., *The Writing of Royalism, 1628–1660* (Cambridge: 2001).

© KONINKLIJKE BRILL NV, LEIDEN, 2017 | DOI 10.1163/9789004326217_002

constitutional and cultural changes of the seventeenth-century.[2] If, ultimately, it is the *interplay* of royalist and parliamentarian political, moral and cultural values that is significant in the formation of the political constitution and the culture that have been inherited today, those values and forms of thought associated with royalist circles have long deserved the more detailed attention that is currently being paid to them.

This collection of essays contributes to this recent, increasingly-nuanced, understanding of royalism, by presenting William Cavendish, his family, household and connections as an aristocratic, royalist case study, relating the intellectual and political underpinnings and implications of their beliefs, actions and writings to wider cultural currents. But the Cavendishes, famously, both valued and were characterised by that 'singularity' that the most prolific author among them, Margaret Cavendish, claimed for herself.[3] Their lives and cultural interventions, while speaking to a shared set of loyalist Stuart values, are at the same time, emphatically individual. Moving between the particularities of William Cavendish's life, writings and cultural production and the relationship of his thoughts and belief system to those of others, the essays that make up this book explore the senses of alternating belonging and exclusion that underpinned his life in different ways, at different moments. In contextualizing the essays that make up *Authority, Authorship and Aristocratic Identity in Seventeenth Century England*, this Introduction will focus on different aspects of his life and of his place in relation to wider social and cultural groups and milieus.

The Socio-political Structure of Seventeenth-century England

Seventeenth century England, as Western Europe as a whole, was a highly stratified society, shaped like a pyramid, with a broad base and a very fine point. An elite caste of large landowners (as exemplified here by the experience of William Cavendish, successively viscount Mansfield, earl, marquis and duke of Newcastle, his family and his second wife, Margaret Cavendish) played a dominant role in the political, social, cultural and economic life of seventeenth-century England. A comparable example of the ways in which aristocratic

---

2   Russell, *Fall of the British Monarchies*, 526. Also quoted by McElligott and Smith, Introduction, 1.
3   Margaret Cavendish, describing how she created her own fashions in dress, writes, 'I always took delight in singularity', *A True Relation of my Birth, Breeding and Life* in *Nature's Pictures drawn by Fancy's Pencil to the Life* (1656), in Graham E. *et al.*, *Her Own Life: Autobiographical Writings by Seventeenth-Century Englishwomen* (London and New York: 1989) 96.

power was achieved and maintained in mainland Europe is provided by
Jonathan Dewald in his *Status, Power, and Identity in Early Modern France.*
Through a focus on the ducal de Rohan family, Dewald reveals ways in which
the political and economic power of the aristocracy also depended on acquisition of social and cultural capital and how, in particular, this was a crucial
aspect of maintaining aristocratic prominence through periods of changing
fortunes and relationships with the monarch.[4] The English ruling class did not,
of course, comprise a homogeneous whole as they varied in terms of wealth,
sphere of social and political influence and career trajectory. Even so, its members were united behind a belief that their authority and fitness to rule were
based upon their social, cultural and economic superiority (hence the title of
this book). In spite of reversals during the Civil Wars, the main trend of the
period was for the elite to deploy their wealth and influence in the political sphere. On a national stage the focus was on the Court and Parliament.
Aristocrats, summoned individually and sitting in the upper house of the leg-
islature, the House of Lords, claimed to be the natural advisors of the monarch
and served on the Privy Council and as government ministers.[5] Indeed, by the
end of the period, they dominated government office. They also dominated the
lower house, the House of Commons, through their kinsmen and clients. Unlike
their counterparts in mainland Europe, the legal privileges of the English elite
were small: they were not exempt from taxation, for instance, and were subject
to the same laws as the rest of the population, facts which shocked Henri, duke
of Rohan.[6] Even so, the law with its emphasis on protecting property buttressed
their position. In Parliament, moreover, their pre-eminence enabled them to
control legislation in their own interest, while at the county level, their hold
over the most important offices—the lieutenancy and the magistracy—gave
them the power to help or hinder the operation of the law.

Just as the Crown exploited the wealth, power and influence of the large
landowners to help them administer the country, so the latter sought the good-
will of the king to bolster their own positions. In an age when the monarch
exercised real power, chose his own ministers and dispensed a great deal of
patronage, members of the elite flocked to the Court where they hoped to find
favour with the king and benefit from his largesse, whether in terms of place,

---

4 Dewald J., *Status, Power, and Identity in Early Modern France: the Rohan Family, 1550–1715*
   (University Park PA: 2015) 3.

5 For a brief history of the creation so the two houses of the UK parliament, see the House
   of Lords' own. *History of the House of Lords*: http://www.lordspublications.parliament.uk/
   pdf/H-076.pdf Accessed 8 March 2015.

6 Dewald, *Rohan Family*, 48.

influence, perks or prestige. In turn, ministers, privy councillors and household officers themselves attracted adherents, anxious for place and preferment through the patronage of a more powerful figure. In the shires, the great house, a visual statement of the wealth and standing of its owner, acted as a centre of political power. From their homes, the leading politicians sought to establish links with all those with influence in the county, if only at a local level. They met their 'lieutenants' there and invited gentlemen they wanted to cultivate to stay as guests, alongside artists, literary figures and intellectuals, clients of their patronage; they organized hunting parties and other entertainments where they could discuss politics, among other matters; and they plotted their campaigns and reported on the meetings they had had with others at such gatherings as the assizes, the quarter sessions, assemblies, race meetings, hunts and even cricket matches. There, they learned not only of the attitudes of the gentry but also of those of the electorate, the size and social complexion of which varied considerably between constituencies, especially parliamentary boroughs. In this respect, political activity centred on the great house drew strength from the social and economic hegemony of its owner. Built according to the prevailing architectural style and filled with artefacts (often acquired on a Grand Tour) that displayed the owner's refined taste, or connoisseurship, the house was not only a cultural object in itself but also a centre of cultural life. Aristocratic patronage of the arts was widespread and some members of the elite employed or gave board to painters, writers and intellectuals and themselves might aspire to virtuosity.[7] Even so, the privilege of having authority over the mass of the population incurred obligations, so the elite subscribed (or at least paid lip-service) to the notion of paternalism, an obligation to look after their dependents, which in a world ordered according to patriarchalist political theory, as well paternalist values, included women. Servants, as members of the aristocratic household, similarly lived in interdependent relationship with their lords and ladies, so that the household as a whole can be perceived as a social microcosm or microstate, operating to embody, represent and further the family's identity and aspirations with something close to a hierarchised hive mentality.

---

7   On connoisseurs and virtuosos see: Hanson C.A., *The English Virtuoso: Art, Medicine, and Antiquarianism in the Age of Empiricism* (Chicago & London: 2009); Swann M., *Curiosities and Texts: The Culture of Collecting in Early Modern England* (Philadelphia: 2001); Swann M., "*The Compleat Angler* and the Early Modern Culture of Collecting", *English Literary Renaissance* 37 i (2007); Yeo R., *Notebooks, English Viruosi, and Early Modern Science* (Chicago & London: 2014).

As the power, authority and influence of the ruling class derived from the possession of land—in a few cases in tens of thousands of acres spread across a number of counties—preserving what land one had, and seeking to extend the acreage, were prime considerations. In her biography of William, Margaret Cavendish carefully lists all her husband's properties (lying in eight counties scattered across the country) that he possessed in the year before the English Civil War broke out. With a rent roll amounting to £22,393 10s.1d. it made him one of the biggest, and therefore one of the wealthiest and most powerful, magnates in the kingdom.[8] And, since the possession of land passed down the generations through inheritance, usually via the custom of male primogeniture, it was important that families were aware of their lineage. A distant cousin might inherit, or an estate might be lost through the lack of a male heir, in which case another family could benefit by a judicious marriage to a female heiress. However, an abiding interest in one's genealogical roots was not prompted solely by economic considerations but also resulted from the pride that elite families took in their ancestry which gave them their special identity and confirmed their status. As Heal and Holmes emphasize in *The Gentry in England and Wales 1500–1700*, 'Lineage, the conjunction of blood and tenure, defines and legitimises individual status'.[9] The periodic visitations by the heralds, the arbiters of status and lineage, between 1530 and 1686 helped police this system, although they could sometimes be bribed or pressured into authorising bogus pedigrees.[10] The construction of detailed illuminated family trees, the writing of family histories and the painting or engraving of coats of arms on monuments, coaches and suitable surfaces in the house reflect the elite's interest in their ancestors and their family connections.[11] Sprung from a cadet branch of a noble family of recent vintage and newly ennobled himself, Cavendish was particularly concerned with lineage. His sense of lineage sustained him in exile, for instance. So, when he published *La Méthode Nouvelle* in 1658 he made sure that its elite readers were aware of his status and authority as soon as they had opened the book. The frontispiece features a mock coat of arms with Cavendish's actual coat of arms as the crest and two horses as supporters drawing back a curtain inscribed with Cavendish's many titles and

---

8   Cavendish M., *Life*, 99–100.

9   Heal F. – Holmes C., *The Gentry in England and Wales 1500–1700* (Basingstoke: 1994) 22.

10   See Cust R., *Charles I and the Aristocracy, 1625–1642* (Cambridge: 2013) for an extensive analysis of the English honours system under Charles I.

11   It was this attitude that Voltaire satirised in *Candide* in relation to the social exclusivity of the French landed classes, when he ascribed the problems of Cunégonde's father to the fact that he could not prove one of the 64 quarterings on his coat of arms.

posts of honour. (1743L: frontispiece. Fig. 1) In France, the de Rohan family even invented a bogus genealogy that set out their descent from an early fourth century king of Brittany called Conan Mériadec. They did so, according to Dewald, because 'the family had to establish versions of its past that erased doubts about its status'.[12]

William Cavendish: A Biographical Summary

William Cavendish, then, stands as a synecdochic figure, a complex individual, whose life and multi-faceted career can also be seen as representative of this larger world he inhabited. (Fig. 2) In a mix of typicality and individuality, his long life (1593–1676) embodies both a continuity of courtly values inherited from the late Renaissance and the necessary adaptations of these occasioned by the changing fortunes of English royalists through the seventeenth century. Characterised, on the one hand, by the historian Keith Thomas as a political and cultural 'dinosaur',[13] he has, on the other hand, been recognised as an influential member of the intellectually forward-looking, 'Cavendish circle', even as early as the 1630s when he and his brother, Sir Charles Cavendish, were at the 'forefront of the new philosophy in England'.[14]

A brief biographical summary suggests this interplay of continuing and renegotiated values in his life, as well as pointing to features of his life that reveal him as both an individual and an aristocratic type.[15] As a son of Sir Charles Cavendish and grandson of Elizabeth Hardwick, Countess of Shrewsbury, and the courtier, Sir William Cavendish, and as a nephew of another William Cavendish, the 1st Earl of Devonshire, Cavendish was born into a family with

---

12   Dewald, *Rohan Family*, 26–27.

13   Thomas K., *The Ends of Life. Roads to Fulfilment in Early Modern England* (Oxford: 2009) 61–62.

14   Raylor T., "Newcastle's Ghosts: Robert Payne, Ben Jonson, and the 'Cavendish Circle'", in Summers C.J. – Pebworth T.-L., *Literary Circles and Cultural Communities in Renaissance England* (Columbia: 2000) 92–114, 94. See also: the special edition on the Cavendish Circle of *The Seventeenth Century*, 9, 2 (1994); and the classic text, Perry H.T.E., *The First Duchess of Newcastle and her Husband in Literary History* (Boston: 1918). On Sir Charles Cavendish, see: Malcolm N. – Stedall J., *John Pell (1611–1685) and His Correspondence with Sir Charles Cavendish: The Mental World of an Early Modern Mathematician* (New York: 2005); Carlyle E. I., "Cavendish, Sir Charles (1595?–1654)", rev. Timothy Raylor, Oxford Dictionary of National Biography (Oxford: 2004) [http://www.oxforddnb.com/view/article/4928, accessed 26 April 2015].

15   See, Hulse L., "Cavendish, William, first duke of Newcastle upon Tyne (*bap.* 1593, *d.* 1676)", *ODNB*, [http://www.oxforddnb.com/view/article/4946, accessed 30 March 2016].

FIGURE 1   *Frontispiece of William Cavendish*, La Méthode Nouvelle et Invention Extraordinaire de Dresser Les Chevaux (*Antwerp 1658*). *All illustrations from the book are reproduced by kind permission of Elaine Walker, one of the contributors to this volume.*

wealth and existing Court and royal associations. He, himself, as a young man, was deeply ambitious for a courtly role.[16] After studying at Cambridge,

16   cf. Worsley L., *Cavalier* (London: 2007) 4. Books which deal with the English and European Courts and courtiers include: Adamson J. (ed.), *The Princely Courts of Europe: Ritual, Politics and Culture under the Ancien Régime 1500–1750* (London: 1999); Asch R.G. – Birke A.M. (eds.) *Princes, Patronage and the Nobility: the Court at the Beginning of the Modern Age c.1450–1650* (Oxford: 1991); Bayreuther, M., *Pferde und Fürsten: Repräsentative Reitkunst und Pferdehaltung an Fränkischen Höfen (1600–1800)* (Würzburg: 2014); Burke, P., *The Fortunes of the Courtier: the European Reception of Castiglione's 'Cortegiano'* (Cambridge: 1995); Cruikshanks E. (ed.), *The Stuart Courts* (Stroud, 2000); Dewald J., *Status, Power, and Identity in Early Modern France: the Rohan family, 1550–1715* (University Park PA: 2014); Elias N., *The Court Society*, transl. from German (Oxford: 1983); Guy J. (ed.), *The Tudor Monarchy* (London: 1997); Howarth D., *Images of Rule: Art and Politics in the English Renaissance, 1485–1649* (Basingstoke: 1997); Peck, L.L., *Northampton: Patronage and Policy at the Court of James I* (London: 1982); Peck L.L., *Patronage and Corruption in Early Stuart England* (London: 1993); Reese M.M., *The Royal Office of the Master of the Horse* (London: 1976); Roche D. (ed.), *Les Écuries Royales du XVIᵉ au XVIIIᵉ Siècle*

FIGURE 2   *Portrait of William Cavendish: original artist unknown (English School), Oil on*
            Canvas, 8.9 × 4.4 cm. Reproduced by kind permission of the Department of
            Manuscripts and Special Collections, University of Nottingham: Accession Number
            Ne4 2/31.

he entered the Royal Mews where he was trained, along with the royal Princes,
Henry and Charles, in the art of the *manège*. It was here that he discovered

---

(Paris: 1998); Starkey D., *The English Court from the Wars of the Roses to the Civil War*
(London: 1987); Strong R., *The Tudor and Stuart Monarchy: Pageantry, Painting,*
Iconography, 3 vols. I: *Tudor* (Woodbridge: 1995) II: *Elizabethan* (Woodbridge: 1995) III:
Jacobean and Caroline (Woodbridge: 1997).

the major talent that became a constant and self-defining feature throughout his life: his expertise in horsemanship. In this, as well as in his intellectual, artistic and literary passions, his values and attitude mirrored those of Prince Henry, son and heir of James I, and were, from this point onwards, integrated with his courtly and political ambitions, ultimately becoming as definitive of him as a significant royalist figure as his later, prominent role in the First Civil War attests.

His involvement in Court circles during the formative period of his life is suggested by his inclusion among the twenty-five contemporaries personally chosen by Prince Henry to attend him at his investiture as Prince of Wales in 1610, and by the creation of Cavendish as a Knight of the Bath for this ceremony. Cavendish was subsequently part of the diplomat Sir Henry Wootton's mission to Italy to discuss a possible marriage between Prince Henry and the daughter of Charles Emmanuel, Duke of Savoy (who wanted to retain Cavendish in his own court). However, it was not until 1638, twenty-six years after the unexpected and untimely death of Prince Henry, and thirteen years after the accession to the throne of Henry's younger brother Charles, that Cavendish's desire for a full Court role was fulfilled: in March the King appointed him sole gentleman of the bedchamber, a few months later governor of Prince Charles (later Charles II) and, in 1641, he became gentleman of the robes to the prince. Amongst other things, Cavendish taught the prince to ride, helped shape his personality and had a formative influence on the development of his values. A genuine sweetness of affection forged between them might be implied by a letter (?1639) from the young prince (b. 1630) to his governor, at a time when Cavendish was unwell and absent from his duties: 'My Lord, I would not have you take too much physic, for it doth always make me worse, and I think it will do the like with you. I ride every day, and am ready to follow any other directions from you. Make haste to return to him that loves you.'[17] The bond suggested here created a continuity of loyalty—but also an expectation of favour that could not always be met—that would endure throughout Cavendish's life.

The Stuart Royal Court, inheriting the structures and functions that had been established in the late fifteenth century, underwent various forms of reconfiguration in the seventeenth century in order to represent the changing role of the monarchy and the administrative needs of the state. This change in and adaptation of the Court is, of course, part of the larger, turbulent history of the changing relations of crown, Court and country that constitute the

---

17   Bryant A. (ed.), *The Letters, Speeches and Declarations of King Charles II* (London: 1935) 3.

history of seventeenth-century England overall.[18] Continuously throughout
the period, however, the Court comprised three departments, or physical locations with their dedicated personnel. The Household, firstly, was a larger, more
lavish version of the households of the aristocracy, and was concerned with
hospitality, cultural activity and display of magnificence. The second department, the Chamber, was made up of the state apartments containing the Privy
Chamber and contained economic and policy-making sub-sections such as the
Exchequer, Chancery and Privy Council. It was responsible for Court ceremony
and controlling physical access to the monarch. Finally, the Bedchamber was
situated at the end of the series of public chambers, the inner sanctum of the
monarch. As their names suggest, these household departments, demarcated
according to spatial distinctions, had been traditionally hierarchised according to proximity to the bodily presence of the monarch and their personnel
were accorded corresponding status. The staff of the Bedchamber, closest
to the personal embodiment of power in the monarch, were the only courtiers with an automatic right to be in the monarch's presence. Consequently,
monarchs had traditionally tended to deploy servants of the Bedchamber as
direct agents, enacting that personal power. But, through the course of the
late-sixteenth century and the reign of James I, as government became more
bureaucratised and complex, both the Chamber and Bedchamber created
increasing numbers of sub-departments. Rivalries ensued between sections
of the Chamber and Bedchamber. In particular, the distribution of power
between members of the Bedchamber, who constituted the personal entourage of the monarch and enacted the royal prerogative, and those belonging to
the Privy Chamber, could shift at different moments. Interpretations of such
internal contests in the royal Court are inevitably aligned with different his-
toriographical approaches to the broader interpretation of events leading to
the Civil Wars.[19] But even a brief outline of the structural rivalries and changes
occurring in the early and mid-seventeenth century gives a sense of how these,
in combination with personal rivalries between courtiers, produced the Court
as a fraught environment. Ability not only to acquire and maintain the monarch's confidence and favour, but also to negotiate departmental and personal
rivalries was paramount for a courtier.

---

18   See Cuddy N., "Reinventing a Monarchy: the Changing Structure and Political Function of
      the Stuart Court 1603–88", in Cruikshanks, *The Stuart Courts*, 59–85.

19   Cuddy "Reinventing a Monarchy", to whom we are indebted here, gives an account of
      different historiographical approaches as well as presenting his own interpretation of the
      politics of the Stuart Royal Court.

In his ambition for a Court position, Cavendish had, in fact, originally desired to be appointed Master of the Horse, 'the third great officer of the Royal Household',[20] responsible for all aspects of the monarch's equestrian and equine needs (ceremonial, sporting, practical, military) and the maintenance of the royal stud and equine estate—a role he perceived as appropriate to his particular horsemanship skills.[21] His actual appointments in the Court were ones that perhaps required rather different abilities and his association with the royal Court was, in fact, troubled, even while in his position as the prince's governor in the Royal Household. Lacking the subtle interpersonal skills of the courtier and alienating people with his bluntness and fragile air of self-importance,[22] he had already found Court life sometimes uncongenial, when his unfortunate (perhaps unfair) implication in the Army Plot, an ill-advised scheme to rescue his erstwhile patron, the earl of Strafford, from the Tower, led to his dismissal in 1641.

Cavendish's determined pursuit of a Court appointment in the 1630s had run in parallel with his artistic and architectural activities. Following in the tradition of his father, Sir Charles Cavendish, and his paternal grandmother, Bess of Hardwick, he actively engaged in the building, extension and restoration of a number of the Cavendish properties in England, before 1645 and after 1660, particularly Bolsover Castle in Derbyshire, Welbeck Abbey and Nottingham Castle in Nottinghamshire, and Newcastle House in Middlesex. Even while in exile in Antwerp in the intervening years, he occupied himself with building, bringing together two of his most favoured activities, equitation and architecture, through the design and commissioning of his Riding House within the rented Rubenshuis where he and Margaret were living.[23] His choice of title, on the first conferment of his nobility as Earl of Newcastle in 1628, points to this central interest in building: New-castle is a punning reference to the geographic location of his mother's Ogle properties in Northumbria, to building as

20   Reese M.M., *The Royal Office of Master of the Horse* (London: 1976).

21   Actual seventeenth-century Royal Masters of the Horse were: George Villiers, Duke of Buckingham to 1628; Henry Rich, Earl of Holland in 1628; James Hamilton, Duke of Hamilton from 1628 until his execution in 1643; Prince Rupert 1653–55, during the period of exile; George Monck, Duke of Albemarle from the Restoration to 1668.

22   Worsley L., *Cavalier* (London: 2007) 134.

23   See Worsley L., "'His Magnificent Buildings': William Cavendish's Patronage of Architecture", in Van Beneden, B., and Nora de Poorter, *Royalist Refugees: William and Margaret Cavendish in the Rubens House 1648–1660* (Antwerp: 2006) 101–104, for an overview of Cavendish's architectural work and Worsley, L., *Cavalier*, 25–54 on Bolsover Castle in particular.

a characteristic personal and familial activity, and to the nature of the propertied embodiment of his status—the very new castles built by the family.

Cavendish's artistic pursuits were not confined to architecture. He was also a playwright, poet and musician himself and an important patron of several English playwrights, including Ben Jonson and James Shirley. His relationship with Ben Jonson was particularly deep, enduring and even informal. The young Cavendish's hospitable and friendly trust in Jonson is instanced in an account written by a travelling companion of Jonson's on a walking journey from London to Edinburgh in summer 1618. This contains the story of how William Cavendish and his first wife, Elizabeth Howard (née Bassett, the widow of Henry Howard, son of Thomas, 1st earl of Suffolk) needed to leave Welbeck Abbey, Cavendish's main residence, for a few days while Jonson was visiting and so 'resigned the whole house to [Jonson] commanding his steward and all the rest of the officers to obey [Jonson] in all things, which authority he did as freely put into execution'.[24] Later, Cavendish also became a significant collector of baroque art, especially of paintings by Antwerp artists such as Anthony Van Dyck and Alexander Keirinex, and a patron of intellectuals including Robert Payne and Thomas Hobbes. More unusually, in spite of prevailing ideas about women's subordinate roles, he was a facilitator of the familial literary production of his daughters, Elizabeth Brackley and Jane Cavendish, as he was later of his second wife, Margaret, aligning the family and household (in this respect, at least), as an intellectual milieu, with those of other aristocratic families such as the Sidneys and Herberts.[25] Networks of sensibility linking a number of courtly families are generally suggested by common patronage of clients and

24   Lynn Hulse suggests that Jonson and Cavendish first met around 1614 (Hulse L., "Cavendish, William, first duke of Newcastle upon Tyne (*bap.* 1593, *d.* 1676)", ODNB, [http://www.oxforddnb.com/view/article/4946, accessed 26 April 2015]. For Ben Jonson's stay at Welbeck, see *Ben Jonson's Walk to Scotland: An Annotated Edition of the 'Foot Voyage'* (Cambridge: 2014) cited in Donaldson I., *Ben Jonson: A Life* (Oxford: 2011) 40–43.

25   The writings of Mary Sidney Herbert (the sister of Sir Philip Sidney who became Mary Herbert, Countess of Pembroke) and her niece Lady Mary Wroth exemplify the way in which, in particular households, women's literary production might be facilitated, even if in complex ways and as a result of particular circumstances. The Herbert household based at Penshurst Place, was a recognised centre of literary and cultural activity. Its hospitality is famously celebrated in Ben Jonson's "To Penshurst". For coterie writing, see Wynne-Davies M, *Women Writers and Familial Discourse in the English Renaissance: Relative Values.* (Basingstoke: 2007).

by shared intellectual interests as well as by their similar household structures and activities.[26]

At the same time, as a local magnate, Cavendish inevitably had a significant role in county and regional politics. Having inherited his father's estates in 1617, he served as Lord Lieutenant of Nottinghamshire in 1625 and also as Lord Lieutenant of Derbyshire in 1628 in place of his under-age second cousin, the earl of Devonshire. As the post made Cavendish the titular head of the counties' militia forces, it involved him in military matters, even if the Deputy-Lieutenants did the actual work of organisation and supply. His actual military career began in his forties, in 1638, when he raised a force of 120 knights and gentlemen, the Prince of Wales's troop, in the face of a threat of war from Scotland. An argument over precedence with Henry Rich, 1st Earl of Holland, the commander of the cavalry units, reflected a prickly sense of honour as well as the personal rivalry between the two men. In spite of a reputation for such prickliness and his earlier fall from grace at Court, during the subsequent Civil Wars, Cavendish, now Marquis of Newcastle, became Commander-in-Chief of Charles I's Northern Army, with some success at first, until his devastating defeat at Marston Moor in 1644, the greatest royalist loss of the First Civil War.

Immediately after this catastrophe, Cavendish fled, initially to Hamburg, then to Henrietta Maria's exiled Court in France and ultimately to Antwerp. Although there is debate about the extent and nature of his role in relation to the exiled Court, even among contributors to this volume, he clearly did involve himself in émigré politics, as befitted a person of his status, if with fluctuating fortunes. While in Antwerp, during a particularly low point in his period of exile, he occupied himself with his horses and horsemanship displays and wrote and published *La Méthode Nouvelle et Invention Extraordinaire de Dresser les Chevaux* (1657–8). Along with his horsemanship, his intellectual pursuits served as significant occupations during his exile. His clients and members of the circle he participated in, which included Hobbes, Descartes and Gassendi, were amongst the most significant political, experimental and

---

26   See Daybell J. (ed.), *Women and Politics in Early Modern England, 1450–1700* (London: 2004) on women and courtly networks, especially Daybell's own essay in the collection, "Suche newes as on the Quenes hye wayes we have mett: the news and intelligence networks of Elizabeth Talbot, countess of Shrewsbury (c.1527–1608)", and Sara Jayne Steen, "The Cavendish-Talbot women: playing a high-stakes game"; and Richards, J. (ed.), *Rhetoric, Women and Politics in Early Modern England* (London: 2006). Although not specifically concerned with the Cavendishes, see also Crawford J., *Mediatrix: Women, Politics, and Literary Production in Early Modern England* (Oxford: 2014), especially "Introduction", 1–29.

natural philosophers of the period. In this respect, his role as a patron throughout his life was important in the development of both English and continental
European thought and culture. After the restoration of the English monarchy, his own return to England and with it the lengthy process of restoring
his own estates, Cavendish (created Duke of Newcastle in 1665) unsuccessfully
offered political advice to Charles II. Sidelined, he largely lived in retirement,
involved—as throughout his life—with his horses and horsemanship, his own
literary, musical, architectural and artistic work and his artistic patronage.

   At least, Cavendish was able to return to and live in his native country when
his former pupil, Prince Charles, became king in 1660. In comparison, the de
Rohan brothers, Henri, duc de Rohan, and Benjamin, duc de Soubise, exiled
after the failure of their third rebellion against the king in 1629 rather than, as
in Cavendish's case, fleeing from victorious rebels, did not have that option.
Soubise never returned from exile (in London) and Rohan only made one brief
visit to France.[27] Whereas Soubise appeared to accept his fate, although complaining of financial problems and inactivity, his elder brother, like Cavendish,
never relinquished his political ambitions nor his links with France.[28] In the
interim, both he and Cavendish, who had taken up residence at centres of
political and cultural significance—the former at Venice and Padua and the
latter at Antwerp—occupied their time reading and writing and discussing a
range of issues with leading European intellectuals.[29]

Margaret Cavendish: A Biographical Summary

Although William Cavendish is an important historical figure because
of his military, political and cultural roles, it is often the literary significance of Margaret Cavendish that today attracts the greatest attention to
Cavendish cultural production.[30] The innovativeness of her writing—and her

---

27   Dewald, *The Rohan Family*, 20.
28   Ibid., 66–67.
29   Ibid., 20, 557, 70–8.
30   See Fitzmaurice J., "Cavendish , Margaret, duchess of Newcastle upon Tyne (1623?-1673)",
      ODNB (Oxford: 2004), [http://www.oxforddnb.com/view/article/4940, accessed 3rd April
      2016], Margaret Cavendish (1623?–1673): doi:10.1093/ref: ODNB/4940 See also: the web-
      site of the International Margaret Cavendish Society (http://internationalmargaretcav-
      endishsociety.org/index.html) which contains a list of resources and a comprehensive
      bibliography (http://jan.ucc.nau.edu/~jbf/CavBiblio.html) of critical writings on Margaret
      Cavendish. [Accessed 24th March 2016]. Further, on issues of particular relevance to

commitment to print publication, rather than manuscript circulation of her writings—establishes her own presence in literary history, as well as illuminating aspects of the overall Cavendish milieu in especially heightened ways. She has, clearly, a particular importance in any exploration of the cultural production of the Cavendish family. So, although her work is not the prime focus of this book, Margaret Cavendish is a presence throughout. Attention to her in this Introduction consequently provides a sense of her role in the broader Cavendish family and ways in which her writings may reveal particular perspectives on the dynamics of Cavendish relationships and the characteristics of their world.

Margaret Lucas (1623?–1673), as the daughter of Thomas and Elizabeth Lucas, was born into a gentry family, based in Colchester (Essex) and London, that had strong royalist sympathies. During the first English Civil War her brother, Sir John Lucas (first Baron Lucas of Shenfield), was Cavendish's Lieutenant-General of the Horse (and was executed after the siege of Colchester in 1648), while Margaret herself left Colchester to join her sister in Oxford, the location

---

the concerns of this book, see: Chalmers H., "Dismantling the Myth of 'Mad Madge': the Cultural Context of Margaret Cavendish's Self-Presentation", *Women's Writing*, Volume 4 [1997] 323–40; Clucas, S. (ed.), *A Princely Brave Woman: Essays on Margaret Cavendish, Duchess of Newcastle* (Aldershot & Burlington, VT: 2003); Cottegnies, L. – Weitz, N. *Authorial Conquests: Essays on Genre in the Writings of Margaret Cavendish* (Madison, Teaneck: 2003); Dowd – Eckerle J.A. (eds), *Genre and Women's Life Writing in Early Modern England: Women and Gender in the Early Modern World* (Aldershot: 2007); Fitzmaurice, J., "Fancy and the Family: Self-Characterizations of Margaret Cavendish", *Huntingdon Library Quarterly*, Volume 53 [1990] 199–209; Justice, G.L. – Tinker N. (eds), *Women's Writing and Circulation of Ideas: Manuscript Publication in England, 1550–1800* (Cambridge: 2002); Larson K.R., *Early Modern Women in Conversation* (Basingstoke: 2011); Masten J., *Textual Intercourse: Collaboration, Authorship, and Sexualities in Renaissance Drama* (Cambridge: 2007); Rees E., *Margaret Cavendish: Gender, Genre, Exile* (Manchester: 2003); Reeves M., "Writing to Posterity: Margaret Cavendish's 'A True Relation of my Birth, Breeding, and Life' (1656) as an 'autobiographical *relazione*'", *Renaissance and Reformation*, Volume 34, 1 (2011) 183–206; Rogers J., "Margaret Cavendish and the Gendering of the Vitalist Utopia", in Rogers J., *The Matter of Revolution: Science, Poetry, and Politics in the Age of Milton* (Ithaca, NY: 1996), 177–211; Rosenthal L.J., "'Authoress of a Whole World': The Duchess of Newcastle and Imaginary Property", in Rosenthal L.J., *Playwrights and Plagiarists in Early Modern England: Gender, Authorship, Literary Property* (Ithaca, NY: 1996), 58–104; Seelig S.C., *Autobiography and Gender in Early Modern Literature: Reading Women's Lives, 1600–1680* (Cambridge, 2006); Smith E., "Genre's 'Phantastical Garb': The Fashion of Form in Margaret Cavendish's *Natures Pictures Drawn by Fancies Pencil to the Life. 2*", *Early Modern Literary Studies*, 11, 3 (2006) 6.1–40.

of the royal Court, in 1642. She became a maid of honour to Queen Henrietta Maria in 1643, and in 1644 accompanied her into exile in France.

It was in the exiled Court of Henrietta Maria that Margaret Lucas met Cavendish, widowed since the death in 1643 of his first wife, Elizabeth, when he joined the Court after his defeat at Marston Moor. After a semi-secret courtship—conducted in a thoroughly literary fashion through exchanges of poems and letters, and opposed by Henrietta Maria and other courtiers—they married in December 1645. They then moved to Rotterdam and finally to Antwerp where they spent the main part of their years in exile, living in the Rubenshuis which they rented from Rubens's widow.

Margaret Cavendish returned to England in 1651 with Sir Charles Cavendish, her brother-in-law, in an attempt to compound for her husband's sequestered estates. She failed in this (although Sir Charles Cavendish was able to buy Welbeck and Bolsover back), but published her *Poems and Fancies*, the first of the extensive series of writings that she produced throughout the rest of her life. Her writings (as well as her person) were immediately controversial, provoking both some ridicule, but also some admiration. The range of her writings is vast: she wrote in a variety of forms—poetry, essays, plays, mixed forms (as in her *The World's Olio*, or hot-pot), biography and autobiography—and with a range of concerns and genres (history, philosophy, natural and experimental philosophy or science, romance, even science fiction). Her reputation today is no longer equivocal or belittling of her. In the last thirty years there has been a (re)discovery of Margaret Cavendish as a major early-modern writer in English. She is now, probably, the most studied and written about seventeenth century female author in English. She is recognised as a serious scientific thinker, a significant dramatist and literary figure, and an important early feminist (if one whose position is complex.) As well as recognising her as an important literary figure in this way, critical attention to her over the last decades or so has increasingly drawn attention to the dialogic nature of her writing and how it engages with the intellectual and cultural work of other members of the Cavendish household and milieu.

Cultures of Patronage, Connoisseurship and Virtuosity

As these brief biographical outlines suggest, the Cavendishes were immersed in—and were sometimes at the centre of—an often esoteric Stuart culture, blending new and old forms of thought and aesthetics. One perspective on this is to see them as participating in a culture of connoisseurship and virtuosity. Marjorie Swann has described the early-modern culture of collecting, central

to ideas of both connoisseurship and virtuosity, as containing several facets:
'Baconian natural history . . .; a premium placed on "wonder" and "wonderful"
physical objects; the importance of textualization in the process of collecting;
and the use of collecting to create new social groups.'[31] These facets are bound
together by a logic associated with a form of self-fashioning that does not
'simply reflect a pre-existing self, but rather functions as a technology through
which selfhood is simultaneously constructed and represented'.[32] The collector, as connoisseur, creates a metonymic identity produced from the acquisition of material objects and which is centred in authorship (both in a textual
sense and in the sense of self-creation). This coming together of authorship, collection and self-imaging provides one understanding of the cultural
activity of the Cavendishes. A single work such as Margaret Cavendish's *The
World's Olio* (1655) can be seen to exemplify the dynamics of such a culture in
a very direct textual manner; almost all of her writing, however, whatever its
ostensible primary genre, might be seen to function in a similar way simultaneously to create herself, a world and the objects of that world textually. For
her, barred from the most exteriorised forms of virtuosity, the self and the text
become its mutually-formative sites.[33] William Cavendish's more dispersed
cultural activities—art collection, experimental science, natural philosophy
(including his 'system' of horsemanship), music, authorship of plays and
poems, architecture and patronage—combine to produce his abiding engagement in varied forms of self-construction and self-representation through
enacting virtuosity.

This concept of the virtuoso is, then, crucially connected to that of connoisseurship and the blend of natural and experimental science, art and self-
creation it implies. In *The English Virtuoso: Art, Medicine and Antiquarianism
in the Age of Empiricism*, Craig Ashley Hanson has pointed out that:

> [t]he earliest usage of the word in an English publication comes from
> Henry Peacham's treatise on deportment, *The Compleat Gentleman*. The
> 1634 edition explains that the possession of such rarities [antiquities
> including statues, inscriptions, and coins], by reason of their dead

---

31   Swann M., "*The Compleat Angler* and the Early Modern Culture of Collecting", *English
       Literary Renaissance* 37, 1 (Dec. 2007): 100–117, 106. See also Swann M., *Curiosities and
       Texts: The Culture of Collecting in Early Modern England* (Philadelphia: 2001).

32   Swann M., "*Compleat Angle*", 106.

33   See Graham E., "Intersubjectivity, Intertextuality, and Form in the Self-Writings of
       Margaret Cavendish", in Dowd M.E. – Eckerle J.A., *Genre and Women's Life Writing in Early
       Modern England* (Aldershot & Burlington, VT: 2007) 131–150.

costliness doth properly belong to Princes, or rather to princely
minds … Such as are skilled in them, are by the Italians termed *Virtuo*.[34]

Peacham's work, in turn, develops thought, already familiar and influential in
England, from Castiglione's *The Book of the Courtier*, first published in 1528.[35]
So, virtuosity becomes explicitly associated with its cognate term, *vertu*, the
central desirable characteristic of the aristocrat, combining moral, physical
and intellectual embodiments of excellence. *Vertu*, by the time Cavendish was
growing up had already lost its earlier military connotations since the firearms revolution had decreased the importance of the role of the cavalry in
which it had traditionally been expressed. The French nobility were particularly affected; not only did firearms render their traditional role as gendarmes
(heavy cavalrymen) obsolete but the rise of the *noblesse de la robe*, ennobled
because they held certain judicial or administrative posts, offered common-
ers a route into the peerage, one that did not require them to display military
prowess on horseback. Their solution was to attach the concept of *vertu* to the
display of horsemanship as demonstrated in the *manège*, which was as time-
consuming as learning to control a powerful steed in battle, while wielding
a heavy lance.[36] Virtuosity, as Hanson's book suggests, meshing practice and
appreciation of the arts and new sciences, not only is evident in royalist cultures of the early seventeenth century, but becomes central to the ethos of the
Royal Society and the intellectual culture of the 1660s. As several of the essays
in this collection suggest, direct participation in this culture—and reaction to
it—is central to the intellectual activities of the Cavendishes.

Perhaps most importantly, it is worth emphasising here the centrality of
notions of authorship in regard to the Cavendishes' participation in the cultural milieu associated with connoisseurship and virtuosity. For Margaret
Cavendish, excluded as a woman from the public roles normally associated
with these forms of cultural activity and production, her creation of a selfhood
through print publication of her writings marks an important moment both
in the history of women's writing and in the establishment of modern notions
of authorship and the movement from manuscript and privately circulated

---

34   Hanson 3.

35   Castiglione B., *The book of the courtier*, transl. Hoby, Sir Thomas, (1561: London).

36   Tucker T.J., "Early Modern French Noble Identity and the Equestrian 'airs above ground'",
      in Raber K. – Tucker T.J., eds., *The Culture of the Horse: Status, Discipline and Identity in the
      Early Modern World* (Basingstoke: 2005) 273–282; Shalk E., "Pluvinel, le renouvellement
      de la noblesse et les premises de L'École de Versailles", in Roche D. – Reytier D. (eds.), *Les
      écuries royales du XVIe au XVIIIe siècle* (Paris, 1998) 169–76.

aristocratic production to participation in a public print culture more generally. Although the Cavendishes' insistence on folio production of their texts served to mark their exclusivity and elite status, the shift that their cultural participation in a print culture denotes is a significant one.

Although this reference to participation in the broader cultures of connoisseurship, virtuosity and entry into print culture might suggest something of the forward-looking aspects of Cavendish cultural work and its base in a method of connection and accumulation, such descriptions of their cultural position do not fully suggest what may seem, in a modern context, the strangeness, or in Conrad Russell's word, the 'peculiarity', of the royalist cultural milieu. As Timothy Raylor suggests in his essay for this volume, cultural royalism did not comprise a cohesive movement based on a coherent epistemology but a sensibility or *mentalité* produced by forms of amalgamation, again characteristic of connoisseurship and virtuosity. So, it is a fictional account of the period that might perhaps reveal some of the strangeness of effect of this most illuminatingly. The 2014 novel, *Viper Wine*, focuses on the lives of the virtuoso son of one of the Gunpowder plotters, Sir Kenelm Digby, an associate of Cavendish, sometimes seen as belonging to the fringes of his 'circle', and Digby's wife, Venetia, a poetic muse of Ben Jonson, who was painted on her deathbed by Antony Van Dyck.[37] *Viper Wine* captures (in part, through deployment of magical realist or postmodern techniques whereby the seventeenth-century is haunted by the future) a sense of the fertile, sometimes febrile, almost hallucinatory, cultural atmosphere that prevailed in the royalist milieu. Cabbalism, Neo-Platonism, alchemy, a baroque aesthetic, medieval codes of honour and chivalry, traditional accomplishments of the aristocrat and courtier (dancing, swordplay, horsemanship), new forms of natural science, poetic and dramatic production, and connoisseurship are all present as elements of the culture surrounding the pre-Civil War, Caroline Court.

Connectivity

Ideas of connectivity are central to all the essays brought together in this collection. A glance at Margaret Cavendish's *The Life of the Thrice Noble, High and Puissant Prince William Cavendish*, a text frequently quoted or referenced by many of the authors in this volume, suggests how different forms of connectivity

---

37   See fn 5 above on virtuosity. Pacchi A., *Introduzione a Hobbes* (Bari: 1971) 16, references
      Raylor 2000, "Newcastle's Ghosts", fn 6, 95 in this context. Sarasohn in this collection refers
      to correspondence between Digby and Cavendish.

themselves intersect. Four pieces of writing preface Margaret Cavendish's 1667 biography of her husband: her dedication of the work to Charles II; a letter addressing William Cavendish himself; a Preface or introduction explaining the aims and form of the work to the reader; and a formal letter from John Rolleston, William Cavendish's secretary, to Margaret Cavendish confirming his acquiescence to her request to him for information and material for the biography. In a way that is entirely characteristic of Margaret Cavendish's deployment of multiple prefatory materials in all of her published writings, each of these provides a different perspective on the text that is to follow. Together, the different prefatory inclusions produce a multi-perspectival context to the production, reading and methodology of the text and may provide a lens through which to view the habits of thought prevalent in Cavendish circles more generally. They also orient Margaret Cavendish herself within core relationships: to the king from whom she is hoping for recognition and favour; to her husband; and to her readers. But it is the inclusion of Rolleston's letter that reminds us most forcibly of the particular household dynamics in which aristocratic cultural production occurred. In her Preface to the reader, Margaret Cavendish explains how Rolleston's role in the production of the *Life* came about:

> I desired my Lord, That he would be pleased to let me have some Elegant and Learned Historian to assist me; which request his Grace would not grant me; saying, That having never had any Assistance in the writing of my former Books, I should have no other in the writing of his Life, but the Informations from himself, and his Secretary, of the chief Transactions and Fortunes occurring in it, to the time he married me.[38]

And in her prefatory letter to her husband she also refers to Rolleston's 'best and truest Observations' as one of her sources.[39] One direct function of these various prefatory materials is, inevitably enough, to provide a sense of the 'truth' of her account. Her precisely chosen word, 'Observations', aligns Rolleston's contribution with a testimonial function that is both legalistic and scientific.[40] In subtly producing Rolleston's testimony as a form of historical scientificism (complementing the authority derived from her own

---

38   Cavendish M., *Life*, Sig b2r.
39   Ibid., single sheet, no sig, following π2v.
40   On establishing 'truth' in early modern natural philosophy, see Shapin S. – Schapiro S., *Leviathan and the Air Pump: Hobbes Boyle, and the Experimental Life* (Princeton: 1985) and Shapin S., *A Social History of Truth: Civility and Science in Seventeenth-Century England*

autobiographical references, attesting to later parts of Cavendish's life and working to legitimise the text overall),[41] Margaret Cavendish links her *Life* with her writings on natural history or experimental philosophy. These, of course, respond, in turn, to the writings of those engaged in these new intellectual fields, especially those associated with the Cavendishes through patronage relationships. But, the invocation of Rolleston's evidence reminds us, too, of the importance of the household itself to the creation and maintenance of aristocratic identities.[42]

Aristocratic identities, as the contextual account above suggests, were produced both as a source of the cultural and political activities and the material forms (buildings, collections of art or marvels, displays and entertainments) through which power was enacted—and as an effect of these. If artistic, intellectual, architectural and cultural production served metonymically to display and extend aristocratic status, power and identity (as many of the essays in this collection demonstrate), it is the aristocratic household that enables, and is central to, this productivity. As with the royal household and court, the aristocratic household, as a microcosm of the wider society, was strongly hierarchical. Those members closest to their aristocratic lords and ladies occupied a position that was highly rewarded, both financially, and through receipt of respect and prestige. Status and values corresponding to the aristocratic codes of loyalty to and honour of their lords informed the identities of gentlemen and ladies making up the 'chief officers' of an aristocratic household. How membership of the aristocratic Cavendish household might offer such a relational identity to men such as Rolleston, is suggested by the expensive, elaborate marble panel in the Warsop Parish church of St Peter and St Paul, Church Warsop (Fig. 3), erected by Rolleston's wife in his memory.[43] It reads:

(Chicago and London: 1994); Shapin S., "The House of Experiment in Seventeenth-Century England", *Isis*, 79, 3, A Special Issue on Artifact and Experiment (1988) 373–404.

41 See Graham 2007 on ways in which Margaret Cavendish used autobiography as both a source and validation of all her writings.

42 See van Benden B. – de Porter N., eds., *Royalist Refugees: William and Margaret Cavendish in the Rubens House 1648–1660* (Antwerp: 2006); Raylor 2000, "Newcastle's Ghosts"; Preface to special edition on the Cavendishes of *The Seventeenth Century* (1994) 141–144; Worsley L., "The architectural patronage of William Cavendish, first Duke of Newcastle, 1593–1676". Unpublished PhD (University of Sussex: 2001); Worsley L., "Building a Family: William Cavendish, First Duke of Newcastle, and the Construction of Bolsover and Nottingham Castles", *The Seventeenth Century* 19, 2 (Autumn 2004), 233–59.

43 On the make-up of the noble household, and how 'chief officers' are represented in the literature of the period, see Burnett M.T., "The Noble Household", chapter 5 of *Masters and Servants in English Renaissance Drama and Culture: Authority and Obedience*,

To the memory of a trusty servant, a loyal subject, a kind master, a faithfull friend, a loving husband and a good Christian. And now reader think not, yet this is to ᵞe memory of MANY but wonder that 'tis to that of ONE. To that of Mr. JOHN ROLLESTON of Rolleston, in Staffordshire well born and well bred. Well knowne & therefore well loved by ᵞe high and mighty. Wm. late lord duke of Newcastle and his noble family as having had ᵞe honour of being his secretary when he himself had yet great one of being Governor to the prince afterwards King Charles the Second as likewise that of secretary, to ᵞe army under his excellencies command in ᵞe late unhappy warrs. His approved honesty and abilities in business rendered him highly usefull to his master and his country particular to the former in ᵞe management and preservation of his estate in a time when ᵞe government: it felt it was too weak to preserve anything from RAPINE and RUINE. The advantages raised to himself out of a long & meritorious service were almost entirely lost upon the declining future of ᵞe royal party at Marston Moor & yet his good service in ᵞe end mett with what he valued above all, ᵞe honour of having been highly trusted and ᵞe comfort of having honestly discharged the trust. To ᵞe many blessings of ᵞe man here remains was added that of a long life he having lived to the age of 84 years: a long but to him a glorious tyme of tryal.

He departed this life ᵞe 22nd of December 1681 in full hopes of a joyfull Resurrection to a much better. Erected (as a MONUMENT of true love) by his entirely beloved wife and sorrowfull widow MRS ELIZABETH ROLLESTON now living in this parish MDCLXXXVI.

The visual and verbal echoes here of frontispieces and prefaces to both William and Margaret Cavendish's published volumes, as well as the extended reference to the Civil Wars and Restoration, inflected through the experience of William Cavendish and his relationship to the monarchy, suggest the cultural radiation of Cavendish values and status through household relationships and into the broader regional community represented by Rolleston's wife, Elizabeth, and the members of the parish to which Rolleston belonged.[44] This memorial

---

(Basingstoke: 1997) 155–191. For a more general historical account of the role of higher servants in the later seventeenth century, see Hainsworth D.R., *Stewards, Lords and People: The Estate Steward and his World in Later Stuart England* (Cambridge: 1992); and Richardson R.C., *Household Servants in Early Modern England* (Manchester: 2010).

44   On Cavendish burial monuments, see: Parry G., "Cavendish memorials" in Special Cavendish Edition of *The Seventeenth Century*, 275–287. On how 'burials reflected a certain version of early modern English social order; they were structured along lines of

FIGURE 3   *The Warsop Parochial Church Council kindly gave us permission to photograph and reproduce an image of the memorial panel to John Rolleston in St Peter and St Paul, Church Warsop. Copyright Elpeth Graham.*

plaque represents Rolleston as both a separate person in his own right (married and buried in his own and his wife's parish) but crucially identified through his role as secretary to William Cavendish. The two different biographical texts, Margaret Cavendish's *Life* and the monument to Rolleston, together suggest how, between the aristocratic heads of household and its members, such as Rolleston, there is a reciprocity, however unequal, of obligation and identity-conferment. [Fig. 4] And, it is through higher servants such as a secretary, an estate steward and a chaplain, that a system of values is disseminated and two-way links are produced between the aristocratic world, often metropolitan or international in its cultural modes, and local communities.[45]

Rolleston's absorption and replication of the values of his lord are, again, precisely suggested by the letter to Margaret Cavendish, included amongst her Prefaces to the *Life*. Addressing Margaret, using the rhetorical mode of *aporia*, he provides a summary of core features and values of Cavendish and his life by describing the very attributes that he says he will not mention:

> And because I humbly conceive, that it is not within the intention of your Graces Commands, that I should give you a particular Relation of His Graces High Birth, his Noble and Princely Education and Breeding, both at home and abroad; his Natural Faculties, and Personal Vertues; his Justice, Bounty, Charity, Friendship; his Right Approved Courage, and True Valour, not grounded upon, or govern'd by Passion, but Reason; his Magnificent manner of living and supporting his Dignity, testified by his Great Entertainments of their Majesties, and his private Friends, upon all fit occasions, beside his ordinary and constant House-keeping and Attendants; some for honour, and some for business, wherein he exceeded most of his Quality; and that he was, and is an incomparable Master to his Servants, is sufficiently testified by all or most of the chiefest of them, living and dying in His Graces Service, which is an Argument that they thought themselves as happy therein, as the World could make them; nor of his well-chosen Pleasures, which were principally Horses of all sorts, but more particularly Horses of Mannage; His Study and Art of the true use of the Sword; His magnificent Buildings.

Rolleston's contribution to both Margaret's and William's published works (and the manuscript writings of other family members) took a direct and

---

family and social class', see: Masten J., *Intertextual Intercourse: Collaboration, Authorship, and Sexualities in Renaissance Drama*, (Cambridge: 1997) 2.

45   Hainsworth, 1–5. See also Raylor 2000, "Newcastle's Ghosts".

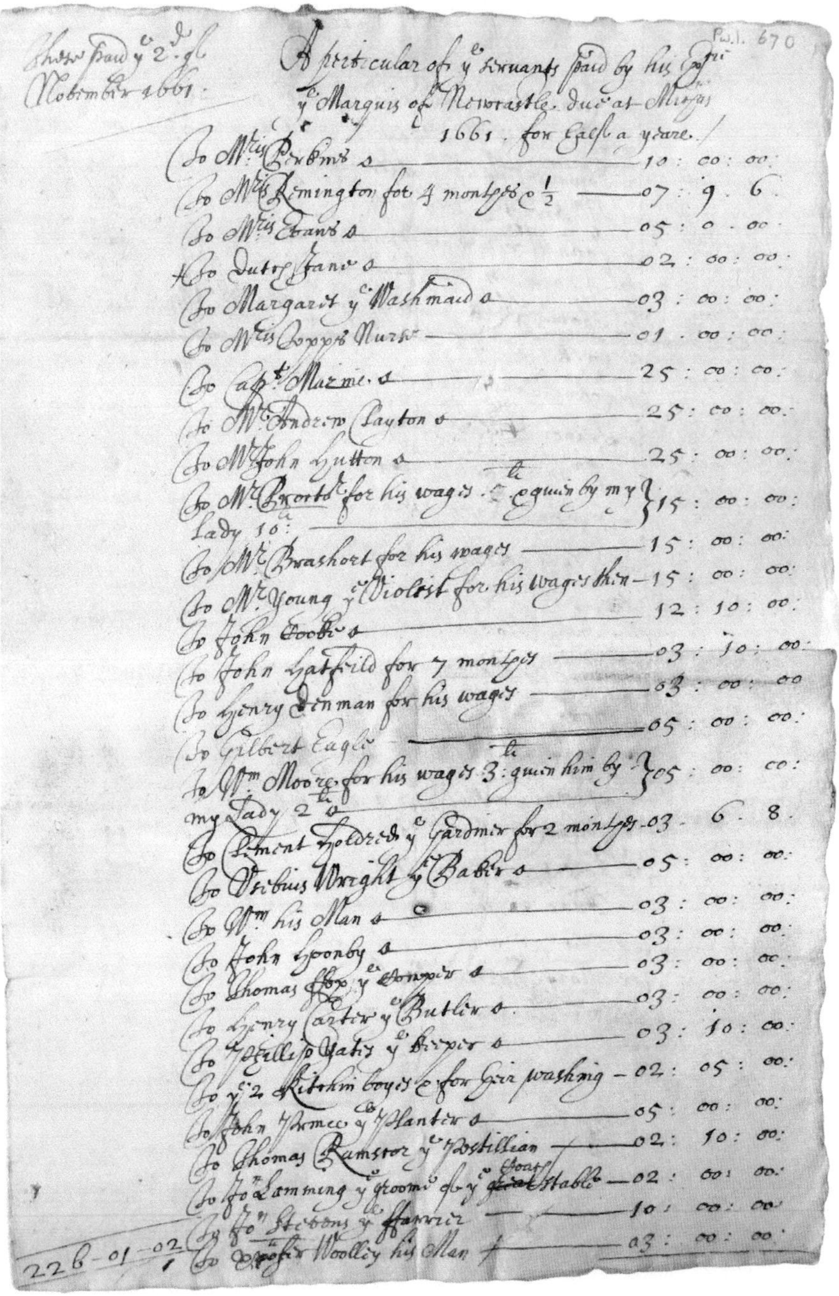

FIGURE 4   *Payments to household servants showing their place in the household through conventions of naming and salaries: Captain Mazin (Cavendish's Master of the Horse), Mr Andrew Layton and Mr John Lutton. Reproduced by kind permission of the Department of Manuscripts and Special Commissions, University of Nottingham, ref. no. Portland Collection, Pw1/670.*

material form, too. It was Rolleston who transcribed Cavendish's literary writings—his poems, plays and masques—and in so doing, corrected spellings and technical errors. His role as a copy editor in revising Cavendish's work brings to light the broader dynamics of textual production in the Cavendish household.

As several significant books and essays have suggested in recent years, Cavendish cultural production cannot be thought of solely—or even mainly— in terms of individual authorship.[46] Lucy Worsley's work on Bolsover Castle highlights household relationships, suggesting that William Cavendish's architectural work was shaped and motivated by his role and responsibilities as the head of an aristocratic family and household who needed to manage the relationships of its members.[47] Or, writing about early modern drama, Jeffrey Masten suggests that, 'collaboration was the Renaissance English theatre's dominant mode of textual production.'[48] And, the acknowledged participation of members of the Cavendish family in each other's dramatic productions occurs regularly. For instance, Margaret Cavendish, in a Preface to her *Playes*, writes: 'My Lord...was pleased to illustrate my Playes with Scenes of his own Wit' (*Playes*, A6); Cavendish's daughters, Elizabeth Brackley and Jane Cavendish are joint authors of *The Concealed Fancies*, with some, but not all, of their individual contributions marked; both Margaret and William Cavendish write in dialogue with Ben Jonson,[49] so that a play such as Cavendish's *Witts Triumvirate, or, The Philosopher* is so firmly imprinted with Jonsonian influences that it might seem, to a modern reader, to be close to plagiarism.[50] Equally, servant or client

---

46   On the significance of revision to literary studies in general, although to literary modernism in particular, see Sullivan H., *The Work of Revision* (Cambridge MA: 2014). On literary collaboration in particular relationship to the Cavendishes, see, amongst many, Raber K., *Dramatic Difference: Gender, Class, and Genre in the Early Modern Closet Drama* (Newark and London: 2001) Chapter 5, where Raber examines Margaret Cavendish's plays as occurring in dialogue with the work of Thomas Killigrew and in relation to William Cavendish, arguing that, in the plays, Margaret 'Cavendish recreates her husband's reputation. As the subject of her text, he is restored to power and made the authority he believed himself before the war', 235. See also Masten, Ch. 5 "Mistris Corrival: Margaret Cavendish's Dramatic Production", 156-164.

47   Worsley L., (University of Sussex: 2001).

48   Masten, 14.

49   See Masten, Chapter 5, esp. 159–60, for a reading of Margaret Cavendish's writing in relation to Ben Jonson and ideas of single and dialogic authorship, 162.

50   On Ben Jonson as the 'inventor' of the idea of plagiarism and Margaret Cavendish's relationship to 'emergent paradigms of authorship' see Masten 159–62.

members of the Cavendish household appear in William Cavendish's non-dramatic, published books: for example, Captain Mazin, Cavendish's Master of Horse, is present in those of van Diepenbecke's illustrations to Cavendish's *Systeme Nouvelle* that show methods of riding and equine training, while in this same text Cavendish also names, and enters into dialogue with, the 'most excellent philosopher master Hobbes' (1743L: 12). Then, as Timothy Raylor has shown in "Newcastle's Ghosts", an important essay on Cavendish textual production, it is likely that Robert Payne, Cavendish's chaplain at Welbeck, who also undertook other roles such as assisting in and contributing to the Cavendish brothers' scientific projects, operated as an editor of Cavendish's literary writings, subtly reworking and improving them.[51] Payne's contribution to Cavendish's writings provides just one particular example of ways in which the hierarchical, but complex and fluid, relationships involving family members, clients, servants and external correspondents, were involved in Cavendish cultural production. Raylor's suggestion that the 'so-called Cavendish, Newcastle, or Welbeck circle is really best understood as an extension of the aristocratic household' implicitly informs the discussion in all the essays in this book. Inter-relationship, in a wide variety of forms, is a concern throughout.[52]

Familial, patronage and household relationships do not occur only through direct collaboration or personal interaction. The sort of participatory sensibility we are describing here also manifests itself as intertextual relationship, appropriation and consciously-voiced dialogism. It similarly informs habits of written style. Reference to a rhetorical mode characteristic of Margaret Cavendish's writing again serves to magnify—and so produce a heightened image of—underlying intertextual relationships operating amongst the Cavendishes and their connections more generally. Just as Rolleston's use of *aporia* in his letter prefacing Margaret Cavendish's *Life* might be understood to imitate the courtly mode of *sprezzatura*, in which apparent ease simultaneously denies but expresses the invisible and unrepresented effort that lies behind it, Margaret Cavendish's style often suggests underlying negotiations of relationship that are at odds with her surface meanings. A single example from the prefatory letter 'To His Grace the Duke of Newcastle' in her *Life* suggests how, even at the level of rhetoric, connectivity is a crucial aspect of all Cavendish work and particularly of Margaret Cavendish's own self-creation.

Concluding this letter, Margaret Cavendish speaks of slights that Cavendish has received. She then (moving on to a habitual concern with the difficulties

51 Raylor 2000, "Newcastle's Ghosts", esp.94–110.
52 Ibid., 114.

that their roles in the world produce for women) compares her own, differently-provoked rebuffs with his, producing an equivalence between their situations—they both, in their different ways, have suffered for their heroism:

> [T]he Censures of this Age . . . stain even Your Lordships Loyal, Noble and Heroick Actions, as well as they do mine, though yours have been of War and Fighting, mine of Contemplating and Writing: Yours were performed publicly in the Field, mine privately in my Closet: Yours had many thousand Eye-witnesses, mine none but my Waiting-maids.[53]

Here, she exploits parallelism, a favourite comparative device of hers, to point up, but also to undercut, differences between the contexts in which men and women operate. In so doing, she implicitly moves her own position from the unseen, private domain in which the activity of her writing occurs into the public world of the battlefield where honour is gained, witnessed and defended. Evocation of censure as the ground of likeness between herself and her husband allows her analogically to shift the site of her activity from the feminine and domestic realm to the world of external action. In such a way her use of similitude serves as a transporting mechanism with a double function. Not only does she figuratively move from one domain to another (thereby hinting at the equal importance of her and William's activities), but she also changes the origin and agency of this move. It is as if the response of a censuring audience makes her work public, rather than the publishing of her work (since the work is actually done modestly in private). This raising of her own work to the status of her husband's, also, of course, produces her own identity through autobiographical reference as a goal in her writing of the *Life* that is equivalent to her more explicit aim of celebrating Cavendish's career, status and selfhood. So, in this text, centrally concerned with an articulation of her husband's identity, Margaret Cavendish also produces, through her use of a comparative device, a form of her own selfhood—a selfhood that is displaced onto the being of others before it is returned to the original locus of self, bearing with it the characteristics of those others. This single, but typical, instance of such a rhetorical manoeuvre serves to indicate something of the complex interplay of different forms of authorship (self-creation and textual) as well as the interaction between people, texts and activities that inform all aspects of the Cavendishes' lives and works. Interpretations of this complexity of exchange, dialogue, interpersonal, textual and intertextual relationship,

---

53   Cavendish M., *Life of William Cavendish*, Sig. b1r—Sig. b1v.

at different moments in the life and afterlife of William Cavendish, form a central concern of the essays in this volume.

The Book, the Essays and Their Themes

The book, then, comprises a series of linked essays, focused on the duke, his family and their connections, highlighting these various issues that relate to our concern with elite authority and aristocratic identity. In order to reflect the varied career of William Cavendish as a *paterfamilias*, horse master, politician, courtier, estate manager, refugee (and even conspirator), as well as his literary, artistic, architectural and scientific interests, we have adopted a primarily thematic approach. This approach is, however, also shaped by a chronological awareness of the dramatic twists and turns in Cavendish's fortunes over time. The highs and lows that William Cavendish experienced naturally affected his political and social standing and, as a consequence, the degree of authority that he and his household wielded. In turn, his view of his personal identity and feelings of self-worth rose or fell according to his particular circumstances.

A defining moment in his life, his defeat at the Battle of Marston Moor, features strongly in this collection: the essays written by Peter Edwards, Elspeth Graham and Andrew Hooper are all concerned with interpreting its implications. Although Prince Rupert shared responsibility for the defeat at Marston Moor, Cavendish took the blow so badly that he immediately went into exile, reputedly unwilling to face the laughter of the Court. Inevitably, his decision to abandon the cause further damaged his reputation, offering a propaganda coup to his opponents—and not merely those in the Parliamentarian ranks. The royalist statesman, Edward Hyde, Earl of Clarendon, for instance, reveals his intense dislike of Cavendish in the assessment he made of him in his history of the Civil Wars, which he began in his own exile in 1649.[54] While admitting that Cavendish was personally brave, he castigates him as an incompetent commander and a dilettante, better suited to the pursuit of pleasure than to the rigours of war. Andrew Hopper's essay here gives a more balanced assessment of his military record, one in tune with recent historians' assessments of his performance as the commander of the king's northern army. Overall, Hopper's conclusion is mixed, the positives and negatives reflecting the strengths and weaknesses of Cavendish's character. He suggests that while it required someone of his status, wealth, connections—and administrative capabilities—to drum up support among the northern gentry and assemble the largest royalist

---

54   Clarendon, Vol. 3, 382–83.

field army, his lack of ruthlessness and tenacity prevented him from making best use of his advantages. Hopper considers, too, the differing accounts of his motives and whether, as some contemporaries and later historians claimed, he created an army that would merely reflect his own grandeur.

Edwards's essay considers the difficulty and consequences of Cavendish's decision to flee into exile after Marston Moor. At a stroke, Edwards points out, he lost everything he held dear: his power and influence; his status and wealth; his reputation and self-esteem; and his possessions, including his beloved horses. Looking back to ways in which Cavendish's personality had caused him problems in his relations with others at Court in the years 1638–41, Edwards suggests his defeat and flight were hardly likely to win him new friends and political influence among the various competing royalist factions abroad. Edwards identifies the despair that Cavendish felt in exile, in one letter gloomily contrasting the indifference of his fellow-countrymen with the generosity of foreigners among whom he was living. Graham's essay similarly takes the defeat at Marston Moor as a starting point in her essay. This considers how the aesthetic modes deriving from Cavendish's immersion in the courtly cultures of the pre-Civil War period, particularly its neoplatonism, were adapted and developed to promote his self-image in the years of exile and into the Restoration period. Graham explores how both a continuing adherence to aesthetic and philosophical forms of thought from the early seventeenth century and an elaborated re-working of these are used by Cavendish, in the context of his core familial and cultural relationships, in the work of attempting to restore his reputation and self-image.

Experience of the period of exile in the 1640s and 50s is, again, central to the explorations of reputation and influence made by Lisa Sarasohn and Madeleine Dewhurst in their complementary essays. Sarasohn, having established the nature of the relationship between Hobbes and Cavendish in the 1630s, links the issues of Cavendish's reputation with the Hobbesian concept of honour, achieved by the acclamation of one's peers and royal favour. She argues that Cavendish failed on both counts. At the Court-in-exile, Cavendish advocated a policy of accommodation with the Scottish Engagers after the execution of Charles I in 1649, in opposition to the anti-Scottish feelings of other influential figures such as Edward Hyde (perhaps contributing to his antipathy towards Cavendish) and Secretary Nicholas. Sarasohn suggests that it was because of Cavendish's decline in reputation that his client, Thomas Hobbes, reputedly snubbed Margaret Cavendish when she returned to London in 1650. Dewhurst, on the other hand, is more positive. She argues that apart from his social status and military experience, which made him an invaluable figurehead, his friendship with the Queen ensured his continuing involvement in émigré affairs. She points to his being a member of the exiled Privy Council from 1650 to at least 1653, and as a figure of authority in the expatriate community, being called upon to maintain law and order. Similarly, she analyses the geographic and political importance of Antwerp as the main location of the Cavendishes' residence during the exile period. She suggests that by 1656, as a result of the settlement of the future Charles II's Court in nearby Bruges, Antwerp's profile was raised among the English refugees.

In debt, and in the changed circumstances of diminished possibilities of direct political activity, or exploitation of his estate-based incomes to promote his image, William Cavendish turned to restoration of his reputation—amongst both English *émigrés* and the European nobility—through more purely cultural forms, both performative and textual. His public displays of horsemanship became especially important. Although he had bought and exercised horses for the *manège* shortly after he had arrived from England, it was only at Antwerp that he began to stage-manage the events. Princes, peers and governors (even the future Charles II) watched him perform and acclaimed him as a master. At the same time, Cavendish sought to capitalise on his fame by writing about his training methods in a lavishly produced and illustrated book, *La Méthode Nouvelle et Invention Extraordinaire de Dresser les Chevaux* (1657–8), which circulated privately among his peers. Don John, the Governor-General of the Spanish Netherlands, even requested a copy of the book before publication and then, having read the manuscript, expressed his great satisfaction with it. No doubt, the contacts that he made through his equestrian activities aided Cavendish's attempts to establish his credibility among his peers and at Court, matters which Dewhurst writes about.

Cavendish's displays and writings on the *manège* created a profound effect on his peers because of the potent symbolism of horses and horsemanship. In an age of poor communications and mass illiteracy, the rulers of early modern England sought to demonstrate their social, economic and political ascendancy in as public a way as possible. If the ostentatious extravagance and political symbolism of a country seat surrounded by landscaped gardens and park were significant metonyms of status, horses arguably were even more important in projecting an image of wealth, status and authority. Horses pulled their owners' gilded and crested coaches, conveyed their retinues of liveried retainers around the country and provided the essential platform for participation in such archetypically elitist pastimes as hunting, hawking, jousting, racing and the *manège*. Among the landed elite good horsemanship not only defined a gentleman but also validated the authority they wielded in the country at all levels of government. As symbols of strength and power, these animals helped to imprint in the mind of the general population the notion that their rulers governed them because of their natural superiority and effortless authority, particularly important in a country without a standing army or professional law-enforcers. To be seen in public riding and controlling such a puissant animal, was to prove that person's fitness to rule. As James I told his son, Henry, 'It becometh a Prince better than any other man to be a fair and good horseman'.[55] The European nobility similarly valued fine horses for their iconic appeal. For Prince Karl Eusebius von Liechenstein (1611–84), one of the most knowledgeable horsemen of his time, fine horses were an essential part of a nobleman's lifestyle and a defining characteristic.[56]

Richard Nash's essay describes how, in his displays of horsemanship, Cavendish was enacting 'a distinctly princely artistic performance of proper management and control'. Pondering why Cavendish preferred the _manège_ over the far more popular sport of horse-racing, he argues that Cavendish viewed racing as a recreational pursuit rather than as an art and one over-concerned with breed identity. Cavendish's empirical approach led him to treat horses as individuals, all of whom could be trained by an expert horseman. In the same way, the absolute ruler's task, in political terms, was to bring out the best in each individual. Nash also discusses the contrasting political standpoints of Cavendish and Thomas Fairfax, his Parliamentarian opponent, reflected in their interpretation of the theory of geohumoralism, the former emphasizing the need to maintain the _status quo_ and the latter pursuing a process of steady improvement through breeding.

If teaching a stallion to perform the refined airs developed skills also necessary to govern subjects, it not only justified aristocratic rule but made it inevitable. As Cavendish stressed, and as Elaine Walker's detailed account of Cavendish's methods indicates, the training process was lengthy, time-consuming and expensive. The ultimate aim was to achieve complete synchronicity between horse and rider so that to the onlooker it appeared that the two acted as one. Cavendish made the analogy with the classical concept of the centaur, a composite being, with a human brain and a horse's body. Walker emphasises Cavendish's belief in the relationship between horsemanship and governance but extends its significance to incorporate his conviction that _La Méthode Nouvelle_ provided a blueprint for the way husbands should govern their family and rulers should preside over their kingdom. It is precisely such an analogy between the relationship of rider and horse with men's governance

---

55   Cited in Reese M.M., _The Royal Office of the Master of the Horse_ (London: 1976) 166.

56   Bayreuther M., _Pferde und Fürsten: repräsentative reitkunst und pferdehaltung an fränkischen Höfen (1600–1800)_ (Würzburg: 2014) 75. The author describes him as 'einer der kompetentesten Pferdekenner und – zuchter seiner Zeit'.

over women that Margaret Cavendish takes issue with, as Alison Findlay argues
in her essay.

Monica Mattfeld, like Walker, focuses on the concept of the centaur in
her essay, arguing that the kinaesthetic relationship that a skilled horseman
enjoyed with the non-human creature evidenced his ability to govern properly.
He was ultimately participating in a display that enhanced his performance
as a 'masculine' man who was governed (that is, was in control of himself)
and, thus, was in turn capable of governing others. Possessing the skills of
the *manège* established an interchange that metaphorically and ontologi-
cally embodied a Hobbesian body politic, providing an avenue for the practice of political, equestrian and masculine governance. As Mattfeld points
out, Cavendish believed that one could not separate politics from honour
nor distinguish between ideal manly behaviour and gentlemanly sovereignty
while mounted or not. For him, to be a gentleman was to be a man of honour and only an honourable person could fulfil his duty to the state and to his
monarch. Sarasohn makes the same point. Indeed, she argues that Hobbes's
notion of the equality of men in the state of nature was informed by his knowledge of aristocratic society, and particularly by his association with William
Cavendish. The men Hobbes described in his political works are motivated
by the desire to be honoured, because honour is an 'acknowledgement of
power' and power guarantees security. At the time Hobbes was formulating his
political theory—*The Elements of Law* (1640) is dedicated to Cavendish—
and he was aware that the latter's honour had been challenged by factions
within the Court. In a sense, the royalists had dissolved into a state of nature
lacking a central authority, a situation in which it was difficult for an aristocratic
courtier to retain or regain his honour. As several essays here suggest, then, such
ideas were pervasive in Cavendish's milieu—and in his own life and thought
they are frequently tied up with his practice of and writing on horsemanship.
The importance to Cavendish of establishing his own identity and values is
clearly discernible in the two horsemanship manuals he wrote. Walker further
suggests that in the French version, published in exile in 1658, he included
engravings of his pre-war possessions to boost his reputation and image among
an exclusive Continental readership, while the English version of 1667, published after his return, served to make his countrymen aware of the contrast
between his reception on the Continent and the way they had treated him.
Edwards argues that the lavish 1658 publication, designed to impress, had a self-
publicising purpose, while in 1667 he was writing to revive interest in the
manège in England. In doing so, he was trying to benefit from the acquisition
of 'cultural capital' that these publications would bring him, putting him at the
head of a line of famous horse masters who had committed their method to

print and, incidentally, displacing Blundeville's manual as the key horseman-ship text in England.

However, as Karen Raber points out, the implications of possessing horse-manship skills and of Cavendish's publishing his 'method' or 'system' are com-plex. Unpicking the connotations of the word 'breeding', Raber shows how it implies conflicting ideas: it refers both to birth (inherent, inborn qualities that cannot be transferred or appropriated) and to education (learned or trans-ferred qualities). To produce an equitation manual in print, especially one whose title includes the words 'method' or 'system', suggesting something that can be reproduced, brings this tension to the fore. Through an extended explo-ration of these ideas and of theories of cultural capital, Raber identifies the risk Cavendish ran of extending the social range of readers beyond the exclusive ranks he wanted to reach and of undermining the very notions of aristocratic superiority that were central to his self-identification through mastery in the *manège*. Ultimately, horsemanship could (and, in time, did) become a com-modity, a mere money-making project.

Alison Findlay's essay approaches this central issue of horse-related cultures and authority rather differently. She focuses on the writings of Margaret Cavendish to provide a relational perspective on Cavendish's immer-sion in the manège. Findlay points to Margaret Cavendish's witty juxtaposition of the idea that man and wife are one flesh with her husband's idea of horse and rider joined in 'but one Body, and one Mind, like a *Centaur.*' Findlay's essay examines Margaret Cavendish's appropriations of horse references as tropes within her own writings to explore how they might be read in the light of her own determination to claim authority—from under the shadow of her hus-band's *manège*—as a writer and in the public sphere. Findlay's essay, in this way, addresses the issues of ownership of artistic and intellectual works in the context of the hierarchic-participatory milieu we have described and tensions between individual and collective authorship, especially in relation to gender.

In her essay, Lisa Hopkins argues that Cavendish's two eldest daughters, Jane and Elizabeth, similarly sought to establish their own identities through author-ship.[57] Focusing on their play, *The Concealed Fancies*, Hopkins emphasizes ways

---

57   Lady Jane Cavendish, later the wife of Charles Cheyne, Viscount Newhaven, was consid-
      ered by her father to be the most literary of his children. She entered into witty poetic dia-
      logue with her father from a young age, as suggested in manuscript materials: WC: 'Sweet
      Jane / I know you are a rare Inditer.—/ And hath the Pen off a moste redye writer. / W.N.';
      JC: 'My Lord / I know you doo but Jest with mee / & so in obdence I right this nothing /
      Jane Cavendysshe.' (NUL, Portland Collection, Pw V 25:21–22). She probably continued to
      write poetry throughout her life, although only a few poems survive. Elizabeth Cavendish

in which they placed themselves firmly within a mainstream dramatic tradition. The intertextual alignment of *The Concealed Fancies* with other dramatic works, from both widely-established and local traditions, not only produces their selves but also, as Hopkins argues, reflects more generally 'the centrality of literary discourse to seventeenth century aristocratic culture'. Hopkins also points out that the sisters based the fictitious characters and the setting on actual members of the Cavendish family circle and their circumstances at the time: their fictional *alter egos*, who are pining for their absent father, are themselves trapped in their home by a besieging army. The play, therefore, as well as being open to a range of specifically literary interpretations, provides readers with unique insights into Cavendish family relationships and, more widely, the dynamics governing the lives of the aristocracy in general. In particular, it reveals the problems faced by intelligent, well-bred young women living in a patriarchal society. While they loved and respected their father, they satirised the difficulties they would encounter on marriage, including the negotiation of a dowry; the conflicting notions of the dynastic imperative and romantic love; the authority of their husband; and the separation from their home and family and with it the thorny question of their relationship with their mother-in-law. Hopkins' essay both acknowledges this direct reflection of traditional aristocratic women's lives and demonstrates how 'the sisters use drama … actively to shape and fashion' them. The essay, in discussing issues of 'literary belonging', argues that their writing allowed them to participate in 'the shared cultural conversation of England's beleaguered aristocracy'.

As a scion from a junior branch of an ennobled family, with even more illustrious connections, Cavendish was keen to establish and enhance his aristocratic credentials. His uncle, also William Cavendish, the head of the senior branch of the family, was ennobled in 1605 and created earl of Devonshire in 1618, shortly after 'our' William Cavendish came into his inheritance. That must have stimulated his own ambition in the pursuit of power and influence, locally, at Court, or in the government, as well his collection of titles and acquisition of land. He also stamped his personality on his building works. If his father planned the Little Castle at Bolsover in conjunction with his architect, John Smithson, it was designed with his son in mind. William had

---

married John Egerton, 2nd Earl of Bridgewater, in 1641. She similarly wrote throughout her life—particularly prayers, meditations, and essays. (The Loose Papers: BL MS Egerton 607, f.30). A collection of writings by both the sisters during the Civil War period, with their individual contributions marked by John Rolleston, and including *The Concealed Fancies*, comprises *Poems Songs a Pastorall and a Play by the Right Honorable the Lady Jane Cavendish and Lady Elizabeth Brackley* (Bodleian Library, MS Rawl., Poet. 16).

to complete the project, and in the interior fixtures and furnishings we can clearly see the expression of his personality and aspirations.

Inheriting a love of architecture from his father, Sir Charles, who was an expert in the language of classical architecture, Cavendish also continued patronage of the Smithson dynasty of builder-architects. Robert Smithson, who assisted in the design and construction of such prodigy houses as Longleat and Wollaton Hall, had also worked on Hardwick Hall for Cavendish's grandmother, Elizabeth (Bess) of Hardwick. John Smithson, Robert's son, helped realise Sir Charles 's plans for improvements at Bolsover and designed the riding school for Cavendish at his main residence, Welbeck Abbey (Nottinghamshire). Adrian Woodhouse, outlining the importance of architectural work to Cavendish, points out that he commissioned the Welbeck riding school as soon as the problems surrounding his father's will (he died in 1617) were resolved in 1620: Smithson's plan is dated 1622 and work probably began in 1623. Adjoining the riding school, Woodhouse shows, Cavendish provided lodgings for his Master of Horse, the Frenchman John Mazin, who enabled Cavendish to refine his system through serving as a model pupil in practical trials. Malcolm Airs's essay extends the consideration of the importance of Cavendish's buildings by looking at the reasons underlying the vogue for building or rebuilding equestrian buildings such as coach houses, stables and riding houses. Often planned as an integral part of the overall design of house and offices, they reflect the iconic value of the animals (and vehicles) housed inside them. His study makes particular reference to the riding schools at Bolsover and Holland House, the home of Cavendish's rival, Henry, Earl of Holland.

As Woodhouse indicates, provision for his horses, however, was only a part of Cavendish's building programme for Bolsover and Welbeck, undertaken to fulfil his aim of creating homes that reflected his wealth and status and which were fit to receive the monarch. He accomplished this successfully, and did indeed entertain Charles I at Bolsover in 1634, a year after he had hosted a visit by Charles I, Henrietta Maria and their party at Welbeck. It was for this visit that Cavendish commissioned Ben Jonson to write his masque, *Loves Welcome*. It had been his mother's death at the end of 1628, just after Cavendish became Earl of Newcastle and lord-lieutenant of Derby, that not only enabled him to enhance his image by buying properties in London and Derby, but also provided him with the funds to commission work on Bolsover Castle making it suitable for a royal visit. Of course, Cavendish, like others who entertained their monarch, hoped that their hospitality would lead to preferment at Court. If he did not obtain the coveted office of the Master of the Horse, he did become the governor of Prince Charles, the heir to the throne.

While Cavendish's building projects provide us with a further example of the forward-looking characteristics that are revealed in his cultural activities and family governance, his conservatism is shown in his traditional view of aristocratic honour, which was being supplanted by a newer version during the course of his lifetime. The chivalric code, to which Cavendish adhered, found echoes in the symbolism that surrounded his installation, along with his companions, into the Order of the Bath. Jim Fitzmaurice links the general appeal of French romances in the seventeenth century to Cavendish's own interest in romance, derived from riding horses. Fitzmaurice explores Cavendish's use of and attraction to whimsy as an under-explored aspect of creating connection and relationship textually and as linked to the importance of such traditional values as loyalty, kindness and honour. Indeed, when, in 1610, Cavendish was made Knight of the Bath as one of Prince Henry's companions, he became a participant in what resembled a scene from *Morte d'Arthur*, or a French romance. The impact of this on the afterlife of the Cavendish sensibility, as Fitzmaurice further notes, is shown by the deep investment of Henrietta Cavendish Harley (Cavendish's great granddaughter) in inherited aspects of romance, creating a world with an imagery now known as Gothic.

While this essay, along with many others in the collection, remind us that Cavendish was an aesthete and a patron of the arts, Timothy Raylor's essay specifically looks at Cavendish's connection with Hobbes in relation to Hobbes's work on the science of motion, which he believed to be the universal cause of all things. As it included moral philosophy, the 'motions of the mind', it dealt with the root causes of human action, and therefore had a political dimension. Raylor assesses the impact that Hobbes's thoughts on the views of both William and Margaret Cavendish and William's brother, Charles, all of whom were keenly interested in the scientific advances being made at the time. Raylor's essay importantly brings to the fore ideas about the nature of the new philosophy, or science, and how we interpret it. It demonstrates the connective nature of the world of the Cavendishes. Not only are people and texts inter-relational, but also in Hobbes' thought, mind and body share a material, connective likeness through their mutual dependence on motion to produce thought and life in the world.

I. *Aristocratic Identity*

∵

Setting the Scenes: The Pre-Civil War Building Works of William Cavendish in Context

Adrian Woodhouse

This article is the first account of William Cavendish's very diverse pre-1642 building projects to anchor them in their personal, regional and even royal contexts. Using newly identified or previously unconsidered contemporary evidence, including forensic analysis of the drawings of the Cavendish family architect, John Smithson, it indicates how Cavendish switched the principal focus of his colossal building expenditure over the period[1] from Bolsover to Welbeck and back again. It highlights works whose importance or even existence have been overlooked and it argues that his constructions, while establishing his identity and increasing his authority, were largely prompted by dynastic and other events over which he had little or no control. It also stresses his good fortune, as he himself appreciated, to have inherited an architect-designer who enabled him to realise his aims, perhaps with some unexpected consequences.

New Patron and the Family Architect

Cavendish's architectural endeavours began after cruel family failure. In early 1617 he was newly influential as executor of the vast, debt-entangled estate of his uncle, Gilbert Talbot, 7th Earl of Shrewsbury, and was preparing to give Countess Mary, his now widowed aunt, Welbeck's customary help with royal visitors at next-door Worksop Manor.[2] Suddenly, his 63-year-old father, Sir Charles, became incapacitated and died on 4 April, just three days before the

---

1 Margaret Cavendish claimed that William had spent £31,000 on his building projects: Cavendish M., *Life of William Cavendish*, 102; the annual earnings of a Bolsover Castle mason were then about £20 vide Douglas Knoop D. – Jones G.P. (eds.), *The Bolsover Castle Building Accounts 1613* (London: 1939) passim.

2 Sheffield Archives (hereafter SA), Arundel MSS W f. 151 confirms countess Mary's now-ignored dower tenure of Worksop; Nichols J.B., *The Progresses, Processions, and Magnificent Festivities of King James the First* (London: 1823) vols. 1–3 passim and HMC, "Portland MSS"

Scotland-bound royal progress was due to arrive.[3] Black-draped Welbeck with its corpse was no place to accommodate any of the court party. With so many members of the entourage having to cram with the king, the Prince of Wales and the favourite, Buckingham, into Worksop, the floor of its third-storey great chamber, then containing the royal throne, collapsed.[4]

The 23-year-old Cavendish and his capable mother, Katherine, who, as his father's sole executrix, initially controlled Welbeck's finances, determined on two emphatic architectural statements to restore family dignity. They would erect a grander monument to Sir Charles than any other constructed for the clan, including that of its house-building matriarch, Elizabeth, William Cavendish's grandmother and the previous Shrewsbury dowager. In addition, they would fulfil his parents' ambitions for the once-royal, recently-Talbot castle of Bolsover, where barely four years earlier his father had begun a picture-book new keep on a great escarpmment commanding Derbyshire. Built as a symbolic *pleasaunce* for the just four-strong Welbeck branch of the Cavendishes,[5] this trumpeted the refined chivalry of Sir Charles, a Padua-educated connoisseur and renowned swordsman, who had fought alongside Sir Philip Sidney, as well as the ancient, much-castled Northumbrian nobility of 'magnetic' Lady Cavendish.[6] These were attributes far more precious to its new master than the freshly minted coronets for cash of William Cavendish, his paternal uncle, owner now of all three houses built by Elizabeth. Naturally, he and his mother had recourse to their family scenographer of the previous two decades, John Smithson.

II (London: 1893) 118, record six royal visits to Shrewsbury houses 1603–1616, including 1604 when Cavendish played host to the three year old Prince Charles.

3   NA, DDP 6/1/19/11, dated 27/3/1617.

4   Cheshire Archives (hereafter CA), ZCR 469/450. I am grateful to Dr James Loxley, its discoverer, for sharing his transcription with me in 2010; customarily a progress house's great chamber was set up by royal officials as a temporary royal "presence".

5   1616 (4 × 4, 4 × 4) is inscribed on the hall fireplace and the building has four towers, four staircases, four main rooms, four family bedchambers and a best bedchamber suite of four rooms. The Julian-style end of 1616 was only days before Sir Charles's death.

6   Talbot Papers, Lambeth Palace Library MSS 3192–32906 and Shrewsbury Papers, College of Heralds, passim chart Sir Charles's two years at Padua (including Venetian and Florentine visits and embracing publication date of Andrea Palladio's *Quattro Libri*) as well as his architectural and musical connoisseurship; BL, Add MS 4161/5 is his letter from Zutphen; Lady Cavendish's Bertram and Ogle forebears held Northumbrian and Parliamentary baronies from the 13th. century and owned Ogle, Bothal and Cockle Castles along many small towers; Ben Jonson described her as 'magnetic' in his epitaph, *Under-woods* (London: 1640) no. 56.

Smithson is first recorded in Sir Charles's employ on 20 October 1597, acting as Welbeck's leading signatory to a lease to extract stone from a marked-out section of the famous Sherwood Forest quarries outside Mansfield.[7] The then thirtyish architect was familiar with their 'White' and 'Red' seams: Mansfield White faced the basement of the spectacular Wollaton Hall near Nottingham, where he had served his seven year apprenticeship and first year as a mason,[8] and red balusters appeared on one of the earliest of his 1590s dynastic set-pieces for the Shrewsburys.[9] Five miles from the quarries a hunting lodge was now to arise on a spectacular site above a new Cavendish park at Kirkby on the Nottinghamshire-Derbyshire border. Surviving drawings for an extraordinary white and red house, with a ground-plan which suggested the barbed head of a cross-bow bolt but with coloured trim and arcaded centrepieces which

---

7   NA, DDP 17/128: the quarry owner was Mansfield's grammar school. Sir Charles's 20 marks fee was the annual salary of its schoolmaster (for whom see the 1633 Welbeck entertainment below).

8   Marshall P., *Wollaton Hall and the Willoughby Family* (Nottingham: 1999) 38; Wollaton is dated 1580–88 over its front door and Smithson's rise in the building accounts from 6d. a day labourer/apprentice in April/May 1585 to 10d. a day junior mason from March 1588 indicates that he was at least twenty by the latter date and that his training and earliest work after qualification had coincided with the construction dates. (NUL, Willoughby Papers, Mi A 3 & 7 passim). In 1585 'Mr Xopher Lovell' or 'Mr Lovel' was ranked above John's father, who remained, as in 1583 and 1584, merely 'Robert Smythson' (NUL, Willoughby Papers, Mi A 60/4 f 6 & 7). Lovell, the son of the queen's master mason, who handled all Wollaton's largest building payments, (NUL, Willoughby Papers, Mi A 1–4 passim), had to leave Nottinghamshire forever in October 1585 and John's father was only elevated to the style 'Mr.' in February 1586. He later received a full-time, salaried, non-building post at Wollaton, which he held until his death, aged about seventy-nine in 1614: see Woodhouse A., *Towers and Compasses: The Lives of John Smithson*, forthcoming.

9   RIBA, Smithson Collection I/26 which with its amendment, II/14, shows Earl Gilbert's heraldic quartering colours in incorrect, then correct , marshalling, and see also II/4 (1) & (2), I/5 and I/6, the last designed before the 1601 will of Elizabeth, Countess of Shrewsbury. All bear either the formal or informal italic handwriting of John Smithson, seen on the majority of Smithson Collection drawings but only correctly identified in 1999 in Woodhouse A., "A Newly Identified Estate Plan by John Smithson, 1608", *Thoroton Society Transactions* 104 (1999), or his various scales which accompany that handwriting. The orthographical identification was accepted by Girouard M., *Elizabethan Architecture* (London: 2009) 491 fn. 4, whose catalogue of the Collection (*Architectural History*, V, 1962) had taken the handwriting to be that of Robert Smythson. Girouard's second assumption, made in 2009 (op cit 491 fn 4), of another, italic hand—on Wollaton ground plan RIBA I/24 (1)—as the father's remains at odds with Robert's long-accessible secretary style of handwriting (NUL, Willoughby Papers, Mi 5/ 165/130).

referenced Palladio's villas of Sir Charles's youth,[10] indicate that the adventurous patron had found his ideal architect.

Thereafter, Cavendish had grown up amidst Smithson's numerous schemes for Welbeck, ranging from a complete rebuilding of the earlier monastic conversion (only the guest wing was constructed) to designing the family's most intimate spaces. These comprised a fitted library and similar 'room of evidences' for Sir Charles; an exquisite, stone-vaulted chamber for Cavendish's mother, Katherine, bearing her Ogle emblems; and paired banqueting pavilions astride a garden canal.[11] The architect also outlined a planned first Cavendish tower-house in north Derbyshire. Moreover, while carrying out delicate business for the Welbeck family in the winter of 1609/10 he made drawings that bore distinct congruity to the attendance of Cavendish, then a Cambridge undergraduate, on Henry, Prince of Wales, at palaces in and around London.[12] Then, Smithson concentrated on Bolsover,[13] where he even conjured perspective to dynastic purpose. Owlcotes, the property of Cavendish's uncle, William (soon to be earl of Devonshire), was shrunk to a tiny eye-catcher directly ahead of the keep's front door and fashionable balcony,[14] between which a red sandstone Atlas, flanked by his Atlas lions, held up impaled (therefore pre-April 1617) Cavendish-Ogle arms.[15]

---

10 Chatsworth Archives, Hardwick MS 7/196v: Countess Elizabeth, October 1597: £300 to Sir Charles for his 'building at Kirkby', of which a huge length of main wall survived until c 1950 (c. 1935 photograph, courtesy of Kirkby Conservation Society, and OS maps up to 1980); RIBA II/11 & 12.

11 RIBA I/23, RIBA II/13 (described, like the library, in CA, ZCR 469/450, which also reveals that arms captured during a notorious 1599 attack on Sir Charles when he visited the Kirkby site were showcased in this 'roome of evidences'), Welbeck's surviving 'Horsemanship Room', which was Katherine Cavendish's chamber; and RIBA III/24.

12 RIBA I/1 is for Blackwell, bought 1607 by Sir Charles from Lord Cavendish (NA DDP/49 passim); vide Smithson's many '1609' drawings at and near Whitehall and St James's, near Richmond and Nonsuch as well as Theobalds and Cambridge, RIBA Collection passim. See also fn. 40.

13 RIBA III/1 (1) and Bolsover's 1613–14 building accounts, headed throughout in Smithson's hand.

14 The directly adjacent pre-1593 Owlcotes house survives beside the still visible platform of the 1593 construction which indicates the precision of the alignment.

15 The modern identification of the original, greatly eroded male figure supporting a globe with the impaled arms above (replaced in 1999/2000 by a faux-stone 'reimagining' of the putative subject) as Hercules is at odds with the positioning of lions to either side of him. Atlas, the Titan condemned to hold up the sky, or celestial globe, was traditionally depicted with lions just so—as can be seen in much 16th/17th cartography, thus giving rise to the term for a collection of maps.

Bolsover 1617–1623

The mausoleum for Sir Charles, containing a towering, standing wall-monument also designed by Smithson, was chosen to be at conspicuous Bolsover, though the dead knight had never had a chance to live there. A chapel of finest ashlar, dated 1618 on a lintel, was attached like a turret-outlier of the castle to the south elevation of the chancel of the church at the other end of the small town. Its frieze of the family motto, set below the crenellations, thus proclaimed to those entering Bolsover not just the body within but new Cavendish ownership of the whole town. The Roman Catholicism of the deceased and his widow appeared more discreetly, encoded by Smithson in a profusion of trinities in the (now much altered) cube interior and on the monument, whose polished marbles and gilding were intended to gleam by the light of Romish candles through the original sepulchral gloom. The cube, whose barrel-vault of black wood and white stucco answered the burial vault below, was originally lit by three tiny windows high on its then three outside walls and viewed from the chancel through arches echoing those over three kneeling sons on the base of the three-tiered tomb. In the middle section of the monument's tripartite inscription twenty-seven of Sir Charles's finer attributes were even marshalled in threes whose sums' sum was his happiness.[16]

In a further piece of dynastic one-upmanship Cavendish, positioning himself among London's cultural élite, commissioned the rest of the monumental inscription from Ben Jonson. Indeed, on 3 August 1618 the new laureate, then enjoying a week at Welbeck during his own progress on foot to Scotland, detoured in his young host's carriage to Bolsover to 'consult' with Smithson about Sir Charles's monument,[17] an unprecedented and symbolic collaboration. The one-time bricklayer, who had long worked with the set-designer turned royal architectural supremo, Inigo Jones, on masques glorifying the father of the nation, was now working with Cavendish's architect to extol Welbeck's *paterfamilias*. Endorsements by the architecturally literate Jonson of Smithson and the new keep as 'an excellent architect' and 'a delicate little

---

16   CA, ZCR 469/450 identifies Henry Lukin, credited in the Cavendish album (now BM Harleian MS 4955) as author of this cube route to Sir Charles's happiness, as Welbeck's mathematics tutor. Description on the monument of a second Charles junior (the first died 1594) without the knighthood he gained on 10 August 1619 (see below) suggests the tomb was then finished.

17   CA, ZCR 469/450. The manuscript states that he was 'carried' to Bolsover and since this was a deviation from his route to Edinburgh on which so much had been wagered the mode of transport was permissible.

house' served doubtless to reinforce the esteem in which Cavendish and his mother held their designer.[18]

In tandem with the chapel, the 'delicate little house' was finished. Its numerological conceit continued with four turret lodges for servants about a crenellated and cross-looped, enclosed forecourt. Behind the keep four rooms for family pleasure were made inside a thick wall, with crenellated walk above, encompassing a second Cavendish Eden which reprised Welbeck's physic garden that boasted a still house[19] and a wall-walk out from the family wing there. Bolsover's garden outline, however, owed something to Padua's walled circular *botanicum* of 1545 as well as the possible shape of the castle's old inner bailey; Renaissance and mock-Gothic ornament were likewise mingled within it. From beneath a second balcony a red sandstone Hercules, slaying the dragon Ladon, guardian of the Hesperides' garden,[20] presided over the plants and a centrepiece fountain,[21] decorated with a red and white stone bestiary of Katherine Cavendish's heraldic antelopes, bulls and busts of bearded, chapleted wildmen.[22] The fountain, like the kitchens, was originally fed from a cistern atop a two-storey turret built just outside the keep, which was supplied

---

18 Ibid., Notes made by Jonson's emanuensis on the trip reflect opinions of the great man himself: a description of Cavendish riding at Welbeck the following day recurs in Jonson's later poem on the subject, Under-woods 53. Very shortly after Jonson's visit Katherine Cavendish became the conscientious godmother to Smithson's younger son, another John, vide Woodhouse, *Towers and Compasses*.

19 A place to distill cordials and other medicinal drinks.

20 The modern identification of the original greatly eroded figure (again replaced in 1999/2000 with a faux-stone putative 're-imagining' of the subject) as Hercules killing the Nemean lion once more appears at odds with the 17th century iconography. In the course of his eleventh labour to steal the golden apples of the Hesperides, beautiful daughters of Atlas and the evening star, Hercules had to kill their dragon Ladon in order to gain the prized fruit. It was this labour, casting him as a harvester, which caused him to be regarded as one of the gods of gardening and thus was the ideal deity to command the Cavendishes' new private paradise.

21 Originally conceived seemingly as a four-jetted, Gothic tower on steps with flying buttresses and miniature cross-looped tourelles (RIBA III/25 (1–3).

22 Katherine Cavendish's serrated-horned, priapic Ogle antelope and wildmen remain prominent in her Welbeck chamber; her Bertram bull was used armorially by her son. Stone fragments of her Bolsover Ogle emblems survived, the dynastic significance unrecognised then or since, until c.1980 in one of the garden rooms and they reputedly remain in storage with English Heritage. For co-eval use at Blicking Hall of emblems on garden pillars, including Hercules, whose name remains a Latin suffix for various medicinal plants, see Henderson P., *The Tudor House and Garden* (London: 1998) 154.

from the substantial surviving spring directly below.[23] Even so, Cavendish at this stage remained true to his father's intention of leaving the family fastness stand otherwise alone on its rock. An 'old house', with named services (including a manorial courtroom) listed in the 1613–14 building accounts as being merely repaired, seemingly stood as a substantial gate-range on the far side of the outer bailey, overlooking the former 'castle ditch' containing the manorial pinfold.[24]

Within the keep lavish decorative schemes refracted another 1618 trophy, a new wife whom Cavendish wanted to please. Shortly before Jonson's visit he had quietly married the widowed Elizabeth Howard (*née* Basset), whose huge landed inheritance meant she had once been destined for Walter Raleigh junior (Jonson's sometime pupil) and recently had been pursued by the usually unstoppable Buckingham as a match for his brother.[25] During her eventful union with the Italophile, the Hon. Henry Howard, the king had stood godfather in Whitehall's Chapel Royal to their short-lived son in the same year that her husband had inherited Clun Castle from his great-uncle, the Earl of Northampton. She had grown accustomed to the greatest luxuries of court and capital so Cavendish and Smithson plundered both for ideas. On 8 November 1618 the architect, perhaps returning from a trip to London with the newlyweds,[26] had access to the presence chamber at royal Theobalds and famously sketched its gilded 'walnut' panelling.[27] This was adapted for Bolsover's dining parlour where Smithson's inlaid fireplace canopy was endowed rather uneasily with alabaster impaled Cavendish-Basset arms held by cherubs.

Other copyings have remained unsung. Elizabeth surely brought to her second marriage '14 Venetian pictures of one bignese', which Henry Howard had acquired in 1614 from his great-uncle's Greenwich Park lodge. So, it cannot just be coincidence that the inventoried contents of that lodge and the opulent

23   *La Méthode Nouvelle*, pl 33. 'The spring against the castle' of the 1613–14 accounts is shown in William Senior's '1630–37' Bolsover map for his survey of Cavendish's lands (private collection) and is now in a private garden.

24   BL, Harleian MS 4955/188, lines 43–50 indicate the keep's 'perfection' without substantial structure beside it until after June 1628; Knoop—Jones, *Bolsover Castle*, passim. The 'castle ditch' in 1613 was 'castle yard' by the time of the 1630s Senior map which still showed the pinfold. See also fn 62.

25   Swinscoe D. *et al.*, Swinscoe, *Blore and the Bassetts*, (Leek: 1998) passim; ODNB entries in the 1891 and 2004 editions on Henry Howard, earl of Northampton, and Sir Robert Howard *passim* for Hon. Henry Howard's inheritance of Clun Castle; Also see McClure N.M., (ed.), *The Letters of John Chamberlain* (Philadelphia: 1939) I, 556, 586; II, 24.

26   Cavendish's marriage was only bruited in London for John Chamberlain to report in the same week in late October 1618 that Sir Walter Ralegh was executed: Mc.Clure, Chamberlain Letters, II, 174.

27   RIBA III/13.

Northampton House on the Strand, recorded in plan by Smithson five years previously,[28] have painted echoes on the plaster and panelling of Bolsover's parlour, ante-room, great chamber, best bedchamber and one of the best closets (this last dated 1619). Moreover, Smithson's celebrated, marble-vaulted closet off the great chamber, inserted below the cornice of an earlier ceiling, was originally remembered as a room he recorded within a house of Lord Rich: presumably lavish Alington House (soon to become Warwick House) in Holborn.[29] Expensive marble copying was certainly planned for a Cavendish property in 1619 when Smithson's 'loving ffrend', the London stone-carver, Thomas Ashby, quoted him £100 for reproducing a segmental-pedimented, Jonesian fireplace in Arundel House on the Strand, which the architect had clearly admired.[30]

It is tempting to assign this Strand imitation, too wide for Bolsover's marble closet, to improvements carried out that year under Smithson's supervision to the first London base Cavendish apparently obtained in artistic, but socially less fashionable, Blackfriars. Jonson made use of this location for his second Cavendish commission, this time celebrating the future of the dynasty in an entertainment for the christening of another Charles Cavendish, with the Prince of Wales as sponsor. On 10 August 1619, James I, again accompanied by Prince Charles and Buckingham, dined at Welbeck, doubtless curious to see the home of Elizabeth's new husband. The content of the laureate's masque suggests very strongly that the advanced pregnancy of Elizabeth during the royal visit to Welbeck had prompted a promise of another royal godparent *if* she bore a son to her second husband and so she made a hazardous journey to give birth in London. The christening entertainment is not only set in a Thameside house, where the mother is still having her *post-partum* lying-in, but incorporates comic nurses recounting anxious earlier speculation about the sex of the baby eventually 'born under' the Plough, the extra-zodiacal constellation ruling 8–15 August and 25 August-10 September in astrology. Alert Jonson also includes in his text a hope that the mother will like whatever her

---

28   "The Inventory of Northampton House 1614", *Archaeologia* (1897) 52, 189; and RIBA 1/12.

29   My thanks to Helen Hughes for information given in 2000 about the cornice;
       on RIBA III/1 (2) the original (crossed through) second line of its verso description, 'My
       Lord Rich's/house/vault at Bolsover', escaped mention in the 1962 catalogue; Rich, whose
       heir travelled with Cavendish to Italy in 1612, was created Earl of Warwick in August 1618
       and Smithson made '1619' record drawings of other Holborn mansions.

30   RIBA IV/11; Smithson's late '1619' drawings used paper with the same watermark as the
       sketch/note by Ashby, whose form of address suggests he had previously worked with
       Smithson.

husband 'takes in hand', presumably building improvements, which, as well as exalted godparents, will make Blackfriars 'compare with' the Strand.[31]

Royal entertaining, expunging memories of April 1617, portended Cavendish's further advancement after his mother cleverly exploited an impasse over the execution of the will of Gilbert, Earl of Shrewsbury. Her son, as executor, could not pay out monies bequeathed to the earl's co-heiresses until his deceased father's estate, which she controlled, received the huge sums Earl Gilbert had owed Sir Charles. Katherine proposed that *if* her son received a peerage brokered with the king and Buckingham by the cash-desperate husbands, Lords Arundel, Pembroke and Ruthyn, she would write off these debts and her son could begin to pay the wives.[32] On 29 October 1620, after much negotiation, Cavendish was elevated to the peerage as Viscount Mansfield. Barely a year later he was putting himself forward as an architectural *cognoscento*, offering advice to Arundel on the most prestigious royal building project of the reign: when Cavendish attended the House of Lords in November 1621 he showed the earl—a member of the committee for building of Jones's Whitehall Banqueting House, then seeking secure supplies of suitable stone—a sample from Steetley near Worksop and Welbeck, the properties of which he highly recommended[33].

Tellingly, when he embarked on the 1621 round of interior decoration at Bolsover, Cavendish chose to place a mythical architect-designer as guardian at the symbolic heart of his keep. In the hall's frescos, with *trompe-l'oeil* vaulting derived from the pictures of the then court darling, Hendrick van Steenwyck II, Vulcan and Hercules flank Smithson's towering, plain stone fireplace. While recent interpretation has suggested that the latter deity represents Cavendish, the significance of the smith-god on the senior (left) side of the hearth has

---

31   Nichols, III, passim for the Welbeck visit from Rufford, home of Cavendish's maternal aunt, Jane, widow of the 8th earl of Shrewsbury; in Jonson's christening entertainment, edited by James Knowles for the *Complete Works of Ben Jonson* (Cambridge: 2012–14), the Plough (vide InteractiveStars.com) is mentioned at l. 24. Other godparents—Lord Bacon and perhaps Lady Arundel, together with Strand residents like the Prince, who had just been granted Denmark (Somerset) House – are mentioned at ll. 19, 20 and 39 and the mother's lying-in is at l. 41; Ll. 231–5. This reflects the aspiration to make Blackfriars comparable to the Strand. Despite the predictions of Jonson's 'mathermatician', the boy died in April 1620 (*HMC*, "Portland MSS" II, 118).

32   *HMC*, "Portland MSS" II, 119.

33   Arundel Castle Archives, Arundel Letters no. 253. Steetley ('Stycklee') in the final detailed fortnight of Smithson's 1613–14 Bolsover account) yields a hard-wearing, fossil-flecked limestone, capable of taking a high polish, hence its extensive, though now unrecognised, use by Smithson at Bolsover. Some of this was lamentably desecrated in the 1999 'restoration', which was ignorant of the stone's provenance.

been ignored. Though associated with fire and equine equipment, Vulcan also served as the patron of stonemasons and carpenters since he devised the palaces on Olympus, built by his Cyclops, and also supplied the furnishings that the immortals desired.[34] Clearly, he was Cavendish's more important household god at Bolsover and his mortal counterpart, Smithson, who had designed even a swing-armed, iron water-boiler for the keep's kitchen below, had recently[35] become a real watchman of the castle himself.

Fully master of his funds after the grant of the peerage had settled his father's estate, Cavendish turned from celebrating or indulging his family by marking his own raised rank at Bolsover with now-forgotten projects infinitely more conspicuous and practical than the tiny viscount's coronets incised *inside* the jambs of the fireplace in his Theobaldian parlour. In July 1622 he secured in perpetuity a more reliable, gravity-fed castle water supply and its course allowed him to improve the approach to his residence.[36] To allow his coach, freshly emblazoned with a coronet, to rumble unhindered by other traffic along the straight half mile from Bolsover's southern boundary to the keep's entrance, he laid an expensive road of square stone setts beside the new pipeline along the edge of the town's scarp to a new gate at the south-western corner of the castle grounds.[37] Punctuating this quasi-triumphal way, Smithson erected four tiny stone turrets with miniature barrel vaults and ingenious dual function: they served as sentry-boxes for castle watchmen as far out as the Cavendish chapel and as housing for settlement cisterns through which the water passed.[38] Once inside the castle grounds the pipe branched northwards from the onward

---

34   The hall frescoes, painted over the original faux-stone scheme, show the same hand as the '1621' great chamber paintings; for Vulcan's commissions for the gods vide Graves R., *Greek Myths* (London: 1954) passim. Vulcan had appeared, less prominently, in the c. 1619 frescos of the best bedchamber's second closet.

35   RIBA III/1 (12); Smithson had bought his first freehold house, which apparently lay just north of the castle, before his daughter was buried in Bolsover on 31 August 1621 (Senior map and Bolsover parish registers).

36   From a never-failing spring on higher ground beyond the church (NA, DDP 50/37). Sir Charles had first planned for this supply nine years earlier (NUL, Portland Papers, Pl E 12/10/1/24).

37   In the Sheffield University Archaeology Department excavations of June 2000 visitors, including myself, could inspect a considerable length of this setted road. The road with its four turrets was still shown on Joseph Colbeck's 1739 Bolsover map.

38   One of the turrets, always known locally as 'watch houses' (my thanks to Peggy White, the custodian at Bolsover 1970–92, for the information), bore a date 1622, while lead pipework and a Cavendish-crested cistern were found in another (Goulding R.W., *Bolsover Castle*, privately printed, 1936 edn., 25). Severe subsidence has ensured that the buried road and turret closest to the castle are now substantially below the south-west gate.

drive to the keep to a second cistern atop the middle of three additional large turrets projecting from the *enceinte's* northern wall. In turn, this enabled the creation in the next turret westwards (at the north-eastern junction of the garden with the outer bailey) of a bathing-house.[39] Accessed by the family from the wall-walk via a cupola-topped staircase and sporting splendid views from its huge windows, this was both highly fashionable and apparently healthy for the constantly child-bearing Elizabeth, whom Cavendish later took to Buxton and the 'Holy Well' near Loughborough. To the same end, he enclosed in stone Bolsover's presumably medicinal 'St John's Well' on the opposite slope of the town's narrow northerly valley.[40]

Welbeck 1623–1628

In the mid-1620s Cavendish's building programme focused on Welbeck's perimeter, although the initial spur for its celebrated hippocentric elements has receded from view.[41] Following another clan calamity, Welbeck acquired flashy neighbours with claims to equine authority. In June 1618, James I's paranoia over Lady Arbella Stuart, even after her death, led him to consign her aunt, Mary, Dowager Countess of Shrewsbury, to the Tower once again. Mary's dower was confiscated to pay a vast fine and eventually the king conferred her lifetime tenure of Worksop Manor on Buckingham, who shortly afterwards passed it on to another royal cousin, the Duke of Lennox.[42] In 1622 the favourite, who was the king's Master of the Horse,[43] began erecting stables at his houses in Essex and Leicestershire, the former building a part of a programme of works

---

39 NUL, Portland Papers, Pw 1/624/1 gives a 1666 date to repairs to the wall on the court side of this 'cestorne house', which is visible on the extreme left of pl. 39 in *La Méthode Nouvelle*. The turret's solid lower level to support the tank (with doorway from the court of c.1666) survives. This image also shows the huge window of the 'bath house' which, with the wall-walk above it, received co-eval repairs (NUL, Portland Papers, Pw 1669). Foundations of a seemingly unrecorded third turret along the northern wall were found during c. 1970 construction of a toilet block (thanks to Mrs White).

40 *La Méthode Nouvelle* pl. 39 and Samuel & Nathaniel Buck, North East Prospect of Bolsover Castle, 1727; BL, Add Ms 4955/164–171 and Sedden P.R. (ed.), "The letters of John Holles 1587–1637", *Thoroton Society*, 31 (1975) 429; Senior's Bolsover map shows 'St Jhos well', now subject of much English Heritage whimsy.

41 Significantly before the publication of Antoine Pluvinel's illustrated book on horsemanship in 1623.

42 CSPD 1618–24, passim, *HMC*, "Portland MSS", II, 119; SA, Arundel MS W/151.

43 He was created duke of Buckingham in May 1623 and the day after the king's cousin, Ludovic Stuart, was made Duke of Richmond and Lennox and Earl of Newcastle.

designed by Jones.[44] Cavendish clearly reckoned that on his home turf he ought to assert his own mastery of horse-flesh because he promptly commissioned Smithson, who thirteen years earlier had recorded Prince Henry's equestrian school at St. James's, to build a royal-scale brick riding house (with eventually lodgings for his own Master of the Horse attached westwards) on the northern side of Welbeck's great (west) court.[45] The king and Prince Charles witnessed the raising of this invocation of the lost royal heir when they dined again at Welbeck (on 10 August 1624) and, doubtless, also saw their host's personal tilting ground, achieved by extending southward the approach to Welbeck's outer (east) court.[46]

Certainly in his first Nottinghamshire architectural statement of identity Cavendish signalled that *his* designer was just as noteworthy as any patronised by the king or favourite. Above the riding-house's main door (derived from Jacques Francart's *Le Premier Livre D'Architecture* of 1617) a Latin inscription recorded Cavendish's erection of the structure in 1623 and named Smithson its 'curatore fabricensi' (keeper-artisan).[47] Although Continental precedent can be found on the Tempietto at Maser where Marcantonio Barbaro placed his own name with that of his family's architect, Palladio,[48] this was the first time a British patron and his designer had been so linked on their building. Recognition of Smithson, like the employment of his own Master of the Horse, served to increase Cavendish's status.

In 1625 Cavendish topped this building display by erecting elaborately ornamented and appointed stables for his fifteen best performance horses on the western side of the great court. Smithson's design, built entirely of stone to reduce fire-risk, was literally an equine keep in view of its domed towers at

---

44   BM Harleian MS 4955/67v, written after 29/10/1620 but before Jane, the dowger Countess of Shrewsbury's , death (December 1625), refers (l. 28) to the ducal tenure of Worksop; Harris J.—Riggott G., *Inigo Jones Complete Architectural Drawings* (London: 1989) cat 42, 43 & 49.

45   RIBA III/15 (3) dated 1622, (4) & (7) dated 1623 (RIBA I/14 is its precursor) and pl. 8 *La Méthode Nouvelle*.

46   Nicols, IV, passim. The royal party was staying at ill-fated Worksop (Richmond had died in February 1624 and his brother, successor as Lennox only, died during the progress at Kirby, Northamptonshire). But, Buckingham avoided encountering Cavendish's architectural challenge: to great surprise he left the progress shortly before the Worksop-Welbeck visit; Senior's Welbeck map (private collection). Cavendish had become such a star in the court tilts at Whitehall that less than five months earlier he had incurred the ire of William Laud, then Buckingham's chaplain, for practising for these on Good Friday.

47   Goulding, *Bolsover Castle*, 10.

48   www.Cisapalladio.org. Entry on the Tempietto. Barbaro's elder brother, Daniele, founded Padua's botanicum and translated Vitruvius.

each corner and cross-loops in the attics, while the luxuries within had Jonson reaching for classical comparisons. A great hall of five 20 feet-high vaults on Tuscan columns stretched like some Steenwyck vista over steeds pampered with constant fresh water, diverted from and back to Welbeck's aquatic system to give a drinking rill beside 'immortal' mangers and a sluice for the floor.[49] Smithson also contrived adjustable ventilation for each horse's head which he artfully concealed in decorated external buttresses that were continued on an adjacent stone seven-bay hay barn.

Not surprisingly, when Prince Charles became king that same year he acknowledged Nottinghamshire's showiest builder as the right man to be its Lord Lieutenant, the first such royal manager in the county for thirty-five years. This prompted further building around Welbeck's great court appropriate to a king's representative, who in spring 1626 also expected to receive the monarch that summer *en route* to a planned second coronation in Scotland. A vernacular gatehouse range abutting the stables' hay-barn was enlarged and topped by miniature shaped and pedimented gables, while a Francartian formal carriage gateway was erected at the east end of the riding house.[50]

Bolsover 1629–1642

Dynastic accident brought Cavendish back to building again at Bolsover. On 7 March 1628, after Richmond's brief tenure of the earldom of Newcastle-upon-Tyne had ended, it was more appropriately conferred upon the only recently created Viscount Mansfield. Then a sudden death three months later required a further statement of Cavendish's authority at the site which gave his second title its extra joke. His cousin, William, 2nd earl of Devonshire, died on 20 June, aged just thirty-eight, and the king quickly conferred the latter's lord-lieutenancy of Derbyshire on Cavendish. As the king's proxy in a second county, he knew that his 'little' house there was simply not big enough for the ceremonial demands of the office, despite a location which enabled him perfectly to show off his new superintendence of the shire.[51] Fortuitously, his mother, created Lady Ogle in her own right in December 1628, died the following April, aged fifty-six. With his Northumbrian inheritance Cavendish could afford to demonstrate his enhanced social and political status by erecting a

---

49 RIBA III/15 and pl. 9 *La Méthode Nouvelle*; Under-woods, 53.
50 *Chamberlain Letters*, 423, pls. 8 and 9 *La Méthode Nouvelle*. Jones had made a similar borrowing from Francart for Richmond 's Holborn mansion in 1622/3: Harris & Riggott, *Inigo Jones*, cat 44 & 45.
51 BL, Harleian MS 4955/188.

hospitality block at Bolsover and buying town residences in Clerkenwell and Derby.[52] Smithson's new task, to provide numerous guest chambers and a hall twice the size of the keep's, had one problem. To take advantage of the view the range had to sit beside the keep but had to avoid eclipsing its predecessor, as was the case with the magnificent castle addition at the seat of Cavendish's Shropshire in-laws, recently sketched by Smithson in August 1627.[53] The architect resolved the problem by designing a less-assertive, many-gabled, double-pile of eleven bays to the west, whose traditional hood-moulds and pillared chimneys jostled fashionable ovolos, but whose Salopian, shaped-gable ends were angled back in obeisance to the keep, thus yielding only nine bays to the east.[54]

However, after several years of construction (the northern end bears the dates 1629 and 1630) a combination of events made Cavendish redirect his building in extraordinary fashion. His status as a northern *magnifico* was under challenge. His friend, Thomas Wentworth, had been appointed President of the Council of the North, the first of many royal offices, in December 1628 and soon displayed his promotion by splendidly extending an acquisition at Ledston near Pontefract. Cavendish's brother, Charles, was also erecting an elegant Smithson 'castle' at Slingsby in the North Riding, thanks to his own legacy from their mother.[55] In response, Cavendish aimed for more intimate royal service, seeking first to become a more suitable replacement for the latest Master of the Horse, the Scottish Marquis of Hamilton. Given six months' notice that he was to accompany Charles I on his journey, via Worksop Manor, (at last) to his Scottish coronation,[56] on 21 May 1633 Cavendish advertised his merits to the king with a Jonson-scripted, post-prandial equine-entertainment in Welbeck's outer court and tiltyard. The action, including a comic schoolmaster of Mansfield and a rustic tilting nostalgic of Elizabethan days, demanded considerable time from the royal spectator. Smithson's design survives for what appears to be an outdoor 'state' or royal dais: an elaborate double staircase up

---

52   He bought Clerkenwell from the estate of Lady Kitson, first mother-in-law of Sir Charles Cavendish, who died in August 1628. He acquired Derby from Cavendish's Devonshire cousin's estate: NUL, Portland Papers, passim.

53   RIBA III/9 shows the entertaining range at Moreton Corbet Castle, home at the time of the then Lady Mansfield's half-sister, Mrs. Andrew Corbet (née Elizabeth Boothby).

54   Pl. 35 *La Méthode Nouvelle* and RIBA III/1 (4). The vaulted kitchens in the basement of the new range were watered as efficiently as the keep's by a spur from the 1622 system to another cistern, housed in a surviving windowless addition to the keep's forecourt wall. English Heritage has since 2003/4 suggested that this was Cavendish's 'bath house' rather than the turret on the north-east corner of the garden.

55   ODNB, Wentworth; vide Woodhouse, *Towers and Compasses* and RIBA III/12 for Ledston and moated Slingsby.

56   *HMC*, "Portland MSS," II, 120.

to a long grandstand, probably encompassing the two small gate-lodges of the outer court, from which the monarch could comfortably watch the action and be watched by the rest of the audience.[57] The king clearly enjoyed his entertainment at Welbeck for during the ensuing two month journey, including a night at Cavendish's Northumbrian Bothal Castle (perhaps recently improved),[58] he indicated that he would like his consort to see it. Coincidentally, the birth of a second royal son accelerated the need for a governor for the Prince of Wales and this offered Cavendish a different avenue for court advancement through which he could restore his pre-eminence north of the Trent. Having accompanied Charles I on his visits to various Scottish fortress-palaces, including Falkland and Stirling with their crude, high-level Mannerist detailing, he decided that his own architect should turn Bolsover into a more splendid one. Attached incongruously to the half-completed entertaining range, there would arise a gigantic state apartment suitable for housing the heir to the throne whose *appanage* lacked a major English castle after the recent sale of Kenilworth by the Crown.[59] The royal couple could even inspect the outlines on paper and on the ground of this architectural hybrid during a day trip to Bolsover from the first royal stay at Welbeck, which would advance most spectacularly Cavendish's fresh bid for the governorship.

Dependable Smithson planned what was required, including alterations to existing lay-outs to suit the Bolsover programme Cavendish apparently intended:[60] the royal couple's dinner in public in the new bigger hall and processions to sweetmeat courses and another Jonson entertainment within and without the keep, the banqueting-house for the day. The double-height princely quarters, which comprised a ceremonial sequence of rooms on its east flank and a vast gallery, plus two closets, affording a view over Derbyshire to the west, though using the same entry as the most recent building, made no

---

57   RIBA III/27. The position of the royal dais in Whitehall's various banqueting houses allowed the royal watcher to be watched by the rest of the audience.

58   Pl. 42 *La Méthode Nouvelle* shows a southern gateway to Bothal's orchards similar to 1633/4 detailing at Bolsover.

59   Kenilworth, where Cavendish's idol, Lord Leicester, famously entertained Queen Elizabeth, had been bought for Henry Prince of Wales in 1612 from Leicester's son. Its next beneficiary, Prince Charles, received a Jonson-scripted entertainment there shortly after his 1624 Welbeck visit. It was sold to its keeper, Lord Monmouth.

60   The bridge linking the garden wall-walk with the entertaining range is dated '1633' above what was first built as a window in the latter. The doorway at the walk's other end [RIBA III/1(8)] matches in its detailing (and pentimenti , unrecorded in 1962) Smithson's drawings of details for the state apartment. The garden was given a grander fountain with large sunken pool, earl's coronet and Hesperidean nymph, as well as elaborate vermiculated decoration within one garden room that was presumably intended for royal use.

attempt to match the latter. At 250 feet the apartment was to be longer than any lodgings yet constructed by the Stuarts in England[61] and its massive, broken-pedimented, blocked and vermiculated plundering of Mannerist Continental designers[62] articulated Cavendish's Ozymandian intentions. The battalions of towering windows, the show-front with a vast central door giving onto a huge viewing platform and buttresses swelling from nowhere, as well as two hackles of machiolations along a flat roof running south from the earlier gables, were to be over-topped again by a central *belvedere* with ornate pedimented balconies to west *and* east.[63] (Fig. 1.1)

FIGURE 1.1   *1650s ink sketch of Bolsover Castle from the west by an unknown hand and adapted by Abraham van Diepenbecke to create his best-known image of William Cavendish, 'Monsieur le Marquis à cheval'. Note that the sketch, although executed to virtually the same dimensions as those adopted by Diepenbecke for his large pencil and chalk drawings, only showed half of the state apartment. This most probably reflected the despoilation of the southern half by the Castle's asset-stripping Parliamentary owner in the early 1650s. Reproduced by kind permission of Alexandra Sitwell.*

61   RIBA III/1 (4).

62   RIBA III/1 (5–7). The style of these is very different from the refined detailing chosen by Sir Charles Cavendish junior at Slingsby.

63   The buttresses are fanciful developments of those on the Welbeck stables. The reverse of the west pedimented balcony and an east one are pencilled ghosts on the 1650s ink sketch now at Renishaw Hall, which provided the basis for pl. 33 of *La Méthode Nouvelle*.

Even more remarkable, the vast new structure's fo'c's'le to the main gate was to be an astonishing chapel of glass, which proclaimed the assured place of authorized spiritual exercise in any Cavendish governorship. This would have appealed to the devoutly Anglican Charles I but was an otherwise odd choice for a patron manifestly insouciant about religious observance. However, this literal forecastle, with its entirely windowed three outside walls and fifty-six foot southern span punctuated by a projecting, twelve-foot round, glazed turret, would be a transparently English response to Jones's Italianate religious building for the Roman Catholic Queen in London. Moreover, the final flourish of Bolsover's own St George's Chapel was intended to exclaim its role in all future perspectives of the castle: the beacon-like turret was to be topped by a 'steeple' aspiring to the height of the keep in one direction and of the parish church in the other. The little prince at prayer would thus have a Cavendish monument far more spectacular than any painted obelisk on Jones's masque scenery celebrating the two previous heirs to the throne.

The spectacular royal day at Bolsover on 30 July 1634, during which the aptly-named Prince's Players from Clerkenwell, the theatre nearest to Newcastle House,[64] performed Jonson's partly building-themed entertainment, turned out to be Smithson's apotheosis. He had created the celebration's various back-drops and, doubtless, collaborated simply with the (now chamber-bound) laureate for the entertainment's *coup de theatre*. Jonson's stage direction for two cupids to come down 'from the cloudes', bearing a second banquet of sweet-meats for the king and queen 'reposing' in the garden presumably on another state-dais, would have been possible by means of a draped builders' cradle descending the keep's southern façade. With Cavendish's approval, Smithson's classical *alter ego* also made a significant appearance: introduced by Jonson's comic personification of Inigo Jones as Bolsover's 'Captain Smith our neighbour Vulcan', he and three assistant Cyclops kept time (measure) for dancing quartets of building craftsmen whose antics preceded the cupids' arrival.[65]

Four months later Smithson died and the 'architector',[66] a veteran of thirty-seven years in Cavendish service, was honoured with burial in the chancel of his patrons' church, just feet from their mausoleum. His plans for the state

---

64   Bentley G.E., *The Elizabehan and Jacobean Stage*, I (London: 1965) 310 & 322 give, without further comment, royal orders/payments and provincial notices identifying the company's accompaniment of the progress only for the fortnight encompassing the eight days spent at Welbeck and Nottingham.

65   'Our neighbour' appears only in the BL, Harleian MS 4955 version of Jonson's text. Smithson, as a senior freeholder (see fn 32), was responsible for raising Bolsover's complement in the county militia, customarily assembled by Lords-Lieutenant for royal visits.

66   Smithson's own description of himself in his will, TNA, PROB 11/66.

apartments were perhaps overseen to completion by his elder son, Huntingdon Smithson, twenty-nine years old and already a 'practicioner of mathematics',[67] after Cavendish was finally appointed Prince Charles's governor in 1638, following yet another entertainment for the king at Welbeck. Ironically, there is no evidence that the future Charles II ever stayed in Bolsover's princely apartments, though his governor's constant attendance on him in and around London until May 1641 might date some of the improvements to Newcastle House, Clerkenwell, which included c. 1640 pilastering to its entrance elevation.[68] However, the insistence over the past 50 years that Cavendish built his second riding house with its ancilliaries on the south side of Bolsover's outer court *before* the Civil War appears misplaced as surviving contemporary evidence indicates the reverse.[69]

A la Recherche des Maisons Perdues

By the time of the Civil War, therefore, Cavendish's constructions had positioned him successively as dutiful son and husband, connoisseur of art and architecture, commander of waters, horses and shires, then finally as governor of the nation's royal future. Indeed, he so identified himself with his buildings that when he wished to show off his expertise in horsemanship to a pan-European audience these constructions, though then apparently lost to him forever, were shown with possessive care and in a detail that no non-royal British buildings had ever received before.[70] Moreover, one can reasonably suggest that the seven large, ink and pencil sketches of Bolsover, from which Abraham van Diepenbecke confected his almost same-size images of

---

67   Huntingdon Smithson was baptised at Wollaton on 28 September 1605, and vide the Senior map of his 1632 survey of Cavendish's Mansell Park near Derby.

68   Clerkenwell entry, Survey of London, British History Online, passim.

69   The Senior Bolsover map does not identify a riding house within the castle's outer court service range, though the Welbeck one is clearly so captioned in the equivalent map. *La Méthode Nouvelle* and the preliminary drawings for its plates also do not show any riding house at Bolsover. The only document referring to 'building' of the Bolsover riding house is undated but two-thirds of the workmen listed (in a later 17th century hand) can be identifed by surname and first name in the 1672 Bolsover hearth-tax returns. Dendrochronology for English Heritage indicated that the main roof timbers in Bolsover's riding house were felled c. 1655–75. 1950s archaeology within the building (briefly referenced in EH's unpaginated Draft Conservation Plan 30/11/98 vol II) found an earlier eastern outline different from its present one. Within a generation of Cavendish's death visiting antiquaries like Bassano and Vertue also noted that he had built the Bolsover riding house after the Civil War.

70   A Freudian 'Ma Maison de Bolsover' slipped through the production process in *La Méthode Nouvelle* pl. 30.

Cavendish performing the most difficult exercises against the backdrop of the castle, were the product of the 'painter' he despatched to England[71] specially to record his by then 'half- pulled down'" fortress-palace[72] and the less-battered buildings surrounding his usual equestrian arena at Welbeck. Man and seat were one in every sense, as Cavendish showed in the book's image of his own apotheosis: when flying on Pegasus *en capriole* towards clouds where classical gods recline he, unlike Bellerophon of myth, stays in the saddle.[73]

However, there is also a significant appearance by one familiar within this particular *tableau* from Cavendish's last masque. Who is the deity front left of the marvelling Olympian assembly on the clouds? Alone of all the gods, he is shown with face obscured[74] since his head is turned back as he emphatically points Cavendish out to Venus and Apollo. It is none other than Vulcan. How fitting a grace-note to his record of his architectural endeavours that Cavendish wished Bolsover's smith-god and keeper-artisan, already portrayed in paint and the lines of a laureate, to harbinger his own aspiration to immortality.

Selective Bibliography

Bentley G.E., *The Elizabehan and Jacobean Stage*, I (London: 1965).

Buck S – Buck N., *North East Prospect of Bolsover Castle* (London: 1727).

Cavendish William, *La Méthode Nouvelle* (Antwerp, 1658).

Girouard M., *Elizabethan Architecture* (London: 2009).

Henderson P., *The Tudor House and Garden* (London: 1998).

HMC, "Portland MSS", II (London: 1893).

Marshall P., *Wollaton Hall and the Willoughby Family* (Nottingham: 1999).

McClure N.M., (ed.), *The Letters of John Chamberlain* (Philadelphia: 1939).

Nichols J.B., *The Progresses, Processions, and Magnificent Festivities of* King *James the First* (London: 1823).

Swinscoe D. *et al.*, *Swinscoe, Blore and the Bassetts*, (Leek: 1998).

Woodhouse A., "A Newly Identified Estate Plan by John Smithson, 1608", *Thoroton Society Transactions* 104 (1999).

---

71   HMC, Portland II, 143. All seven sketches are now at Renishaw Hall, Derbyshire, while only two of the Diepenbecke chalk drawings derived from them survive in European museums.

72   Cavendish, M., *Life of William Cavendish*, 91, and Margaret Duchess of Newcastle, "A Dialogue between a bountiful knight and a castle ruined in war", *Poems and Fancies* (London, J. Martin & J. Allestrye:1653).

73   *La Méthode Nouvelle*, pl. 4.

74   In 16th and 17th century group portraiture an obscured face was traditionally a symbol for somone already dead.

CHAPTER 2

Whimsy and Medieval Romance in the Life and Writing of William Cavendish

James Fitzmaurice

William Cavendish was a man who appreciated whimsy. He did not lay the foundations for the architectural conundrum of a 'holiday home' that is Bolsover Castle, but he did see construction to the completion of its initial stages in 1619, and he was responsible for much of the building's decoration. Bolsover is a whimsy, a surprising and pleasantly entertaining oddity, but it also works practically as a retreat from the generally predictable and mostly work-a-day world of estate management associated with the main Cavendish residence, Welbeck Abbey. Bolsover is romantic in the sense that it recalls the architecture of castles contained in tales of chivalry. It fits in with the medievalism that found a place in court life in the late sixteenth and early seventeenth centuries in England, but Bolsover also is intentionally odd in several respects. It has a Gothic hall marked by vaulted and ribbed ceilings as well as a bailey girdled by a wide wall on which people can walk. The hall is too small to function as a place for servants to eat and sleep, so it is likely that it was mostly used for other purposes such as mock Medieval banquets to which Francis Andrews may allude in a poem on the building.[1] The interior of the bailey wall has large niches apparently designed for trysts to be conducted by faux knights and ladies.[2] The hall is also a room for visually educated aristocrats to

---

1 Andrews, in comparing Hardwick, Worksop, Welbeck, Bolsover, and Rufford, finds that Bolsover is a better building than the rest for 'feast'. Andrews explains that Welbeck is 'for use' and Bolsover 'for sight', which I take to mean Welbeck provides the cash for Bolsover as, to use Andrews's words, a 'pretty' "maid". Text in: Fowler A., *The Country House Poem, A Cabinet of Seventeenth-Century Estate Poems and Related Items* (Edinburgh: 1994) 159. The manuscript may be found in BL, MS Harley, 4955. For more details on the manuscript and on Andrews, see Hilton Kelliher's "The Newcastle Manuscript", *English Manuscript Studies*, 4 (1993) 134–173.
2 These possibilities were discussed in detail by a group of National Trust staff, architectural historians, and literary scholars at a conference at Bolsover in January of 2013. Geoffrey Trease says of Bolsover that it is 'a fanciful structure conceived rather in the romantic spirit

---

FIGURE 2.1   *Detail of the vaulted ceiling in the hall of the Little Castle at Bolsover.*
COPYRIGHT JAMES FITZMAURICE.

appreciate, for the actual masonry vaulting of the ceiling is continued into a
whimsical set of *trompe-l'oeil* wall paintings depicting a vaulted ceiling. (Fig. 2.1)

The word 'romance' for those living in the early seventeenth century called
to mind Sir Philip Sidney's *Arcadia* and, later, multi-volume prose narratives in
French such as Madeleine de Scudéry's *Grand Cyrus*. Dorothy Osborne's correspondence with William Temple in the early 1650s is full of discussions of
the French romances, but she is careful to avoid being labelled a 'romancy'
lady. She loves to read of long ago and far away but she does not confuse her
elevated passions inspired by *Grand Cyrus* with the *sang-froid* she felt while
instructing her brother to work out a jointure with Temple's representatives.
Cervantes' knight of La Mancha, of course, was a reader of romances who was
both foolish and lovable, but some foolish readers were just fools. By the end
of the century, the reading of romances was certainly a dubious activity. In
Thomas Shadwell's play *The Lancashire Witches* (1682), for instance, Isabella
scoffs at a penniless woman who will have a difficult time finding a husband.

---

of the *Faerie Queene* than with any eye to defence'. *Portrait of a Cavalier: William Cavendish:
First Duke of Newcastle* (London: 1979) 38.

Isabella cynically asks, 'Canst [anyone] think [men] are such romancy Knights to take Ladies with nothing?' Even Cavendish's second wife, Margaret, writing in *World's Olio* (1655), takes a negative view, explaining that 'romancy' is an 'adulterate' genre.[3]

Much criticism of the readers of romance was, however, more fashionable than actual. Nobody really wanted to be quite as cynical as Shadwell's Isabella. Margaret Cavendish, for all her apparent willingness to depreciate romance in *World's Olio*, wrote and published two substantial prose romances herself. Found as pieces of extended fiction in *Nature's Pictures* (1657), each involves an orphaned young woman who finds it necessary to outwit those who would ruin her life. In the second of these tales, "Assaulted and Pursued Chastity", the heroine ends up setting her would-be seducer straight and then marrying him, in the manner of Marina from Shakespeare's co-authored romance, *Pericles*. Nevertheless, Margaret's heroine, we are told, would never waste time reading a romance. Margaret's readers must have giggled at the various ironies involved in this sentiment, since they were themselves reading a romance about a woman who hated reading romances. Romance, one might say, was in the air, even if people claimed, with a wink, that it had nothing to do with them.

Medievalism, Prince Henry and James I

Cavendish's first recorded exposure to romance in direct, physical connection with horsemanship came when he was seventeen. The young William Cavendish went through an initiation ceremony that might have come from Thomas Malory's *Morte d'Arthur*. Lucy Worsley and Tom Addyman describe a part of what happened.

> In [June of] 1610, William... took part in a ritual based on the cleansing, vigil and creation of a medieval knight when he was made Knight of the Bath as one of Prince Henry's companions. Once he had won his spurs, William frequently took part in the court's jousting and tilting, 'Running at the Ring' in 1616 and failing to 'runne at Tilt' on the King's Day as expected in 1618.[4]

---

3   Cavendish Margaret, *World's Olio* (London: 1655) 27.
4   Worsley L. – Addyman T., "Riding Houses and Horses: William Cavendish's Architecture for the Art of Horsemanship", *Architectural History*, 45 (2002) 218.

William's failure to run the tilt in 1618 seems an exception to his general rule of keeping as close to the royal family as possible, often by exploiting his expertise in horsemanship. William's biographer, Geoffrey Trease emphasizes the visual aspects of the pageantry involved in William's initiation:

> After, one might imagine, a somewhat restless and murmurous night, the youths rose, donned grey-hooded gowns, and in this unwonted monkish attire filed into the chapel to take the oath. Then, blossoming into crimson taffeta and white sarsenet, they returned to Durham House, so that they could ride [horseback] ... to the palace through admiring crowds to the thrilling blare of trumpets.[5]

Trease, one might guess, overdramatizes the emotional force of the midnight vigil. Perhaps in actuality the young men played jokes on each other or simply slept soundly. But to what more practical end and how was William made one of the colourfully-clad, horsemen-companions to Prince Henry? First, how did William come to be chosen for knighthood? William's father, Charles Cavendish, was still living in June of 1610 but was not in a political or social position to place his son in a princely entourage. William's uncle, Gilbert Talbot, was much better situated with respect to James I, who no doubt had some say over which young men were invited to become knightly retainers of Prince Henry and which were not. The circumstances are a little complicated, but a brief explanation follows. Gilbert's father, George Talbot, had played benefactor and host to James I's mother, Mary Queen of Scots, for fourteen years at Sheffield Castle. 'Benefactor' really is the right word rather than 'jailer', for George helped to support Mary's retinue financially and generally gave her the run of the lands surrounding the castle, where she was kept as anything but a close prisoner. She saw herself as a queen and that is how she was, on most accounts, treated.[6] Thus, it may be said that the Talbots and Scottish royalty had a substantial and longstanding connection. Gilbert also had provided a place for James I to pause when he travelled south after the death of Elizabeth I to become King of England. James did not just have a brief stay for one night on that occasion in April 1603 and he was not lodged at Sheffield Castle. Rather, Gilbert brought James to what had become the favoured residence, Worksop Manor, where an entertainment was staged. A year later, the four-year-old child, who would later become Charles I, was taken on the journey south and

---

5   Trease, *Portrait*, 29.
6   George's epitaph in Sheffield Cathedral describes at length how much expense was involved in keeping Mary happy.

also stayed at Worksop. The eleven-year-old William Cavendish both observed and took a part in the festivities in 1604. William's parents were not present, but William wrote to his father in French to give a report. Geoffrey Trease translates what William wrote as follows:

> I [William] thought it my duty to write to you by the bearer what honourable entertainment my Lord Duke [of Albany, eventually Charles I] and his company have received at Worksop, and how my brother and I received much honour, comporting ourselves so well that the Scottish noblemen were astonished, principally in the French language, in which his governor is perfect.... I offer thanks for the honour that [Gilbert and Mary Talbot] do me in considering me fit to entertain such a prince.[7]

William, at the age of eleven shows an enormous amount of self-confidence. He is not shy about reporting his apparent success and might even be seen as a little arrogant in feeling qualified to offer an evaluation of the French of the prince's governor.

The second question: what practical end was there in having William Cavendish become a companion of Prince Henry? If Gilbert Talbot wanted to place a young agent in the swirl of London's royal politics, one who was full of self-confidence, he could not have chosen anyone better than his nephew. As a member of the newly established court of Prince Henry at Richmond, William would not have served at that of James I, but interaction among the various courts, including the queen's, was frequent. In any event, William took leave of Prince Henry two years after the initiation in order to accompany Sir Henry Wotton to Savoy as part of an entourage engaged in negotiations surrounding a proposed match for the Prince. William, thus, went from honour to honour, responsibility to responsibility in connection with Henry. William also became ever more the insider in royal politics. Perhaps most interesting is that the initiation of William as a knight blurred the line between romance and reality. When the vigil and vows were finished and the horseback ride through the streets of London had been completed, William really was a knight, a Knight of the Bath. This title was not pretend or make-believe. It was not 'romancy'. At the same time, I have no doubt that William was wise enough to understand that his knighthood derived its significance not from any actual military exploits that he, himself, had undertaken. Rather his knighthood, in practical terms, functioned as a part of his uncle's political apparatus.

---

7   Trease, *Portrait*, 24.

This is, of course, not to assert that William and Henry were not friends or that the choice of William to become a knight was made solely by Gilbert Talbot and James I. Certainly, William was known to Prince Henry, who could have refused him as a follower. Henry, though only fifteen, knew his own mind and asserted himself strongly with his father, with whom he more or less openly disagreed on occasion, if the Venetian ambassador is to be believed.[8] There is also evidence to suggest that William and Henry liked one another. On 6 January 1610, William and Henry tilted together at the Banqueting House at Whitehall at a spectacular event designed to emphasize the fifteen year old Prince Henry's chivalric virtues. He and six others, including Cavendish, took on 56 opponents across a barrier, a form of tilting which did not feature horses but involved vigorous non-lethal sword play and 'pushing' with pikes over a barrier or fence.[9] It is likely that William, not yet Sir William, distinguished himself with sword and pike and earned the respect of the prince. Certainly, William claimed swordsmanship as a special skill for the rest of his life.[10]

The tilting event is mostly remembered today because of the accompanying *Speeches at the Barriers*, a masque written by Ben Jonson.[11] The scenery and costumes were designed by Inigo Jones, with the general atmosphere of the event evoking chivalric romance. Jonson, who did not much care for Arthurian material, nevertheless made use of a story line he found in *Les Prophécies de Merlin* and borrowed from other chivalric sources. Jonson, as it turned out, was in an awkward position because of the politics of the situation. James I did not want to be pushed into a religious war on the Continent by Parliament, but the adherents of the prince saw in that young man the makings of a great Protestant military leader. Jonson has been given credit by at least one critic for being wily enough to avoid taking sides between king and prince in the masque.[12] William was certainly in a position to see the practical interaction between script writing and political disagreement.

---

8   The Venetian ambassador noted that Henry 'found some difficulty in obtaining the King's consent, but his Majesty did not wish to cross him'. *Cal. State Papers Venetian*, 11, 401.

9   Young A., *Tudor and Stuart Tournaments* (London: 1997) 178–83.

10   'The arts Newcastle excelled in himself were swordsmanship [and horsemanship]'. Grant D., *Margaret The First* (London: 1957) 59.

11   See David Lindley's introduction to *The Barriers*, in Bevington D. – Butler M. – Donaldson I. (eds.), *The Cambridge Edition of the Works of Ben Jonson*, 3 (Cambridge: 2012) 519–22.

12   Ibid., 522.

Whimsy and Ben Jonson

There is not a great deal of whimsy apparent in *The Barriers*, although the event quite obviously was steeped in the imagery attending the re-enactment of chivalric romance. Three years later, in late December 1613, William is likely to have been present for another royal performance scripted by Jonson, *A Challenge at Tilt*. Much of the dramatic accompaniment to the actual tilting is whimsical, as is most of *The Irish Masque*, which was performed between the first and second parts of *A Challenge*. The occasion for *A Challenge* was the wedding of Robert Carr and Frances Howard, the daughter of Thomas, Earl of Suffolk.[13] While Carr famously enjoyed the favour of James I, the wedding was highly controversial. Frances had been married to the Earl of Essex in 1605, but the two did not live together and an annulment was granted in 1613 on the basis of the earl's supposed impotence. The annulment came about only after the intervention of the king, and a number of those invited to the wedding, mostly adherents to Essex, refused to accept invitations. Ben Jonson, as a writer of masques and royal entertainments, clearly had a tricky social situation on his hands. Whimsy, I will suggest, could have been used by Jonson to defuse, or at least reduce the tensions of the fraught Carr and Howard marriage. In the case of *The Irish Masque*, whimsy might have helped to make light of the difficulties that James I was having with a newly created Parliament in Dublin.

Before I begin with Jonson's scripts and their performances, however, I would like to try more precisely to characterize 'whimsy' as a seventeenth-century word and as a literary form. In the early part of the century, whimsy often referred to a state of mind to be avoided. Whimsy suggested giddiness or dizziness, along with a general loss of mental control. Jonson's character Volpone indicates that whimsy is a sort of foolishness with erotic overtones: 'I can feele a whimsy i'my bloud. I know not how, / Success hath made me wanton'.[14] Jonson uses the word again, in *Bartholomew Fair*, when Edgeworth says to Ursula, 'We shall ha' smocks, Urs'la and good whimsies, ha?' Ursula replies, 'Come, you are i' your bawdy vein!'[15] The *OED* states that the 'whimsies' in the quotation from *Bartholomew Fair* are 'wenches', but 'erotic experiences' would work as well. At the same time, whimsy did not need to be either giddy or bawdy. A second usage for the word is sometimes connected to Miguel de

---

13   For a fuller description of the circumstances of the tilt, consult David Lindley's introduction in *The Cambridge Edition*, 4 (Cambridge: 2012) 227–29 and also Lindley's *The Trials of Frances Howard: Fact and Fiction at the Court of King James* (London: 1993).

14   Act 3, scene 1 of *Volpone*. *Cambridge Edition*, vol. 3, p. 99.

15   Act 2, scene 4 of *Bartholomew Fair*. *Cambridge Edition*, vol. 4, p. 319.

Cervantes' *Don Quixote*, the first part of which was published in English in 1612. An English version of the second part and a reprinting of the first, also in English, followed along quickly. *Don Quixote* was widely read in England, and the physician, Edmund Gayton, seems to have tried to play upon its popular appeal by publishing *Pleasant Notes upon Don Quixote* in 1654. Gayton says of the character of Ducinea de Toboso, 'I love Tobosa, and I know not why, Only I say, I love (whimsyly)'. Dulcinea is a muscular and loud-voiced country girl, whom Don Quixote has seen only fleetingly, but he both falls in love with her and imagines her to be a delicate and shy princess. Quixote, one might say, is a whimsical character, but as the quote from Gayton shows, Quixote is whimsical in the sense that he entertains Cervantes' readers. Quixote does not understand or enjoy his delusions himself.

Whimsy of the second, less sexualized sort is to be seen in the visual arts of the time. Cavendish's journey to Savoy with Sir Henry Wotton undoubtedly took the two through Flanders on their way home. Both had travelled through France on the outward voyage and the return was to be made by another route. In Flanders Wotton's party would have come in contact with paintings like Pieter Bruegel's much copied *Netherlandish Proverbs*, in which odd, comic images, including pies perched on a steeply pitched roof, dominate. Some art historians would say that beneath Bruegel's imagery is a serious moral message, a message that predominates and therefore attenuates any entertainment value involved. I would not completely deny the existence of the moral lessons, but am not inclined to see the odd images as being merely vehicles for didacticism. As Svetlana Alpers writes of another painting by Bruegel, 'no [ordinary viewer] could keep a solemn face' in spite of '[one modern scholar's] exaggerated solemnity'.[16] In short, I see whimsy of the second sort in *Netherlandish Proverbs* and I expect that Cavendish would have seen it too.

Whimsy was not always the dominant theme when it was employed in the visual arts, however. Whimsy is tucked away or even hidden in an oil painting of Welbeck Abbey completed during the time of William Cavendish. The painting, displayed in the entry hall of Welbeck today, depicts it as a large house, in front of which stand various small figures going about their business as individuals or talking in groups. It may be that some of these figures are family members. If, however, the viewer looks carefully at this large painting, a tiny, unobtrusive

---

16   "Bruegel's Festive Peasants", *Simiolus Netherlands Quarterly for the History of Art*, vol. 6, nos. 3 and 4 (1972–1973), p. 165. Walter S Gibson, in a similar vein, writes, 'It is widely assumed that most of Bruegel's pictures express profound philosophical or moral concepts... Unfortunately [this view is not] supported by what Bruegel's contemporaries thought about either peasants or personifications': Gibson W.S., *Bruegel* (London: 1977) 11.

FIGURE 2.2 *Man urinating. Private Collection.*

man can be seen, back to viewer, apparently urinating on the side of the building. Such is the opinion of Lucy Worsley, who thinks the urinating man is a servant.[17] (Fig. 2.2) This is a bit of whimsy placed in the painting, I imagine, with the understanding that it would be missed by anyone seeing the picture for the first time. William and other family members, then, were in a position to point the fellow out to selected visitors. The little man would have been good for a chuckle. This small bit of whimsy is not without some precedent in European painting. Indeed, the author of a paper given at the Renaissance Society of America in 2012 asserts the existence of what appears to be a minor tradition of tiny men urinating against buildings in Italian Renaissance paintings.[18] It is a tradition about which few English visitors to Welbeck would have known, so there was plenty of opportunity for surprise.

Men urinating were commonly depicted in Netherlandish painting of the time. Rembrandt's print, *Man Urinating* (1631), is quite typical. Presumably, this sort of art was intended for the walls of taverns or for rooms in houses where men gathered to drink and jest. These generally large figures offer no surprise to viewers and not much oddity. While they might be amusing, they fall short of whimsy on the other two accounts. The large painting of Welbeck Abbey is, of course, art of a different sort. Its subtle whimsy is in keeping with a place where estate management was the rule of the day but where

---

17   Worsley L., *Cavalier: A Tale of Chivalry, Passion, and Great Houses*, (London: 2007) colour plate 4 between 76–77.

18   See Trowbridge M., "The Micturating Man and the Artist Doctor: Reading Urine in Roger van der Weyden's *St Luke Drawing the Virgin*", Renaissance Society of America programme for 2012, 153.

the occasional joke was not inappropriate. There were far fewer restraints at Bolsover Castle.

During the 1640s, Cavendish wrote a set of poems that he called his 'phansies', and these poems eventually were transcribed into a beautiful scribal volume by his secretary, John Rolleston. A certain amount of whimsy makes its way into this verse, much of which was written for Margaret Lucas, who became his second wife. 'Fancies', however, would be the wrong word to describe the elements of the architecture of Bolsover or the little man in the painting of Welbeck if we stick to the way Cavendish used the word 'fancies' of his poetry. Rather, his verse fancies are emanations from his imagination and are better understood as having mostly serious philosophical import. They can be surprising—and do involve oddities—but they go beyond being pleasantly entertaining. Cavendish's verse fancies also are quite personal and tied to him as an individual. They do not function as continuation, as is the case with the architecture and decoration of Bolsover, of a tradition that involved his father, Charles Cavendish.

Whimsy, as found in the life of William Cavendish, involved an element of play, especially if we posit that he enjoyed the game of pointing out the little man in the painting of Welbeck to guests new to the house. The Dutch historian, Johan Huizinga, in a landmark study published in 1938, *Homo Ludens*, looks at play across the centuries. For Huizinga, play is necessarily competitive and must involve losing as well as winning. To the extent that whimsy functions as a form of play in the life of William Cavendish, the stress is not on winning and losing but on shared good fun.

Jonson's A Challenge at Tilt and The Irish Masqe

I now would like to return for a closer look at the way in which Jonson may have tried to use *A Challenge at Tilt* to reduce the social tensions surrounding the Carr-Howard nuptials. I then will offer a passing glance at the politics of *The Irish Masque*. With *Challenge*, it might be argued that Jonson was merely writing a whimsy of a sexual sort. His motivation in that case was to indulge his penchant for bawdy drama. It is quite possible that both motivations coexisted, as he wrote his scripts. *A Challenge* begins with two actors dressed as servants. The actors are scuffling as they enter, and oddly, they carry bows and quivers. The audience would have had to take a moment or two to figure out that the servants were actors and not two members of the household staff. This is the sort of trick played on audiences that we find in modern drama like Tom Stoppard's *The Real Inspector Hound*, but it is also a theatrical gambit that enjoyed a long tradition in royal entertainments.[19] In any event, the two characters each claim to be Cupid. The first Cupid says that he is a helper to the groom and the second maintains that he is an attendant of the bride. Both claim to be the sole son of the Goddess of Love. Surprise is increased—and perhaps a little indignation generated—when the second Cupid, addressing the ladies, almost immediately threatens to disrobe: 'Sure they are these garments that estrange me to you! If I were naked, you would know me better. No relic of love left in an old bosom here? What shall I do?'[20] It is easy to imagine the second Cupid singling out an elderly lady in the audience as he speaks the words 'old bosom here', while beginning to undo buttons of his tunic. The first Cupid says, 'My little shadow is turned furious', and the modern sense of 'angry' for 'furious' is not intended. Rather, the second Cupid is, in the view of the first, 'being daft' or furious in a verbal echo of Ariosto's description of the deranged Orlando Furioso. The sight of a man dressed as a servant making such an overture to an aristocratic lady and beginning to remove his clothes would have been hilarious, especially given the taboo against sex between male servants and their mistresses. The erotic nature of the dialogue of *A Challenge*, however, shifts from joking to elegant verbal picture as evoked by the first Cupid, who waxes eloquent:

> Was there a curl in [the bridegroom's] hair that I did not sport in or a ring of it crisped that might not have become Juno's fingers? His very undressing, was it not love's arming? Did not all his kisses charge and his touch attempt? But his words, were they not feathered from my wings and flew in singing at her ears, like arrows tipped with gold?[21]

Jonson might have hoped that those in the audience who reluctantly accepted their invitations to the wedding of Carr and Howard, given its social circumstances, would have forgotten their qualms by this point and would have laughed heartily at the sexual jokes. The plan also may have been that these people would have had feelings of a more refined sort awakened by the elevated language of the first Cupid, language reminiscent of an erotic epyllion.

---

19   Herford and Simpson assert that 'the abrupt entrance of the disguised persons—a company of ostensible strangers—into the festive hall was a piquant moment, which, again the later masque persistently maintained': Herford C.H. – Simpson P., *Ben Jonson: The Man and His Work* (Oxford: 1925) 251.

20   *Cambridge Edition*, 4, 232.

21   Ibid., 233.

Of course, we have no independent evidence about audience reaction so it is unclear if Jonson was successful. Given the supposed sexual rapacity of the bride, the bawdiness of the masque could have had the potential for embarrassing everyone present.[22] But there is no evidence for this reaction either.

Jonson fell out of royal favour with the advent of the court of Henrietta Maria and did not enjoy the attention of Charles I in the way that he had been admired by James I. Jonson, at Cavendish's urging, nonetheless, carried on writing racy dialogue in the 1630s for *The King's Entertainment at Welbeck*— but there will be more detail on this entertainment later in the present essay. For the moment it is mostly important to observe that it is likely that the bawdiness of *A Challenge* was at the very least perceived to be enjoyable by Cavendish or it would not have been repeated in the entertainment some twenty years later. He undoubtedly knew that Charles I was less inclined to ribaldry than James I, but, at the same time, ribaldry was something of an anti-Puritan quality that he claimed for himself.[23] Cavendish's comedy of the early 1640s, *The Variety*, contains two characters that represent different aspects of his personality. One, called Sir William, is full of nostalgia for the early years of the seventeenth century. The other, Master Newman, angrily decides to take up 'roaring and whoring' after apparently losing favour with the lady he loves.[24] Master Newman, however, does not actually engage in these activities and ends up marrying the lady whom he thought he had lost. Thus *The Variety* is a play that Cavendish would have expected to have found favour with Henrietta Maria because it not only brings up bawdy behaviour merely to dismiss it but also portrays its author as a man whose nostalgia for the time of James I is entirely forgivable. Cavendish, naturally, could have miscalculated the effect on Henrietta Maria, but she and he became close allies during the Civil Wars and much of their cordial correspondence survives. It is, I think, impossible to know if this alliance was strengthened or weakened by Henrietta Maria's memory of ribald passages in *The Variety*.

---

22   David Lindley calls into question the commonly held view that Frances Howard was promiscuous. Rather he sees her as a woman whose life became the material for public fictions of a sexual nature. Lindley does not deny the possibility that there is truth in the allegations that she was promiscuous, but he understands most of the evidence that has survived today as shaped by the nature of storytelling at the time. See in particular the introduction to Lindley, *Trials of Frances Howard*.

23   Ironically, Charles I may have been less than completely chaste, himself. See Poynting S., "Deciphering the King: Charles I's Letters to Jane Whorwood", *The Seventeenth Century*, 21, 1 (2006) 128–140.

24   *The Varietie, a Comedy*, 1649 [n.p.] 63. Quoted from EEBO.

To return to the first part of *A Challenge*, the entertainment ends with the second Cupid formally accusing the first of falsehood and asking that the first appear at the beginning of the New Year with ten knights to defend himself. This challenge is accepted and the performance of the two disguised servants gives way to dancing. *The Irish Masque* was performed after the first part and before the second part of *A Challenge*, but I will continue on to the second part, which is not only sexually suggestive and surprising but even more odd than the first. The first Cupid enters alone and addresses the ladies, with whom he flirts, as did the second Cupid before. The first Cupid is no longer dressed as a servant and wears wings:

> Now, ladies, to glad your aspects once again with the sight of love and make a spring smile i'your faces, which must have looked like winter without me, behold me not like a servant but a champion… tickling your soft ears with my feathers and lying little straws about your hearts to kindle bonfires shall flame out your eyes… bending those stiff piccadills of yours… whipping your rebellious farthingales with my bowstring.[25]

Many in the audience would have found it delightfully odd that the apparently humourless first Cupid has transformed himself into a sexual joker, and this theatrical gambit works nicely in producing a combination of momentary confusion and surprise.[26] The second Cupid soon appears and at this point does become angry, quite probably because his role as sexual jester with the ladies has been usurped. Soon, however, the second Cupid makes a foray into his opponent's territory by claiming 'masculine eloquence' for the ladies in the face of supposed feminine beauty and cheerfulness to be found on the side of the groom. Oddity clearly follows on oddity.

The second Cupid's inversion of gender stereotypes causes the first Cupid to lose self-control and opens an opportunity for the first to respond with a pair of phallic puns:

> FIRST CUPID I will break my quiver into dust first… or be torn to pieces with harpies, marry one of the Furies, turn into chaos again, and dissolve the harmony of nature.

---

25   Ibid., p. 234.

26   David Lindley, editor of the *Cambridge Edition* of *Challenge*, also finds Jonson's approach to be confusing and also takes Jonson's motive to be theatrical, though Lindley does not bring up the topic of whimsy: *Cambridge Edition*, 4, 234.

> SECOND CUPID Oh, most stiffly spoken, and fit for the sex you stand for! Well, give the sign, then: let the trumpets sound, and upon the valour and fortune of your champions put the right of your cause.[27]

At this point, there is a flourish of trumpets and the tilting begins. Once completed, the two Cupids make brief ambiguous references to the outcome of the contest, and Hymen appears to set all straight between the two of them. Both Cupids, says Hymen, have a legitimate claim to be sons of Venus for they are, in fact, brothers. The first is Eros, while the second and taller of the two is Anteros, a pair who will reappear in Jonson's Bolsover entertainment in 1634. With the completion of Hymen's speech, *A Challenge* is over and Jonson has produced the sort of happy ending that James I and many others would have expected. Hymen's feel-good eloquence, however, may have been less effective in smoothing over the social awkwardness attached to the Carr-Howard match than was the whimsical battle of wits of the two Cupids. This is not to say that Jonson patched up the dispute, but only to suggest that for the duration of *A Challenge* resentment could have been attenuated. Whatever the outcome or Jonson's intentions, it is clear that Jonson simply liked writing Jonsonian comedy in which the sexual sort of whimsy played a part.

The Irish Masque was presented in a political environment dominated by news of a failed Irish Parliament, a catastrophe, in fact, which must have rankled with James I. As with *A Challenge*, the performance begins with a surprise and seems to use whimsy to deal with a difficult situation. The masque opens with a citizen being chased by four Irishmen. The first lines are spoken by the Irishman, Dennis, who having finished the chase and lost the quarry, looks around somewhat vacantly and says in broad dialect,

> For Creesh's sayk, phair ish te king? Phich ish he, an't be? Show me te shweet faish, quickly. By Got, o'my conshence, tish ish he! An tou be King Yamish, me name is Dennish: I serve Ty Mayesty's own cashtermonger, be me troth.[28]

Dennis, poor soul, is the only one in the room who does not know which person is King James. Dennis, true to Irish stereotype, swears casually and profusely. He also takes the trouble to introduce himself directly to James I in a piece of grossly indecorous and uncourtly behaviour. Even his language is oddly intimate as he asks to see the 'sweet face' of the king. James I would

---

27   Ibid., 236.
28   *Cambridge Edition*, 4, 243.

have roared with laughter. Jonson's sense of what might be appropriate subject matter for the occasion, of course, teeters on the edge of being ill-judged,
for he has Dermock, another Irishman, say, 'For by Got, tey love tee [James]
in Ireland'.[29] All evidence, given the disaster with the Parliament in Dublin,
pointed the other direction. The king was thoroughly disliked in Ireland, or
at least had no control over Irish politics. Still, I think, James I roared with
laughter simply because it was better to laugh than become angry—and he
was a man who could be teased. Nevertheless, some in the audience had their
doubts about the politics of *The Irish Masque* or were simply not amused.
One member wrote,

> The loftie maskers were so well liked at court the last weeke that they
> were appointed to performe yt again on Monday, yet theyre deuice
> (which was a mimicall imitation of the Irish) was not so pleasing to many
> which thincke it no time (as the case stands) to exasperate that nation
> [Ireland] by making yt ridiculous.[30]

I am not so sure that it was only the leaping dances of the masquers that
brought about the second performance. Rather, I think that the majority of
the audience, perhaps taking their cues from James I, liked the 'device' of the
whimsical Irishmen.

Cavendish echoes the opening of *The Irish Masque* at the beginning of the
second scene of *The King's Entertainment*, which he, himself, wrote about
1660 for an unrecorded royal performance. Royal entertainments were far less
fashionable in 1660 than they had been in the years when *A Challenge* and
The Irish Masque were performed, but a Cavendish theatrical signature was
nostalgia, in this case nostalgia for an outdated dramatic form. The first scene
of *The King's Entertainment* is serious but the second involves a bumptious
Welshman whose speaking in dialect is reminiscent of the Irishman Dennis
from *The Irish Masque*:

> A Welsh-man enters attired in a freez Cote, white Welch flannell for
> his Stockins, a great Welch Dager at his back, and a Monmoth Capp
> on his head.

---

29   Ibid., 247.
30   Herford – Simpson, *Ben Jonson*, 10, 541.

Wel—"Gott pless your Majesties worship, I am a Wells-man, that is a shentlemans, look you now. For wee are all Shentlemens in Walls, and pigg pedegres as up Thomas, up Richard's, up William's, up Robert's, and almost aule Christen names. Yet I never heard of up Charles, yet by the plessings of Got, Charles is up and is up in spight of aule the uglie Treasons and rebellious in the Orlde."[31]

The Welshman, like Dennis in *The Irish Masque*, addresses the king in familiar tone and in dialect. The Welshman is perhaps overly inclined to invoke deity, but mostly the audience is invited to laugh at his presumption in saying that he never heard of an 'up' Charles. What is meant here, according to Lynn Hulse, is 'ap' Charles or 'son of' Charles.[32] Of course, the power of the joke is increased by the fact that Charles II was indeed 'up' and the Parliamentarians down with advent of the Restoration. The main difference between the opening of *The Irish Masque* and the scene from *The King's Entertainment* is that the Welsh had supported Charles I against Parliament while the Irish had made trouble for his father and went on to rebel against Charles in 1641. Cavendish, thus, was not taking chances with angering the king, as had been the case with Jonson. Cavendish also liked to work in dialect from time to time and the French accent of his Dancing Master in the Restoration revival of *The Variety* helped to bring about an enormous theatrical success. Indeed, the title of the play was changed for the Restoration from *The Variety* to *The French Dancing Master*. Cavendish, Lynn Hulse tells us, reworked a good deal of old material that he, himself, had formerly written for new plays.[33] In the case of Restoration royal entertainment, Cavendish reworked, not what he had written, but some of the dramatic techniques that he found in *The Irish Masque*.

Jonson's Welbeck and Bolsover Entertainments

It is time now to look more closely at the two entertainments written by Jonson in the 1630s for Welbeck and Bolsover. William Cavendish was Earl of Newcastle. As such, he was in a position to sponsor entertainments of his own in bids to increase his social standing and to strengthen his political connections to a new king, Charles I, and to the queen, Henrietta Maria. Cavendish's main hopes for the 1630s were to become Master of the Horse to Charles or,

---

31   I have slightly modernized the edition of Hulse L., *Viator*, 26 (1995) 389–90.
32   Ibid., Hulse, 371.
33   Ibid., 375.

failing that, governor to Charles's son Prince Charles, or both. After much worry and at least one despairing letter to his first wife, Elizabeth Bassett, William did become governor to the prince but he was never to be Master of the Horse. Cavendish, we might imagine, made various attempts to carry his case forward in these ambitions, but the two efforts that stand out most distinctly involve a pair of entertainments written by Jonson for royal visits to Welbeck in 1633 and to Bolsover in 1634. Some have suggested that the entertainments were a blunder, since Cavendish did not become Master of the Horse, but perhaps they worked in his favour, but just not well enough.

Charles I's visit to Welbeck was undertaken as part of a journey that culminated with his coronation as King of Scotland. Jonson's entertainment, performed on 31 May, has been seen by scholars to be both comic and an attempt by Cavendish to claim for himself the role of local magnate, much as the Earl of Leicester had done with the Kenilworth Entertainment in 1575.[34] The Welbeck entertainment was probably more whimsical in a bawdy way than it should have been, given Charles's more staid taste than that of his father, James I, but Charles did return the following year for the second entertainment, staged at Bolsover, bringing along Henrietta Maria. If Charles found the first offensive, why did he return for more? Although Lucy Hutchinson has been much quoted as saying that that Cavendish wasted his money in various efforts to impress Charles and Henrietta, Hutchinson probably wrote under the influence of bitterness brought about by the failure of the Commonwealth as a republican project.[35] The money spent, perhaps £5,000 for the Welbeck entertainment and £15,000 for Bolsover's, did cause Cavendish to economize for the next few years to pay his debts, but it also helped to cement a relationship between him and his sovereigns for a long time to come.[36] My sense is that Charles, who, as I have noted, did not find bawdy performance enjoyable, nevertheless, would have appreciated the reference to his father's more ribald taste. The tilting of the Welbeck entertainment also recalled the fashion for chivalric romance in

---

34   See James Knowles' introduction to the Welbeck entertainment in *The Cambridge Edition*, vol. 6, p. 661.

35   'A foolish ambition of glorious slavery carried [Newcastle] to court, where he ran himself much into debt to purchase the neglects of the king and queen and the scorns of proud courtiers'. Quoted From Grant, *Margaret the First*, 60.

36   The amounts come from William's life written by Margaret Cavendish and have seemed to some to be too large to be accurate. Brown believes that the full cost of the royal visit and not just the performances was involved. The king did stay for six days and had a retinue that probably numbered in the hundreds: Brown C.C., "Courtesies of Place and Arts of Diplomacy in Ben Jonson's Last Two Entertainments for Royalty", *The Seventeenth Century* (Autumn, 1994) 151.

the time of James I. Cavendish and Ben Jonson, were, after all, old friends and were admirers of James I. To some degree, nostalgia was involved, as Anne Barton has suggested of Cavendish's play, *The Variety*.[37]

While the Welbeck entertainment has been taken to be comic, the bawdy aspects of its whimsy have been overlooked. The entertainment begins, in the manner of *The Irish Masque*, with two characters who do not know which person in the audience is the king. This connection has been noted but what has been missed is what might be called the 'vicitie' of the entertainment. As the performance ends and before a gentleman appears to deliver the final, serious-minded concluding remarks, there is a song which contains these lines:

> Let's sing about, and say Hey—troll!
> Troll to me the bride-ale bowl.
> . . . .
> With, here is to the fruit of Pem,
> Grafted upon Stubb, his stem,
> With the Peakish nicetie,
> And old Sherwood's vicitie." (ll. 250–258)[38]

Jonson's editors, following the OED, sometime say that 'vicitie' is a non-signifying word put into the song for rhyme, but, in my view, it refers in a jocular way to Cavendish's anti-Puritanical appreciation for bawdiness in drama. Cavendish might well be identified with the bridegroom Stubb, who is said in the entertainment to be short but not quite a 'shrimp' (l. 126).[39] Cavendish's vicitie, or bawdiness, was later to be much remarked upon by the Puritans in pamphlet literature, but it was something of a badge of honour for him.[40] If Stubb of Nottinghamshire (Sherwood) in a loose way is a stand-in for Cavendish (who identified himself with Sherwood), it might be asked who is meant by Pem, the elderly May Queen from Derbyshire (the Peak), to whom Stubb is to be married? I am inclined to see Pem as recalling Christian Bruce Cavendish, Countess of Devonshire, who lived at nearby Hardwick Hall.

---

37   Barton A., *Ben Jonson, Dramatist* (Cambridge: 1984) 301.

38   *Cambridge Edition*, 6, 678.

39   There also may be a local allusion, since Stubb Hollow, home of Stubb in the entertainment, could point to Stubbs Hall in West Yorkshire, not overly far from Welbeck.

40   Lucy Worsley writes, 'He has put so much effort into making the point that pleasure can be more important than virtue because he has to counter the popular perception of himself as a great-pleasure seeker. In his wall paintings, he takes pride in his image as a womanizer'. Worsley, *Cavalier*, 105.

The Devonshires only moved their main residence to Chatsworth at the end of the seventeenth century. Christian, after the death of her husband and before her son's majority, was very definitely the most powerful person in Derbyshire. As a woman, she could not be the Lord Lieutenant of that county, so there was, in effect, a temporary 'marriage' between William and Christian, in which he acted as Lord Lieutenant for both shires in consultation with her. Certainly the office of Lord Lieutenant is frequently mentioned in the entertainment and it is clear that Cavendish and Christian were political allies, as may be seen in their letters.[41]

Would Christian Bruce Cavendish have liked being compared to the aging ale-wife and May queen Pem? That depends on whether or not she could take a joke. The whimsy displayed in *The Irish Masque* required that James I allow himself to be teased, so it would seem that there was a tradition in which being the butt of a rude joke was part of royal and aristocratic life—at least in some circumstances. It may be useful to recall that there is an elderly May queen in *The Kenilworth Entertainment*, and Buckingham played the part of a robber in Jonson's *Gypsies Metamorphosed* (performed 1621). One need not always be figured as beautiful or virtuous. Although the Welbeck entertainment makes risqué references here and there, ultimately it is not as bawdy as it might have been. I suggested some years back that the script of the Welbeck entertainment at one time was outrageously bawdy and that cutting was necessary to tone down the erotic references contained therein.[42] I will say now that the eroticism of the uncut script is quite whimsical in a sexual way. Below, may be found an example taken from what I believe to be a cut passage, something which survives as an isolated item in the family archive in the British Museum (Harley 4944, fo. 53v). The Moon addresses a group of aristocrats in a hall:

> I had something else to say,
> But have lost it on the way,
> I shall think on't ere't be day.
> The Moon commends her
> To the merry beards in hall
> Those turned up and those that fall,
> Morts and Merkins that wag all,
> Tough, foul, or tender.

---

41   See NUL, Portland MSS, Pw1. 56–66.

42   I am happy to say that I have received some support for this suggestion from *The Cambridge Edition*, 6, 657. My point was first made in Fitzmaurice J., "William Cavendish and Two Entertainments by Ben Jonson", *The Ben Jonson Journal*, 5 (1998) 63–80.

There is a good deal more bawdry, but this snippet is probably enough to give an idea of what was originally intended for the Welbeck entertainment.[43] It is unlikely, however, that either Charles I or Henrietta Maria would have found this very bawdy sort of whimsy amusing. William knew just how far to go and when to stop, so the passage had to go. But, of course, he did not discard the passage altogether. He kept it among his manuscripts for perusal by later generations. And, naturally, it could be employed in performance if the right occasion arose.

The Welbeck entertainment is centred round the riding of horses in a tilt against the quintain. The tilt would have recalled earlier tilts in the style of chivalric romance undertaken for James I and even Elizabeth I, and it would have played up Cavendish's interest in horsemanship for the assembled crowd as well as for the king. The tilt would have been tricky to perform, since the script called for some of the riders to do well but for others to endure a bucking horse or fall to the ground. One successful rider, Blue Hood, pokes 'Sir Quin' in the 'Q' rather than the shield, and 'Q' seems to be a pun on the French for 'bottom', a mild bit of naughty language. All in all, it would have been a very entertaining show with much clowning by skilled riders.

The second entertainment, the one staged for the royal couple at Bolsover Castle in 1634, shows very little bawdiness and is more in keeping with the sort of elevated love associated with the court of Henrietta Maria. The performance can be seen to contain whimsy, though one apparently whimsical passage has not found favour with modern scholars. Neither James Knowles nor Cedric Brown feels that the speech of Colonel Vitruvius works very well, and I am inclined to agree.[44] Vitruvius is intended as a satire on Jonson's rival, Inigo Jones, and it might have surprised the royal couple but they would not have found it amusing. It has no nostalgia value. The final speech of the entertainment, delivered by Philalethes, would not have been objectionable and it is definitely could be played as whimsical. Philalethes suggests that there is a

---

43   Because there are mechanicals in the Bolsover entertainment, this isolated manuscript item could have been omitted from it rather than from the performance at Welbeck. That is, the character Moon from the passage would fit with the mechanicals in the Bolsover entertainment. The editors of the *Cambridge Edition* (6, 657), however, connect the manuscript item to Welbeck because the item seems to be a companion to another apparently excised poem, which refers to the coronation in Scotland. The coronation took place in 1633 shortly after the Welbeck performance. The manuscript item, of course, might have been included in one entertainment and then the other and then excised but kept. William Cavendish kept large numbers of fragments from dramatic pieces that he, himself, penned. For a printing of many these fragments, see Hulse L., (ed.) *Dramatic Works by William Cavendish*, Malone Society Reprints 158 (Oxford: 1996).

44   See *Cambridge Edition*, 6, 684.

'divine school of love' at Bolsover and that it does not allow poetry. The two main characters of the entertainment, Eros and Anteros, have been speaking in verse, which Philalethes says will not gain them credit at 'court'. Further, the school of love, if the two learn its complex ways, will cut these characters off from the ale-drinking people of Derbyshire, where Bolsover is located. I am inclined to see Eros and Anteros as being intended to recall William Cavendish and his brother, Sir Charles. William, as has been noted, was short and Sir Charles was a dwarf. Height is mentioned as the two vie for a palm and, as was the case with the Welbeck entertainment, helps to make the biographical connection.

Philalethes's advice to Eros and Anteros can be read as containing an outline of Cavendish's dilemma regarding Henrietta Maria. He may try to fit in with the values of her court, but his being a (worldly) poet makes him an outsider. Cavendish could resign himself to the rusticity of Derbyshire, where he owned a good deal of land, but he preferred to find a way to please her. If Philalethes' speech is delivered in a wistful tone, Cavendish would seem to be in a very sad predicament. Still, one should not take the speech of Philalethes as the final word on his relationship with Henrietta Maria. Cavendish was, as I have noted, a frequent correspondent with her during the Civil Wars, when military alliances were paramount and schools of elevated love were less important. The sadness of Eros's and Anteros's (i.e., Cavendish's) condition could have been a relatively obvious comic pose even when the Bolsover entertainment was staged, the whimsical *faux* dejection of a rejected platonic lover. Quentin Bone believes that Henrietta Maria flirted with Cavendish in correspondence during the Civil Wars, perhaps to gain his cooperation.[45] Bone also notes that flirtations of this sort were common in French royal courts. The Henrietta-Cavendish flirtation probably went both ways and had an early onset.

Conclusion

Cavendish, himself, took up writing comedies late in the 1630s, though his friend and literary mentor Ben Jonson died in 1637. It once was common among scholars to find as significant the fact that he received help from the dramatist, James Shirley, during these pre-war years and from another playwright, Thomas Shadwell, during the Restoration. Nevertheless, the suggestion by Douglas Grant that his helpers did the real writing has no basis in the evidence. Indeed, to say that Cavendish's successful comedy *The Variety*, could not have been written without Shirley is like asserting that T.S. Eliot could not

---

45   Bone Q., *Henrietta Maria: Queen of the Cavaliers* (Urbana: 1972) 166–67, fn. 105.

have completed *The Wasteland* without Ezra Pound. In each case, there is an author and an editor, but the author should be given a far greater share of the credit for the work than the editor.[46] Cavendish's later writing, as I observed earlier in this essay, betrayed his continued interest in whimsy, but his attention to romance clearly diminished. It is not that he forgot about his days in the chivalric court of Prince Henry. Rather, that period in his life became a part of his general theatrical use of nostalgia. In *The Variety*, a character who resembles Cavendish likes to dress up as if he were the Earl of Leicester. Leicester was an Elizabethan rather than Jacobean, but the sense of nostalgia is much the same. This character, called Manley, confirms Cavendish's continued use of the whimsical, for Manley is surprising, odd and entertaining. Manley is also very sympathetic. We are delighted when he wins the heart of the canny and desirable Lady Beaufield as the play comes to a close. She is wise enough to know Manley's value and by extension the value of the literary taste of earlier monarchs.

It is probably safe to say, then, that Cavendish simply let chivalric romance drift into the background of his life while remaining a committed horseman. He wrote, and in 1658 published, a book on horses but that book contains practical advice on what we today would call dressage. If the book was intended to enhance his standing among the aristocracy, it was not through reference to chivalry but through William's intimate acquaintance with the facts of training horses. It remained for his great-granddaughter, Henrietta Cavendish Harley, Countess of Oxford, to revive the idea of Medieval romance among the Cavendishes by installing a Gothic ceiling at Welbeck in the eighteenth century. But that is another story.

Selective Bibliography

Barton A., *Ben Jonson, Dramatist* (Cambridge: 1984).

Bevington D. – Butler M. – Donaldson I. (eds.) *The Cambridge Edition of the Works of Ben Jonson* (Cambridge: 2012) 7 volumes.

---

46   Following Henry Ten Eyck Perry, Douglas Grant takes the view that *The Variety* was 'largely the work of Shirley'. Grant also finds the play 'tedious and coarse'. The word 'coarse', it would appear, refers to sexual whimsy. Grant, writing in the 1950s, betrays a prudery that is no longer dominant in literary criticism and that is slightly laughable these days. Quotation from Grant: *Margaret the First*, 160. Perry simply notices plot similarities between *The Variety* and what is to be seen in Shirley's plays. Plot similarities do not constitute convincing evidence of actual ghost writing. Perry H.T.E., *The First Duchess of Newcastle and her Husband as Figures in Literary History* (Boston & London: 1918) 104.

Bone Q., *Henrietta Maria: Queen of the Cavaliers* (Urbana: 1972).

Fitzmaurice J., "William Cavendish and Two Entertainments by Ben Jonson", *The Ben Jonson Journal*, 5 (1998) 63–80.

Fowler A., *The Country House Poem, A Cabinet of Seventeenth-Century Estate Poems and Related Items* (Edinburgh: 1994).

Herford C.H. – Simpson P., *Ben Jonson: The Man and His Work* (Oxford: 1925).

Hulse L., *Viator*, 26 (1995) 311–405.

Hulse L., (ed.) *Dramatic Works by William Cavendish*, Malone Society Reprints 158 (Oxford: 1996).

Lindley D., *The Trials of Frances Howard: Fact and Fiction at the Court of King James* (London: 1993).

Poynting S., "Deciphering the King: Charles I's Letters to Jane Whorwood", *The Seventeenth Century*, 21, 1 (2006) 128–140.

Ten Eyck Perry H. *The First Duchess of Newcastle and her Husband as Figures in Literary History* (Boston & London: 1918).

Trease G., *Portrait of a Cavalier: William Cavendish: First Duke of Newcastle* (London: 1979).

Trowbridge M., "The Micturating Man and the Artist Doctor: Reading Urine in Roger van der Weyden's *St Luke Drawing the Virgin*", Renaissance Society of America programme for 2012.

Worsley L. – Addyman T., "Riding Houses and Horses: William Cavendish's Architecture for the Art of Horsemanship", *Architectural History*, 45 (2002).

Young A., *Tudor and Stuart Tournaments* (London: 1997).

CHAPTER 3

'An After-Game of Reputation': Systems of Representation, William Cavendish and the Battle of Marston Moor

Elspeth Graham

What are the personal implications of being held responsible for defeat in a history-changing battle? Over the past few decades historians, cultural historians and literary critics have paid increasing attention to how the British Civil Wars (1638–1651), and more specifically the English Civil War (1642–1651), were experienced by individuals.[1] Among the many personal responses to civil war that are documented, and that might be imagined, is a particular cluster of concerns with matters of reputation, status and integrity of the self that is apparent in the writings of defeated royalists.[2] In his *The History of the Rebellion and Civil Wars in England*, Clarendon remarked (in relation to Colonel Richard Feilding who was—in Clarendon's view, unfairly—disgraced after the royalist surrender of Reading), 'So fatal are all misfortunes, and so difficult a thing it is to play an after-game of reputation, in that nice and jealous profession'.[3] The need to repair a personal reputation can be recognised not just as a difficulty facing Fielding in an immediate military context, but as a central preoccupation of royalist writing in the much broader context of the loss of a political, cultural and ontological system, based on notions of order and degree, in which management of reputation had been crucial. In the system of allegiances, patronage, reward and favour that had characterised the court and that was necessary to 'a monarchy without a fully salaried bureaucracy',[4] matters of reputation and image-making had underpinned the administrative organisation of the court as a political body, and had been central to the identities, advancement and

---

1   On the experience of the Civil Wars, see particularly, Carlton C., *Going to the Wars: The Experience of the British Civil Wars, 1638–1651* (London & New York: 1992); Bennett M., *The Civil Wars Experienced: Britain and Ireland, 1638–1661* (London: 2000); and Purkiss D., *The English Civil War: A People's History* (London: 2006).

2   Cf. de Groot J., *Royalist Identities* (Basingstoke: 2004) 1–7.

3   Hyde Edward, Earl of Clarendon, *The History of the Rebellion and Civil Wars in England*, (ed.) Macray W.D., 6 vols. (Oxford: 1888) III, 30.

4   Butler M., "Ben Jonson and the Limits of Courtly Panegyric", in Sharpe K. – Lake P. (eds.), *Culture and Politics in Early Stuart England* (Basingstoke: 1994) 91.

© KONINKLIJKE BRILL NV, LEIDEN, 2017 | DOI 10.1163/9789004326217_005

survival of individuals. As a royalist sense of the collapse of order deepened through the course of the war's lost battles, the fracturing of the court as family and household by the removal of Henrietta Maria to France in 1644, and the execution of Charles I in 1649, the need to create compensatory and restorative images grew more urgent, complex and troubled, as the publication of *Eikon Basilike* emphatically signalled.

This essay examines issues of reputation and self-imaging in the career and writing of the royalist courtier, playwright, poet, musician, master of horsemanship and military commander, William Cavendish, Earl (1628), Marquis (1643), and Duke (1665) of Newcastle. Born into a family with court associations, Cavendish had aspirations towards a significant role at court from his youth. His career as a courtier, however, involved periods of favour (highpoints included his being chosen, at the age of seventeen, as one of the twenty-five contemporaries of Prince Henry to attend him at his investiture as Prince of Wales in 1610, and his creation as Knight of the Bath for this ceremony; and, twenty-six years later, his appointment as governor of Prince Charles, the future Charles II); an extraordinarily high level of personal financial expenditure (both in direct contribution to the royal war effort and in relation to the production of self-promoting events and entertainments); and periods of exclusion from favour (as a result of impolitic alliances, his tendency to provoke jealousies at court, and his insensitivity to—even impatience with— some of the complexities of rivalries and allegiances that characterised court life).[5] From 1642 and the start of the English Civil Wars, nevertheless, Charles I placed reliance on him as Commander-in-Chief of the Northern Army and gave him powers equivalent to those of a viceroy in the North. He had some success in early battles until 1644, when Cavendish and Prince Rupert, in an unclear and uneasy chain of command, led the northern royalist armies into catastrophic defeat at Marston Moor. By focusing on his literary, architectural and artistic production and patronage as aspects of his long career of aspirational image-making, this article considers Cavendish's 'after-game of reputation' during his exile after Marston Moor.

---

5   For biographical accounts see: Trease G., *Portrait of a Cavalier: William Cavendish, First Duke of Newcastle* (London: 1979); Hulse L., "Cavendish, William, first duke of Newcastle upon Tyne (*bap.* 1593, *d.* 1676)", ODNB, http://www.oxforddnb.com/view/article/4946 William Cavendish (*bap.* 1593, *d.* 1676): doi:10.1093/ref:odnb/4946 (accessed 29 Dec., 2010); Worsley L., *Cavalier: The Story of a Seventeenth-Century Playboy* (London: 2007). On Cavendish's political position in relation to the court at various times in his life see Sarasohn L.T., "Margaret Cavendish, William Newcastle, and Political Marginalization", *English Studies*, 92:7 (2011), 806–817.

Marston Moor

The battle of Marston Moor (2 July 1644), the decisive engagement in the more protracted struggle for possession of York, and consequently northern England, is generally seen as a turning point in the First English Civil War, and perhaps the British Civil Wars overall. It was certainly the largest set-piece battle of the Civil Wars, and is sometimes accounted the largest battle ever fought in England.[6] The number of battlefield casualties was certainly the greatest of the Civil Wars: between 4,000 and 6,000 of the 40,000 soldiers engaged were left dead or fatally wounded at the close of battle. And Marston Moor was, of course, a major loss for the royalist side. The vast majority of those killed—all but 300—were royalist troops. As Oliver Cromwell (whose military reputation and ultimate rise to power were grounded in the battle) described it, Marston Moor resulted in, 'an absolute victory obtained by the Lord's blessing' and for the parliamentary army, a 'great victory . . . such as the like never was since this war began.'[7] But, the decisiveness of the battle and the extent of the slaughter are not its only significances for historians. As John Barratt has remarked, 'The effects of Marston Moor spread like ripples for the remainder of the war',[8] or as Peter Newman has rather more forcibly suggested, Marston Moor constituted a catalytic moment: 'After it, nothing was to be the same.'[9] Not simply its military, but its political consequences, both immediate and long-term, were emphatic. Through his comparative allusion to the battle of Hastings, Newman identifies Marston Moor as one of the few single-day events that demonstrably brought about long-term change in British history. If we accept the idea that the Civil Wars constituted 'perhaps the single most important event in [British] history', creating the system of government, indeed the nation, that modern Britain has inherited, as well as 'creat[ing] by influence' the French

---

6   Newman P.R. – Roberts P.R., *Marston Moor 1644: The Battle of Five Armies* (Pickering, U.K.: 2003) viii. On the numbers of soldiers involved see also Gaunt P., *The English Civil Wars 1642–1651* (Oxford, 2003) 42. These numbers broadly correspond with those given by Carlton, *Going to the Wars* 121–122.

7   Cromwell's letter to his brother-in-law, Colonel Valentine Walton, informing him of his son's death at Marston Moor, in Lomas S.C. (ed.), *The Letters and Speeches of Oliver Cromwell: With Elucidations by Thomas Carlyle* (London: 1904) I, 176–77. This letter also gives a sense of the experience of the battle and of the wars. For the horror of Marston Moor, see in particular, Purkiss, *The English Civil War*, 328–337. On the experience of this battle also see Carlton, *Going to the Wars*, 119–129 and Bennett, *The Civil Wars Experienced*, 28–43 on Marston Moor and the north of England.

8   Barratt J., *The Battle for York: Marston Moor 1644* (Stroud: 2002) 158.

9   Newman and Roberts, *Marston Moor 1644*. viii–ix.

and American revolutions,[10] those few, violent, bloody hours at Marston Moor on a summer's evening in 1644, can be recognised as history-changing.

And if this important battle, as an immediate effect, established Cromwell's reputation, its outcome had a correspondingly diminishing effect on the reputations of the royalist commanders. In popular and parliamentarian consciousnesses, Rupert, Prince and Count Palatine of the Rhine, Charles I's nephew and foremost general, had been considered invincible, even diabolically aided, until this point. Rupert's military training from his early teens and his experience in the Thirty Years War differentiated him from other royalist army grandees, who had status but no actual military experience. In addition, his energy, physical appearance and personality (epitomising him as a cavalier), and most particularly his habit of always taking his favourite dog (a female, rare-breed poodle named Boy, perceived as a familiar) into battle with him, consolidated the satanic image, first suggested by his family nickname, *Robert le diable*. For parliamentarians, Marston Moor (where Boy was killed) shattered this image of supernaturally-aided invincibility; for Prince Rupert himself, the sense of responsibility for defeat was personally devastating, even though he went on substantially to rebuild the royalist war effort in the south of England. In the disputes and recriminations that followed Marston Moor, Prince Rupert's judgment in—even his authority for—engaging the parliamentarian army at that moment (and in opposition to the inclination of Cavendish, the northern commander) were questioned.[11] It was said that Rupert carried Charles I's letter, which he took to be the warrant for engagement at Marston Moor, on his person for the rest of his life.[12]

The reputation of William Cavendish, who both disagreed and miscommunicated with Rupert before the battle, who quarrelled violently with Rupert immediately after it and who (most damningly) went into exile within days of it, was more deeply damaged.[13] As John Barrett puts it, Cavendish has been 'one of the most vilified of all the Royalist commanders'.[14] While some modern historians have re-evaluated his efficacy as a military commander generally,

---

10   Purkiss, *The English Civil War*, xxi; 2–3.

11   See Barratt, *The Battle for York*, 79 for discussion of whether the king's letter to Prince Rupert should have been considered a warrant for battle and for the text of the letter. The letter is also given in Young P., *Marston Moor 1644: The Campaign and the Battle* (Kineton: 1970) 86–87. Clarendon also refers to the letter, Clarendon, III, pp. 378–379.

12   For a particularly lucid account and a nuanced interpretation of these issues, as well as of the battle itself and its aftermath, see Barratt, *The Battle for York*, 76–80, 154–56.

13   Ibid., 141–2.

14   Ibid., 29.

and his role at Marston Moor and immediate post-battle decision to flee into exile in particular, the assessments of many contemporaries established a picture of Cavendish as a hedonistic dilettante, full of a grandiose self-conceit, motivated by desire for the trappings of power, whose departure into exile significantly undermined royalist morale and effectiveness.[15] While Clarendon's account of the royalist defeat at Marston Moor itself is even-handed in attributing blame to both Prince Rupert and Cavendish,[16] it was his more equivocal portrait of Cavendish's overall role as a military commander that established this enduring character:

> He liked the pomp, and absolute authority of a general well, and preserved the dignity of it to the full . . . But the substantial part, and fatigue of a general, he did not in any degree understand . . . nor could submit to, but referred all matters of that nature to the discretion of his lieutenant general King . . . In all actions of the field he was still present, and never absent in any battle; in all which he gave instances of an invincible courage and fearlessness in danger; in which the exposing himself notoriously did sometimes change the fortunes of the day when his troops began to give ground. Such articles of action were no sooner over than he retired to his delightful company, music, or his softer pleasures, to all which he was so indulgent, and to his ease, that he would not be interrupted upon what occasion soever; insomuch as he sometimes denied admission to the chiefest officers of the army, even to general King himself, for two days together; from whence many inconveniences fell out.[17]

In these, and in further, well-known, *faux-sympathique* comments on Cavendish's character and flight into exile after the battle, Clarendon set the tone for much subsequent writing on him:

> All that can be said for the marquis is, that he was so utterly tired with a condition and employment so contrary to his humour, nature and education, that he did not at all consider the means or the way that would let

---

15   Ibid., 141–159; Newman – Roberts, *Marston Moor 1644*, 134 on Cavendish's departure into exile signalling the collapse of the royalist war effort in the north and influencing others; Grant D. (ed.), *The Phanseys of William Cavendish, Marquis of Newcastle addressed to Margaret Lucas and her Letters in Reply* (London: 1956) defends Cavendish's flight and mentions his example to other royalists, xiv–xv.

16   Clarendon, III, 375–380.

17   Ibid., III, 382–83.

him out of it, and free him forever from having more to do with it. It was
a greater wonder that he sustained the vexation and fatigue of it for so
long, than that he broke from it with so little circumspection.[18]

The corroborating assessments of other royalist contemporaries, emphasising
Cavendish's temperamental incompatibility with the demands of military
command, confirmed such a view. Sir Philip Warwick, for instance, who liaised
between Charles I in Oxford and Cavendish in the north-east before Marston
Moor, wrote: 'His edge had too much of the razor in it, for he had the tincture
of a romantic spirit, and had the misfortune to have something of the poet in
him.'[19] But it was, in fact, this very relationship between the poetic and the
military that came to be at the heart of Cavendish's own work of reputational
repair in the decades that followed.

Reputation and Its After-Game: Paris

Cavendish's often-quoted comment, reputedly made immediately after
Marston Moor, 'I will go into Holland ... I will not endure the laughter of the
Court',[20] suggests that his immediate response to the catastrophic losses of
the battle (all but thirty of the 4,000 soldiers in his Whitecoat army died), as
well as the personal and propaganda losses it brought about, was motivated
primarily by reputational concerns alone. His instinctive reaction, as it was
reported, relates not to the loss of men, nor to the royalist cause overall, nor
to Charles I himself (who was, in fact, generous-spirited about Marston Moor,
writing to thank Cavendish) but to intra-court politics, rivalries and associated contests of style and culture. His flight, in actuality to Hamburg at first,
where he arrived six days after the battle, and then to Henrietta Maria's exiled
court in France, nearly six months later, suggests an ambivalent quest for both
escape and self-restoration within an established royalist environment. That
matters of reputation should have been reported as paramount in Cavendish's
response to defeat at Marston Moor is perhaps made inevitable by the extravagance and nature of his pre-Civil War self-promotional activity.

Cavendish's past career of aspirational flamboyance, along with the necessary attempt to restore his reputation and to re-establish himself in continental royalist circles while in exile, worked in tension with his post-Civil War

---

18   Ibid., III, 380–1.
19   Sir Philip Warwick, *Memoirs of the Reign of King Charles the First* (Edinburgh: 1813) 235.
20   Warburton E. (ed.), *Memoirs and Correspondence of Prince Rupert and the Cavaliers*
       (London: 1849) II, 468.

silence in relation to his military role, his honour-based refusal to enter into recrimination or self-justification. Cavendish never provided his own direct account of, and self-justification for, his role in the Wars. Rather, his responses are produced obliquely. Just as his daughter, Jane Cavendish, had written in celebration of her father's victory at the Battle of Adwalton Moor in 1643, it was his wife who provided the most extensive defence of his lifelong loyalty to the Stuart monarchs.[21] Margaret Cavendish's *Life of William Cavendish* embodies this indirectness by its very status as a work that is apparently both recognised and legitimated by Cavendish himself, yet distanced from him and established as having an (at least, semi-) independent authority. Her dedication to her husband reproduces this ambiguous position through, on the one hand, her appeal to the authenticity of her account as deriving from the evidence of Cavendish and his secretary, John Rolleston, and on the other hand, her reference to the inhibitions produced by Cavendish's embargo on any recriminatory or disparaging comment:

> My Noble Lord,
>
> It hath always been my hearty Prayer . . . That God would be pleased to enable me to set forth and declare to after-ages, the truth of your loyal actions and endeavours, for the service of your King and Country; For the accomplishing of which design, I have followed the best and truest Observations of your Secretary John Rolleston, and your Lordships own Relations, and have accordingly writ the History of your Lordships Life, which although I have endeavoured to render as perspicuous as ever I could, yet one thing I find hath much darkened it; which is, that your Grace commanded me not to mention any thing or passage to the prejudice or disgrace of any Family or particular person (although they might be of great truth, and would illustrate much the actions of your Life) which I have dutifully performed to satisfie your Lordship, whose Nature is so Generous, that you are as well pleased to obscure the faults of your Enemies, as you are to divulge the vertues of your Friends; And certainly, My Lord, you have had as many Enemies, and as many Friends, as ever

---

21   Cavendish Jane, "On the 30th June to God", Yale University Library, Osborn MS b. 221. Transcribed in Millman J.S. – Wright G. (eds.), *Early Modern Women's Manuscript Poetry* (Manchester: 2005) 93; quoted by Knowles J., "'War is all the World About': The Cavendishes, Civil Wars and Culture Wars", in van Beneden B. – de Poorter N. (eds.), *Royalist Refugees: William and Margaret Cavendish in the Rubens House, 1648–1660* (Antwerp: 2006) 28 and Bennett, *The Civil Wars Experienced*, 34.

any one particular person had; and I pray God to forgive the one, and prosper the other...[22]

It is this disjuncture between Cavendish's established proclivity for glorifying self-representation and the empty space created by his determined refusal explicitly to justify his actions at, and after, Marston Moor that manifests itself in his post-1644 writings and cultural activities with their complex play between past and present identities.

Cavendish's first wife had died in 1643 and it was at the exiled court of Henrietta Maria that he met and wooed Margaret Lucas, a lady-in-waiting to the queen, as his second wife. His love poems to her, collected as *The Phanseys of the Marquesse of Newcastle* (?1647), are a work not only of courtship, but of self re-creation from the severed metonyms of his past identity.[23] If a courtship might always be assumed to involve some sort of self-revelation and self-presentation, the highly literary courtship of Cavendish and Margaret Lucas functions to create a relationship that is especially intense in its production of an identity that acknowledges, but also refashions, the situational identity of each partner and of them as a couple. Cavendish's marriage to his first wife, Elizabeth Howard (née Bassett), the widow of Henry Howard, third son of the first Earl of Suffolk, had bolstered his aristocratic and courtly connections. The marriage also brought him, as well as five surviving children, money to finance his architectural work and his efforts to secure royal favour through lavish royal entertainments at his homes and his contribution to the royalist war effort.[24] His courtship of, and marriage to, Margaret Lucas, fulfilled a quite different identity-related need. Thirty-one years younger than Cavendish, the shy Margaret Lucas, anxious and silent in the context of the political, gossipy Paris court of Henrietta Maria, appeared to him, in her

---

22   Cavendish M., *Life of William Cavendish*, sigs a1r–a1v. It was perhaps Cavendish's adamant refusal to enter into self-justification or corresponding blame of others and his refusal to cooperate in providing material for his *History of the Great Rebellion and Civil Wars* that, along with post-Restoration rivalry, coloured Clarendon's account of Cavendish. Cf. Hopper A., "William Cavendish, Marquis of Newcastle, as a Royalist General" in this volume 216–17.

23   *The Phanseys of the Marquesse of Newcastle Sett by him in verse* (BL, Add. Manuscript 32497). Seventy four of the love poems to Margaret Lucas/Margaret Cavendish are collected, along with her letters in reply (from BL, Portland Manuscript List 1 B), in Grant. References in this article to Cavendish's poems, where included in Grant, are to that edition. Poems not included in Grant are referenced to the BL Manuscript.

24   See Hulse, *ODNB* on Cavendish's reported financial contributions to Charles 1's cause.

words, 'such a Wife as he might bring to his own humours'.[25] As an object of love, Margaret Lucas could serve to reinforce aspects of Cavendish's damaged identity. Her own family connections—she was the sister of Sir John Lucas (first Baron Lucas of Shenfield), who had been Cavendish's Lieutenant-General of the Horse—could be positively associated with aspects of his military role (related to his horsemanship, his greatest acknowledged talent).[26] Her own literariness responded to 'that something of the poet in him' that Sir Philip Warwick had described pejoratively. Perhaps even Henrietta Maria's disapproval of their courtship also re-animated in him that very 'romantic spirit' of adventurous noncompliance with courtly consensus and opinion. The courtship correspondence itself (his poems; her letters) reveals her as providing a dialogic amplification to his utterances. She is not just a blank page onto which he could project his self (she was always more independent-minded than that would suggest), but someone who responds to his blend of wit with—sometimes courtly, sometimes gossipy—expressions of love, by intensifying and elaborating his conceits, producing herself with her 'mallancolly humer' and her 'contempaltions . . . on nothing but dessolutions',[27] as a temperamental complement to his witty, sanguine, worldy-wise person:

> My lord I have not had much experanse of the world, yet I have found it such as I could willingly part with it; but sence I knew you I fear I shall love it to well becaus you are in it; and yet me thinks you are not in it because you are not off it, so I am both in it and out off it, a strang enchantment.[28]

The play with neoplatonic notions of being 'in' and 'off' the world, the puns on world, signifying both the world of the court and the terrestrial world, and the melancholic tone precisely respond to his characteristic presentation of himself as having been fully incorporated into the world through his estates and homes, his conflicted relationship to the court and its culture, and his possession of a sanguine temperament.

Cavendish was an instinctively systemic and a naturally conservative thinker. Crucial to his work of self-construction and projection in written, architectural and visual forms in the pre-Civil War period had been his capacity for

---

25   Margaret Cavendish, *A true relation of my Birth, Breeding, and Life*, appended to *Natures Pictures* (Printed for J. Martin and J. Allestrye, London: 1656) 375.

26   See Barratt, *The Battle for York*, 117 on Lucas' being, 'always among the horse', and so lacking in conversational skills.

27   Grant, *The Phanseys of William Cavendish*, 104.

28   Ibid., 110.

deployment of easily-recognised and well-established systems of meaning that served to codify his self-image with economy and versatility. Neoclassicism, play with humoralism, and architectural embodiments of self had been at the core of his earlier self-representations. In his *Phanseys* he redeploys elements of these very same systems of meaning, manipulating them to reposition himself, but conserving the crucial components of identity he had figured through them. As Timothy Raylor has suggested, the opening of Cavendish's courtship poem 'Love's Muster' directly invokes Bolsover Castle, his favourite residence and the site of the entertainment he had provided, in his quest for royal favour, for Charles I and Henrietta Maria during their visit of 1634:

> I'le Muster Up my senses with delight;
> My taste, my touch, my smell, Hearing, and sight,
> All att one tyme; height's pleasure shall obtayne,
> With gentle strokes Upon my Ravisht Brayne.
> Best Various Pictures wee will have; nay, more,
> The Roofe with story fill'd, and gilt o'er.[29]

Raylor observes that this unconventional ordering of the senses, 'My taste, my touch, my smell, Hearing, and sight' corresponds precisely (if in reverse) to the sequence used by Ben Jonson in *Love's Welcome at Bolsover*,[30] the spectacular entertainment, including banquets, songs, dances and speeches, staged at different places in the castle that was *Love's Welcome*:

> 1. Ten. When were the Senses in such order plac'd?
> 2. Ten. The Sight, the Hearing, Smelling, Touching, Taste,
>
>   All at one Banquet'.[31]

Since the Pillar Parlour at Bolsover, 'originally called "the lower dining room" and ... used for intimate banquets and entertainments', is decorated with a depiction of the five senses, also in this order, it is possible—likely—that the opening song from *Love's Welcome* was performed to the king and queen

29   Ibid., 56–57.

30   Raylor T., "'Pleasure Reconcil'd to Virtue': William Cavendish, Ben Jonson, and the Decorative Scheme of Bolsover Castle", *Renaissance Quarterly*, 52 (1999) 402–39.

31   Ben Jonson, *Under-Woods. Consisting of Divers Poems* [1640], (Cambridge: 2011) 160.

in this room.[32] While several of Cavendish's courtship poems explicitly draw attention to his 'Misfortunes', 'the gretest Monarks' frownes',[33] and his dispossessed state (his flight into exile had been almost immediately followed by the surrender of his main estates and homes, Welbeck Abbey and Bolsover Castle, to parliamentarian troops), 'Love's Muster' serves to restore his past glories—both buildings and royal favour—textually. He inscribes Margaret Lucas into the buildings that had, in a particularly strong sense, embodied his past identity.

That Bolsover Castle functioned as a metonymic extension of Cavendish's identity is suggested more strongly still by further features of its decorative scheme and their emblematically witty use of similar systems of meaning. At the left of the entrance porch to the Little Castle at Bolsover, the oldest part of the building used for intimate and extravagant entertainments, the anteroom contains a series of depictions of the Four Temperaments. Three of the paintings contain a scene populated by figures representing the attributes of a depicted humour. Missing from the fourth picture is an equivalent set of figures representing the sanguine. As both Timothy Raylor and Lucy Worsley have observed, this missing temperament was perhaps embodied in the person of Cavendish himself, who would complete the sequence when he stood, on occasions such as the royal visit, below this painting.[34]

These sorts of exchanges between material, textual and visual projections of identity are not simply incidental. Cavendish's deployment of humoral systems and his sense of his own sanguine humour (the humour which suggests amorousness, equability, cheerfulness, a rosy complexion, cordiality, ability to adjust easily, optimism and generosity) had been central to his self-imaging from early in his career and provided a template for his behaviour throughout his life, even in times of adversity. In all his portraits he is shown with rosy cheeks, a quite specific marker of his temperament. Even those who were critical of Cavendish tended to speak of him in terms of the corresponding negative attributes ascribed to a sanguine temperament: proneness to hedonism, lust, dilettantism, and carelessness. The story that he lost the Battle of Marston Moor because he 'sneaked off to his coach for a quiet smoke' at the crucial

---

32 Worsley L, *Bolsover Castle* (London: 2000) 19.

33 'A Songe', Grant, *The Phanseys of William Cavendish*, 22.

34 Raylor, "Pleasure Reconcil'd to Virtue", 402–39. See also Brown C.C., "Courtesies of Place and Arts of Diplomacy in Ben Jonson's Last Two Entertainments for Royalty", *The Seventeenth Century*, 9, ii (1994), Special Issue: The Cavendish Circle, Raylor T. (ed.) 147–71; Worsley, *Bolsover Castle*, 16.

moment, although almost certainly not true, accords precisely with the sort of behaviour associated with sanguine types.[35]

Cavendish's deployment of emblems of his humorally-defined temperament in the fabric of Bolsover, and his performative displays of his self, along with his evocation of Bolsover and all that it represented of him in 'Love's Muster', are also indicative of his loyal patronage of Ben Jonson. Jonson, the great playwright of the humoral, provided influential models for Cavendish's own writing (as well as for the works of those, such as Shadwell, to whom he later gave patronage), and served him as one of his major image-makers. Cavendish's absorption of Jonsonian style, his sustained emulation of Jonson throughout his own career of playwriting, through the years of exile and into the Restoration, as much as his employment of Jonson during the latter's own years of difficulty, all suggest his constancy in using, perhaps even his conservative adherence to, the systems of thought most fashionable in his youth, in spite of his interests in, and patronage of, new scientific thought.[36]

Jonson was centrally involved in Cavendish's self-imaging and self-advertisement in the entertainments for Charles I and Henrietta Maria. The opening scene of *Love's Welcome* presents the particular neoplatonic notion of love that was fashionable in royalist circles and particularly endorsed by Henrietta Maria:

> Bas.   Love is a circle, both the first, and last
>   Of all our Actions, and his knots, too, fast.
> 1.[Ten]   A true-love Know, will hardly be unti'd,
>   And if it could, who would this Payre divide.[37]

This compliment to the king and queen is at the heart of this entertainment's play with neoplatonic ideas of love. The highest love, in neoplatonic

---

35   The phrase is from Purkiss, *The English Civil War*, 330. See also cf. Trease, *Portrait of a Cavalier*, 99. The story is originally taken from Clarendon, *Notes on Events in the North*, Bod. MS 23, f. 23 or, and is repeated in most modern accounts, although Cavendish's defeat is no longer attributed to his going for a smoke.

36   Cavendish wrote a comic interlude entitled "A Pleasante & Merrye Humor off a Roge" while in exile and after the Restoration produced the comedies *The Humorous Lovers* (Printed by J.M. for H. Herringman at the Sign of the Blue Anchor, London: 1677) and *The Triumphant Widow, or, The Medley of Humours* (Printed by J.M. for H. Herringman at the Sign of the Blue Anchor, London: 1677). Although Cavendish consistently adhered to the cultural and epistemological systems of his youth, he was also interested in new scientific thought. He was an associate of, among many, Hobbes, Mersenne and Descartes. See Timothy Raylor's essay in this volume.

37   Jonson, *Under-Woods*, 160.

epistemological systems, occurs when friendship or amorous love is united with spiritual love (mirroring the love of God) between individuals. This love then operates as a circuit of love that spirals round towards perfectibility. Ultimately, it raises those who love above the sphere of the corruptible world into heaven. Cavendish, then, in completing the sequence of the Temperaments in the Ante Room of Bolsover Castle in the 1630s provided that sort of completion that aspires to perfection. And, the performance of *Love's Welcome*, staged around the castle as a series of speeches, songs, dances, in a circle of welcome and festivity, embodies again the notion of a circle of love (between king and queen, monarch and subjects, the divine and the human). In the later poem, 'Love's Muster', Cavendish similarly plays with ideas of love being linked to the senses that come together in completeness in the brain. Implicit in the poem, of course, is the idea that the couple, uniting through the pleasures of the senses, are part of this achievement of completeness that will elevate them above the corruptible world.

The veiled and apparently slight allusion to Bolsover Castle in the allusion to the senses of 'Love's Muster', carries with it a whole world of meaning. It performs the work of textually restoring a lost environment, bringing it into present play, and resinscribing Cavendish in the very systems of meaning that had established him. The poem itself, by invoking the castle, then comes to replace the actual Bolsover as a projection of Cavendish's self. It also incorporates Margaret Lucas into the fabric and systems of this world. Simultaneously, through its neoplatonic elaboration of her as being 'some Unexpressible thinge', Cavendish elevates her, in accordance with the neoplatonic idea of a love that produces transcendence of the world, to 'something that's divine'.[38] It is this play with neoplatonic conceits that Margaret Lucas recognises in her own responsive play with ideas of being not 'in' or 'off' the world, and her implicit reference to neoplatonism's fundamental insistence on degree and on the relationship between the corruptible world and the world of the spirit. Since neoplatonism is crucially a philosophy of synthesis, primarily involving a synthesis of classical and Christian thought and figures, but also tending to promote synthesis as a general mode of amalgamation of opposing ideas into new hybridities or paradoxes, it is especially conducive to elaboration of the sorts of conceits that are exchanged between Cavendish and Margaret Lucas. The exchanges between them as lovers, but equally those exchanges between material, textual, visual and incorporated self-images that occur here in their textualised courtship, are generated by their mutual participation in this shared system of thought.

---

38   'Love's Creature', Grant, *The Phanseys of William Cavendish*, 11.

Since their courtship is conducted secretly, and—at least on Margaret Lucas' part—anxiously in the context of gossip and political manoeuvring in the exiled court, matters of current reputation, past glories and past losses of reputation are fully present in their writings.[39] Cavendish, throughout the poems written to Margaret Lucas before and immediately after their marriage, recreates himself for her and in relation to her, in all his temperamental sanguinity, and through memory of his past worldly achievement. The poems operate as a means of wittily acknowledging but also transcending the losses of Marston Moor and exile.

The majority of the manuscript poems (which were never intended for publication) that make up *The Phanseys of William Cavendish* are love poems to Margaret Lucas before their marriage, or to her as Margaret Cavendish shortly after they were married. Although a few miscellaneous poems such as the tale, 'The Beggars' Marriage', later published in Margaret Cavendish's *Nature's Pictures drawn by Fancies Pencil to the Life*,[40] and the final, bawdy poem on John Evelyn's and Mary Browne's marriage in 1647, are included amongst the later items in the collection, the lyric entitled 'The Battle' appears as strikingly anomalous.[41] It ruptures the sequence of love poems, largely made up of lyrics with titles such as 'Love's Thoughts', 'Love's Answers', 'Love's Creature' and 'Love's Excuse'. It begins conventionally enough, suggesting how a parting between lovers troubles the speaker's sleep:

> When parted, Eare since, my sad hart did ake
> Such Melancholly dreames, and soe a wake
> My perturb'd Phansyd sleepe, whose motion thought . . .[42]

But the next line's shift to depiction of dreams of war, and its reference to 'bloody battles', immediately disrupts the poem, irretrievably changing its whole tone and overall concern. What follows is description that becomes, line by line, more directly experiential in tone. From the routinely phrased, 'Seeing

---

39   See, for instance, Margaret Lucas' letter no. 7, Grant, *The Phanseys of William Cavendish*, p. 104; and Cavendish's much more insouciant 'A Songe', written after their marriage, ibid., 22, which specifically references the queen, the court, Baron Jermyn, and others.

40   Cf. Grant, Introduction, *The Phanseys of William Cavendish*, xxxi.

41   As Grant, ibid., remarks, the conclusion of the collection with the poem on Evelyn's marriage which occurred in 1647 suggests that all the previous poems were written earlier than this. See Grant *The Phanseys of William Cavendish*, xxx–xxxi, for his identification of the structure of the manuscript collection.

42   Newcastle, *Phanseys*, BL, Add. MS, 32497, fo. 80v–r.

some fight like lions, some faint harted', the poems quickly moves on to the bodily mutilations and dismemberments of a battle field:

> In seurall Posturs, one an other Graspinge
> Minglinge defeates, most now for life are gasping
> A Musketeer heer lyinge, by a Pike
> Ther horse ore throne, heer one another strike
> Heere ours above, and √thir ours there was Under
> Cannons thick clouds of lightnings, flashe of thunder
> Heer Musketts fire, there Pikes doe make a stand
> Heer Crye for quarter, ther att no Comand
> Heer they doe fight, and ther doe runne away
> Some call for helpe, and some will not obay
> One wants a legge, another wants an Arme
> One Cries retreat, another Cries Alarme
> A Gored body here lies could and dead
> One's bowels out, an other wants his head[.]

It seems that as the poem progresses from its conventionally courtly start, something uncontrollable erupts. Although it is always dangerous to infer an unmediated immediacy of personal feeling in any text, Cavendish's reference to a dream of battle does seem to have opened up an overwhelming personal memory of the trauma of war that overrides the demands of love conventions here. Familiar traces of neoplatonic play are certainly evident in lines such as 'Stifld with mists of Powder, steame of soles / Minglinge with th'Enemy, from on to th other', with their implicit reference to the amalgamation of opposites and their figuration of gunpowder as the matter of souls transmigrating to heaven, but in this poem Cavendish's insistently-valued sanguinity appears to have yielded to uncontainable feeling. The description of the sensory experience of the battlefield here is quite unlike the elegant itemisation of the senses in 'Love's Muster'. For all the military connotations of its title, 'Love's Muster' is a witty, self-referencing love poem; 'The Battle' is a war poem. Because it is so unexpected and anomalous in this collection, it is difficult to read 'The Battle' as anything but personal testimony. The mixings between sides, between moral and political positions, that are described in the final lines of the poem are not created as plays of wit, but as the experienced confusion, mental and physical, of an actual battle:

> Noyse, drowndinge noyse, not knowinge on another
> Some butt with halfe Immortalls, for their breath

The Other halfe, but lingringe them from death
None knowinge what for to call bad, or good
Rivers, for water, now all running blood
His doubtfull Victory neyther to yeeld
Neyther durst say, yett Eyther won the feild[.]

This is not a poem to be written to a lover. An awareness that this poem had transgressed the conventions of love poetry, becoming something quite different, is suggested by the manuscript transcription. The closing lines appear:

~~And so's our love, when happily we meete~~
~~He yield, as Prisner, att thy conquring feete[.]~~

In the revised transcription, the deletion of the closing couplet acknowledges that no conventional simile could ever draw such a poem back to the courtesies of a love genre.[43] In the Introduction to his edition of Cavendish 's *Phanseys*, Douglas Grant discusses the literary merit of the poems in spite of their deliberate, aristocratic amateurishness.[44] 'The Battle' is certainly one of the most unpolished of the poems: the banality of rhymes, for instance ('orethrowne in holes'/ 'steame of soles' [soules], or 'could [cold] and dead'/ 'wants his head'), might appear comical if not for the experiential immediacy to the writing. But the content of 'The Battle' in combination with the regular slightness of its rhymes and form actually gives force to the poem; it reads as surprising, moving and powerful. And this one poem, disturbing in feeling and disturbing of convention, suggests that concern with reputation, status and self-image is not, after all, Newcastle's sole response to the trauma and loss of Marston Moor.

Reputation and Its After-Game: Antwerp

In 1648, William and Margaret Cavendish (married since late 1645) moved to Antwerp where they lived until 1660 in the Rubenshuis, the 'Italianate palazzo', built by Rubens that comprised house, studio and a home for Rubens's

---

43   For an analysis of the different roles that members of Cavendish's household played in the transcription and amendment of his manuscripts, see Raylor, T., "Newcastle's Ghosts: Robert Payne, Ben Jonson, and the 'Cavendish Circle'", in Summers C.J. – Pebworth T.- L., *Literary Circles and Cultural Communities in Renaissance England* (Columbia: 2000) 92–114.

44   Grant, *The Phanseys of William Cavendish*, xxii.

extensive collection of antiquities, books and paintings.[45] In spite of his financial difficulties, the renting of the Rubenshuis from the artist's widow allowed
Cavendish to restore himself situationally and symbolically. Rubens had been
associated with the Stuart court from the early 1620s, occupying a dual role as
court artist and European peace-negotiator and was commissioned by Charles I
to paint the ceiling canvases celebrating the reign of James I, including the
especially-celebrated centre piece, 'The Apotheosis of James I', for Inigo Jones's
Banqueting House. It is James I's particular role as a peace-maker, as well as
Rubens's own diplomatic role, that provide the informing themes for the
Banqueting House ceiling with its emphasis on peace.[46] At the end of Rubens's
stay in London in 1629–30, Charles I had knighted him in recognition of both
his art work and his skilful diplomatic negotiation and had received, as a reciprocal gift from Rubens, a painting, 'Minerva Protects Pax from Mars': 'a painted
plea for peace'.[47] As both a master of baroque painting and an internationally-
recognised diplomat, Rubens provides a perfect figure of association for the
exiled Cavendish, himself an established collector of baroque art (especially
by Antwerp painters)—if a rather less successful diplomat and peace-maker.

Situated in Antwerp, rather than Paris, Bruges or The Hague, the locations
of the main 'English' exiled courts that were 'packed with transplanted English
courtiers playing political games, seeking alliances that might extend their
power and enjoying themselves at luxurious ... festivities',[48] the Rubenshuis
becomes a substitute for the lost Bolsover and Welbeck. Living here allowed
Cavendish to establish his own realm of influence, to be in contact with the (now-
exiled) Stuart court, but apart from it, and to pursue his own self-determining
and identity-promoting interests in the way that he always had done. While
in Antwerp, Cavendish particularly devoted himself to his horses and development of *manège* techniques: the occupation that had always represented
his greatest passion and his highest, and most reputationally-secure, skill.
In 1658, a decade after writing his *Phanseys*, he published his influential horsemanship treatise, *La Méthode Nouvelle et Invention Extraordinaire de Dresser
les Chevaux*. This was originally written in English and translated into French
for the purpose of this continental edition. After the Restoration, when
Cavendish was re-established in his English residences and estates, the treatise

---

45   Donovan F., "Rubens, Sir Peter Paul (1577–1640)", *Oxford Dictionary of National Biography*,
      (Oxford: 2004; online edn, Oct 2008), http://www.oxforddnb.com/view/article/63010
      (accessed 25 Sept 2012), Sir Peter Paul Rubens (1577–1640): doi:10.1093/ref:odnb/63010.

46   See Donovan *ODNB* for further details of Rubens' role.

47   Donovan *ODNB*.

48   Van Beneden, "Introduction", van Beneden – de Poorter, (eds.), *Royalist Refugees*, 10.

was translated back into English and altered somewhat for a 1667 version: *A New Method and Extraordinary Invention to Dress Horses*. The 1658 French edition, unlike the later English language edition, was flamboyantly illustrated, containing a series of copperplate engravings by Petr Clouvet (and others) that were based on designs made by Abraham van Diepenbeke, a former pupil and assistant of Rubens. Van Diepenbeke, who had produced both family and equine portraits for Cavendish in England before the Civil Wars and during his exile, worked, as Anthony van Dyck and Ben Jonson among others had done in the past, as an image-maker for Cavendish, collaborating closely with him and providing portrait-based illustrations for his horsemanship treatise and many of Margaret Cavendish's books.[49] These illustrations are informed by a sophisticated aesthetic of sublimation.

Through its illustrations *La Méthode Nouvelle*, while exploiting that hybridity of form always made available by neoplatonic epistemic and aesthetic systems, returns to the foundational tropes and emblems established in Bolsover Castle and by Ben Jonson. In *La Méthode Nouvelle*, however, a more mediated, a more fully sublimated, self-articulation is visually imaged than in earlier schemes of self-representation. The plates in *La Méthode Nouvelle* now create not an echoing reminder of the past but something closer to a corporeal hybridisation of Cavendish's self which is always on the brink of transfiguration. The broken bodies of "The Battle" come ultimately to be replaced by a transformed body. In the opening illustrations to *La Méthode Nouvelle*, Civil-War battles and the memory of defeat and loss are boldly countered by plates such as "La Bataille Gagnee". [Fig. 3.1]

This illustration explicitly challenges the idea of Marston Moor as the reputation-defining moment of Cavendish's life through its assertive celebration of an earlier (although unspecific) victorious battle. At the same time as it insists on Cavendish as triumphant military commander, it relegates the military, positioning the tumbled bodies, smoke and battle-action of war on a lowered background, separated from the representation of Cavendish himself by the line marking the contour of the raised foreground on which he rides, and by the caption, 'LA BATAILLE GAGNEE'. The military is then further distanced by the depiction of the foregrounded Cavendish and his horse performing a *levade*, one of the *manège's* 'airs above ground'. Practice of the arts of the *manège*, the subject of Cavendish's treatise, constitutes in itself an aestheticisation of older battle skills and manoeuvres. The movements and airs of the

---

49   For further description and analysis of Cavendish's horse treatises, including discussion of the aesthetics of the baroque and the sublime, see Elspeth Graham, "The Duke of Newcastle's 'Love [...] for Good Horses': An Exploration of Meanings", in *The Horse as Cultural Icon*, 327–350.

FIGURE 3.1 *"La Bataille Gagnée". From William Cavendish,* La Méthode Nouvelle, *plate 1.*
COPYRIGHT ELAINE WALKER.

manège are elaborated versions of those movements that had traditionally been necessary to horses engaged in battle: their need to turn and halt rapidly, to charge, to jump or to rise in a rear to avoid obstacles. The changes of leg, the controlled paces, the equal responsiveness and flexibility of the horse on both reins (or both directions in a circle or on a curve), as well as the more spectacu-larised 'airs above ground' of the *manège's levade, capriole, ballotade* and *crou-pade*, are all highly skilled, performative elaborations of these more functional battle actions.[50] Cavendish here, then, dressed in armour and overlooking a scene of warfare, is both linked to battle, but positioned above and beyond it. The inclusion of Cavendish's crest in the top left corner of the illustration, bal-ancing the angelic, cloud-enfolded figures in the top right-hand corner, hero-ically elevates him above the battle scene while the angel's trumpet and the

---

50   For the use of horses in battle in the seventeenth century and earlier, and changes in related horsemanship skills and cavalry practices, see Boehrer B.T., "Shakespeare and the Social devaluation of the Horse", in Raber K. – Tucker T. (eds.) *The Culture of the Horse* (New York: 2005) 91–111; and Robinson G., "The Military Value of Horses and Social value of the Horse", in *The Horse as Cultural Icon,* 351–376.

crown of laurels positioned above Cavendish's head directly depict heavenly celebration of his victory. The trees, rocks and figure of the African page-boy that frame Cavendish and his horse represent the nature of the earthly, corruptible world; they also, through their compositional positioning, form a path of ascension to the heavenly. And it is Cavendish himself, and his horse, overlooking the battle and united in their performance of the *levade*, that provide the unifying element of the illustration, providing lines of connection between foreground and battleground, the corruptible world and heaven. Most emphatically of all, the illustration suggests Cavendish's own transcendence over the affairs of the world through its central depiction of the harmoniously-balanced joint figure of himself and his horse.

Just over two decades earlier, Ben Jonson had celebrated Newcastle's horsemanship skills in his "An Epigram to William, Earle of Newcastle", which begins:

> When first my Lord, I saw you backe your horse,
>   Provoke his metal, and command his force
> To all the uses of the field, and race,
>   Me thought I read the ancient Art of thrace,
> And saw a Centaure, past those tales of Greece,
>   So seem'd your horse; and you both of a peece!
> You shew'd like Perseus upon Pegasus[.][51]

Unsurprisingly, the mythical, hybrid figure of Pegasus was also referenced in the architectural decoration of Bolsover's Pillar Parlour with its carved stonework of winged horses, along with fruit and flowers. [Fig. 3.2]

In the new context of exiled life, residing in the baroque Rubenshuis, and in his need to restore his projected self-image post-Marston Moor and to establish himself in continental aristocratic circles, Cavendish, through van Diepenbecke's designs, redeploys these images. In their portrayal of Cavendish as a great master of the art of horsemanship, and of the mythic equine figures of the centaur and Pegasus, the illustrations to *La Méthode Nouvelle* develop neoplatonic imagery to new heights, producing a vision of Cavendish that refers to the past, but re-embodies him in a sublime, spectacular form. [Fig. 3.3] This extraordinary illustration brings together a vision of Cavendish's transcendence, a precise depiction of the *capriole* as a *manège* movement (as performed by Pegasus: 'Le Cheval de pegase qui volle en Capriole') and a witty play on the notion of apotheosis. The image is composed around those neoplatonic circles and spirals that create perfection and transcendence: the semi-circle

---

51   Jonson, *Under-Woods*, 86–87.

FIGURE 3.2 *Stonework winged horses in Bolsover's Pillar Parlour.*
COPYRIGHT ELSPETH GRAHAM.

of submissive and worshipping horses performing their own 'demi-airs', *cour-bettes* (without the 'aid' of riders);[52] the flying birds of the background; and the sweep of the landscape that cradles the central image of Cavendish astride Pegasus. The cloud of glory surrounding Cavendish-Pegasus elevates their composite body towards the heavens, mirroring the clouds of the heavenly fir-mament itself, from which the gods, looking down, are ecstatically delighted by Cavendish's skill. Cavendish, in riding the horse, is shown as giving, through his precisely-depicted position and use of aids, the signal for the *capriole*. He guides the horse. But Pegasus enfolds him in his wings and his own flight is emphasised by the flow of mane and tail, mirroring the fluidity of his ascen-sion, as well as by the birds of the background. This is an image of pure reci-procity between Cavendish and Pegasus, between the human, the natural and the heavenly. It is this complete harmony of being that produces transcen-dence, and something close to transfiguration.

Cavendish's apotheosis here immediately recalls both Rubens's ceiling at Whitehall, and Cavendish's own painted ceilings at Bolsover which refer-enced Whitehall. Bolsover's Elysium Room ceiling depicted classical gods and goddesses in an upwardly spiralling heaven, while the Heaven Room ceiling contained a portrayal of Christ's ascension to heaven. Other illustrations in *La Méthode Nouvelle* contain direct representations of Cavendish's pre-Marston Moor residences: Welbeck and, most particularly, Bolsover. Here, in this plate

---

52   Aids: the rider's seat, hand, spurs, whip. Cavendish always emphasises the literal meaning
       of 'aids' as 'helps' to the horse.

FIGURE 3.3 *Cavendish riding Pegasus. From William Cavendish,* La Méthode Nouvelle, *plate 4.*
COPYRIGHT ELAINE WALKER.

that envisions Cavendish's apotheosis, the reference to Bolsover is oblique, just as it was in "Love's Muster". It serves in the same way, however, simultaneously to reinscribe Cavendish in his identity-conferring homes and to produce a reminder of what has been lost. And the potential grandiosity of this illustration with its vision of heavenly elevation and its reference to royal palaces, as well as his own residences, is ultimately undercut by its wit, its playfulness. Cavendish's equine audience here constitutes an earth-bound circle of adoration. The horses are firmly linked to the corruptible world by the insistent shadowing of their bodies that is noticeable in all the illustrations and by the reinforcement of this in the plate's written text with its direct reference to 'Les Chevaux corruptibles'. The equine circle may indeed be a circle of perfected love, but it is one grounded in the corruptible world. And horses are horses. It is hard to read this as not containing Cavendish's own self-deprecating joke that wittily co-exists with his aggrandising self-promotion.

A further plate depicting Cavendish driving a chariot drawn by centaurs makes this more explicit. [Fig. 3.4] The familiar Neoplatonic motifs are present here once more: flocks of birds spiralling upwards; a semi-circular, enclosing

FIGURE 3.4 *Cavendish riding in a coach drawn by centaurs receives the homage of his horses.*
From William Cavendish, La Méthode Nouvelle, *plate 3.*
COPYRIGHT ELAINE WALKER.

landscape; and a completed circle of horses paying homage to Cavendish. Here, however, the bodily humour becomes more apparent. The ring of horses' croups facing the viewer creates a physical joke that works in counterpoint with the vision of bodily hybridisation and potential transfiguration that is suggested by the mythical figures of the centaurs. That the bawdy was a significant element of Cavendish's aristocratic persona is evident not only in his poem on Evelyn's marriage in the *Phanseys*, and in his dramatic works, but also in his deployment of a bawdy wit in his architectural work at Bolsover. The original design by Cavendish's builder-architect, John Smythson, for the Venus fountain in the centre of the Little Castle's walled garden, 'shows remarkable naked ladies sitting in the niches squirting water.'[53] A further visual joke in the positioning of the fountain might also be suspected: there is a direct sight line from the window of the Little Castle's stool closet to the fountain. [Fig. 3.5]

---

53   Worsley, *Bolsover Castle*, 28.

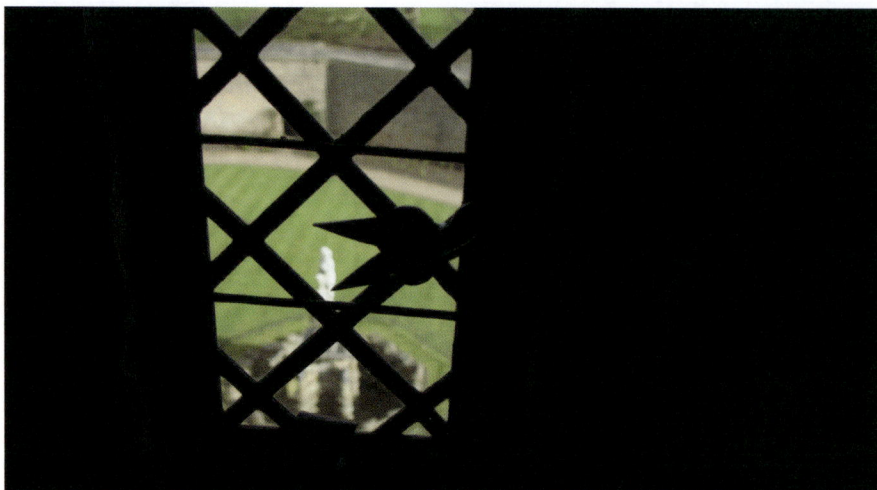

FIGURE 3.5 *Bolsover Castle's Stool Closet looking onto the Venus Fountain.*
COPYRIGHT ELSPETH GRAHAM.

Bodies and buildings, through this consistent series of allusions used in a variety of contexts over three decades, seem to function as especially potent signifiers of Cavendish's identity. The hybrid bodies of the divine winged horse, Pegasus, and the centaurs in the illustrations to *La Méthode Nouvelle*, not only represent an elegant version of Cavendish's play with body images but also provide a particular development in his forms of self-projection. Jonson's references to centaurs and Pegasus in his epigram to Cavendish are part of a general series of references to famed classical horses. The visual portrayals of these mythic equine figures in the van Diepenbeke designs work in more particularised ways. Pegasus, in Greek mythology, was sired by Poseidon and foaled by the Gorgon Medusa in her archaic form as either a beautiful woman or, sometimes, a centaur. Essential to his being is Pegasus's godly breeding, his association with inspiration and fame and his hybrid nature that in itself transcends limitation, since he belongs to two different elements—earth with his hooves, and air with his wings. Conventionally, his hybrid nature and his ability to traverse different elements, produce him as a symbol of wisdom and of poetry, those epistemological and aesthetic domains that themselves produce transcendence of fixity in a single realm of being. So, Cavendish's riding of Pegasus aligns his horsemanship with the poet in him, and presents him as a mobile being, not simply as someone of adaptable sanguine temperament, but as someone who transcends the limitations of time, place and element. In one particular Greek myth, Perseus is captured by Bellerophon and allows Bellerophon to ride him to defeat a series of monsters, including the Chimera. In the seventeenth century, the Chimera was, in turn, routinely seen as an embodiment of the deception, hypocrisy, fraud and misrepresentation of the corruptible world. The image of Cavendish riding Pegasus provides, at this level, a quite direct representation of his elevation above the misrepresentations and the pettiness, as he saw it, of the post-Civil Wars world of exile. At a more abstract level, the illustrations' attention to themes of hybridity and mobility produces a reasserted vitality in Cavendish. Thomas Hobbes, Cavendish's *protégé*, had suggested as a central concept in his *De Corpore* that, 'life was but matter in motion, that there was "a continual relinquishing of one place, and acquiring of another" by bodies', as Jane Bennett puts it.[54] Almost every element of *La Méthode Nouvelle* serves to project this notion. From the treatise's central concern with horsemanship and the elegant controlled movements of the *manège*, to the mythologising portrayal of Cavendish himself driving or riding the hybrid figures of Pegasus and centaurs, the text associates Cavendish with transformative, sublime movement. And, if the neoplatonic sublime always suggests the move to the spirit from the body, to heaven from the corruptible world, the illustrations to *La Méthode Nouvelle* might also be seen to refer to that relationship between the material and spiritual that is at the heart of alchemical processes of sublimation, the transformation of base metals to gold. For all its affirmation of movement, *La Méthode Nouvelle* also retains direct reference to the identity-giving, fixed locations and allegiances of Cavendish's past. Bolsover Castle, Welbeck Abbey and the landscapes of Derbyshire and Nottinghamshire are all present. Indirectly, so, too, is the thought of Cavendish's former image-maker, Ben Jonson. (It was Jonson's satire, *The Alchemist*, that Cavendish borrowed from extensively in his *Witts Triumvirate, or, The Philosopher*, written for a performance before Charles I and Henrietta Maria in 1635/6.)

The images of *La Méthode Nouvelle* serve in a multi-layered manner to restore the body fragmented by battle and the collapse of the royalist body politic, to reassert the possibilities of transfiguration; and to hold in a suspension the memory of those buildings and locations that had previously given Cavendish his place in the order of the world. Although the 'after-game of reputation' continued to be coloured by Marston Moor for Cavendish throughout his exile and even beyond the Restoration, it was the poet, the lover—and the

---

54   Bennett J., *Vibrant Matter: a Political Ecology of Things* (Durham, NC & London: 2010), 55. Her reference is to Thomas Hobbes, "De Corpore", in Molesworth W. (ed.), *The English Works of Thomas Hobbes* (London: 1839) I, part. ii, 8.10.

horseman—in him that provided a means to negotiate his reputational concerns and to display 'to the World', as Margaret Cavendish put it in her post-Restoration encomium: 'the Merits, Wealth, Power, Loyalty, and Fortunes of My Noble Lord, who hath done great Actions, suffered great Losses, endured a long Banishment, for his Loyalty to his King and Countrey; and [who] leads now, like another Scipio, a quiet Countrey-life'.[55]

Select Bibliography

Barratt J., *The Battle for York: Marston Moor 1644* (Stroud: 2002).

Bennett J., *Vibrant Matter: a Political Ecology of Things* (Durham, DC & London: 2010).

Bennett M., *The Civil Wars Experienced: Britain and Ireland, 1638–1661* (London: 2000).

Brown C.C., "Courtesies of Place and Arts of Diplomacy in Ben Jonson's Last Two Entertainments for Royalty", *The Seventeenth Century*, 9, ii (1994), Raylor T. (ed.), Special Issue: *The Cavendish Circle*.

Butler M., "Ben Jonson and the Limits of Courtly Panegyric", in Sharpe K. – Lake P. (eds.), *Culture and Politics in Early Stuart England* (Basingstoke: 1994).

Carlton C., *Going to the Wars: The Experience of the British Civil Wars, 1638–1651* (London & New York: 1992).

Cavendish Jane, "On the 30th June to God", Yale University Library, Osborn MS b. 221.

Cavendish Margaret, *A true relation of my Birth, Breeding, and Life*, appended to *Natures Pictures* (Printed for J. Martin and J. Allestrye, London: 1656).

Cavendish Margaret, *The Life of the Thrice Noble, High and Puissant Prince William Cavendishe* (Folger Shakespeare Library, Call no. or shelfmark: 131518; Wing N853: London, 1667).

Cavendish William, *The Humorous Lovers* (Printed by J.M. for H. Herringman at the Sign of the Blue Anchor, London: 1677).

Cavendish William, *The Phanseys of the Marquesse of Newcastle Sett by him in verse* (British Library Add. Manuscript 32497).

Cavendish William, *The Triumphant Widow, or, The Medley of Humours* (Printed by J.M. for H. Herringman at the Sign of the Blue Anchor, London: 1677).

De Groot J., *Royalist Identities* (Basingstoke: 2004).

Donovan F., "Rubens, Sir Peter Paul (1577–1640)", *Oxford Dictionary of National Biography*, (Oxford: 2004; online edn, Oct 2008), http://www.oxforddnb.com/view/article/63010 (accessed 25 Sept 2012), Sir Peter Paul Rubens (1577–1640): doi:10.1093/ref:odnb/63010.

---

55   Cavendish M., *Life of William Cavendish*, Sig. d1v.

Edwards P. – Enenkel K. – Graham E. (eds.), *The Horse as Cultural Icon: The Real and the Symbolic Horse in the Early Modern World* (Leiden: 2012).

Gaunt P., *The English Civil Wars 1642–1651* (Oxford, 2003).

Graham E., "The Duke of Newcastle's 'Love [. . .] for Good Horses': An Exploration of Meanings" in Edwards P. – Enenkel K. – Graham E., (eds.) *The Horse as Cultural Icon* (Leiden: 2012).

Grant D. (ed.), *The Phanseys of William Cavendish, Marquis of Newcastle addressed to Margaret Lucas and her Letters in Reply* (London: 1956).

Hobbes Thomas, "De Corpore", in Molesworth W. (ed.), *The English Works of Thomas Hobbes* (London: 1839).

Hulse L., "Cavendish, William, first duke of Newcastle upon Tyne (*bap.* 1593, *d.* 1676)", *Oxford Dictionary of National Biography* (Oxford: 2004; online edn, Jan 2011, http://www.oxforddnb.com/view/article/4946 William Cavendish (*bap.* 1593, *d.* 1676): doi:10.1093/ref:odnb/4946.

Hyde Edward, Earl of Clarendon, *Notes on Events in the North*, Bod. MS 23, f. 23.

Hyde Edward, Earl of Clarendon, *The History of the Rebellion and Civil Wars in England*, ed. Macray W.D., 6 vols. (Oxford: 1888).

Jonson Ben, *Under-Woods. Consisting of Divers Poems* [1640], (Cambridge: 2011).

Knowles J., "'War is all the World About': The Cavendishes, Civil Wars and Culture Wars", in van Beneden B. – de Poorter N. (eds.), *Royalist Refugees: William and Margaret Cavendish in the Rubens House, 1648–1660* (Antwerp: 2006).

Lomas S.C. (ed.), *The Letters and Speeches of Oliver Cromwell: With Elucidations by Thomas Carlyle* (London: 1904).

Millman J.S. – Wright G. (eds.), *Early Modern Women's Manuscript Poetry*, (Manchester: 2005).

Newman P.R. – Roberts P.R., *Marston Moor 1644: The Battle of Five Armies* (Pickering, U.K.: 2003).

Purkiss D., *The English Civil War: A People's History* (London: 2006).

Raylor T., "'Pleasure Reconcil'd to Virtue': William Cavendish, Ben Jonson, and the Decorative Scheme of Bolsover Castle", *Renaissance Quarterly*, 52 (1999).

Raylor T., "Newcastle's Ghosts: Robert Payne, Ben Jonson, and the 'Cavendish Circle'" in Summers C.J. – Pebworth T.-L., *Literary Circles and Cultural Communities in Renaissance England* (Columbia: 2000) 92–114.

Sarasohn L.T., "Margaret Cavendish, William Newcastle, and Political Marginalization", *English Studies*, 92:7 (2011), 806–817.

Trease G., *Portrait of a Cavalier: William Cavendish, First Duke of Newcastle* (London: 1979).

Van Beneden B. – De Poorter N. (eds.), *Royalist Refugees: William and Margaret Cavendish in the Rubens House, 1648–1660* (Antwerp: 2006).

Warburton E. (ed.), *Memoirs and Correspondence of Prince Rupert and the Cavaliers* (London: 1849).

Warwick Sir Philip, *Memoirs of the Reign of King Charles the First* (Edinburgh: 1813).

Worsley L., *Bolsover Castle* (London: 2000).

Worsley L., *Cavalier: The Story of a Seventeenth-Century Playboy* (London: 2007).

Young P., *Marston Moor 1644: The Campaign and the Battle* (Kineton: 1970).

CHAPTER 4

The Concealed Fancies and Cavendish Identity

Lisa Hopkins

The Concealed Fancies, a play co-written by Cavendish's two eldest daughters, Lady Jane Cavendish and Lady Elizabeth Brackley, probably in 1644, is radically informed by the two girls' status and experience as members of their family. The play can be seen as operating on three different levels, which collectively work to show us what it meant to be a female member of the Cavendish family during the First English Civil War. Firstly, it offers us a series of closely observed and detailed portraits of individuals and reflects on the nature and circumstances of the domestic theatrical performances which were so important in the life of that family. Secondly, the play deliberately and self-consciously draws our attention not only to its familial affiliation but also to its literary ones, constructing for itself a literary genealogy with almost as much enthusiasm as it does a literal one, and in so doing it allows us to glimpse something of the centrality of literary discourse to seventeenth-century aristocratic culture. Finally, as I shall argue here, we need to consider not only the ways in which *The Concealed Fancies* resembles other plays but also the ways in which it differs from them, because it is in these changes and developments from earlier models that I think we can see most clearly how the sisters use drama not only to reflect on their Cavendish identity but actively to shape and fashion it. Writing becomes for them a way of asserting that which they most value and of testifying their continuing commitment to participating in the shared cultural conversation of England's beleaguered aristocracy. It is these issues of literary belonging and intertexuality that I shall focus on in the main part of my essay. *The Concealed Fancies* is, I shall argue, a play which benefits from and invites a reading which both situates it firmly within mainstream dramatic tradition and also pays attention to its distinctive literary sensibility.

Family

The arrangement of appropriate marriages was central to aristocratic identity in the period, and the idealised marriage of Charles I and Henrietta Maria was also crucial to royalist ideologies of the relationship between the body politic and the royal body natural. With the turmoil of the Civil War and Henrietta

© KONINKLIJKE BRILL NV, LEIDEN, 2017 | DOI 10.1163/9789004326217_006

Maria's flight to France in 1644, both of these issues came under threat. In *The Concealed Fancies*, the meanings and purposes of aristocratic marriage and the idea of the household as a microcosm are both explored in a self-consciously literary way, the production and consumption of literature being in themselves bonding and defining activities for the Cavendish household. The main plot of the play centres on the courtship of the two fictional sisters, Luceny and Tattiney, by their suitors, Courtley and Presumption, and clearly affords, amongst other things, a means for the two actual sisters, Jane and Elizabeth, to express the intellectual sympathy and mutual devotion which is evident throughout their lives and writings. The subplot introduces three female cousins, who to some extent seem to offer additional portrayals of the two Cavendish daughters and of their younger sister, Frances: Alison Findlay argues that Jane clearly played Luceny and Sh., Elizabeth took on the role of Tattiney and Cicelly, and Frances was Is.[1] Moreover, the two brothers are clearly based on their own two brothers, Charles and Henry, who are gently sent up, the elder being ridiculously romantic and the younger comically prosaic and practical, in ways which may well represent the two young men's actual characters.[2] Their aunt Elizabeth Grey, Countess of Kent, may be implicitly referred to in the list of cosmetics (1.ii.43)[3] and is explicitly so when we hear of 'my Lady Kent's cordials' (III.iv.56–7). The name of one of these, 'Gilbert's water' (III.iv.59), may perhaps recall the countess's father, Gilbert Talbot, 7th earl of Shrewsbury, who had been both the stepson and son-in-law of the sisters' great-grandmother, Elizabeth, Countess of Shrewsbury, and from whom their grandfather, Charles Cavendish, had bought Welbeck and Bolsover;[4] Kamille Stone Stanton suggests that the point about the experiment with the cordials is that they are alcoholic and that this relates to Cavalier drinking games,[5]

---

1 Findlay A., "'She gave you the civility of the house': Household performance in *The Concealed Fancies*", in Cerasano S.P. – Wynne-Davies M. (eds.), *Readings in Renaissance Women's Drama: Criticism, History, and Performance 1594–1988*, (London & New York: 1988) 260.

2 Findlay, "She gave you the civility of the house", 269.

3 Susan Cerasano and Marion Wynne-Davies comment in their note on this passage that 'Lady Tranquillity's cosmetics are not unlike the potions described in *A Choice Manual of Rare and Select Secrets in Physick and Chyrurgery* by Elizabeth Grey, Countess of Kent, a book which is referred to at III.iv.56': Cavendish Lady Jane – Brackley Lady Elizabeth, *The Concealed Fancies*, Cerasano S.P. – Wynne-Davies M. (eds.), *Renaissance Drama by Women: Texts and Documents*, (London: 1996) fn. 23, 210.

4 Warren R.O., "A Partial Liberty: Gender and Class in Jane Cavendish and Elizabeth Brackley's *The Concealed Fancies*", *Renaissance Papers* (2000) 155–167, 158.

5 Stanton K.S., "The domestication of royalist themes in *The Concealed Fancies* by Jane Cavendish and Elizabeth Brackley", *Clio* 36, ii (2007) 195.

but the evocation of family is I think at least as important. More controversially, it is often and not unreasonably assumed that the troublesome Lady Tranquillity is modelled on the sisters' future stepmother, Margaret Lucas.[6] If true, it would lend retrospective savage irony to Tattiney's remark that 'I hate see a fond fool, let it be he or she' (Epilogue 75–6), for Samuel Pepys acidly castigated Margaret as a fond fool when he dismissed her biography of her husband as 'the ridiculous history of my Lord Newcastle wrote by his wife, which shows her to be a mad, conceited ridiculous woman and he an ass to suffer her to write what she writes to and of him'.[7] Even the play's marriage-plot is concerned less with the romance of either of the individual unions than with the role played by marriage in the formation of new families. Presumption assures Courtley that 'if she do but behave herself ugly, then I'll tell her that was like a good wife and an honourable stock to bear children on withal' (III.iii.36–7), later adding that 'if she do not give respect to my mother and sisters, I will tell her she hath not deserved to enter into my honourable old house' (III.iii.39–42).

The most important family member in the sisters' eyes, however, was without question their father, William Cavendish. Courtley warns Presumption that this is something they need to reckon with: 'You know her father is an understanding gentleman; his discourse uses not to be dull, catechising; and they very much with him' (III.iii.53–6). And he is proved abundantly right; the filial devotion evinced by both sets of sisters, fictional and real, is indeed so great that Catherine Burroughs detects a barely sublimated incest fantasy in the play.[8] Moreover, the play goes to great pains to clear Cavendish from any hint of possible blame or suggestion that there might be potential cause for daughterly dissatisfaction. Alexandra Bennett observes that the reference to '18. or 22. youth' 'supports the contention that *The Concealed Fancies* was written after the fall of Welbeck' (c. August 1644) and notes that during this time Jane 'managed to send her father some badly needed money out of her marriage portion and by selling some of her jewelry and plate'.[9] In the play, however, Luceny says confidently that 'my father intends to give me a great

---

6   The idea that Lady Tranquillity should be read as Margaret is controversial, but is supported by Alison Findlay in *Playing Spaces in Early Women's Drama* (Cambridge: 2006) 49.

7   Latham R. – Matthews W. (eds.), *The Diary of Samuel Pepys* 9 (London: 1976) 123.

8   Burroughs C., "'Hymen's Monkey Love': *The Concealed Fancies* and 'Female Sexual Initiation'", *Theatre Journal* 51, i (March 1999) 22.

9   Bennett A.G., "'Now let my language speake': The Authorship, Rewriting, and Audience(s) of Jane Cavendish and Elizabeth Brackley", *Early Modern Literary Studies* 11, ii (September 2005) Online: http://extra.shu.ac.uk/emls/11-2/benncav2.htm.

portion' (1.iv.38), a comment that would in the circumstances be tantamount to a statement of blind faith, insisting on Cavendish's affection for Jane and refusing to acknowledge his reduced ability to do anything about it. There can certainly be no doubt that their father is, at this stage at least, far more highly valued by the fictional—and implicitly by the actual—sisters than their rather thinly delineated suitors are:

> *Tattiney.* Aye, but I know who governs us both.
> *Luceny.* Who prithee? Let me hear.
> *Tattiney.* Monsieur Calsindow.
> *Luceny.* Ho! My father, indeed. And that gentleman shall be my alpha and omega of government.
> *Tattiney.* What, shall not Mr. Courtley be your governor when you're married?
> *Luceny.* How often, sister, have yo[u] read the Bible over, and have forgotten man and wife should draw equally in a yoke?
>   (II.iii.29–38)

The invocation of biblical discourse, so often drawn on in early modern England to legitimise a wife's subjection to her husband, proves here to be a double-edged sword as it also and even more urgently authorises the idea of the omnipotence of God, so often figured as a father. This idea is underlined by the reference to 'alpha and omega', which, as used in Revelation 22, refers there to Christ. Margaret Ezell points out that in a number of the poems written by the sisters (probably mainly, if not entirely, by Jane) Cavendish 'takes on explicitly God-like responsibilities and powers',[10] so rather than bolstering the husband's authority, this passage works rather to bolster the father's.

Although I have suggested that the play is extensively concerned with the Cavendish family, it is worth noting that there is another family involved, and I think one should pause to consider what the circumstances surrounding that involvement may have been. By the time the play was written the younger sister, Elizabeth, was already married, although as she was considered too young to be bedded, she was still living at home, something which Alison Findlay suggests is pertinent to the play: 'Coterie jokes undermine Presumption's words. For example, his determination that "she shall not stay with her own friends or family after she is married" is flatly contradicted by Elizabeth's experience,

10   Ezell M.J.M., "'To Be Your Daughter in Your Pen': The Social Functions of Literature in the Writings of Lady Elizabeth Brackley and Lady Jane Cavendish", *Huntington Library Quarterly* 51, iv (Autumn 1988) 291.

since she did just that'.[11] For the younger daughter to be married before the elder was highly unusual, and it would seem likely that the match had been offered first to Jane but that she had declined, presumably because she considered affection to be important in a marriage and was not convinced that she would be able to feel it for the proposed bridegroom. In fact, although this could not have been predicted at the time of the play's composition, Jane did not marry until she was in her early thirties, an advanced age for a bride by seventeenth-century standards. The bridegroom, Charles Cheyne, was a mere gentleman rather than an aristocrat, but he did come of a family with impeccable royalist credentials, and that criterion had weighed profoundly with Jane. Jane's own marital history thus seems to suggest that what she at least looked for was a combination of personal compatibility and familial suitability, and that is also the goal of Luceny and Tattiney in *The Concealed Fancies*. They, too, are acutely aware they will not simply be marrying individuals but forming a whole raft of ties: Luceny's preparations for marriage extend to planning how when she meets her future mother-in-law, 'Though I look obedient and civil to her, I will let her discretion understand in silence, that I know myself, and that I deserve thanks for coming into her family' (1.iii.124–7).

Culture

To develop Luceny's point, she is confident that she can wordlessly communicate with Courtley's mother because of their shared cultural code which ensured that two aristocratic women would instinctively understand each other's meaning. In this instance, she relies specifically on her ability to modulate her demeanour and physical appearance, which lie at the heart of her strategy. Thus, she confuses Courtley because 'I looked soberly, as if I would strictly observe him, yet dressed myself contrary to his instruction, and my behaviour was according to my dress' (Epilogue 14–17). It is, however, equally appropriate to think in terms of the way that identities are constructed through the sophisticated manipulation of shared cultural—specifically literary—discourse, because that is, to a large extent, the central idea of the play and seems to have been something of a *leitmotif* of Cavendish family life, as well as something which they could depend on sharing with other aristocratic families. Margaret Ezell, observing that the play has a family audience, wonders whether 'in this instance, the cosy domesticity of the term may mislead us concerning the

---

11   Findlay, *Playing Spaces*, 51.

critical sophistication of the audience intended'.[12] Cavendish, himself was both a patron of playwrights and a playwright in his own right, whose work the sisters certainly read: in his funeral sermon for Jane, the elder daughter, Adam Littleton observed that 'She took, when Young, special delight in her *Father's Excellent Composures'*.[13] In addition, Elizabeth's husband, Lord Brackley, was a member of the household for which Milton's *Comus* had been written and had himself played the elder brother, while Alexandra Bennett notes that at least one sister, probably Jane, was engaged in a literary correspondence with his sister Lady Alice Egerton, who had played the Lady.[14] To say that the sisters wrote for and of family, therefore, is by no means simply to position them within a domestic and implicitly private sphere, since this was no ordinary family and the ways in which it wrote and thought were sophisticated, skilled and self-conscious. Indeed, Cerasano and Wynne-Davies have proposed that 'the Cavendish family should be considered alongside the Sidneys as a literary grouping, which encompassed both male and female authors',[15] and which was fundamentally structured by the importance of literary culture to aristocratic identity.

Sidney family writings and those with connections to that family feature in a number of earlier literary texts, among which this play very deliberately situates itself. When the three sisters are under siege, Cicilley says to Sh, 'You mean how did you look in the posture of a delinquent? Faith, as though you thought the scene would change again, and you would be happy though you suffered misery for a time' (III.iv.6–10). Sh replies that she was able to do this because 'I practised Cleopatra when she was in her captivity, and could they have thought me worthy to have adorned their triumphs I would have performed his gallant tragedy and so have made myself glorious for time to come'. (III.iv.13–16) Cleopatra was a figure recalled in many contexts in seventeenth-century England, not least in the presence of a Cleopatra tapestry at Hardwick (now lost), which we can be almost certain that the sisters would have seen.[16]

---

12   Ezell, "To Be Your Daughter in Your Pen", 285–6.

13   Smith E., "The Local Popularity of *The Concealed Fansyes*", *Notes and Queries* 53, ii (June 2006) 190.

14   Bennett A., "Filling in the Picture: Contexts and Contacts of Jane Cavendish", *Literature Compass* 5, ii (2008) 344.

15   Cerasano – Wynne-Davies (eds.), *The Concealed Fancies*, 127.

16   For a description of the Cleopatra panel and its iconography, see Frye S., *Pens and Needles: Women's Textualities in Early Modern England* (Philadelphia: 2010) 61. For a suggestion about its possible fate, see Hopkins L. – MacMahon B., "'Come, what, a siege?': Metarepresentation in Lady Jane Cavendish and Lady Elizabeth Brackley's *The Concealed Fancies*", *Early Modern Literary Studies* 16, iii (2013). Online: https://extra.shu.ac.uk/emls/journal/index.php/emls/article/view/83 .

Who, though, is the referent of 'his'? Daniel? Brandon? The editors' note in the Cerasano and Wynne-Davies edition is 'Played the part of Cleopatra, perhaps in Shakespeare's *Antony and Cleopatra* since the authors appear to make other allusions to his plays'. This is certainly an attractive possibility, not least because Shakespeare's was unquestionably the pre-eminent version of the story, to such an extent that Daniel seems to have been prompted to revise his own version after seeing Shakespeare's,[17] and it was Shakespeare's version for which the sisters' stepmother Margaret Cavendish would later record her particular approbation, asking 'Who could describe Cleopatra better than he hath done?'[18] Moreover, the Earl of Pembroke, the husband of Cavendish's cousin, Lady Mary Talbot, was one of the two dedicatees of the First Folio (he was also the son of the Countess of Pembroke) so, in a sense, Shakespeare, too, could count as family drama.

One might be very tempted to speculate on the name of the female cousin identified only as 'Sh'. Catherine Burroughs suggests that Sh.'s "shortened name evokes secrets, 'Shhh'".[19] However, since it is hard to think of a woman's name of the period beginning with 'Sh', would a better model be the form of abbreviation which consists of the first and last letters of a name, and could one possibility therefore be Susannah, a possible spelling of the name of Shakespeare's own daughter? Susanna Shakespeare did not die until 1649 and in July 1643, she was living at New Place with her daughter and son-in-law when the queen was accommodated there. John Stubbs observes of Henrietta Maria's visit to New Place: 'it is not inconceivable that a touch of cultural tourism crept into the queen's itinerary. Shakespeare was still far from being the institution he became in the eighteenth and nineteenth centuries, but the queen, besides being fond of the theatre, presided over a court in which his works had vehement advocates, imitators and plagiarists'. (Stubbs also notes that Suckling, a friend of the Cavendishes, was 'portrayed by Van Dyck with the folio text open before him'.)[20] Certainly Cavendish's *The Variety* calls for a folio to be brought on stage, and the sisters would undoubtedly have been interested in a fellow daughter of a literary father, especially one called William. Shakespeare himself seems to be clearly remembered elsewhere in the play;

---

17   See the introduction to Samuel Daniel, *Cleopatra*, edited by Lucy Knight as part of the MA Shakespeare and Renaissance Literature degree at Sheffield Hallam University, 2011. Online: http://extra.shu.ac.uk/emls/iemls/renplays/cleopatra.html.

18   For a discussion of this, Romack K, "'I wonder she should be so infamous for a Whore?': Cleopatra Restored", in Romack K. – Fitzmaurice J. (eds.) *Cavendish and Shakespeare, Interconnections*, (Aldershot: 2006) 194.

19   Burroughs, "Hymen's Monkey Love", 27.

20   Stubbs J., *Reprobates: The Cavaliers of the English Civil War* (London: 2011) 341–2.

many critics have commented on the debt to *The Taming of the Shrew*,[21] seen clearly in passages such as that where Presumption tells Courtley that

> I mean to follify her all I can, and let her know that garb, that doth best become her, is most ill-favoured. So she shall neither look, walk, or speak, but I will be her perpetual vexation; then send her into the country, where I will stay with her a month, then tell her my occasion draws me to rown, and so leave her to contemplate me in my absence, and to obey my family.
>
> (III.iii.10–18)

At the heart of both *The Taming of the Shrew* itself and also of the history of reaction to it is the question of Petruchio's and Katherine's relationship and to what extent he genuinely tames her. Petruchio's own metaphors for the relationship are taken from the animal world, in which, as in the Riding School of Bolsover, horses had to be broken before they could be ridden. But Katherine is not an animal, and the analogy might well seem, therefore, wildly inappropriate if one were to suppose Petruchio to mean it seriously. What *The Concealed Fancies* suggests, though, is that what characters say may not always be a safe index to what they mean, particularly in questions of courtship and marriage. As we have already seen, Luceny notes in the epilogue how she has thoroughly bamboozled Courtley by a careful strategy of mixed signals. Then, when Courtley tells her she is finely dressed, she replies 'I am glad you said so, for now I shall understand you by contraries. So, sister, I knew he was to seek about again for a new good counsel' (Epilogue 22–5). As this shows, this is a game of which the sisters are already experts; the sooner the suitors learn to keep up with them at it, the better it will be for them.

The Taming of the Shrew is also a play in which we are constantly reminded that individuals are part of a community. Early in the Induction, the lord, surveying the disreputable-looking Christopher Sly, asks,

> What think you, if he were conveyed to bed,
> Wrapped in sweet clothes, rings put upon his fingers,
> A most delicious banquet by his bed,

---

21   See for instance Ezell, "To Be Your Daughter in Your Pen", 289, Burroughs, "Hymen's Monkey Love", 24, and my own "Judith Shakespeare's Reading: Teaching *The Concealed Fancies*", *Shakespeare Quarterly* 47, iv (Winter 1996) 400. Ezell also quotes some of 'The Antemasque' to the pastoral in which witches talk of how 'This is a brave world... now' (287).

> And brave attendants near him when he wakes,
> Would not the beggar then forget himself?[22]

You are what you are, it seems, only in relation to others, and certainly this play
is remarkable for the number of other characters, who surround its main characters. When Petruchio and Katherine reach his home, Grumio commands,
'Call forth Nathaniel, Joseph, Nicholas, Philip, Walter, Sugarsop, and the rest'
(IV.i.79–80), and Petruchio himself asks

> Where's my spaniel Troilus? Sirrah, get you hence,
> And bid my cousin Ferdinand come hither.
> One, Kate, that you must kiss and be acquainted with.
>   (IV.i.136–8)

So that is six servants, who are named, plus 'the rest', one cousin and a dog
inhabiting Petruchio's household. We do not meet most of these characters,
but reference to them does create an impression of people living firmly within
a household community.

Particularly important in this society is the rôle of fathers. When Petruchio
first hears of Katherina, he says,

> I know her father, though I know not her,
> And he knew my deceasèd father well.
>   (I.ii.100–1)

Later, he says to Baptista:

> You knew my father well, and in him me,
> Left solely heir to all his lands and goods.
>   (II.i.116–7)

Similarly, Tranio declares,

> Baptista is a noble gentleman,
> To whom my father is not all unknown.
>   (I.ii.237–8)

---

22   Hibbard G.R. (ed.), William Shakespeare, *The Taming of the Shrew*, (Harmondsworth:
     1968), Introduction 1, 35–9. All further quotations from the play will be taken from this
     edition and reference will be given in the text.

Like Beatrice acknowledging Claudio as her cousin, Petruchio, after the wedding, acknowledges that he has formed a relationship with Baptista as well as with Katherine when he exhorts the guests to 'Dine with my father' (III.2.195). Moreover, when he hears that Vincentio is Lucentio's father he says,

> And now by law, as well as reverend age,
> I may entitle thee my loving father.
> The sister to my wife, this gentlewoman,
> Thy son by this hath married.
>   (IV.v.60–63)

Later, Lucentio begins the process of reintegrating his and Bianca's relationship back into the community after their runaway marriage by commanding,

> My fair Bianca, bid my father welcome,
> While I with self-same kindness welcome thine.
>   (V.ii.4–5)

This is an emphasis which makes *The Taming of the Shrew* a particularly appropriate intertext for *The Concealed Fancies*, because there, too, the characters are acutely aware that marriage is a relationship not just between individuals but between family groups.

An emphasis on the importance of the wider community is also a feature of John Fletcher's sequel to *The Taming of the Shrew*, *The Tamer Tamed*. This is, I think, another probable source for *The Concealed Fancies*, and an important one, because both it and *The Concealed Fancies* share a project of not merely recalling Shakespeare but writing back to him, and both also couple a story of courtship and marriage with the motif of a house under siege. In *The Tamer Tamed*, a widowed Petruccio remarries and gets a taste of his own medicine, when the women fortify the house against the men, under the direction of 'Colonel Bianca' (1.3.66). The female defenders proceed to observe all the protocols of a full-blown siege, with a properly stipulated duration—'A month's siege will not shake us' (1.3.258)—and all due formalities. As Bianca vows, 'They stand upon their honours and will not give up without strange composition, I will assure you. Marching away with their pieces cocked, and bullets in their mouths, will not satisfy them' (1.3.59–62).[23] This is a comic and metaphorical version of the events which for the sisters are literal and very far from comic.

---

23   All quotations from the play are taken from Daileader C.R. – Taylor G. (eds.), John Fletcher, *The Tamer Tamed*, (Manchester: 2006). Soldiers from a garrison who marched away with

The Concealed Fancies also contains an allusion to a different play with a military background, *Othello*, in the exchange between Friendly and Proper:

> *Friendly* . . . Where's our officers?
> *Proper*. Why, the old man is at the works.
> *Friendly*. Have we not more?
> *Proper*. Yes, his clerk who, you know, is an ancient.
>   (III.i.5–8)

There is an obvious joke about the lack of distinction between the 'old man' and the 'ancient', and an equally obvious registering of the hideousness of the situation, in which these people are the only ones available to man the defence. Nonetheless, it is difficult not also to hear an echo, however faint, of the rank held by Iago in *Othello*, perhaps with the recollection that Iago proved more of a liability to the defence of Cyprus than an asset.

It is no coincidence that *Othello* too is a play about marriage, and here again I think the sisters are not merely echoing Shakespeare but writing back. *Othello* shows a marriage in which romantic love fails to survive under the pressure of external influences. The most obvious source of disruption is Iago, but initial opposition to the marriage comes most strongly and visibly from Desdemona's father, Brabantio, and reminders of his failure to sanction it resurfaces repeatedly in the play, at key points in the narrative. To remember this, throws into sharp relief the contrast with *The Concealed Fancies* where the approbation of Monsieur Calsindow is a prerequisite for the eventual solemnisation of the marriages of his daughters. Moreover, the sisters undoubtedly intended Cavendish to play Monsieur Calsindow, making his physical presence as necessary to the play as it is to the Anteroom at Bolsover, where the frescoes show three of the four humours emblematised by human figures, with the fourth left blank to be supplied by and incorporated in Cavendish himself. Ultimately, his flight after the battle of Marston Moor would have rendered this impossible, effectively making the play unperformable, but the intention is, I think, clear. This was a play written not only *about* the sisters' father but *for* their father, and his role would have served to underline and emblematise the importance of family approval as well as of individual affection in the contracting of marriages.

Other dramatists may be remembered too—I have argued elsewhere for possible intertextualities with *The Changeling* and *The Duchess of Malfi*[24]—

---

their firearms cocked and with bullets in their mouth had obtained an honourable surrender. Clearly, this was not enough for Bianca.

24   Hopkins, "Judith Shakespeare's Reading", 402.

and in particular there are allusions to other writings with connections to the Cavendish family. Kamille Stone Stanton compares *The Concealed Fancies* to Shirley's *Bird in a Cage*,[25] but I think, as I have discussed elsewhere, that the similarities with John Ford's *The Fancies, Chaste and Noble* are at least as strong.[26] The sisters' stepmother, Margaret Cavendish, was also to echo Ford in her play *The Unnatural Tragedy*, but she chose a very different play, *'Tis Pity She's a Whore*,[27] to whose traumatic narrative she might perhaps have been attracted by her own experience of desecration and violation of household gods: Alison Findlay notes that during the Civil War 'Margaret probably witnessed the ransacking of buildings and gardens, and then breaking into the family tomb in the church'.[28] *The Fancies, Chaste and Noble* is a very different sort of play. Its emotional heart is three sets of family relationships: that between the marquis of Siena and his three nieces, the Fancies of the title; that between the heroine of the main plot, Castamela, and her brother Livio; and that between the heroine of the subplot, Flavia, and her brother Romanello, the repairing of which proves Flavia's sole consolation for the loss of the husband, whom she loved but who sold her to another man. So different is *The Fancies* from *'Tis Pity* that it might well seem the work of a different playwright, with a very different set of values and interests. In particular, in both *'Tis Pity She's a Whore* and *The Broken Heart* sibling bonds are stretched and distorted; in *The Fancies, Chaste and Noble* they hold firm, and so too do those between the uncle/marquis and his nieces and nephew. I think it is no accident that it is this, one of the quietest and most family-oriented of Ford's plays, to which the sisters were apparently attracted.

Other plays and entertainments seem also to be remembered, and again in ways which emphasise direct or indirect associations with the Cavendish family and its concerns. *Love's Welcome to Bolsover* and *The King's Entertainment*

---

25   Stanton, "The domestication of royalist themes", 182.

26   Hopkins, "Judith Shakespeare's Reading", 403–404.

27   On the similarities between *The Unnatural Tragedy* and *'Tis Pity She's a Whore'* see, for instance, Corporaal M., "An Empowering Wit and an 'Unnatural' Tragedy: Margaret Cavendish's Representation of the Tragic Female Voice", *Early Modern Literary Studies* special issue 14 (May 2004). Online: http://extra.shu.ac.uk/emls/si-14/corpempo.html. For the suggestion that it may faintly encode events in the Sentloe family see Hopkins L., "Crime and Context in *The Unnatural Tragedy*", *Early Modern Literary Studies* special issue, 14 (May 2004). Online: http://extra.shu.ac.uk/emls/si-14/hopkunna.html.

28   Findlay A., "'I hate such an old-fashioned House': Margaret Cavendish and the search for home", *Early Modern Literary Studies*, special issue, 14 (May 2004). Online: http://extra .shu.ac.uk/emls/si-14/findhate.html.

at Welbeck are also evoked in Luceny's line 'when the species returns back, my face methinks should be converted into debaseness' (1.iv.65–7). Emily Smith, quoting an elegy for Jane which contains the lines 'whatsoe're her *Fancies* stamp did own, / Was *Sterling Coin* to be refus'd by none', suggests that this 'refers to a moment in *The Concealed Fansyes* in which one of the heroines analogizes courtship with commerce by using terms of economic exchange (*species* and *debaseness*) metonymically to represent her entry into the sexual marketplace'.[29] However, the person whose face is actually on coins is the monarch, and what we hear in this line is probably the not ill-grounded fear that very soon Charles I's head would no longer appear on the coins of the realm. As Robin Warren notes, 'even as the play jeers at men's lofty station (and equally lofty self-regard), it also speaks again and again in defense of an embattled king'.[30] Moreover, Warren suggests that the sisters 'may have been recalling a scene from *Love's Welcome* in which two cupids descend from the sky when they staged a similar entrance for the suitors'.[31]

Even closer are the parallels to William Sampson's 1636 play, *The Vow Breaker*, and it may perhaps be pertinent to note that Sampson had collaborated with Gervase Markham, whose falconry manual seems to have provided a source for *The Taming of the Shrew*.[32] *The Vow Breaker*, as its subtitle, 'The Fair Maid of Clifton', suggests, tells the story of Anne Boot, a young girl from Clifton, just outside Nottingham. Anne is courted by Young Bateman, but he is forced to leave her when he follows Sir Gervase Clifton to the Siege of Leith. In his absence Anne, partly of her own free choice and partly under pressure from her father, marries instead the wealthy Jarman. Young Bateman returns on the wedding day, warns Anne that she will soon come to grief, and hangs himself. Anne, now pregnant, becomes increasingly melancholy and penitent and sees his ghost wherever she goes (though we do not). As soon as the child is born, she drowns herself in the Trent. This may well be the same story as that told in the now lost play, *Black Batman of the North*, but if the sisters were familiar with the story at all, I think we can be confident that it was through Sampson that they knew it. Firstly, the title page assures its readers that the play was acted many times, but there is no apparent record of any London performance, and it would in fact have been of interest mainly, if not exclusively,

---

29   Smith, "The Local Popularity of *The Concealed Fansyes*", 191–2.

30   Warren, "A Partial Liberty", 155.

31   Ibid., 164.

32   Morris B. (ed.), William Shakespeare, *The Taming of the Shrew*, (London: 2003), note on IV.i.175–98.

to Nottinghamshire audiences. Indeed, the last act virtually forgets about the Boot/Bateman story and stages instead an episode in which the local inhabitants plead with the visiting Queen Elizabeth to have the Trent made navigable.

Secondly, Sampson, as Margaret Ezell notes, was a member of Cavendish's literary circle,[33] and *The Vow Breaker*, like *The Concealed Fancies*, tells a story in which a siege disrupts Nottinghamshire country life and courtships. It harks back to the age of Elizabeth, as Cavendish's own play, *The Variety*, does, and mentions Mary, Queen of Scots, who was held captive mainly at Sheffield Manor in the care of the George Talbot, 6th Earl of Shrewsbury, the 4th husband of the sisters' great grandmother. It foreshadows *The Concealed Fancies* in various allusions, one of which is to monkeys. Ursula asks, 'Why should not I have my monkey to play withal?' and Young Bateman condemns Anne as 'More prime than goats or monkeys in their prides'.[34] There is also talk of women 'keeping a handsome chamber-maid' (I.iv.27) and 'turn[ing] nun' (I.iv.59); mention of cordials (III.iii.129–30) and, above all, reference to fancies which cannot be seen. When Old Bateman asks 'Whom converses she withal?' Ursula replies 'To her unseen fancies' (III.iii.70–1), and he later says to Anne herself 'Distemper not yourself at fancies' (III.iii.123). It would be tempting to see an anticipation of 'Newcastle's Lambs', to whom Alison Findlay also sees a possible allusion in *The Concealed Fancies* in the apparent whiteness of the nuns' habits,[35] in Clifton's boast that he has

> Five hundred and fifty tall white coats,
> Fellows that will face a murdering cannon
> When it blows rank into the air as chaff.
> Yet dreadless they shall stand it and not shrink.
> Right Nottinghamshire lads.
>   (I.ii.43–7)

I have been unable to discover any mention of the white coats of 'Newcastle's Lambs' before the war itself, but Newcastle the place is certainly mentioned— Boote tells Anne 'Thy husband, wench, this morn journeys to Newcastle' (II.iii.158). Moreover, the play shows itself interested in traditions of Robin

---

33   Ezell, "To Be Your Daughter in Your Pen", 285.

34   Griffin P.A., *A critical edition of William Sampson's 'The Vow Breaker' 1636* (unpublished PhD thesis, Sheffield Hallam University, 2009), I.i.211–12 and II.ii.159. All further quotations from the play will be taken from this edition and reference will be given in the text.

35   Findlay, 'She gave you the civility of the house', 262.

Hood when Miles asks 'Am I not going to buy ribbons and toys of sweet Ursula for the Marian, and shall not I play the hobby-horse?' (v.iii.31–3). *The Vow Breaker*, then, looks like another intertext for *The Concealed Fancies*, and thus reminds us that the Cavendish sisters formed part of several overlapping communities and that the literary influences to which they were subject could be local as well as national.

Identity

The Vow Breaker also tells a story about an unhappy marriage, this time one that breaks down because it does not enjoy the support of both families. 'Their parents jarred, and never could agree / Till both of them were drowned in misery' ('The illustration', 5–6):

> The moral is, maids should beware in choice
> And where they cannot love, divert their voice.
> Parents must not be rash nor too unkind,
> And not for wealth to thwart their children's mind.
>   ('The illustration', 11–14)

It is also worth noting that there *is* an 'illustration' in the first place, and that it is also accompanied by a 'Prologue to Censurers', which concludes,

> If, in his scenes, he any vice have hit,
> To you far better known than to his wit,
> Take't to yourselves alone; for him, his pen
> Strikes at the vices, and not minds the men.
>   (23–6)

This didactic mode of dramaturgy would have been very familiar to the sisters, as it is the standard approach of Jonsonian theatre, which presents itself as designed to identify and correct vice and folly. It is, however, not the mode which the sisters themselves have chosen. *The Concealed Fancies* pokes fun at the sisters' fictional representations of themselves as much as at those of their suitors, and its aim is not to modify behaviours and identities but to negotiate and confirm them, which it does by means of reference to literary tradition rather than to a moral schema. A crucial element of this negotiation of identity is the sisters' willingness to present themselves as women writers, despite the fact that this role was potentially problematic: in *The Tamer Tamed*, Sophocles's ultimate insult for Maria is 'I wonder that she writes not' (4.4.168). For us, the figure of the woman writer is of course strongly associated with feminism, and there is certainly something that sounds like early feminism in *The Tamer Tamed* when Bianca adjures,

> If we believe, and you prove recreant, Livia,
> Think what a maim you give the noble cause
> We now stand up for.
>   (2.1.79–81)

However, this is not something the sisters are interested in pursuing, any more than they wish to follow the example of Jonsonian didacticism. There is no pervasive feminist sensibility of sisterhood in this play of the kind which might have created a fellow-feeling with Lady Tranquillity or with Toy, and no interest in negotiating any position for women which does not involve embracing the norms of traditional patriarchal marriage; what the sisters are interested in is, very specifically, being traditional aristrocratic wives, whose sole deviation from the norms of that role is an interest in writing—and even for that there were reasonably respectable precedents in the shapes of the Countess of Pembroke, Elizabeth Cary and Lady Mary Wroth.

There is one more thing which the play notably does *not* do. *The Concealed Fancies* itself, and both *The Vow Breaker* and *The Tamer Tamed*, echo *Othello*. In *The Vow Breaker*, Lord Grey says to Bateman 'for thy merit, retain an ancient's place' (I.iii.14) and Bateman himself calls Anne and Jermane 'More prime than goats or monkeys in their prides' (II.ii.159). Most suggestively, Ursula in *The Vow Breaker* observes 'We must be coupled in wedlock your Barbary horse and Spanish genet' (I.i.146–7) and Jaques in *The Tamer Tamed* says of the women 'They are a genealogy of jennets' (2.3.49). Both echo Iago's disparaging language about the marriage of Othello and Desdemona, but both also introduce a motif of horses. This is, in fact, only one of many uses of horse imagery in *The Tamer Tamed*. The motif is first introduced when Petruccio asks 'On my wedding night am I thus jaded?' (1.3.290); subsequently, Jaques compares his mistress to 'a resty jade; / She's spoiled for riding' (1.4.17–18), Roland calls Moroso 'the stallion' (1.4.44) and declares 'when I credit woman more, / May I to Smithfield, and there buy a jade' (1.4.64–6) before vowing that 'henceforth a good horse shall be my mistress' (2.2.31), Bianca tropes Livia as Sinon (2.1.30) and Petruccio as 'the wooden jade' (2.1.31), and Roland's definition of a shrew is that 'She flayed her husband in his youth, and made / Reins of his hide to ride the parish' (2.3.44–5). Most intriguingly, one of Maria's demands is hunting horses (2.5.139), and Petruccio assures Sophocles that

>   She means to ride a great-horse.
> *Sophocles.*   With a side saddle?
> *Petruccio.*   Yes, and she'll run a-tilt within this twelvemonth.
> *Maria.* [*To horseman*] Tomorrow I'll begin to learn.
>   (3.3.70–72)

We can be quite certain that the sisters were familiar with the vocabulary of riding, but they show no interest in using it in the play. This might be partly attributable to context, in that the war had given the word 'horse' new connotations much darker than those of the dressage—the royalist garrison at Pendennis Castle in Cornwall was reported to be eating horseflesh—but I think there may be also another reason. That the sisters do not apply animal-based metaphors to human relationships should not, I think, surprise us, but perhaps it is worth noting that in this respect, too, they are not espousing the same kinds of cause as the militant women of *The Tamer Tamed* are. For Maria, access to 'a great-horse' seems to function as a marker of equality which implicitly serves to reverse the roles of husbands and wives and eliminate the difference between them. Jane Cavendish and Elizabeth Brackley, by contrast, do not desire access to a great horse, and the taming they propose for their respective suitors is a far milder form than that which Livia and Maria administer. Nevertheless, we are able to see that better if we compare their play with Fletcher's.

Conclusion

The Concealed *Fancies* is, then, a play which benefits from and, I think, invites a reading which both situates it firmly within mainstream dramatic tradition and also pays attention to its distinctive literary sensibility. In the process of self-fashioning which it limns, Shakespeare is undoubtedly an important precedent: it is practising Cleopatra which sustains Sh. in her captivity. However, *The Concealed Fancies* is not in Shakespeare's shadow; rather it could be seen as something of a writing back, evoking *The Taming of the Shrew* and *Othello* primarily in order to suggest its own difference from them. In so doing, it aligns itself with a Cavendish family tradition which sees Welbeck and Bolsover as significant seats of literary production in something of the same way as Wilton had been—as being, as it were, producing theatres rather than simply receiving ones. As well as implicitly affirming the value and importance of women's writing, the play thus specifically endorses the value of *Cavendish* writing, positing for it a place at the table of a national literary and cultural conversation in which aristocratic identity is shaped through a shared participation in literary discourse.

Selective Bibliography

Bennett A.G., "'Now let my language speake': The Authorship, Rewriting, and Audience(s) of Jane Cavendish and Elizabeth Brackley". *Early Modern Literary Studies* 11.2 (September 2005). Online: http://extra.shu.ac.uk/emls/112/benncav2 .htm.

Bennett A.G., "Filling in the Picture: Contexts and Contacts of Jane Cavendish". *Literature Compass* 5.2 (2008) 342–352.

Burroughs C., "'Hymen's Monkey Love': *The Concealed Fancies* and 'Female Sexual Initiation'". *Theatre Journal* 51.1 (March 1999) 21–31.

Cavendish Lady Jane – Brackley Lady Elizabeth, *The Concealed Fancies*, in Cerasano S.P. – Wynne-Davies M., (eds.) *Renaissance Drama by Women: Texts and Documents* (London: 1996).

Ezell M.J. M., "'To Be Your Daughter in Your Pen': The Social Functions of Literature in the Writings of Lady Elizabeth Brackley and Lady Jane Cavendish", *Huntington Library Quarterly* 51.4 (Autumn 1988) 281–96.

Findlay A., "'She gave you the civility of the house': Household performance in *The Concealed Fancies*", in *Readings in Renaissance Women's Drama: Criticism, History, and Performance 1594–1988*. Cerasano S.P. – Wynne-Davies M. (eds.) (London & New York: 1988) 259–271.

Findlay A., *Playing Spaces in Early Women's Drama* (Cambridge: 2006).

Hopkins L., "Judith Shakespeare's Reading: Teaching *The Concealed Fancies*", *Shakespeare Quarterly* 47.4 (Winter 1996) 396–406.

Smith E., "The Local Popularity of *The Concealed Fansye*", *Notes and Queries* 53.2 (June 2006) 189–193.

Stanton K.S., "The domestication of royalist themes in *The Concealed Fancies* by Jane Cavendish and Elizabeth Brackley", *Clio* 36.2 (2007) 177–197.

Warren R.O., "A Partial Liberty: Gender and Class in Jane Cavendish and Elizabeth Brackley's *The Concealed Fancies*", *Renaissance Papers* (2000) 155–167.

CHAPTER 5

Flogging a Dead Horse?: Margaret Cavendish and the Pursuit of Authority

Alison Findlay

'Horse-flesh is not mans-flesh' was the unequivocal declaration of Margaret Cavendish in her *Philosophical and Physical Opinions*, where she discredited the idea of metamorphosis,[1] yet her husband's devotion to *manège* suggested a different view. His *New Method* to dress horses argued that there could be nothing 'more Glorious or Manly' to celebrate 'great Marriages of Princes' than to see man and horse in perfect unity: 'to see so Excellent a Creature, with so much Spirit, and Strength, to be so Obedient to his *Rider*, as if having no Will but His, they had but one Body, and one Mind, like a *Centaur*?' (1667: 13) This essay explores a textual dialogue between Margaret and William Cavendish on issues of authority which is articulated through their discussions of, and references to, horses in their writings.

The unity that William Cavendish describes did not happen by nature, of course; it was a battle of wills and the result of the man's assertion of his over that of the horse. William's words are informative here:

> Certainly there is no Horse but will Strive at the first in the Dressing, to have his own will, rather than to *Obey* your *will*; nor doth any Horse love *Subjection*, nor any other Creature, until there is no Remedy, and then they *Obey*; and the Custom of *Obedience* makes them *Ready-Horses:* They will Strive all the Wayes possibly they can, to be Free, and not Subjected; but when they see it will not be, then they *Yield*, and not before. (1667: 200)[2]

---

* In other essays in this collection the subject is normally referred to as 'Cavendish' but here he is named 'William' or 'William Cavendish' since the essay is concerned with both Margaret and William Cavendish. Margaret Cavendish is, correspondingly, referred to as 'Margaret' or 'Margaret Cavendish'.

1 The comment appears in Chapter 84 "Of Metamorphosing of Animals and Vegetables" in *The Philosophical and Physical Opinions, written by her Excellency, the Lady Marchionesse of Newcastle* (London: 1655) 48.

2 In the context of modern horse knowledge, it is usually understood that a rider has to be accepted as a horse's herd leader in order to produce the horse's obedience.

© KONINKLIJKE BRILL NV, LEIDEN, 2017 | DOI 10.1163/9789004326217_007

I am interested in the double recognition William makes in his view that no horse 'nor any other Creature' loves 'Subjection' to the will of a man. Each creature will naturally 'strive all wayes possibly they can to be free and not Subjected'. Firstly, the slippages between the horse and 'any other Creature', here and elsewhere in his text, reveal, as Elaine Walker has suggested, that this is not just a book about horsemanship but about the art of government.[3] Walker has pointed out the connections between the liberal methods adopted by Cavendish's *New Method* and the political advice he offered to Prince Charles (later Charles II), whom he taught to ride while his governor. In the *New Method*, the author signs off the opening dedication to 'His Most Sacred Majesty Charles the Second,' as '*Your Majesties most Obedient Creature*' explicitly submitting himself to the king's authority as 'the most Comely *Horseman* in the World', able to govern his subjects with knowledge and understanding. (1667: 7, a2v) Cavendish's dedication 'To the Readers' praises the king as 'an *Excellent* Judge' of horses and '*both of* Men, *and* Business; *of* Things *of* Use, and *of* Recreation; *of* Necessity, *and of* Ornament'. The essence of good government, the *New Method* explains, comes from understanding the horse or the subject(s) to be managed: '*It being very certain, That all Men undertake to* Ride *them, but very few* Know *them, or can tell what they are good for*'. (1667: c2r–v) Via use of metaphors and similies the *New Method* presents the art of *manège* as a transferable skill. William Cavendish anthropomorphises horses, reiterating the view that 'they wanted nothing of a Reasonable Creature, but Speaking', and pointing out, for example, that horses should not be overworked since 'Have not Schollars Play-dayes? and certain Hours of Rest in their daies of *Study?* All *Trades-Men*, Holy-dayes to Rejoyce themselves in? *States-Men*, Divertisments from Business? And Good *Preachers* Preach not every *Sunday?*' (1667: b2r, c2v; 39) Such details advertise the fact that William is writing about authority in the widest sense.

William's use of equine metaphor for government had precedents in classical and religious authority. Richard Middleton advised Prince Charles, newly elevated as '*heire apparant* to the Crowne of Great BRITAINE', that '*Pythagoras* was wont to say· That no horse, without a bridle, could well bee gouerned; nor any felicitie, without great wisdome, well swayed'.[4] Philip Edwards, minister of St Saviour's Southwark, drew on both Proverbs 26:3 and Psalm 32:9 to counsel

---

3   Walker E., "'The Author of their Skill': Human and Equine Understanding in the Duke of Newcastle's 'New Method'", in Edwards P. – Enenkel K.A.E. – Graham E. (eds.), *The Horse as Cultural Icon: The Real and the Symbolic Horse in the Early Modern World* (Leiden: 2012) 327–50.

4   Middleton Richard, *The carde and compasse of life Containing many passages, fit for these times. And directing all men in a true, Christian, godly and ciuill course, to arriue at the blessed and glorious harbour of heauen* (London: 1613) A2.

the necessity of actively asserting power over inferiors since theirs 'is no willing nor voluntarie subiection, but by force and constraint: for the horse must haue his rough rider, or else the snaffle will not hold him in; and the mule as *Dauid* saith, *Psal.* 32.9. must haue his mouth bound with the bitte and bridle lest hee come neere thee with his heele'. Edwards reminded his readers that, above all, God controls individual affections as a master-horseman, for 'the strong horse whose neying is fearefull, and swalloweth the ground for fiercenesse, would quickly turne his heele vpon the reprobate, if the Lord held him not by the hoofe: for wee see how euen the smallest creatures are armed to annoy them when God letteth the raines loose but a little'.[5]

William Cavendish's recognition that every creature will strive 'all wayes possibly they can to be free and not subjected', thus rehearses a wider consciousness of the faultline in patriarchal authority which made it necessary to manage obedience. Man and horse, ruler and subordinate are not one being, like the Centaur, but two distinctive entities. William Cavendish carefully outlines the means to achieve control:

> It is Impossible to Dress any Horse, but first he must Know, and Acknowledge me to be his Master, by Obeying me: That is, He must *Fear* me, and out of that *Fear, Love* me, and so *Obey* me. For it is *Fear* makes every Body *Obey*, both Man and Beast... *Love* doth no Good, but *Fear* doth All.[6]

The basis of William's recipe for control, inducing fear to produce love, again derives from scripture and religious exegesis. Believers were regularly exhorted to *'love and fear the Lord'*,[7] the minister William Erbury reminding his readers that fear is not 'to drive me from God, but to draw me to him' although 'when thou most beleeves that thou lie in the arms of his love' one should 'fear the more' the danger of committing sins.'[8] Likewise, a wife should *'fear or reverence her husband'* as Launcelot Andrews spelled out in his *Learned and Pious Exposition of the Ten Commandments* (1650): 'that as he hath the government, so he hath power and authority, which she must fear', and should 'never follow

---

5   Edwards Philip, *Certain godly and learned sermons, preached by that worthy seruant of Christ M. Ed. Philips in S. Sauiors in Southwarke* (London: 1607) 499; 507.

6   Ibid., 200.

7   Nicholas Bouwnd's *A storehouse of comfort for the afflicted in spirit*, for example, was published *'for the further good of all those that loue and feare the Lord'* (London: 1604).

8   Erbury William, *The great mystery of godliness Jesus Christ our Lord God and man, and man with God; one in Jesus Christ our Lord* (London: 1640).

her own will hereafter, but must be subject to her husband'.[9] This gendered message was carried through into some very rigorous forms of control, most notoriously in the scold's bridle and the tradition of mocking the husband's failure to govern his wife in a skimmington ride, where he was mimicked riding backwards on a horse. It passed down through conduct books, notably William Whately's, *A Bride Bush or a Wedding Sermon* (1617), which declared:

> It sufficeth not that her obedience reacheth to all things that are lawful, unless it be also willing, ready, without brawling, contending thwarting, sourness ... Then it is laudable, commendable, a note of a virtuous woman, a dutiful wife, when she submits herself with quietness, cheerfully, even as a well-broken horse turns at the least turning, stands at the least check of the rider's bridle, readily going and standing as he wishes that sits upon his back. If you will have your obedience worth anything, make no tumult about it outwardly, allow none within.[10]

Whately's celebration of the wife or horse's willingness to be ruled masked a recognition of their natural resistance to subordination. The same insecurity about patriarchal authority informs R.D.'s sermon on *Matrimoniall Honour*, which refers back to Proverbs 26:3 noting that the rebellion of horse, ox and ass 'is moderated, and a shaddow of our Lordship over them restored'.

Given that the horse is, implicitly and explicitly, a cultural icon for those subjected by patriarchal control, in particular wives, how does the horse feature in the prolific writings of William's second wife, Margaret Cavendish? By looking at some examples, I would like to suggest that the horse—that creature who, William recognised, 'will Strive all the Wayes possibly they can,' to each 'have his own will'—can be read as a trope through which Margaret's own determination to claim authority is negotiated. Her authorship of philosophy, prose fiction, epistolary exposition, orations, poetry and drama constituted a will to 'be Free, and not Subjected' (like the horse), to keep an imaginative freedom under the shadow of her husband's *manège*. It was, of course, William who managed the process of getting her writing into print, encouraging her efforts and financing publication, just as he invested energy and finances in building up his riding school. His status, after the publication of the *New Method*, was celebrated by the Masters of Cambridge whose letter

---

9   Andrews Launcelot, *Learned and Pious Exposition of the Ten Commandments* (London, 1650) 143. On the issue of a horse's 'fear' of its rider, see again Walker Elaine, "'The Author of their Skill'" 332–337.

10   Whateley William, *A Bride Bush or a Wedding Sermon* (London: 1617) 43.

observed that riding experts, noblemen and princes 'as soon as ever they hear the Name of Duke *William*, they bow to your Sovereignty, and falling infinitely short of your Glory, they confess you the most absolute and only Master, and themselves your Pupils.'[11] It was in the presence of such celebrated authority that Margaret had to configure her own literary endeavours.

Margaret's familiarity with her husband's *New Method* and practice made her allusions to horses precise. She knew the manner of a horse's characteristic movements 'to gallop, to amble, to trot, to runn, to leap, to kick, and the like', as outlined in the section 'Of The Natural Paces' in *A New Method*. (1667: 146–55)[12] Margaret's writings also suggest her understanding of the value her husband placed on his horses. In *Observations Upon Experimental Philosophy* (1666), to illustrate a case of justice within injustice, she pointedly offers the example of a man who 'hath a Horse which he esteems, and hath a love or (as it were) an affection to' and, when forced to sell the horse, 'asks a Price according to his Affection, not according as he is really worth'. Her cameo prefigures William's protestation that he '*would not have taken any* Money' for his beautiful 'Grey Leaping Horse' for '*he was above Price*'. (1667: c1v–c2)[13] Her cameo of 'The Self-conceited Fool' mercilessly mocks anyone who has no real knowledge of horses and boast of 'his House, his Horse, his Dog,' not for their innate virtues, 'that his Horse is the strongest, or soundest, or best natur'd, or choyccst colour'd, or perfectest shaped, or fullest of spirit, or swiftest of race, or surest of foot' but just his own will in esteeming it so.[14] This could be a jibe at a wealthy rival from the *nouveau riche*, more richly endowed with credit but not endowed with William's judgement. Alternatively, it could also be a playful way of teasing William about his own dreams of investing in architecture and horses and dogs for his estates.

In her *Orations of Divers Sorts* (1662), Margaret echoes her husband's advocacy of good horsemanship as the most effective means of control. The General's Oration to his soldiers advocates that the man who can 'Manage a Horse' as well as his sword,

> hath a Double Advantage, if he can Ride well, and hath a good Managed Horse, that Obeyes well the Hand and the Heel, that can tell how to Turn,

---

11   *A Collection of letters and poems written by several persons of honour and learning, upon divers important subjects, to the late Duke and Dutchess of Newcastle* (London: 1678) 50.

12   Cavendish Margaret, *Philosophical and Physical Opinions*, 45.

13   Cavendish Margaret, *Observations Upon Experimental Philosophy* (London: 1668) 71.

14   Cavendish Margaret, *The worlds olio written by the Right Honorable, the Lady Margaret Newcastle* (London: 1655) 68.

or to stop on the Hanches, or to go Forward, or Side-wayes, and the like:
The truth is, a good Horse-man, although not so well Skill'd in the Use
of the Sword, shall have Advantage of an Ignorant Horse-man, although
well Skill'd in the Use of the Sword.

The comparison of horse and sword, and the superiority of *manège* to swordsmanship, might in this passage again emphasise a cooperative working relationship between master and subordinate. Like Whateley's sermon and other
cultural guides on subjection, Margaret's text implicitly places value on understanding the subject as the key to effective government. Other metaphoric
references to horses suggest that Margaret sees *manège* in traditionally conservative terms as a means to maintain hierarchy across class and gender lines.
In Letter LXI of the *Sociable Letters*, for example, her persona tells Madam the
correspondent that the fault of insubordinate servants really lies with their
masters and mistresses whose neglect of government leaves them open to
temptation 'for there is an old true Saying, The Masters Eye makes the Horse
Fat'.[15] In another letter, children and peasants are equated in their inability to
manage horses. Peasants 'or such mean bred Persons . . . have no skill to use
a Sword, nor know not how to manage an Horse, unless a Cart-Horse, & that
better in a Cart than when astride'.[16] Horsemanship is inextricably tied to a
traditional, patriarchal hierarchy in such allusions.

Margaret pays deference to her husband's authority as the basis for her
allusions to horsemanship. In *Sociable Letters* her narrator persona is quick to
point out that although it may be thought 'not Fit, nor Proper for a Woman
to Discourse or Write of Duels or Wars, nor of Horses or Swords', she enjoys
'a greater Privilege than other Women in this Discourse', because of William's
expertise:

> for my Husband hath been a General of an Army of 30000 men, and hath
> fought Battels; also he is Master of those two Arts, the Use of the Sword,
> and the Manage of the Horse, as there is not any man, nor hath never
> been, so well Known, Skilful, and Practised, as he, so that he is the best
> Horseman and Swordman in the World.[17]

Margaret echoes her husband's compliments to Charles II as 'the most
Comely *Horseman* in the World', with the implicit acknowledgement of his
absolute authority. For all her praise of William in this fictional persona,

---

15   Cavendish Margaret, *Sociable Letters* (London: 1664) 125.
16   Ibid., Letter CCXI, 143.
17   Ibid., Letter LXVII, 145.

Margaret Cavendish also—perhaps equally self-consciously—figures female wit as independent and inherently subversive. Her play, *The Several Wits*, features a conversation on the virtues and dangers of witty self-expression between Monsieur Discretion and the appropriately-named Lady Volante. Use of the French term *volante* (flying) for a fast horse predates the famous 1885 American Derby winner by 286 years,[18] and Margaret alludes here (and in *Natures Daughters*) to Shakespeare's *Henry V*, where the Dauphin praises his horse as '*le Cheual volante,* the Pegasus', whose majesty has inspired him to write a sonnet. The whole world 'familiar to us and unknown' should 'wonder at him', the Dauphin claims: 'Turne the Sands into eloquent tongues, and my Horse is argument for them all'.[19] Margaret Cavendish extends his elision of horsemanship and oration in a dialogue where Discretion tells Lady Volante that her eloquence will get her fame 'and esteem of the world'. However, her wit must be very carefully managed, lest it run wild:

> Lady, I would not have your wit out-run your prayse, which it will do, if you spur it too hard, for wit must be used like a strong spirited horse, it must be restraind with a bridle, not prick'd with the spur, least it should run away, and fling the Rider, which is, the Speaker, into a ditch of disgrace; neither must it run wildly about, but must be wrought, to obey the hand and the heel, which is, time and occasion, to stop, and to change, as when to speak, and to whom to speak, and on what to speak, and when to make a stop of silence, otherwise, it will run out of the smooth paths of civility, or the clean wayes of modesty: Besides, wit must not only be taught, to amble in rhime, and to trot in prose, but to have a sure footing of sense, and a setled head of reason, least it should stumble in disputes, or fall into impertinent discourses; likewise, wit may be taught to go in aires of fancies, or low, upon the ground of proof.

Monsieur Discretion has no hesitation in imagining Lady Volante in the controlling position of rider, a real master of command, an authority in speech and

---

18   Lucky Baldwin's horse Volante won the American Derby in 1885 and gave its name to the Volante Handicap, inaugurated in 1969 and retitled as the Oak Tree Derby in 1997. Baldwin had financed the building of the Baldwin Theatre which opened with *Richard III* in 1876, so it seems likely that his horse was named after that in *Henry V.*

19   These lines are attributed to the Duke of Bourbon throughout the scene in the 1599 Quarto text of the play but in the First Folio they are assigned to the Dauphin. Margaret comments on *Henry the Fifth* in Letter CXXIII in *Sociable Letters* (1664) 244–8 and her references to Shakespeare's 'Book' and his 'Works' (247) suggest she would have been reading the single-volume *Collected Works* in the Folio. The Folio is quoted from here.

self-government. Nevertheless, she expresses doubts about women's horsemanship or power to adopt a strong managerial role, saying 'Sir, you must consider, that women are no good managers of wit, for they spoyl all their tongue rides on, hackneys it out, untill it becomes a dull jade'.[20]

Given Margaret's commitment to writing as an expression of her wit, one suspects that, here, the Lady doth protest too much. In Shakespeare's *Much Ado About Nothing*, a play Margaret knew, the proto-feminist Beatrice reverses the usual gendered hierarchy in her first 'skirmish of wit' with Benedick. She responds to his insult about her volubility, 'I would my horse had the speed of your tongue, and so good a continuer', by likening him to a 'jade' or unruly horse that deviously tries to unseat the rider.[21] Margaret's writing, I suggest, conducts a similarly subversive campaign, citing and challenging the conventional trope of horsemanship by repeatedly figuring the independent wit or spirit of the supposedly subordinate 'creature'.

Her first volume of *Playes* (1662) begins with three gentlemen discussing female wit and playwriting. The First Gentleman readily acknowledges that 'men will not allow women to have wit, or we men to have reason, for if we allow them wit, we shall lose our prehemency'. The texts which follow constitute a challenge to male 'prehemency' in playwriting, beginning with a teasing reference to William Cavendish's play *The Variety*. The Second Gentleman complains 'theres not enough variety in an old play to please me'. The First Gentleman counters 'There is variety of that which is bad, as you have divided it, but it seemes you love youth and variety in playes, as you doe in Mistresses'. William's play thus stands as an emblem of the cavalier attitude which assumes women cannot take the authorial reins into their own hands and 'write a good Play'.[22]

Margaret's technique of subversively citing the horsemanship metaphor for patriarchal authority can be seen most fully in the play *Nature's Daughters, Beauty, Love and Wit* (1662), where William Cavendish's views on the importance of the *manège* as a mark of superior class and gender are articulated by the dramatic character of Lord Noblissimo and his group of courtiers. Noblissimo contends that what is essential 'for a Right bred Gentleman is to know the use of the Sword', and 'also to know how to mannage Horses', since such skills enable both attack and self-defence. Maintaining one's status as

20   Cavendish Margaret, *Playes written by the thrice noble, illustrious and excellent princess, the Lady Marchioness of Newcastle* (London: 1662) 96.

21   Shakespeare William, *Much Ado About Nothing*, ed. McEachern Claire, Arden Shakespeare (London: 2007) 1.1.135–9.

22   Cavendish Margaret, *Playes* (1662) 2.

much as one's physical wellbeing is Noblissimo's primary concern, as revealed in a full defence of the aristocratic hierarchy:

> if there be no difference of persons, there will be no Supremacy of Power, if no Supremacy, no Royal Government; for as the Sword maintains the Prerogative of the Crown, so it doth the Honour of a Gentleman; and as the Sword keeps up the dignity of the Crown, so a Sword keeps up the Heraldry of a Gentleman; and no man ought to be accounted a Gentleman, that knows not how to use his Sword, and manage his Horse.[23]

An ideal model of horsemanship is celebrated in Noblissimo who seems to have a riding school like William's. Noblissimo's First Gentleman remarks 'Your Lordship rid to day beyond *Perseus* on his Pegasus' and Noblissimo, modestly deferring, 'No Monsieur, he went (if Poets speak truth) in higher Capreols than ever I shall make my Horse go'. The Gentleman insists, however, on Noblissimo's superior control of his animal, which, though less extravagant, had the precision of the diagrams outlined in William's *Method*: 'He might go higher my Lord, but never keep so just a time, and place, as to pitch from whence he riss, his feet in the same Circle, his legs in the same lines, and your Lordship in the same Center.'

The image of Noblissimo as the constant centre, around which the horse moves in perfectly described circles evokes the diagrams in the first edition of William's *La Nouvelle Méthode* (Antwerp, 1658). They illustrate how, for example, the horse dances round a grand circle in a 'grand galop', stopping at the four points of the compass to give 'un petit galop' or 'un terre terrre'. The perfectly controlled circumferences of horse and rider are a microcosm of the pattern of order in the heavens, whose perfect harmony appeared in the so-called music of the spheres, a common metaphor for macrocosmic order in early modern writing. To make the analogy unmistakable, Monsieur Noblissimo remarks 'The truth is, my Horses went well to day; they were like Musical Instruments, fitly strung, and justly tun'd', and his Gentleman obsequiously notes 'And your Lordship, like a skillfull Musician, played rarely thereon'.[24] The final compliment echoes William's own remarks on the musical harmony that could be achieved between man and horse. Reporting on a display of horsemanship on the Spanish horse, Superbe, he declared that 'no Musitian could keep Time

---

23   Cavendish Margaret, *The First Part of Nature's Daughters, Beauty, Love and Wit in* Playes (London: 1662) 497.

24   Cavendish Margaret, *Playes* (1662) 500.

better' (1667: b2v) and William concludes the third and final part of the book with an extended comparison between riding and musicianship. 'There is no man, that hath not a *Musical Head*, that can be a good *Horse-man*, because all Horses ought to go in a just and Musical time,' he notes, recommending subtle use of the hands and heels, 'or else it will be *Ill Musick* on Horse-Back'.

Margaret's cameo dramatisation of the *New Method* and William as Noblissimo, its perfect 'Center', is not as reverential as it first appears. The figure of the horseman as a semi-divine hero '*Perseus* on his Pagasus', who can defeat the monstrous female gorgon and rescue the heroine Andromeda, is undercut by a second level of allusion, to *Henry v*. Here, the Dauphin describes his '*cheval volant*' as 'the Pegasus' with nostrils of fire. He continues in equally hyperbolic style:

> When I bestryde him, I soare, I am a Hawke: he trots the ayre: the Earth sings, when he touches it: the basest horne of his hoofe, is more Musicall then the Pipe of *Hermes* ... It is a Beast for *Perseus:* hee is pure Ayre and Fire; and the dull Elements of Earth and Water neuer appeare in him, but only in patient stillnesse while his Rider mounts him: ... It is the Prince of Palfrayes, his Neigh is like the bidding of a Monarch, and his countenance enforces Homage .... Nay, the man hath no wit, that cannot from the rising of the Larke to the lodging of the Lambe, varie deserued prayse on my Palfray ... 'tis a subiect for a Soueraigne to reason on, and for a Soueraignes Soueraigne to ride on.[25]

Margaret's representation of Monsieur Noblissimo's riding academy employs strikingly similar terms to those used by the Dauphin. This may be a shared joke with William, based on their common knowledge of Shakespeare's play. The Dauphin's extravagant praise of his horse is echoed not just in the preface to the *New Method*, but in the instructions. William advises the rider how to control a leaping horse: 'stay him there upon the *Hand*, as if he hung in the *Ayre*', for example. (1667: 296)

In *Henry v* the Dauphin's arrogance is criticised not only by comparison with the humility of King Henry but by his fellow French nobles. The Constable interjects, acerbically, 'Indeed my Lord, it is a most absolute and excellent Horse' and 'You have good judgement in Horsemanship'.[26] That Margaret rec-

---

25   *Mr William Shakespeares comedies, histories, & tragedies Published according to the true originall copies* (London: 1623) 81–2 (3.7.14–17).

26   Ibid., 82.

ognised and exploited the irony in Shakespeare's portrait of equine adulation, is suggested by a comment in *Sociable Letters*, that 'Shakespear had a Clear Judgement, a Quick Wit' and that 'the Wit and Language' in his history plays was 'all his Own'. There may be an acknowledgement of her own witty allusions in *Nature's Daughters* when she notes 'that those, who Writ after him, were Forced to Borrow of him'.

Margaret's equivalent to the Constable of France's deflating comments in *Henry V* is the voice of Nature's eldest daughter, Wit. Her proper name, Madamoiselle Grand Esprit, evokes the indubitable equine spirit or mettle and Margaret uses her, arguably, as a dramatic representation of her own authorial wit, to comment on Noblissimo's ideals. Grand Esprit brings ideas of phallocentric power firmly down to earth with a series of questions about man's subordination to a feminised Nature: 'What Man is, or ever was, that knows what Nature is, or from whence her power proceeds? ... Or whether her work is prescribed, or limited? Or of what she works on? Or what instruments she worketh with? Or to what end she works for?' Grand Esprit then goes on to remind her audience that 'we are apt to think our selves Gods in the pride of prosperity; we strive to make our selves Gods in the hight of worldly power; and we do not only strive to make our selves equal with the Gods, but to raise our selves above the Gods'.[27] Moreover, speaking in congratulation of her sisters' weddings, Lady Grand Esprit argues controversially, that even when 'Souls, Bodyes, and Affections, are united as one' as they must be, 'yet at the best marriage is but the womb of trouble, which cannot be avoided'. The 'trouble' she identifies, even in the ideal union, is loss of autonomous voice. She objects that 'marriage is the grave of Wit; for which I am resolved for my part to live a single life, associating with my own Thoughts, marrying my self to my own Contemplations, which I hope to conceive and bring forth a Child of Fame that may live to posterity and keep alive my Memory'.[28]

We cannot know to what extent this dramatisation advertises Margaret's own difficulties in reconciling an ideal alliance of 'Souls, Bodyes and Affections' with William and the maintenance of an autonomous wit. The prefaces to her published writings, and her autobiographical text, appended to her *Life of William*, both suggest that she shares Lady Grand Esprit's ambitions.[29] In dedicating her first publication, *Poems and Fancies* to 'All Noble and Worthy Ladies',

---

27   Cavendish Margaret, *Playes* (1662) 496; 502.

28   Ibid., 525.

29   Cavendish M, *Life of William Cavendish*.

for example, she tells them 'all I desire is Fame and Fame is nothing but a great noise, wherefore I shall wish my Book may set a work every Tongue'.

Although man and wife were supposedly one flesh, Margaret's references to horses repeatedly refute William's ideal of horse and rider joined in 'but one Body, and one Mind, like a *Centaur*'. The fact that many of them occur in situations of battle may say something about Margaret's personal struggle for literary authority, wittily incorporated into the immediate contexts of the English Civil Wars. The title character of her play *Lady Contemplation* embodies a wild, in the sense of utopian, female wit like that envisaged by Madam Grand Esprit. Speculation allows Lady Contemplation to imagine saving her husband by taking up the reins of command herself.[30] The heroine contemplates the prospect of her husband being captured in battle after his horse collapsed in the enemy territory, and casts him in the conventionally feminine role of victim in distress:

> his horse riding thorow Rivers of blood, those Rivers rising so high, as his horse was forced to swim; but the blood growing thick to a jelly, obstructed his way, which made his horse furious, which fury added to his strength, forced a passage over a hill, or heap of slain bodies; but the horses spirits being spent with fury and labour, fell strengthless to the ground, with my Husband upon his back.[31]

Although the Lady cannot carry a sword, her pen allows her to write a woman into the saddle from which commanding position, she addresses the rest of the company, 'arm'd as a Soldier', undaunted by authority she has assumed and confidently promising 'to give you victory by my Conduct'.[32] Erica Mae Olbright[33] comments that this play uses sex to present a fantasy of class permanence and although she does not discuss the Lady Contemplation plot, it is easy to see how this fantasy of control mirrors that of royalist hierarchy that was so closely connected with the metaphor of horsemanship. Lady Contemplation comments self-consciously on the power of speculation (or fiction) to provide space for commanding female roles to emerge. The vivid picture gets even

---

30   In actuality, however, we know that members of his family were concerned about Margaret's influence over her husband. Some servants at Welbeck even plotted against her, though the conspiracy was discovered.

31   Cavendish Margaret, *Playes* (1662) 222.

32   Ibid., 222.

33   Olbright Mae, "Using Sex: Margaret Cavendish's *The Lady Contemplation* and the Authorial Fantasy of Class Permanence", *Pacific Coast Philology* 38 (2003) 77–98.

more animated as she imagines persuading the Chief Commander to let her lead a rescue attempt, and take over as head of the army so that 'that all the rest of the Commanders cry'd or call'd out, that none was so fit to Lead and Command them as I'. Having strategically arranged her troops and delayed engaging her army, she says,

> I led the Van my self, and was Accoutred after this manner: I had a Masculine Suit, and over that a cloth of silver Coat, made close to my waste, which reached to the ankles of my legs; and those Arms I wore being all gilt, were Back, Brest, Gorget, Pot and Gantlet, all being made light according as my strength would bear: In my hand I carried my Sword; for being not accustomed, I could not wear a sword by my side, as men do, but whensoever rested, I tyed it to my Saddle-bow, and on my Head-piece I wore a great Plume of Feathers: As for my Horse, he was cole-black, only a white star on his fore-head, and three white feet; my Saddle was crimson Velvet, but so imbroidred with silver and gold, as the ground could not be seen.[34]

Further into the volume of plays, contemplation is translated into action through the dramatic persona of Lady Victoria who leads the cavalry in an all female army to save her husband in *Bell In Campo*. In the rules announced to the company of women, Lady Victoria includes the command that all the members of the company should be 'imployed in some Masculine action' in their spare time as 'Tripping, Wrastling, Running, Vaulting, Riding, and the like exercise'.[35] (*Playes* 1662, 592).

Since women can command inferiors—equine or human—ably (a truth which was manifest to every seventeenth-century woman who managed a household and servants), male attempts to exercise absolute authority in the household were inevitably somewhat specious. In *The Matrimoniall Trouble Part II*, Margaret advertises this truth in her portrait of Sir Edward Courtly who desperately tries to hold onto the reins of government in his household in a literal way, telling Lady Jealousy:

> Well, I will pardon you this time; and know, Wife, that though I am willing to part with my Breeches and Doublet to give them you, yet I will never part with my Sword and my Spurs, which is my Courage and my Management:

---

34   Cavendish Margaret, *Playes* (1662) 222.
35   Ibid., 592.

> And I will give you all liberty in Vanity, but not in Dishonesty; you shall
> keep the Purse, but not manage the Horse.[36]

Managing his stable is a symbolic substitute for not being able to manage his
wife's behaviour, which has taken control of his finances and even his clothes.

Women's ability to assume effective (if devious or covert) government within
the household, makes poor *manège* by men all the more intolerable. Cavendish
offers a pointed critique of the horsemanship analogy for husbandly authority
by drawing a contrast between *manège* and dancing:

> for those Fashions that are Proper for Dancing, are not Proper for Riding;
> as for Example, Pumps are of no Use a Horseback, nor Boots, nor Spurs
> in a Galliard, or Courant, unless it were to Tear the Ladies Gown the man
> Dances withall, for he cannot well cut a Caper in a pair of Boots and
> Spurs, nor a Horseman Spur a Horse with a pair of Pumps.[37]

In spite of William's insistence in the *New Method* that *manège* should be a
gentle art, it will not work on the dance floor. The exercise of and tools of force
will only 'Tear the Ladies Gown the man Dances withall' and spoil the dance.
Margaret's subtle use of analogy (in contrast to the repressive force attributed
to the male dancer) suggests that William's thesis of *the manège* as a transferable skill might not work in the context of male-female relationships. For all
its refinement as an elaborate form of terpischoran display, as demonstrated in
the courts of Europe,[38] the skills of *manège* would spoil the harmony of com-
panionate marriage symbolised by the dance.

Margaret's critique of male authority is more explicit in *The Matrimoniall
Agreement.* This short story features a man who is sexually unfaithful, so his
wife takes control of the situation by deciding to be unfaithful too. Here the
man's lack of self-government demotes him to the position of the horse.
The husband's friends persuade him:

---

36   Ibid., 460.

37   Cavendish Margaret, Letter cxxviii, *Sociable Letters* (1664) 260.

38   On dancing horses as a form of courtly spectacle see Van Orden Kate, *Music, Discipline,
      and Arms in Early Modern France* (Chicago: 2007). The website http://www.press
      .uchicago.edu/ucp/books/book/chicago/M/bo3533738.html offers a one-minute video
      clip. Accessed 10th January 2015.

What do our Wives know what we do? Besides, said they, Wives are only to keep our House, to bring us Children, not to give us Laws. Thus preaching to him, he at last followed their Doctrine, and improved it so well, that he became the greatest Libertine of them all; like a Horse that having broken his Reins, (when he finds himself loose) skips over Hedges, Ditches, Pales, or whatsoever is in his way; and runs wildly about, until he hath wearied himself.[39]

Although it is the husband who appears to have absolute agency to make or break the laws, in this story it is obviously the wife who should be given the authority to hold the reins in the marriage. When the wife confronts him with his infidelities and considers punishing him, she pointedly asks him 'Do you know what is in my Power', and he acknowledges 'Yes ... a great part of my Estate'.[40] Her infidelity is presented as, ultimately, a less damaging alternative.

In contrast to texts like this which offer bold critiques of patriarchal *manège*, Cavendish's literary personae, both characters and authorial, are more equivocal. The Preface to *The World's Olio*, for example, argues, on the one hand, that female complaints that men have 'from their first Creation usurped a Supremacy to themselves', may be justified. Rule by 'Tyrannical Government', denying women education and practice in government 'so that we could never come to be free, but rather more and more enslaved, as subjects' (A4), should be resisted. Such resistance is inevitably limited, however, since women have no natural inclination to rule. Margaret turns to a horsemanship analogy again to make her point: 'neither can Women bring the furious and wild Horse to the Bit, quenching his fiery Courage, and bridling his strong swift Speed. This is the reason we are not so active in Exercise' (A4v). Given a lack of active exercise in *manège*, women's best option is to assert their authority in the non-material world. Women's thoughts are free 'those can never be inslaved' Cavendish's preface goes on to say (A5), an idea that is taken up in her fantasy writing.

Travellia, the cross-dressed heroine of *Assaulted and Pursued Chastity*, offers an idealised image of what woman's material resistance against male tyranny could be within a fantasy world realised in fiction. As a 'young generall', Travellia arranges her male forces carefully and 'commanded all the cuirassiers

---

39   Cavendish Margaret, *Natures picture drawn by fancies pencil to the life being several feigned stories, comical, tragical, tragi-comical, poetical, romanicical, philosophical, historical, and moral* (London: 1671) 205.

40   The possibility that a child not of his own flesh and blood might inherit the estate, perhaps.

should stand in the forefront to bear the shock'.[41] She pointedly tells the men that 'All noble spirits hate bondage, and will rather die than endure slavery', drawing a parallel between her own assigned position as subject and her resistance to it and the prince. Finally she offers a tactical use of horse to outwit the Prince's army:

> [She] sent some flying horse to give the onset, and then to run away which the other army seeing thought it was out of fear and followed them as in pursuit which haste disordered and broke all their ranks, which the Queen's army no sooner saw but it marched in good order to meet them … which made them become absolute masters of the field.[42]

Travellia achieves absolute mastery of the field in this story in literal and ideological terms. An even more grandiose fantasy is imagined in the *New Blazing World* when the Empress and the soul of the Duchess fly above William Cavendish's riding house:

> the Duke came out of the house into the Court to see his horses of manage; whom when the Duchess's soul perceived, she was so overjoyed that her aeriel vehicle became so splendorous, as if it had been enlightened by the sun; by which we may perceive that the passions or souls of spirits can alter their bodily vehicles.[43]

Utopian fantasy allows Margaret Cavendish a rare new perspective: to look down on her husband's *manège* from above, a prospect which makes her 'aery vehicle', her own body, glow as though it were the royal sun itself, able to shine beneficently down upon him. It is she rather than he who occupies the position of Perseus here. A rude anonymous poem of the time satirised Margaret's writing as emasculating William:

---

41 Cuirassiers were cavalrymen dressed in three-quarter armour unlike most mounted soldiers, who by the mid-seventeenth century only wore a corselet , that is, a breast and back pieces, a 'pot' on the head and a thick buff coat. Heavily armoured troopers disappeared during the course of the sixteenth and seventeenth centuries as the spread of firearm weapons rendered armour useless. Moreover, lightening the rider allowed them to ride lighter, more nimble horses into battle. In the context of this quotation, however, the reference to cuirassiers serves to emphasise how, as they were more heavily armoured, they could 'bear the shock' better.

42 Cavendish Margaret, *The Blazing World & Other Writings*, (ed.) Lilley Kate (Harmondsworh: 1994) 197–8.

43 Ibid., 194. Margaret's use of her wit to create a fantastic 'volante' or carriage, predates the earliest entry in the OED by over a hundred years.

Newcastle and's Horse for entrance next strives
Well Stuff'd was his Cloakbag, and so was his Breeches
And unbutt'ning the place where Nature's Posset-maker lives
Pull'd out his Wife's Poems, Plays, Essays and Speeches.[44]

Conclusion

Writing—funded and encouraged, of course, by William—did give Margaret an undoubted illusion of autonomy. In the preface to *The Blazing World*, she famously proclaims that she is 'as ambitious as ever any of my sex was, is or can be; which makes, that although I cannot be *Henry the Fifth* or *Charles the Second* yet I endeavour to be *Margaret* the *First*' by making her own world to govern.[45] In the world of seventeenth century England, any such dream of absolute authority, of taking the reins of government was, as Margaret knew, a case of flogging a dead horse (a phrase which appears in 1638 in Richard Brome's *The Antipodes*).[46] For all William's innovative *New Method* which recognised the will to freedom, the wisdom of the horse and faultlines in patriarchal authority, Margaret Cavendish could not assume the controlling position of the rider in real life. In the Preface to *Sociable Letters* she chooses a telling metaphor to express her disdain for her critics. 'I matter not their Censure, for it would be an Endless Trouble to me, to Answer every ones Foolish Exception; an Horse of a Noble Spirit Slights the Bawling of a Petty Cur, and so do I.[47]

Selective Bibliography

Andrews Launcelot, *Learned and Pious Exposition of the Ten Commandments* (London, 1650).

Bouwnd Nicholas, *A storehouse of comfort for the afflicted in spirit*, for example, was published 'for the further good of all those that loue and feare the Lord' (London: 1604).

Brome Richard, *The Antipodes* (London: 1640).

---

44   Cited in Classen Constance, *The Colour of Angels: Cosmology, Gender and the Aesthetic Imagination* (London: 1998), 101, who discusses the importance of fantasy to Margaret.

45   Cavendish Margaret, *The Blazing World & Other Writings* 124.

46   Brome Richard, *The Antipodes* performed in 1638 by the King's Men (London: 1640). Blason says that 'All went, as they say, for a dead horse' B1v.

47   Cavendish Margaret, *Sociable Letters* (1664) sig. C2.

Cavendish Margaret, *Natures picture drawn by fancies pencil to the life being several feigned stories, comical, tragical, tragi-comical, poetical, romanicical, philosophical, historical, and moral* (London: 1671).

Cavendish Margaret, *Observations Upon Experimental Philosophy* (London: 1668).

Cavendish Margaret, *Playes written by the thrice noble, illustrious and excellent princess, the Lady Marchioness of Newcastle* (London: 1662).

Cavendish Margaret, *Sociable Letters* (London: 1664).

Cavendish Margaret, *The Blazing World & Other Writings*, ed. Lilley Kate (Harmondsworh: 1994).

Cavendish Margaret, *The First Part of Nature's Daughters, Beauty, Love and Wit* in Cavendish Margaret, *Playes* (London: 1662).

Cavendish Margaret, *The life of the thrice noble, high and puissant Prince William Cavendishe, Duke, Marquess and Earl of Newcastle* (London, A. Maxwell: 1667).

Cavendish Margaret, *The Philosophical and Physical Opinions, written by her Excellency, the Lady Marchionesse of Newcastle* (London: 1655).

Cavendish Margaret, *The worlds olio written by the Right Honorable, the Lady Margaret Newcastle* (London: 1655).

Cavendish William, *A New Method and Extraordinary Invention to Dress Horses, and Work Them according to Nature, as Also, To Perfect Nature by the Subtilty of Art: Which was never found out but by the Thrice Noble, High and Puissant Prince, William Cavendishe* (London: 1667).

Classen Constance, *The Colour of Angels: Cosmology, Gender and the Aesthetic Imagination* (London: 1998).

Edwards Philip, *Certain godly and learned sermons, preached by that worthy seruant of Christ M. Ed. Philips in S. Sauiors in Southwarke* (London: 1607).

Erbury William, *The great mystery of godliness Jesus Christ our Lord God and man, and man with God; one in Jesus Christ our Lord* (London: 1640).

Middleton Richard, *The carde and compasse of life Containing many passages, fit for these times. And directing all men in a true, Christian, godly and ciuill course, to arriue at the blessed and glorious harbour of heauen* (London: 1613).

Olbright Mae, "Using Sex: Margaret Cavendish's *The Lady Contemplation* and the Authorial Fantasy of Class Permanence", *Pacific Coast Philology* 38 (2003) 77–98.

Shakespeare William, *Mr William Shakespeares comedies, histories, & tragedies Published according to the true originall copies* (London: 1623).

Shakespeare William, *Much Ado About Nothing*, ed. McEachern Claire, Arden Shakespeare (London: 2007).

Van Orden Kate, *Music, Discipline, and Arms in Early Modern France* (Chicago: 2007).

Walker E., "'The Author of their Skill': Human and Equine Understanding in the Duke of Newcastle's 'New Method'", in Edwards P. – Enenkel K.A.E. – Graham E. (eds.), *The Horse as Cultural Icon: The Real and the Symbolic Horse in the Early Modern World* (Leiden: 2012) 327–50.

Whateley William, *A Bride Bush or a Wedding Sermon* (London: 1617).

11. Politics and Authority

∴

Courtly Rivalry: The Context for William Cavendish's Equestrian Buildings

Malcolm Airs

The remarkable equestrian buildings of William Cavendish can only be properly understood within the broader contemporary context of the veneration of the horse as a symbol of status and manhood and the care that was lavished on its architectural presentation. In seeking to provide that context it is necessary to consider the various ways by which his contemporaries responded to that obligation. The Great Horse, whether for riding or for pulling a richly decorated coach, was an essential possession of the English courtier household in the early modern period. It fulfilled a multitude of roles relating to skill, pleasure, status and rank. It embodied the virtues and taste of the owner and symbolised his elevated position in society. The origins for the admiration of the Great Horse lay with military prowess in the medieval period, based on their iconic role of carrying noble, plate-armoured men-at-arms, wielding a lance, into battle. However, as the firearm revolution increasingly rendered heavily armed and armoured cavalry obsolete during the course of the sixteenth century, such horses were no longer required. The term, 'Great Horse', did survive but was applied to parade horses or to those involved in virtuoso displays of skilled horsemanship, whether at the tilt or in the *manège*.[1] These aristocratic pastimes demanded new breeds of horse who were not only well-built but were also nimble and dexterous. They were greatly prized as valuable gifts that demonstrated allegiance and friendship. As they represented substantial financial investment, they were of pivotal importance in the self-fashioning image of the nobility and the aspirational gentry. Of course, the élite kept a range of

---

1 Treva Tucker argues that the French aristocracy lost their two defining qualities of military service and *vertu* (manliness) with the demise of the heavily armoured cavalry in the early sixteenth century. Mastering the refined skills of the *manège* enabled them to exhibit many of the same qualities inherent in the notion of *vertu* and to execute them with the courtly qualities of grace (*grazia*) and without effort (*sprezzatura*). Tucker, T., "Early modern French noble identity and the equestrian 'airs above the ground'", in Raber K. – Tucker T., eds., *The Culture of the Horse* (Basingstoke: 2005) 275–280.

horses, whose size, strength and conformation varied according to function but for whatever purpose they were used, their owners demanded the best.[2]

It is not surprising, therefore, that owners sought to house these magnificent beasts in carefully designed structures which catered not only for their welfare but also provided an opportunity for proud theatrical display. The 'stable revolution' that Giles Worsley identified in the Tudor and Jacobean period was not simply concerned with practical improvements in feeding and drainage arrangements, important though these developments were.[3] It was also a reflection of an extraordinary campaign of country house building in which equestrian buildings played a significant part. Stables were just as much an essential component of the country estate as both the house itself and the formal gardens and decorative lodges which formed their setting. It is a safe assumption that their appropriate architectural treatment and positioning were carefully considered by those who were responsible for commissioning the new houses, even if this is not always explicit in the surviving record. The careful delineation of the stables in the 1580 symmetrical plan for service buildings on the four principal axes of Wollaton Hall, Nottinghamshire, in the Smithson drawing in the RIBA collection is proof enough of that even if, in the execution of the building programme, the concept was dropped.[4]

Given their functional purpose as well as their potential for aesthetic pleasure, stables are particularly vulnerable to remodelling and replacement due to changing fashions in equine welfare and architectural taste. As a consequence, many of the renowned stables of the sixteenth and seventeenth centuries, such as those at Petworth House (Sussex), Theobalds (Hertfordshire), Fonthill House (Wiltshire) and Burley-on-the-Hill (Rutland), have been long demolished and can only be recalled through fragmentary documentation, estate surveys and topographical paintings.[5] Even where their basic fabric survives, many stables have been so radically altered that it is often difficult to reconstruct their original form. The stables at Osterley Park (Middlesex) can be cited as an exemplar of the sort of periodic change that has taken place over the centuries since its original construction. As a result of the recent analysis by Paul Drury and Richard Peats it is now possible to understand the complexities of

2   Edwards P., *Horse and Man in Early Modern England* (London: 2007) 3.

3   Worsley G., *The British Stable* (New Haven & London, 2004) 21.

4   RIBA Drawings Collection, Smythson I/25.

5   See particularly Harris J., *The Artist and the Country House* (London, 1979) and Knyff Leonard & Kip Jan, *Britannia Illustrata* ... (London, 1707, facsimile reprint Bungay, Suffolk: 1984).

this important building with a high degree of confidence.[6] Placed in a prominent position so that it was clearly visible on the approach to his new house, it was built around three sides of an open courtyard for Sir Thomas Gresham, the Elizabethan merchant and financier. Dendrochronological research confirms that all three sides of the courtyard were built to a uniform design in 1566. The preceding year Gresham had entertained Queen Elizabeth on progress at his newly completed house and could only offer temporary stable accommodation for her retinue. The knowledge that she would visit Osterley again in 1567 seems to have prompted Gresham to embark on the construction of the stable complex. Examination of the structure suggests that it was built at great speed with the design evolving even as the work proceeded in order to ensure suitable accommodation for the royal household on their second visit. (Fig. 6.1) As first finished, it seems to have provided temporary lodgings in the projecting west wing with a barn for fodder in the matching east wing and a grand stable in the connecting north range with two staircase towers in the re-entrant angles. Having fulfilled its immediate need to host the queen, the building was then adapted on a more permanent basis to serve the estate. A second barn was added to the north-east in 1567/8 and the eastern staircase tower was rebuilt on a larger footprint to allow the formation of an access passage.

Early in the seventeenth century the stables were refitted with heel posts for the horses and the central door case was inserted to give greater architectural emphasis. The next major change took place around 1714 when the estate was in the ownership of the Child family of bankers. The north wall of the stables was rebuilt following a collapse and the central clock tower was added. It was probably at this time that the stalls arcade, the principal decorative feature of the interior, was installed and the upper storey was converted into a hay loft. In the middle of the eighteenth century the barn in the east range was converted to create the Grand Stable with its Doric arcade, and a coach house was formed at the south end. Since that date there have been a number of minor alterations but the essential Tudor character of the building has remained intact. Gresham's stable was notable as the largest known non-royal stable yard in the Elizabethan period. Despite the subsequent alterations and the loss of the house that it was built to serve, it continues to impress as a magnificent architectural embellishment of his estate. Clearly, it had a practical function but it was also a statement of his allegiance to the Crown, whose finances he had successfully managed on the Antwerp money market.

---

6   Drury McPherson Partnership, *The Stables, Osterley Park, Isleworth, Middlesex, Conservation Plan, 2009.*

FIGURE 6.1 *The stable courtyard at Osterley from the south showing the rebuilt eastern tower and the added central doorcase and clock turret.*
COPYRIGHT MALCOLM AIRS.

It is unfortunate that the original decorative scheme of the interior of the stable at Osterley does not survive. We know very little about how the interiors of sixteenth century stables were presented, and the fittings that do survive from the early part of the seventeenth century, such as the stalls at Dunster Castle (Somerset), dating from 1617 are at best incomplete. (Fig. 6.2) A tantalising indication of their opulence is provided by an estimate of 12 October 1623 for the fitting out of the stable range at Blickling Hall (Norfolk). This was built as part of a symmetrical approach to the entrance front of the new house under construction for Sir Henry Hobart, Lord Chief Justice of the Common Pleas. The placing of the stable in this prime location and its adornment with newly-fashionable shaped gables and decorative brick diaperwork is in itself indicative of the architectural importance attached to its function. The care that was taken with its architectural appearance was carried through into the internal fittings which were designed to show off the horses to their best advantage. The two-storeyed range incorporated various other offices with a floor to ceiling height on the ground floor of ten feet. (Fig. 6.3) The stable compartment, however, was made two feet higher to provide a more impressive setting for the eighteen horses that it housed. The internal walls were plastered and the floor was planked with wood in conformity with best current practice. The stable was 105 feet long and entered in the centre. The stalls on either side of the entrance 'acording to the plote' were highly decorative 'with pillers of dorica and arches over the Capitals with arkatrive freese and Cornish with french Racks and maingers with pillers and arches with heel peeses for the horse and bars between them...'.[7]

Sadly, these decorative fittings no longer survive nor does Hobart's 'stable at Highegate' which provided the inspiration for the design. However, the description with its classical vocabulary and its references to hanging bales and heel posts can be illuminated by consideration of the fittings of a small group of other stables of the period. Invariably, Doric was the chosen order for the arcading, no doubt because it symbolised the robust strength that was expected of a prize horse. Examples include the little-known early seventeenth century stable block at Shapwick Manor (Somerset), the stables at Whitmore Hall (Staffordshire), possibly built before 1597 and with a matching arcaded rack and manger,[8] and the stables at Peover Hall (Cheshire) of 1654.[9] (Fig. 6.4)

---

7   The estimate in the Norfolk Record Office (MC3/53) is transcribed as an appendix to Stanley-Millson C. – Newman J., "Blickling Hall: The Building of a Jacobean Mansion", *Architectural History*, 29 (1986) 33–35.

8   Illustrated in Worsley, *British* Stable, 36–37.

9   Ibid., 38–39.

FIGURE 6.2 *Interior of the stable at Dunster Castle with heel posts and hanging bales.*
COPYRIGHT MALCOLM AIRS.

FIGURE 6.3 *The stable range at Blickling Hall flanking the approach to the entrance of the house.*
COPYRIGHT MALCOLM AIRS.

FIGURE 6.4 *Stalls arcade at Shapwick Manor.*
COPYRIGHT MALCOLM AIRS.

The stable at Shapwick has a plain plaster ceiling above the cornice of the arcade and at Peover Hall there is a more ornate plaster ceiling decorated with strapwork and floral motifs. As Worsley comments, 'The treatment is what one would expect of a domestic interior, not a utilitarian space. There is no reason to believe that the Peover stables were exceptional and they clearly demonstrate that display was an important factor even in gentry stables'. A similar aspiration can be deduced from the alterations that Thomas Howard, Earl of Suffolk, made to his lodging range at Audley End (Essex) sometime before 1616 in order to create a grand stable and coach house. (Fig. 6.5) He introduced two canted bays with shuttered fenestration on either side of a large central entrance. The bays probably functioned as architectural spaces from which visitors could admire the horses in the two stable ranges, entered internally through dramatic arched openings on either side of the central coach house.[10]

The arcade to the stalls in the north range of the stable at Osterley was probably part of the refurbishment which took place *c.* 1714 and suggests that the established vocabulary of appropriate decoration persisted into the eighteenth century. Certainly the Grand Stable that was inserted in the east range later in that century perpetuated the tradition, with an arcaded screen to the stalls articulated by Doric pilasters. The design has been identified with the plate published in 1731 by Isaac Ware in his book on the *Designs of Inigo Jones and others.*[11] Ware does not give the source for his design but it can be demonstrated that it was part of the interior decoration of the stable and coach house range built in 1638–40 by Henry Rich, 1st Earl of Holland, at Holland House, a few miles down the road from Osterley.[12] (Fig. 6.6) Together with Blickling, this is the other major documented equestrian building of the first half of the seventeenth century. It was an immensely impressive structure, some 240 feet long with projecting flanking wings and an emphasised centrepiece.

Placed in view of the new west wing that Holland added to his house at the same time, the brickwork of the east elevation was painted in ochre to enhance its appearance on the approach from the house, whilst the rest of the building was left uncoloured. From the building accounts,[13] the surviving fabric and the plan and elevation published by Ware, it is possible to reconstruct the lavish interior of the stable, which occupied the southern half of the building.

---

10   Worsley, *British Stable,* 41; Drury P. – Smith P., "The Audley End Stable Block in the 17th Century", *English Heritage Review,* 5 (2010) 45–81.

11   Worsley, *British* Stable, 143.

12   Airs M., "Inigo Jones, Isaac De Caus and the Stables at Holland House", *The Georgian Group Journal* XII (2003) 141–60.

13   Leeds City Library, TN/EA/13/74.

FIGURE 6.5   *Audley End stable and coach house with added projecting viewing bays.*
COPYRIGHT MALCOLM AIRS.

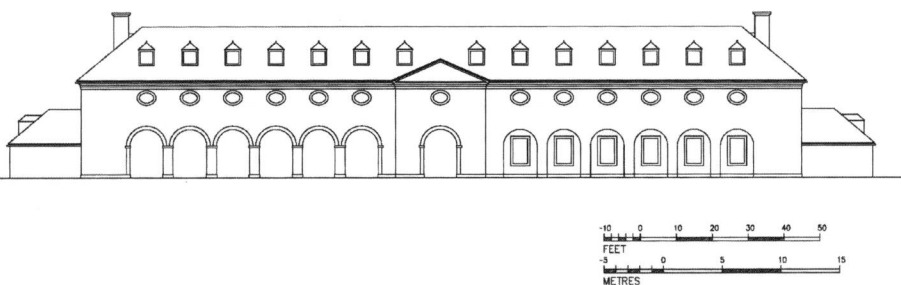

FIGURE 6.6   *Holland House stable and coach house. Reconstructed west elevation with the coach*
house to the left and the stable to the right of the central entrance.
REPRODUCED BY KIND PERMISSION OF MIKE THRIFT.

As drawn by Ware, the four brick arches, which framed the stalls, were defined
by Doric pilasters with central keystones and a moulded brick cornice above.
Each compartment was divided into two by hanging bales with heel posts
topped by 'great balls'. Richard Vesey, the carpenter, was paid just over £169 for
these, together with 'the double rack and manger 169 foote being made of the
best oken timber and the rack with a deepe architrave freeze and cornish and
having strong shutters to keepe in the strawe under the manger...'[14] The walls
and piers were lined with moulded panelling and all the woodwork, including
the fittings and the doors, were painted 'a sad Timber color in oyle' by no less
a craftsman than Matthew Goodrich, the assistant to John de Critz, the King's
Serjeant Painter.[15] The internal height of the stable was an impressive eighteen
feet and, together with its painted and carved decoration, it must have made
an opulent setting for the admiration of the eight Great Horses that it housed.
(Fig. 6.7)
　　The northern half of the building was a coach house entered by 'six paire
of great coach-house doores with doorecases to them' thirteen feet high and
ten feet wide also painted in the same colour scheme. Other than a double-
boarded partition, which divided it into two compartments, the account is
silent about its internal decoration but this was the largest and most architecturally ambitious coach house known to have been commissioned in the
period. Built by craftsmen from the Royal Works and possibly designed by
Inigo Jones or his collaborator, Isaac De Caus, it was a product of Holland's

14　　Ibid. fo. 8.
15　　Ibid., fo. 13.

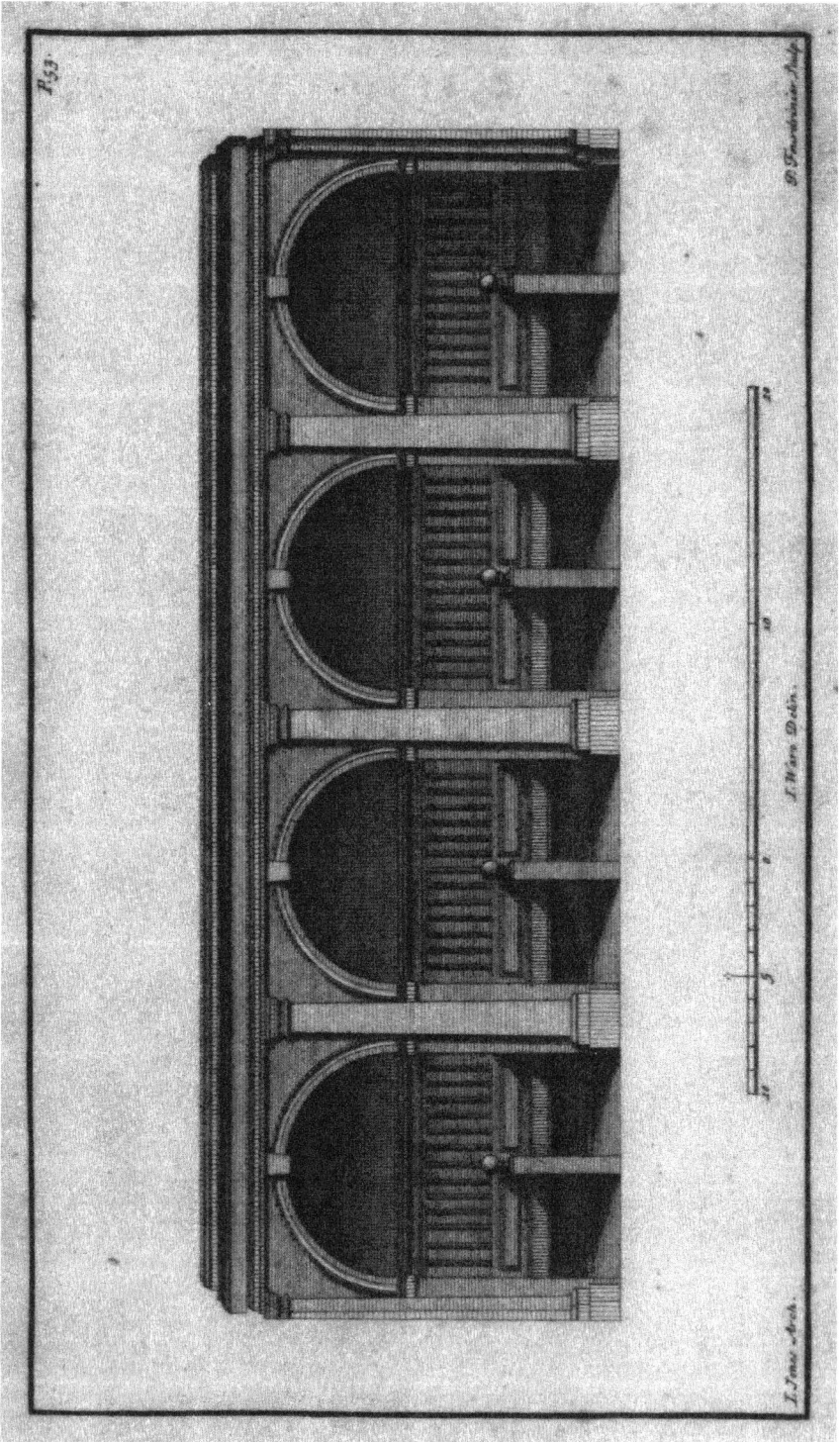

FIGURE 6.7 *Holland House stable. Engraving of the internal elevation of the stalls from Isaac Ware,* Designs of Inigo Jones and others.

easy access to influential officers of the court, even though it was commenced shortly after it was reported that he had 'retired to his house at Kensington in disgust' when he failed to gain the post of Lord High Admiral.[16]

The six coaches that it could accommodate would have been the height of luxurious expenditure. Sprung coaches with four large wheels were a comparative novelty. Introduced to England in the mid-sixteenth century, so quickly did they become assimilated into aristocratic culture that by 1617 one commentator claimed that there were 'few Gentlemen of any account ... who have not their coaches'.[17] They provided an opportunity for elaborate displays of wealth through their painted and gilded decoration, their luxurious upholstery and the matching teams of four to six horses. No doubt, the stables at Holland House were designed to accommodate and show off these precious beasts.

However, there were critics who saw the popularity of the coach as a decadent symptom of the decline of manly virtues. John Aubrey in his brief life of his neighbour Thomas Tyndale (1588–1672) records him complaining that

> Now-a-dayes every one, forsooth! Must have coaches, forsooth! In those dayes [at Queen Elizabeth's court] Gentlemen kept horses for a man-at-Armes, besides their Hackney and hunting horses. This made the Gentry robust and hardy and fitt for service ... Our Gentry forsooth in these dayes are so effeminated that they know not how to ride on horseback.
>
> The advantage that King Charles I had: Gentlemen ... kept good horses, and many horses for a man-at-Armes, and men that could ride them; hunting horses. Now we are come all to our Coaches forsooth! Now Young men are so farre from managing good horses, they know not how to ride a hunting nag or handle their weapons. So God help the King ...[18] Moreover, writing on Sir Philip Sidney, Aubrey cites Dr Pell, who had heard from ancient gentlemen that at that time a young Cavalier would as soon as ride out in a petticoat and waistcoat as be seen in a coach.[19]

As a leading exponent of the *manège*, one can be reasonably sure that Cavendish subscribed wholeheartedly to these critical sentiments. As he declared in his 1667 manual on horsemanship, 'What could be more comely or Pleasing than to see Horses go in all their several Ayres? And to see so excellent a creature with so much spirit to be so obedient to his rider?' (1667: 13) By then, he had

---

16   The Earl of Ilchester, *The Home of the Hollands 1605–1820* (London, 1937) 12.

17   Moryson Fynes, *An Itinerary* (London, J.Beale: 1617) III, 62.

18   Dick O.L. (ed), *Aubrey's Brief Lives*, (New Hampshire: 1999) 301.

19   Ibid., 279–80. I am grateful to David Adshead for drawing my attention to this entry.

a life-time of experience to draw upon, having, in his own words, 'Practised, and Studyed Horse-manship ever since I was Ten years old.'[20] That would have been at the end of 1603, the year that Henri IV of France sent over Monsieur de St. Antoine to the English court to teach the nine year old Prince Henry and a select group of high-born youths the art of the *manège* as an essential part of their education. As James I told his son, 'It becometh a Prince better than any other man to be a fair and good horseman.'[21] Presumably, the twenty-five high-born youths, including Cavendish, who were created Knights of the Bath when Henry was invested as Prince of Wales in June 1610, came from this circle.[22]

Henry, 1st Earl of Holland, was another of Prince Henry's companions who were created knights in June 1610, and this suggests that he, too, had belonged to the group who were educated in the *manège* by St. Antoine. Unfortunately, equestrian related issues were to cause a rift between him and Cavendish. As young men they had both been enthusiastic jousters and had participated together in the tilt, but in later life the reputation of Cavendish as a horseman far surpassed that of Holland. Both had voracious political ambitions but neither of them obtained the office that they coveted at court and they both took their failures badly. In spite of entertaining the king lavishly at Bolsover and Welbeck in 1633 and 1634, Cavendish did not obtain the hoped-for post of Master of the Horse. In 1636 he was moved to write to his wife from London that 'I find a Great dell of venum Agaynste mee ...'[23] We have already noted Holland's sulky absence from court when he embarked on his building project. In February 1639 they were rivals for the post of commander of the cavalry in succession to the Earl of Essex in the army being raised to face the rebellious Scottish Covenanters.[24] Although Holland had briefly been Master of the Horse in 1628, Cavendish clearly had better credentials and was bitterly 'disappointed & therby a litle (with noe little reason) discontented' when Holland was appointed.[25] No doubt the resentment was still simmering when Cavendish, having raised a force of 120 knights and gentlemen, joined other

20   He was baptised at Handsworth near Sheffield on 16 December 1593: Trease, G., *Portrait of a Cavalier: William Cavendish, First Duke of Newcastle* (London: 1979) 18; 41.

21   Strong, R., *Henry Prince of Wales and England's Lost Renaissance* (London: 1986) 41–42; 63–65; Reese M.M., *The Royal Office of the Master of the Horse* (London: 1976) 166.

22   Strong, *Prince Henry*, 65.

23   Hulse L., "William Cavendish c. 1593–1676", ODNB (Oxford, 2004) X, 654–63.

24   Fissel, M.C., *The Bishops' Wars: Charles I's Campaigns against Scotland 1638–1640* (Cambridge: 1994) 25.

25   Smuts M., "Henry Rich 1590–1649", ODNB (Oxford: 2004) XXXXVI, 664–68; Worsley L. – Addyman T., "Riding Houses and Horses: William Cavendish's Architecture For The Art of Horsemanship", *Architectural History* 45 (2002) 224.

cavalry units under the command of Holland at Berwick in June. Holland placed Cavendish's detachment at the rear of the cavalry advance and such was his humiliation that he challenged his general to a duel which was only prevented by the personal intervention of the king.[26]

The rivalry between the two men can be used as a background against which to consider the remarkable equestrian building activities of Cavendish. As far as we know, there were no grand coach houses at Welbeck or Bolsover or even at his London house in Clerkenwell. The obsession of Cavendish with horsemanship was focused on stabling and the provision of specialised buildings in which to demonstrate the art of the *manège*. At Welbeck, where he had spent his formative years, he commissioned John Smithson to design a riding house, which was built between 1621 and 1623. It is perhaps an indication of his priorities that he built the riding house first before he began the altogether grander stable range (described below) a couple of years later in 1625. The riding house, in contrast to the stable, was a comparatively simple building, measuring 120 foot by 40 foot and decorated with finials and a mannered pedimented doorcase. Internally, there was an impressive hammer beam roof with a cornice at the head of the walls on both sides. The wall at one end was pierced by a circular window, matched by a decorated arched window and pedimented doorcase at the other end. A raised viewing gallery was inserted in the 1660s for the elderly earl to enjoy the spectacle from an elevated position.

Elements of the structure still survive in a much altered form but most of the other riding houses built by his contemporaries have been demolished as the fashion for the *manège* waned. They include a group of royal examples at Richmond, Charing Cross and Newmarket built in the decade after 1610 but they were never common amongst the aristocracy. Viscount Cranborne proposed one at Hatfield but it is uncertain whether it was ever built. Lord Percy built one at Petworth (Sussex) around 1620 and considered another for his Thameside seat at Syon (Middlesex) a few years later. The Earl of Northampton built two, one at Ludlow Castle in 1618 as part of a proposed riding academy, and another on his country estate at Castle Ashby (Northamptonshire) in the same decade.[27] The latter survives in an altered form, as does the riding house at Wolfeton House, Charminster (Dorset), built in the 1590s for the Trenchard family, which has recently been confirmed as the earliest known riding house in the country, pre-dating that built for Prince Henry at St James's Palace in

26   Hulse, "William Cavendish", *ODNB* X, 654–63.

27   Worsley G., "Inigo Jones and the Hatfield Riding House", *Architectural History* 45 (2002) 230–37.

1607.[28] (Fig. 6.8) However, the royal riding house, though very similar in design to the one at Wolfeton, was somewhat larger, measuring 128 feet by 43 feet against 100 by 35 feet.[29]

The total of known private riding houses on country estates is pretty small, their scarcity due partly to loss over time but mainly because interest in the *manège* among the English aristocracy was never as high as it was on the continent.[30] Yet, over the course of his lifetime Cavendish is associated with no less than three of them, all in different locations. Welbeck was the first, and the riding house that he established in Ruben's studio in Antwerp during his years of exile was almost certainly the second. This must have been an especially theatrical space. It was renowned throughout Europe and it attracted a constant stream of visitors. As Cavendish himself noted with pride in the English edition of his book on horsemanship, it 'was often so full, that my Esquier... had hardly Room to Ride'.[31] The third riding school that he built at Bolsover has been subjected to lengthy scholarly debate as to its true position in this sequence. Lucy Worsley and Tom Addyman set out the case for a date in the 1630s but, as Adrian Woodhouse argues in an earlier chapter in this book, it was almost certainly built in the 1660s after his return to England.[32] It can be seen as the culmination of his equestrian ideal, conceived after the publication of the first edition of his treatise and heralding his re-establishment on one of his ancestral estates. Architecturally, it is far more ambitious than his first riding house at Welbeck, with showy elevations exhibiting mannerist details in the central doorcase and the dormer windows. The interior decoration by way of contrast was relatively restrained with plain plastered walls and ceiling concentrating the attention of the spectator on the intricate exercises executed by the horses and their riders. The only concession to display was the decorative frame of the viewing gallery, emphasising the privileged status of those who had access to this prime space and perhaps reflecting Cavendish's advancing years, as at Welbeck where a similar gallery had been inserted around the same time.

---

28   Rodwell K.A., "The Architecture of Entertainment: Two Examples of a Late Sixteenth-Century Building Type", *Archaeological Journal* 148 (1991) 269–95. For the date see *Vernacular Architecture* 44 (2013) 83–84. There was possibly another early 17th century riding house in Dorset at Wimborne St Giles, built for Sir Anthony Ashley, but this has later been converted into stables, *RCHM Dorset* (1975) v, 97.

29   Strong, *Prince Henry*, 64.

30   See Edwards below, 301.

31   Worsley – Addyman, *Riding Houses*, 217.

32   Ibid.; see Woodhouse above, 58.

FIGURE 6.8 *Wolfeton riding house.*
COPYRIGHT MALCOLM AIRS.

Adjoining the riding school at Welbeck is a slightly lower building with a dor-mered roofline called 'La boutique de Marechall' on Diepenbeke's illustration, where Cavendish's Master of the Horse lodged in generous accommodation with direct access to the riding school. John Mazin, a Frenchman, occupied this post. Although he first appears in the records in 1632 as John Mazin 'of Welbeck, gent', he had probably resided at Welbeck since the building of the riding house.[33] As Cavendish's protégé, he acted as 'guinea pig' for his master's methods and is depicted in many of the plates that accompany the French version of his manual, executing various *manège* movements. Naturally, Cavendish praised the skill of his pupil, declaring that 'the best Horse-man, that ever I know, is one of my own Breeding, and rides by my Method'. He served under Cavendish as Captain of a troop of horse and went into exile with him after the defeat at Marston Moor on 2 July 1644. Given Cavendish's asser-tion that horses trained in the *manège* made excellent cavalry mounts, it would be interesting to know how Mazin fared on the battlefield.

At Bolsover the stable at the western end was an integral part of the overall design, unlike the two building campaigns at Welbeck. (Fig. 6.9) It was given an imposing entrance doorway from the courtyard, which matched the entrance to the riding school and through which the earl and his guests could pass to admire the tethered horses within. The fittings have long since been removed but they were undoubtedly of a similar character to the decorated fittings that have been noted elsewhere. Certainly, the fragment of surviving cornice at the east end suggests a high standard of finish. It was a much more mature design than his earlier stable at Welbeck. Although that stable was demolished in the mid-eighteenth century when the riding school was converted into more mod-ern stabling, its appearance is known from John Smithson's plan and elevation of 1625 and the illustration by Abraham Diepenbeke in Cavendish's *Méthode Nouvelle et invention Extraordinaire de dresser les chevaux* of 1658 where a groom is shown proudly leading a handsome stallion in the foreground.[34] (Fig. 6.10) Some modifications seem to have been made to Smithson's design in the execution of the building but in Diepenbeke's elevation it was a singular building with a curious mixture of motifs. The high windows were crowned with alternating triangular and segmental pediments in the classical idiom introduced by Jones at his Whitehall banqueting house. The central entrance also had a segmental pediment but the hayloft was ventilated by a row of

33   Worsley, L., *Cavalier: A Tale of Chivalry, Passion and Great Horses* (London: 2005) 296, fn. 7.

34   Smith P., "Welbeck Abbey and the 5th Duke of Portland: Eccentricity or Philanthropy", in Airs M. (ed), *The Victorian Great House* (Oxford, 2000) 151; RIBA Drawings Collection, Smythson III/5–6.

FIGURE 6.9 *Bolsover stable and riding house.*
COPYRIGHT MALCOLM AIRS.

FIGURE 6.10 *Welbeck stable. From William Cavendish,* La Méthode Nouvelle, *plate 9.*
COPYRIGHT ELAINE WALKER.

gun-loops with rusticated pilasters below. The two flanking circular towers were terminated below the eaves of the main body of the stable with shaped onion domes. The interior had a stone-vaulted ceiling and the heel posts and mangers were also of stone, unlike the wooden fittings which were universal in all the other contemporary stables. Another unusual feature was the diversion of a stream through the building to take away the waste from the horses. It must have been a striking building in which to display his horses to privileged guests. The gun-loops, domes, pilasters and the vaulted interior might well have been self-conscious symbols of medieval chivalry already present in the Little Castle at Bolsover, and the running water might equally be a reference to the cleansing of the Augean Stables by Hercules as Worsley and Addyman suggest[35] but there can be little doubt that it graphically demonstrates Cavendish's obsessive concern for the care and display of his horses.

The focus of the building activities of his contemporaries was mainly on their houses, in tune with the sentiment of Sir Henry Wotton that 'Every Mans proper *Mansion* House . . . [is] the *Theater* of his *Hospitality* . . . an *Epitome* of the whole *World* . . .'[36] Their service buildings, including stables and in some instances coach houses, were complementary components of their architectural vision. Certainly, Cavendish did not neglect his obligation to provide a domestic stage suitable to his rank. At Bolsover he completed the work started by his father on the Little Castle, created the walled garden and built the magnificent terrace range. At Welbeck he made various alterations and additions to his ancestral home in order to entertain the king in 'such an excess of feasting, as had never before been known in England'.[37] In London he built a new house in Clerkenwell in order to pursue his ambitions at court. On his return from exile he made further domestic additions to Bolsover, and late in his life he embarked on a new mansion at Nottingham Castle. But what set him apart from his contemporaries was the sheer number of buildings that he devoted to his beloved horses. He established no less than three riding houses and a similar number of grand stables. Although he never built a coach house, he did create a five mile racetrack at Welbeck with six meetings a year. In his devotion to the architecture of the horse he was truly exceptional even in an age of great aristocratic builders.

Like Osterley, Audley End and Blickling, the approach to Welbeck was carefully contrived to ensure that Cavendish's equestrian buildings featured prominently in the vision of his visitors. They would have been left in no doubt that

---

35   Worsley – Addyman, *Riding Houses*, 224.

36   Wotton Henry, *The Elements of Architecture* (London, John Bill: 1624) 82.

37   Hulse, "William Cavendish", ODNB X, 654–63.

they were entering the household of a man who took pride in his horsemanship. Welbeck was entered by taking a route through an architectural gateway into the Great Court defined by the riding house and Captain Mazin's lodging on the north side and the stables on the west side. Having crossed the court and admired both sets of buildings, the gatehouse to the mansion was tucked away in the south-eastern corner. At Bolsover, the riding house and stable range dominated the approach from the town and formed the southern side of the entrance court, with the grand state apartments away to the west. As at Welbeck, it was the impressive provision for his horses that was encountered before entering the domestic part of the house. The distinctive mannerist architecture of both sets of equine buildings offers a tantalising glimpse into the cultural mind of Cavendish. It was far removed from the aesthetic taste of his great rival, Henry Holland, as displayed in the courtly classicism of his stable and coachhouse range at Holland House and reflects a unique and very personal contribution to the architectural patronage of the seventeenth century.[38]

Selective Bibliography

Airs M., "Inigo Jones, Isaac De Caus and the Stables at Holland House", *The Georgian Group Journal*, XIII (2003).

Drury P. – Smith P., "The Audley End Stable Block in the 17th Century", *English Heritage Review*, 5 (2010).

Edwards P., *Horse and Man in Early Modern England* (London: 2007).

Harris J., *The Artist and the Country House*, (London, 1979).

Rodwell K., "The Architecture of Entertainment: Two Examples of a Late Sixteenth-Century Building Type", *Archaeological Journal*, 148 (1991).

Worsley L. – Addyman T., "Riding Houses and Horses: William Cavendish's Architecture For the Art of Horsemanship", *Architectural History*, 45 (2002).

Worsley G., "Inigo Jones and the Hatfield Riding House", *Architectural History*, 45 (2002).

Worsley G., *The British Stable*, (New Haven & London, 2004).

---

38   For a discussion on the architectural taste of Cavendish, see Lucy Worsley, "The Architectural Patronage of William Cavendish, Duke of Newcastle (1593–1676)", *Trans. AMS*, 50 (2006) 37–68.

CHAPTER 7

William Cavendish, Galileo, Hobbes and the Mechanical Philosophy

Timothy Raylor

William Cavendish's patronage of what we call science but which he and his contemporaries incorporated under the broad banner of 'philosophy' encompassed a wide range of theoretical and practical disciplines. These embraced such areas of natural philosophy as alchemy, chemistry and optics, both practical (telescopy and lens grinding) and theoretical (the operation of light, as a route to a more general study of the processes of sensation and reaction); closely connected to these interests was a keen concern with physiology and psychology, both human and animal, and ethics. Other broadly philosophical interests included the civil science of politics (in which he wrote two famous letters of advice to Charles II), the *manège* (on which he published two huge printed volumes) and swordmanship (on which 'noble science' he wrote a long, unpublished manual). Assisting him in these enterprises was a disparate group of thinkers, among whom were direct dependents like Robert Payne, who served him during the 1630s not only as chaplain, but also as secretary, chemical operator and literary assistant; more distant clients like Walter Warner, who explored questions of optics and perception on his behalf, and Thomas Hobbes, who contributed to these discussions and also, more famously, elaborated at Welbeck the foundations for a science of politics—foundations ultimately written up and circulated as *The Elements of Law* (1640).[1] Also involved were

---

* A version of this argument was presented at a conference on Cavendish's cultural patronage at Oxford in 2002. I am most grateful to Malcolm Airs for the invitation to speak there. Thanks to Stuart Huntley for discussions about and demonstrations of Cavendish's fencing technique, to Elaine Walker for information about his horse-training methods and to Adrian Woodhouse for explaining to me the workings of the Bolsover water supply. Noel Malcolm offered helpful comments on an earlier version of the argument. All errors and misjudgements are my own.

** In most of the essays in this volume the subject is called 'Cavendish' but here, where necessary, he is named 'William' or 'William Cavendish' to distinguish him from his brother, Sir Charles Cavendish.

1 On Payne, see Thomas Hobbes, *The Correspondence* 2 vols., (ed.) Malcolm N. (Oxford: 1994) II 872–77; Feingold M., "A Friend of Hobbes and an Early Translator of Galileo: Robert Payne

---

international correspondents like René Descartes, who answered Cavendish's queries about psychology, physiology and the passions (particularly in regard to animals) during the middle 1640s, and who later in that decade attended a dinner at Cavendish's Paris establishment aimed at reconciling him with Hobbes.[2] To the modern historian, Cavendish's range of contacts and affinities forms a bewildering congeries that does not readily lend itself to analysis and classification.[3]

In addition to its alarmingly miscellaneous (one is tempted to say indiscriminate) character, the fragmentary nature of the available evidence inhibits the construction of a complete and coherent account of Cavendish's scientific patronage. We rely upon hastily scribbled notes among his surviving papers; upon allusions in his writings in other fields and other genres—in particular, upon his extensive literary works; upon brief asides in the sizeable *oeuvre* of his loquacious second wife, Margaret; and upon inferences from the surviving papers of his brother, Sir Charles. But most of all we rely upon snippets of surviving correspondence by others: upon letters written to and from his several estates by members of his circle, the largest number of which cover a brief period of only two or three years in the middle 1630s. As the fragmentary nature of the surviving evidence allows one to put together only a few pieces of what is clearly a much larger picture, the risk of distortion is high. Can we be confident that the preponderance of evidence for scientific patronage from the earlier years of Cavendish's career and the almost complete absence of evidence of similar interests in his later years reflects a substantive shift in his intellectual priorities as opposed to a fluke in the surviving documentation? Lisa Sarasohn believes that we can be; and she has erected on this foundation a well-argued reading of Cavendish's patronage that highlights a radical shift

---

of Oxford", in North J.D. – Roche J.J. (eds.), *The Light of Nature* (Dordrecht: 1985) 265–80; on Warner, see Prins J., "Walter Warner (ca. 1557–1643) and his Notes on Animal Organisms" (PhD dissertation, University of Utrecht, 1992). For a brief, valuable sketch of Ben Jonson's involvement with members of the circle, see Donaldson I., *Ben Jonson: A Life* (Oxford: 2011) 409.

2 Adam C. – Tannery P. (eds.), René Descartes, *Oeuvres*, rev. ed., 11 vols. (Paris: 1996) IV, 188–92, 325–30, 568–77; Clark A. (ed.), John Aubrey, *'Brief Lives', chiefly of Contemporaries, set down by John Aubrey, between the Years 1669 & 1696*, 2 vols. (Oxford: 1898) 1, 366; Hobbes, *Correspondence*, II, 827.

3 Since first writing this paragraph a valuable and sumptuously illustrated overview of the period of Cavendish's exile has appeared: Van Beneden B. – de Poorter N. (eds.), *Royalist Refugees: William and Margaret Cavendish in the Rubens House 1648–1660* (Antwerp: 2006); so also has Lucy Worsley's racy, fictionalised *Cavalier: A Tale of Chivalry, Passion, and Great Houses* (London: 2007).

after the Restoration, from science to the arts: a shift she accounts for by reference to the establishment of the Royal Society, which, she argues (in the wake of Steven Shapin and Simon Schaffer) centralised and institutionalised scientific research, thus creating an atmosphere hostile to the operation of individual patrons.[4] One wonders, however, whether Cavendish noticed or, if so, was ruffled by any such large-scale, long-term shift towards the institutionalisation of knowledge.[5] Indeed, he remained active as a sponsor of his wife's natural philosophical speculations and publications throughout the 1660s.

The fragmentary character of the evidence involves another stumbling block for the construction of a coherent account of Cavendish's scientific patronage: lack of direct access to his perspective on such matters. Most of the available evidence derives from family members and associates, all of whom had, to varying degrees, their own intellectual agendas. Accounts of Cavendish's scientific patronage—obliged to rely heavily upon the papers of his brother, Sir Charles—invariably either assume, imply or conclude that Sir Charles, rather than William, was the real force behind the brothers' sponsorship of scientific research.[6] The absence of a clear delineation of the goals and priorities driving the latter's scientific interests, moreover, almost obliges the interpreter to search for a single unifying principle to account for their bewildering range. Thus, for example, Richard Tuck suggested in 1988 that the Welbeck interest in optics and mathematics was probably grounded in the brothers' awareness of 'the *military* implications of both', adding that 'the Cavendish brothers were heavily involved in military matters'.[7] In 1989 Tuck strengthened the claim, implying that the entire range of the Cavendish brothers' scientific research could be explained as the product of 'a consuming interest in military technology', an interest to which Tuck now subordinated William Cavendish's passion for horses, which were, he notes, 'still centrally important in warfare'.[8] While the last claim is no doubt true, there is little

---

4   Sarasohn L.T., "Thomas Hobbes and the Duke of Newcastle: A Study in the Mutuality of Patronage before the Establishment of the Royal Society", *Isis*, 90 (1999) 717, 735–7.

5   I propose an alternative view of this period in "William Cavendish as a Patron of Philosophers and Scientists", in Van Beneden – de Poorter, *Royalist Refugees*, 82.

6   Jacquot J., "Sir Charles Cavendish and his Learned Friends", *Annals of Science* 8 (1952) 13–27, 175–91; Feingold, "A Friend of Hobbes", 275. There is now a full, scholarly edition of Sir Charles's correspondence with the mathematician, John Pell: Malcolm N. – Stedall J., *John Pell (1611–1685) and his Correspondence with Sir Charles Cavendish: The Mental World of an Early Modern Mathematician* (Oxford: 2005).

7   "Hobbes and Descartes", in Rogers G.A.J. – Ryan A. (eds.), *Perspectives on Thomas Hobbes* (Oxford: 1988) 28.

8   Tuck, R. *Hobbes* (Oxford: 1989) 12–13.

evidence in his extensive writings on the *manège* to suggest that Newcastle's intense and lifelong passion for horses was driven exclusively or even primarily by a narrow concern for their military utility.[9] Although he regularly mentions the military utility of the *manège*, this is never his prime focus.[10] Military science was far from the centre of Cavendish's concerns: indeed, Clarendon would later complain that, even in executing his role as commander-in-chief of the king's northern forces during the civil war, he possessed neither interest nor real expertise in military matters.[11]

For the reasons I have outlined, I do not propose in this paper to attempt anything like a complete overview of Cavendish's scientific patronage but rather to take a close look at what appears to me to be the most assiduously pursued and significant aspect of that patronage. This concerned his early interest in what we now, somewhat loosely and anachronistically, think of as the mechanical philosophy: the attempt to offer accounts of natural phenomena based exclusively on the analysis of bodies in motion, stripped of any reference to spiritual powers or occult forces, and then to extend mechanical explanations into new areas.[12] To do so I shall be tying together and endeavoring to synthesize arguments and evidence that I have advanced in a series of publications;

---

9   Walker E., *'To Amaze the People with Pleasure and Delight': The Horsemanship Manuals of William Cavendish, Duke of Newcastle* (n.p.: 2010) 20; 28–32. On Cavendish's horsemanship there is a burgeoning literature, see, especially, Worsley L. – Härting U. – Keblusek M., "Horsemanship", in Van Beneden—de Poorter *Royalist Refugees*, 37–54; Raber R.K., "'Reasonable Creatures': William Cavendish and the Art of Dressage", in Fumerton P. – Hunt S. (eds.), *Renaissance Culture and the Everyday* (Philadelphia: 1999) 42–66; Graham E., "The Duke of Newcastle's 'Love [...] for Good Horses': An Exploration of Meanings", in *The Horse as Cultural Icon*, 37–69; Walker E., "'The Author of their Skill': Human and Equine Understanding in the Duke of Newcastle's 'New Method'", in *The Horse as Cultural Icon*, 327–50, and various essays gathered in this volume.

10   See, for example, the reference to its use in warfare or single combat at the end of a long discussion of its more general value as a marker of gentle status in Cavendish (1667: 48). Elaine Walker notes that the implied reader of Cavendish's works on the *manège* is a man of noble or gentle status (*'To Amaze the People'*, 46).

11   Macray W.D. (ed.), Edward Hyde, Earl of Clarendon, *The History of the Rebellion and Civil Wars in England Begun in the Year 1641*, 6 vols. (Oxford: 1888) III, 382–83.

12   On the terminological difficulties involved in using the phrase, see Gabbey A., "What Was 'Mechanical' about 'The Mechanical Philosophy'", in Palmerino C.R. – Thijssen J.M.M.H. (eds.), *The Reception of the Galilean Science of Motion in Seventeenth-Century Europe*, Boston Studies in the Philosophy of Science, 239 (Dordrecht, Boston & London: 2004) 11–23.

to these I shall be adding a few new pieces of information.[13] My account will argue for Cavendish's significance as a motivating force both in importing and translating into English works of Galilean mechanics and in promoting the application of mechanistic methods to fresh areas. But, it will also attempt to establish that while he may have inspired such adaptations within his circle, it was Hobbes who, in the mid-1630s, first brought to his attention the possibility of a mechanical philosophy of nature.

Cavendish, Patronage and Mechanical Philosophy

William Cavendish was, by the later-1630s, the sponsor or recipient of several works of Galilean science and, loosely construed, mechanical philosophy. Four documents are especially important. The first is a translation, prepared in 1635 by the Cavendish family chaplain, Robert Payne, of a work by Benedetto Castelli on the measurement of moving water, the *Demostrazioni geometriche della misura dell'acque correnti* (Rome, 1628):

1. Equall sections, equally swift, void equall quantity of water, in equall time.
2. Sections equally swift, that voyd equall quantity of water, in equall time, are equall.
3. Equall sections, that void equall quantity of water, in equall time, are equally swift.
4. When the Sections are vnequall, but equally swift; the quantity of water which passes by the firste shall haue the same rate to the quantity of water which passes by the second: that the first section hath to the second.[14]

This is the earliest dated of the documents of Welbeck mechanism, and it is, I suggest, the source and inspiration for the other three. The others, despite

13   Raylor T., "Thomas Hobbes and 'The Mathematical Demonstration of the Sword'", *The Seventeenth Century*, 15 (2000) 175–98; Raylor T., "Newcastle's Ghosts: Robert Payne, Ben Jonson, and the 'Cavendish Circle'", in Summers C.J. – Pebworth T.-L. (eds.), *Literary Circles and Cultural Communities in Renaissance England* (Columbia & London: 2000) 92–114; Raylor T., "Hobbes, Payne, and *A short tract on first principles*", *The Historical Journal* 44 (2001) 29–58.
14   British Library, Harley MS 6796, fols. 309–16 (310v). The translation is dated 1635. (Obsolete contractions are here, and in subsequent quotations from manuscript, silently expanded.)

their disparate subject matter, share the common approach of taking the geometrical method of mechanics—a method of deductive mathematical reasoning—from its traditional use as a tool for the analysis of the motions of simple machines and apply it to such far-flung and disparate fields as physiology and psychology, horsemanship and fencing. Underlying this application is the assumption or expectation that all phenomena, even animal movements or psychic impulses, could be treated as mere matter in motion, and analyzed as one might a lever or an arrangement of beams and weights. These tracts deploy the mechanical method of subjecting physical phenomena to geometrical reasoning, providing sure demonstrations by building up from a small set of (supposedly) self-evident principles through a series of numbered propositions and corollaries, to indisputable deductive conclusions.

Payne's translation of Castelli's work can be compared to his own essay, also probably dating from the middle 1630s, 'touching the facility or Difficulty of the Motions of a Horse on streight lines, & Circular': an eccentric, not to say Quixotic, attempt to subject equine motion to a mechanist analysis in terms of ease and naturalness. Despite its mechanist aspirations, this account proceeds from a bedrock of scholastic assumptions about the greater ease and naturalness of rest over motion and of rectilinear over circular motion in physical (as opposed to celestial) bodies:

1. The most naturall & easy posture of the body of a Horse, at rest, is in a streight line: for in that posture every Horse, standing still, and at liberty, naturally putts himself.
2. All voluntary motion of his body hath somewhat of difficulty in it...
3. Of such motions, that is more difficult, to which the body, limmes, ioynts, or other instruments of motion, are naturally less fitt & pliant.
4. Since every Motion hath in it some difficulty, the greater, or swifter, the Motion, the greater is the difficulty to performe it.[15]

The essay seems to provide a loosely mechanistic account for principles of equine motion that William Cavendish deployed in his writings on the *manège*.[16]

---

15   Strong S.A. (ed.) *A Catalogue of Letters and Other Historical Documents exhibited in the Library at Welbeck* (London: 1903) 55, 237–40. The document was evidently at Welbeck in 1902; its present location is not known. On the date and authorship of this document, see Hobbes, *Correspondence*, ii, 875.

16   Walker, *'To Amaze the People'*, 36–8.

A similar reliance upon scholastic assumptions, which vitiates the attempt to provide a thoroughly mechanist account of light, sensation and the passions of the soul also shapes the third document. Recent research suggests that the so-called "Short Tract on First Principles", traditionally attributed to Hobbes is, in fact , another work written at Cavendish's behest by Payne:

5. Equall Agents are such as haue equall power.
6. Equall Agents, equally distant from the patient, moue it equally.
7. Equall Agents, vnequally distant from the Patient, moue it vnequally
8. Vnequall Agents, equally distant from the Patient, moue it vnequally.[17]

The formal, structural similarities between this passage and the excerpt quoted above from Payne's translation of Castelli are too striking to require much by way of comment.

The fourth and last document I wish to consider is Thomas Hobbes's recently identified essay on the location of the point of greatest strength in a sword, written during the mid-1640s, and which consists in the application of a problem in contemporary mechanics—a problem circulated by Marin Mersenne and discussed, *inter alia*, by Descartes—to the concerns of the practising swordsman:

When two swords meete, (supposinge the strength of the men equall) the effect of the strength wherewith one sword presseth is to the effect of the strength wherewith the other sword presseth, in proportion reciprocall to the distances of the point where the swords meete from the perpendiculars of the mens shoulders.[18]

The novel and intellectually daring extension of the method of mechanics to the spheres of physiology and psychology, to horsemanship and fencing, is perhaps the most distinctive product of Cavendish's scientific patronage. Written in Hobbes's hand, Cavendish marked it up for inclusion at the front of

---

17 British Library, Harley MS 6796, fols. 297–308 (297r). For the date and attribution of this
    tract to Payne, see Raylor, "Hobbes, Payne, and *A short tract*" and Malcolm N., "Robert
    Payne and the Short Tract", in *Aspects of Hobbes* (Oxford: 2002) 80–145. For the most per-
    suasive attribution of it to Hobbes, see Schuhmann K., "Le *Short Tract*, première oeuvre
    philosophique de Hobbes", *Hobbes Studies*, 8 (1995) 3–36.
18 British Library, Harley MS 5219, fols. 1–7 (1r). For the date, attribution, and context of this
    work, see Raylor, "Hobbes and 'The Mathematical Demonstration'".

his own treatise on fencing, "The Truth off the Sorde".[19] The mere existence of documents that are so clearly written to address his peculiar range of concerns weighs strongly against the prejudice that Newcastle's influence on the scientific researches of those in his circle was negligible.

Cavendish's Writings

Having established something of the coherence and wide-ranging application of Cavendish's concern with mechanics, I next wish to examine its effects upon his own writings on the sciences of the sword and of the *manège*, before turning to consider its probable causes and its overall significance for the introduction and development of the mechanical philosophy in England.

It is tempting to infer that Payne's tract on the motions of a horse and Hobbes's on the strength of the sword must have laid the methodological foundations for the development of Cavendish's much-vaunted new systems of swordsmanship and the *manège*. Sarasohn, for instance, suggests that 'Newcastle tried to establish himself as a philosopher in his own right by applying Hobbesian ideas' to his studies and following, in the process, 'a deductive methodology'.[20] This suggestion seems open to question in several respects. First, I find it hard to see that Cavendish had any pretensions to being a philosopher in any of the variants in which that role was then conceived.[21] He disdains the impractical learning of the schools, which encourages readers of Caesar's *Commentaries* to believe 'that they are greater soldeiers then Cesar, Pompey, Brutius, Caseus'; to Cavendish 'the greatest Clarkes are not the wiseste men'.[22] He sees himself, rather, as a great aristocrat, a prince even, a title he adopted in the later 1650s, over the doubts and concerns of the Garter King at Arms.[23] Intellectual interests were pursued in a resolutely amateur manner, and with careful regard for his social status. Although his wife would, in her biography of him insist that he was 'a good Natural and Moral Philosopher', this was not, she admitted, the product of study or labour but of 'his own natural understanding

---

19   Raylor, "Hobbes and 'The Mathematical Demonstration'", 175–77.
20   "Hobbes and Newcastle", 715, 732.
21   For those variants, see Condren C. – Gaukroger S. – Hunter I. (eds.), *The Philosopher in Early Modern Europe: The Nature of a Contested Identity* (Cambridge: 2006).
22   Slaughter T.P., *Ideology and Politics on the Eve of the Restoration: Newcastle's Advice to Charles II*, American Philosophical Society, Memoirs, 159 (Philadelphia: 1984) 22, 21.
23   British Library, Additional MS 70499, fols. 347–48; Additional MS 37998, fol. 82.

and observation': innate ability and experience were all that were required.[24] Cavendish was quick to provide such insights; to his client-assistants he left the working out of the details.[25] Where he asserted expertise was not in the academic or philosophical arena, but in that of the physical exercises he considered as markers of nobility: the *manège* of Great Horses and the use of the sword (1667: 5–14).[26] Secondly, as his readers know only too well, there is—despite his claims to have discovered new 'methods' of horse- and swordsmanship—nothing remotely deductive or even methodical in his writings. His approach is, by his own admission, unsystematic and anecdotal. Introducing his 1667 volume on the *manège*, Cavendish announces (rather than, strictly speaking, apologises for) the lack of organizational method therein:

> I have divided this whole Book in four Parts, and every Part in many Sections, and Paragraphs, wherein I never intended to observe any exact Method; I beseech my Readers, to take in good part, That I have however set down, as clearly as I could, without the Help of any other Logick, but *what* Nature *hath taught me, all the* Observations *about* Horses, *and* Horse-manship; *which I have made, by a long, and chargeable, though I must needs say, very pleasant, and satisfactory*, Experience. (1667: c2v).

Finally, as this excerpt makes evident, his new methods are founded not upon deductive methodology but upon personal experience. Upon realizing that all that had previously been said or written on the subject was deficient, he applied himself to study 'all the *Particulars* that concern the *Mannage*; that at last I Found this *Method*, which is as *True*, as it is *New*, and is the *Quintescence of Horse-manship*'. (1667: 42) Not scientific deduction, but practice is the source of his new method. But, not all practical experience is equally authoritative; innate aristocratic brilliance is also required. This is clear from Cavendish's insistence that one cannot simply buy one's way into success at the *manège*: 'For if *Good Qualities* could be Purchased with *Money*, every *Rich Citizen* would be a *Fine Gentleman*' (1667: 47). The same implication hovers around his wife's attribution of his new method to 'his own ingenuity and practice'—the term

---

24   Firth, ed., *Life of William Cavendish*, 106.
25   On Cavendish's use of assistants, see Raylor, "Hobbes, Payne, and *A short tract*", 46–47; and more generally, Raylor T., "Newcastle's Ghosts", 92–114.
26   Raylor, "Hobbes and 'The Mathematical Demonstration'", 177.

'ingenuity' carrying with it not only the sense of quickness or wit but also that of nobility of status.[27]

The impact of the theoretical works of Payne and Hobbes upon Cavendish's new methods is difficult to determine with certainty, but it was probably local and superficial. It is certainly possible that Payne's essay on the movements of a horse on straight lines and in circles, with its lengthy discussion of movement around a pillar, might have contributed to the method, with its apparently novel use of the single pillar; but it is equally possible that the essay was written to provide a physiological underpinning for conclusions Cavendish had already reached through his own experience and practice.[28] As far as I can see, nothing in either of his works on horsemanship is necessarily contingent upon Payne's essay.[29] Moreover, Cavendish attributes his new method to his discovery of the differential between the width of the horse's shoulders and that of its haunches—a matter not touched upon by Payne.[30]

Much the same may be said of the method of fencing discussed at length in Cavendish's unpublished treatise, "The Truth off the Sorde", the body of which does not appear to depend in any way upon Hobbes's essay on the strength of the sword. And yet, Hobbes's essay evidently had some impact on the shape of the final text of that treatise. Firstly, it is marked up for incorporation, without attribution, in the prefatory matter for that treatise, and is re-titled by Cavendish for that purpose "the mathematicall Demonstration off The Sorde".[31] It is evidently presented as a proof, a demonstration, of the general validity of a mathematical approach to swordsmanship, on the grounds that this is an area in which mathematical demonstration is possible. In addition, although it does not appear to be the foundation for the method discussed in the body of the treatise, it seems to have prompted Cavendish to add a prefatory discussion to his treatise, treating the movements of fencer in terms of planes, perpen-

---

27   Firth, ed., *Life of William Cavendish*, 113; *OED*, 'ingenuity', i (senses associated with 'ingenuum') and ii (senses associated with 'ingenium'). Karen Raber in "Cavendish's Horsemanship Treatises and Cultural Capital" argues for the democratizing effect of Cavendish's publication of his method; she is, however, sensitive to the complex implications of key terms such as 'breeding'.

28   This much is suggested by the passage quoted above, although, given Cavendish's tendency to incorporate silently the ideas of his associates, such evidence should be treated with caution.

29   I am grateful to Elaine Walker for discussions on this point.

30   NUL, Portland Papers, PwV 21, fol. 185v.

31   British Library, Harley MS 4206, fol. 9r; Harley MS 5219, fol. 1; Raylor, "Hobbes and 'The Mathematical Demonstration'", 192.

diculars and screws—the simple machines of mechanics.[32] Ultimately, however, as Stuart Huntley suggests, the place occupied by Hobbes's essay within Cavendish's treatise is not so much foundation as 'decorative flying buttress'.[33]

In both cases, therefore, the mechanist analyses supplied by Cavendish's clients seem to provide a kind of general warrant for an approach and for conclusions derived independently from his own experience. While these analyses had some impact on the presentations of the finished works, only in the most general and superficial manner do they appear to have informed those new systems themselves.

Evaluation of Cavendish's Role

The second issue I want to consider is the broader and perhaps more important question of Cavendish's role in the introduction and first attempted exposition of a mechanical philosophy in England. The textual evidence points to a moment, in the mid-1630s, at which works of Galilean mechanics were brought to Welbeck and translated (presumably for William Cavendish's benefit rather than that of his scholarly brother); their procedures and techniques then being extended, at William's behest, to the examination of equine and human motion. The evidence suggests that Cavendish underwent something of a conversion to mechanism in the mid-1630s. Up to that time his scientific interests appear to have been limited to questions of optics and sensation. There is, on the one hand, no evidence that he had any interest in mechanics, even in places where we might expect to find this; on the other hand, he appears up until this time to have been positively hostile to the application of geometrical techniques to physical bodies. But in and around 1635 we notice both a sudden fascination with Galilean mechanics and a concern with the possibility that geometrical analysis might help one determine the truth about matters of natural and moral philosophy.

Let us look first at the situation before 1635. We know that prior to 1635 Cavendish was interested in questions of optics and sensation. Hobbes claims that at Welbeck as early as 1630 he had expounded his theory that light and sound were but fancies in the brain produced by motion in the medium, though there is no suggestion that this was presented as part of a general

---

32   British Library, Harley MS 4206, fols. 10v–20r: an insertion, apparently a later addition, in
      the hand of an amanuensis, who worked for Cavendish during the middle and later 1640s;
      Raylor, "Hobbes and 'The Mathematical Demonstration'", 180.

33   Private correspondence, 20 December 2002.

mechanical philosophy. It seems, rather, to have been a hypothesis, the implications of which Hobbes had not yet developed.[34] It was in keeping with these optical interests that Cavendish charged Hobbes with acquiring for him a copy of Galileo's *Dialogo* in January 1634, a request which Hobbes was unable to fulfill because of the scarcity of the volume. Published in March 1632, the book had caused an immediate sensation, selling rapidly before a curial order in August suspending sales stopped supply.[35] Writing to Cavendish on 26 January 1634, Hobbes expressed hopes for the translation of the work currently being undertaken: 'I doubt not but that the Translation of it will here be publiquely embraced, and therefore wish extreamly that Dr Webbe would hasten it.'[36] The translator to whom he refers has been tentatively identified as Joseph Webbe, the Padua-trained physician, theorist of language teaching, astrologer and suspected papist, who was, in the summer of 1631, apparently assisting Cavendish at Welbeck in the construction of optical instruments.[37] An English translation of the *Dialogo* that survives as British Library MS Harley 6320 has generally, though once again tentatively, been identified as Webbe's.[38]

MS Harley 6320 is neither signed nor explicitly identified as the work of Webbe; but several features serve to associate it with Cavendish. Firstly, the rear

---

34   Hobbes, *Correspondence*, I, 102–103, 108.

35   Hobbes, *Correspondence*, I, 19; Galileo Galilei, *Dialogue Concerning the Two Chief World Systems*, transl. Drake S. Stillman (Berkeley & Los Angeles: 1967) xxiii. In his letter, Hobbes notes that he has heard rumours about the order ('I heare say it is called in, in Italy'). If Cavendish never managed to secure a copy of the first edition of the *Dialogo*, the family library sale catalogue of 1718 nevertheless suggests that someone in the family (perhaps Sir Charles) acquired a copy of the Latin translation of 1635, along with numerous other texts on mechanics, both ancient and modern. These included an edition of the works of Archimedes, works by Guido Ubaldo del Monte (the *Mechanicorum liber* of 1577 and the paraphrase of Archimedes of 1588), a copy of Galileo's 1638 *Discorsi e dimostrazioni matematiche*—a work 'concerning Two New Sciences pertaining to Mechanics & local motions'—as well as Mersenne's 1639 French abridgement of that seminal work; *Bibliotheca Nobilissimi Principis Johannis Ducis de Novo-Castro, &c.* (London: 1719) 20, 22, 24, 26.

36   Hobbes, *Correspondence*, I, 19.

37   Hobbes, *Correspondence*, I, 20 fn. 10; British Library, Additional MS 70499, fol. 145r (letter from Richard Andrews, 22 June 1631); Salmon V., "Webbe Joseph (*d. c.* 1630)", *ODNB, online* (accessed 11 Dec. 2013); Woolfson J., *Padua and the Tudors: English Students in Italy, 1485–1603* (Toronto & Buffalo: 1998) 281. On Webbe's theories of language teaching, see Salmon V., *The Study of Language in 17th-Century England* (Amsterdam Philadelphia: 1988) 4–31.

38   Hall M.B., "Galileo's Influence on seventeenth-century English scientists", and Drake S., "Galileo in English Literature of the seventeenth century", in McMullin E. (ed.), *Galileo, Man of Science* (New York & London: 1967) 406–7, 420; Hobbes, *Correspondence*, I, 20 fn. 10.

cover of the original binding (preserved inside the modern binding) is stamped with the initials 'W N'. Secondly, the manuscript exhibits the distinctive calligraphic features of texts prepared for Cavendish in what we might term the Welbeck house style. The prime exponent of that style was Cavendish's secretary, John Rolleston, who perfected his technique during the 1630s while working on the so-called "Newcastle Manuscript" of literary works by Donne, Jonson and others.[39] Although the translation is not in Rolleston's hand, it is copied in his distinctive manner, with elaborately elongated and clubbed ascenders and descenders, dotted D and C and otiose flourishes over terminal italic e.[40] The location of the manuscript in the Harleian collection of the British Library is congruent with this theory: many of the Harleian manuscripts were at one time at Welbeck, before passing into the Harley family by marriage.[41] That the conjectural identification of the translator as Webbe is also correct is confirmed by a poem preserved in Rolleston's hand among Newcastle's papers at Nottingham University Library, in which Cavendish thanks a Dr Webbe for a translation of what is evidently Galileo's *Dialogo*: 'Now Galileo, All his Booke a longe, | By Thee, speakes purely our best English tongue.'[42] Webbe's translation was evidently complete by the end of 1635 (old style, that is by 24 March 1636 new style), because a character in Cavendish's play, *Wits Triumvirate*, the manuscript of which is dated with that year, refers to a translation of the work having been completed: 'And for his book, although it was translated, it shall not be printed here'.[43] We might also note that a visiting Englishman informed Galileo himself in late November 1635 that the work had been translated into

---

39 On Rolleston and the features of this house style, see Kelliher H., "Donne, Jonson, Richard Andrews and The Newcastle Manuscript", *English Manuscript Studies 1100–1700* 4 (1993) 134–73 (145–50); Hulse L., "'The King's Entertainment' by the Duke of Newcastle", *Viator* 26 (1995) 359–64.

40 The hand of the translation may be distinguished from Rolleston's by means of its short-bodied h, a time-saving trick that had been recommended by the Italian writing master, Giovan Francesco Cresci: see Osley A.S., *Scribes and Sources: Handbook of the Chancery Hand in the Sixteenth Century* (London & Boston: 1980) 115.

41 On the sources of the collection, see Wright C.E., *Fontes Harleiani* (London: 1972); other Welbeck documents in the collection include MSS Harl. 3360, 4206, 4245, 4955, 6083, 6796, 7180.

42 NUL, Portland Papers, Pw V 25, fols. 14r–15r (14r).

43 Nelson C.A., (ed.), *A Critical Edition of Wit's Triumvirate, or The Philosopher*, 2 vols., Salzburg Studies in English Literature: Jacobean Drama Studies, 57–58 (Salzburg: 1975) I, 47–49 (date); II, 284 (IV.ii.375–6) (quotation). Nelson did not identify the play's author; for the attribution, see Kelliher, "Donne, Jonson, and The Newcastle Manuscript", 150–51.

English.[44] Although Webbe had left Padua before Galileo began his telescopic investigations, perhaps his Italian contacts might help to explain his acquisition of so scarce a volume as the *Dialogo*?[45]

Cavendish's poem not only confirms the long-suspected link between Webbe, Cavendish and the Harleian manuscript, it also sheds light on the context and purposes of the translation, substantiating the notion touched upon in *Wits Triumvirate*, that the translation was for private rather than public consumption.[46] The aristocratic Cavendish had no concern for the dissemination of new knowledge. Indeed, in his letter of advice for Charles II he would argue for the importance, for the sake of political stability, of limiting access to education by reducing the number of grammar schools and scholars.[47] In addition, it suggests something of the character of Cavendish's interest in the work: this was not in its mechanics, its analysis of celestial and terrestrial motion, but in its contribution to practical and theoretical optics:

---

44   Favaro A., *Le Opere di Galileo Galilei*, 20 vols. (Florence: 1890–1909; repr. 1929–39) xvi, 355/ no. 3217.

45   Mordechai Feingold suggests that many Englishmen, who studied at Padua during Galileo's residence there, may either have attended Galileo's public lectures or sought private tuition; "Galileo in England: The First Phase", *Novità Celesti e Crisi del Sapere, Annali dell'Istituto e Museo di Storia della Scienza* (1983) 411–20 (414).

46   The decision not to publish appears to have been unconnected with the appearance of a Latin translation of the original in 1635.

47   Slaughter, *Ideology and Politics*, 20. In her essay in this collection, "Cavendish's Horsemanship Treatises and Cultural Capital", Karen Raber argues against this view, treating Cavendish's 1658 *La Méthode Nouvelle* as an attempt to broadcast his method of equitation through publication. It is, however, arguable whether that work was really designed to broadcast the method, as opposed to asserting his mastery of it to an elite readership. And it is questionable whether the book was, in the modern sense, published, as opposed to privately printed. A full bibliographical study of the printing of the volume and an inventory of its surviving exemplars is required. Among evidence for private printing should be noted: the lavish size and beauty of the volume, with its elaborate plates illustrating Cavendish's aristocratic credentials and estates, which far outweigh the bare requirements of illustrating specific manoeuvres. For a discussion of the plates, see Walker, 'To Amaze the People', 140–63; Cavendish's defraying the cost of publication (Letter to Sir Edward Nicholas, 15 Feb. 1656, printed in Firth, ed., *Life of William Cavendish*, 206); the assignation of authority and privileges to Cavendish himself (1658: [2]fir–[2] f2v); For Cavendish's possession of the plates after publication (they survived in his family, to be reused for the 1737 reprint) see Cavendish (1743) iv; and, finally, the personal presentation of many (though not necessarily all) copies of the edition, see Steinkraus W.C., "Foreword" (1743L: iii); Walker, 'To Amaze the People', 5.

With this Booke, Natures secretts I will Diue;
With helpe of bettter, clearer, Perspectiue,
To see remotest Bodies; A Shipp Sayle
In Seas, see Earth, ruff Rockes, Curl'd woods, Hill Dale:
Men in Citties, walking by Moone light Day;
See them busy, but heare not what they say.
So multiply each thing in euery kind;
Like Swine wee shall bee, sighted see the wind,
Thinne Ayre, nay thinnest Beames, and how they lurke,
Which way they flowe, and which way they doe worke.[48]

What Cavendish hopes for from his translation of the *Dialogo* is new telescopic and microscopic insights (the reference to 'multiplication' is to 'multiplying glasses', or microscopes); his goal is a proper understanding of the nature of light. Cavendish's *Dialogo*, thus, looks like nothing so much as a fresh instalment of the *Siderius Nuncius* of 1610, with its startling telescopic revelations.[49] He shows not the slightest concern with what most would regard as the core of the book: the analysis of bodies in motion. Nor is there evidence for any such interest among the allusions to Galileo in Cavendish's play, *Wits Triumvirate*, which references Galileo's astronomical discoveries and his theory of tides.[50]

Further support for the view that, prior to 1635, Cavendish was largely indifferent to mechanics and unimpressed by the pretensions of those who would employ mathematics to account for bodies in motion comes from another source: Ben Jonson's complimentary epigram to Cavendish ('They talk of fencing and the use of arms', written probably in or soon after 1628) and his play *The New Inn* (written, probably with Cavendish in mind, in late 1628– early 1629).[51] These closely related documents suggest that, in the late 1620s, Cavendish could be counted on to despise those who fenced mathematically: the play makes much sport of those who do, alluding in Act II, Scene v to a duel between Euclid and Archimedes.[52] By the time he wrote his "Truth off

---

48   NUL, Portland Papers, Pw V 25, fol. 14v.

49   A copy of this work is listed in *Bibliotheca Nobilissimi Principis Johannis Ducis de Novo-Castro*, 24 (no. 210).

50   Nelson, *Wits Triumvirate*, I, 16–17.

51   Bevington D. – Butler M. – Donaldson I. (eds.), Ben Jonson, *The Cambridge Edition of the Works of Ben Jonson*, 7 vols. (Cambridge: 2012) vii 207; vi, 172; Riggs D., *Ben Jonson: A Life* (Cambridge, MA: 1989) 302; Rowe N., "'My Best Patron': William Cavendish and Jonson's Caroline Drama", *The Seventeenth Century* 9 (1994) 201–6.

52   Ben Jonson, *Works*, VII, 228.

the Sorde" in the middle 1640s, however, while reserving particular scorn for the elaborate geometrical confections of such works as Girard Thibault's 1628 *Académie de l'espée*, Cavendish, nevertheless, stridently insisted that in answer to the question 'muste one fighte mathematicalye I saye yes'.[53]

The immediate occasion of Cavendish's conversion to the mechanical philosophy seems to have been an encounter with Galilean mechanics that followed his acquisition of a translation of the *Dialogo*. As noted earlier, in 1635 Robert Payne translated into English a short treatise on hydromechanics by Galileo's star pupil, Benedetto Castelli. The "Geometricall demonstrations of the measure of running-waters" was taken from Castelli's *Demostrazioni geometriche della misura dell'acque correnti*, published in Castelli's *Della misura dell'acque correnti* of 1628. It seems likely that the impetus behind the interest in Castelli came not from William Cavendish but from Sir Charles, who took a profound interest in the mathematical sciences, both pure and applied (he later corresponded with Mersenne about questions in Galileo's mechanics), and also from Payne, who shared these interests and, in fact, made his translation from his personal copy of Castelli's work.[54] The relatively unlearned William, however, is a more obvious recipient of Payne's translation than the scholarly Sir Charles.

Castelli's work is generally regarded as the foundational text of the discipline of hydromechanics in its successful employment of the geometrical method to calculate the rate of a river's flow. The encounter with Castelli appears to have had a profound effect on Cavendish, sparking an interest in Galilean mechanics and a sense of its potential to settle those questions about light and sensation with which he had, for some years, been exercised—and perhaps also afford appropriate foundations for the right method of dressing horses. We find evidence for Cavendish's burgeoning interest in Galilean mechanics in Payne's translation, in November 1636, of Galileo's treatise *Le meccaniche*.[55] And, we find evidence for his sense of the general potential of the method in the other treatises Payne probably wrote for Cavendish at about this time: the "Short Tract on First Principles", and the "Considerations touching the... motions of a horse". Their close similarities in both form and method point to the conclusion that they represent attempts by Payne to extend the method of Galilean mechanics to areas of particular interest to Cavendish. The abandonment of the "Short Tract" in the midst of an attempt to define the faculties and

---

53   British Library, Harley MS 4206, fol. 8v.

54   Malcolm, "Robert Payne and the 'Short Tract'", 144. Payne's copy is now in the Savilian Collection of the Bodleian Library.

55   British Library, Harley MS 6796, fols. 317–30.

passions of the soul suggests that Payne was stumped by the difficulty of moving his mechanical analysis from physical to psychic phenomena.[56]

As I read the evidence, therefore, a fortuitous combination of texts, actors and interests at Welbeck led, in the middle 1630s, to the first English attempt to apply mechanist approaches to fields beyond those of traditional mechanics. While the attempt to furnish a mechanist account of 'the facultyes & passions of the soule' in the "Short Tract" may have been abandoned, the relatively late date of Hobbes's essay on the strength of two swords suggests that the application of mechanist approaches to other physical problems remained a continued preoccupation for Cavendish.

Evaluation of Hobbes's Role

Although it is not my purpose here to offer an account of Hobbes's more extensive effort to develop a full-blown analysis of the physical world in terms of bodies in motion, it seems appropriate to conclude this investigation by considering his role within the process I have just sketched out. Hobbes is, as I mentioned earlier, traditionally credited with the "Short Tract", which is seen as a turning point in his philosophical development. But if that work is in fact Payne's, we might reasonably wonder what part Hobbes played in the Welbeck effort to elaborate a mechanical philosophy.

The answer I think is that he contributed in four ways. Firstly, it seems clear that it was Hobbes who first—as early as 1630—introduced the Cavendish brothers to the possibility of a mechanical philosophy by introducing them to the idea that secondary qualities are nothing but psychic motions: 'that Light is a fancy in the minde, caused by motion in the braine'.[57] He claims as much on two separate occasions and I see no reason to disbelieve him.[58] But this insight—startling though it is—does not necessarily either depend upon or entail a fully mechanist account of the physical world. Galileo, for example, had offered a strikingly similar account of secondary qualities in *Il saggiatore* (1623), without pursuing the epistemological implications of his tantalising

---

56   That work on the "Tract" was abandoned is apparent both from structural anomalies in the text and from the fair condition of the manuscript; Malcolm, "Robert Payne and the 'Short Tract'", 134.

57   British Library, MS Harley 3360, fol. 3r.

58   Hobbes, *Correspondence*, I, 102–3, 108; Malcolm, "Robert Payne and the 'Short Tract'", 115–16.

remarks. His account almost certainly underlies Hobbes's.[59] But was Welbeck, as is traditionally believed, the source of Hobbes's knowledge of Galileo, or was it Hobbes who introduced Galilean science to Welbeck?[60] An allusion in a letter written during the summer of 1636 might suggest Cavendish's direct knowledge of *Il saggiatore*. Writing to Hobbes, he suggested 'That the variety of thinges is but variety of locall motion in the spirits or inuisible partes of bodies. And That such motion is heate'.[61] In chapter forty-eight of *Il saggiatore*, Galileo had written on the thesis 'Motion is the cause of heat', briefly expounding (for the first time since classical antiquity) a theory of the subjectivity of sensible qualities: 'many sensations which are deemed to be qualities residing in external subjects have no real existence except in ourselves, and outside of us are nothing but names'.[62] Galileo included the sensation of heat in this category, attributing it to the motion of tiny particles; Cavendish follows him in this. But, he adds to Galileo's analysis the idea that sensation is explainable solely in terms of motion, and he takes the novel step of inferring all sensation to derive from matter in motion, which motion he identifies as heat. In its emphasis on the universality of motion the allusion, then, appears to be more Hobbesian than Galilean.[63] And it seems to confirm Hobbes's claim that it was he who introduced to Welbeck the fundamental insight about the primacy of motion.

But, was this insight sufficient in and of itself to stimulate the attempt to construct a mechanical philosophy? Not, perhaps, in 1630. The evidence furnished by Hobbes's autobiographical account of investigating natural philosophical questions with Marin Mersenne in 1634 (questions which he claims to have investigated on the basis of his insight about motion) and the evidence of his surviving fragmentary manuscript works from this period, suggests that, in 1630, Hobbes had no coherent philosophy of motion; all he had was an insight on which such a philosophy might be built. Not until the European tour of 1634 does he seem seriously to have begun to pursue the elaboration of such an account which from that insight involved him in a twenty-five years' struggle to erect a coherent physical and metaphysical system. But, while he may not have provided a sufficient stimulus in 1630, he may yet have done so in the middle of the decade.

---

59   Malcolm, "Robert Payne and the 'Short Tract'", 123.
60   Hall wondered 'whether Hobbes's great interest in Galileo did not stem from the Cavendish brothers', "Galileo's Influence", 406; cf. Feingold, "A Friend of Hobbes", 273.
61   Hobbes, *Correspondence*, I, 33.
62   Galileo Galilei, et al., *The Controversy on the Comets of 1618*, transl. Drake S. – O'Malley C.D. (Philadelphia: 1960) 312.
63   Malcolm, "Robert Payne and the 'Short Tract'", 123.

The efficient cause of the Welbeck effort to establish a mechanical philosophy was, I have argued, the appearance there in the mid-1630s of Castelli's
Demostrazioni geometriche and perhaps also of Galileo's *Le meccaniche*. This
leads us to Hobbes's second likely contribution: the provision of texts. From
October 1634 through to October 1636 Hobbes was travelling in France and Italy
as tutor to the young Earl of Devonshire. His first and last stop on this tour was
Paris, where he spent time with Marin Mersenne, who had in June 1634 published his translation, with elaborate commentary and additions, of Galileo's
Le meccaniche. At that very time, Mersenne was enthusiastically attempting to
develop a mechanical philosophy for, according to his biographer, 1634 was the
year of his 'conversion' to mechanism.[64] It is generally believed that Hobbes
was the source of the Italian text of *Le meccaniche*, from which Payne made his
translation, dated 11 November 1636.[65] Since Hobbes returned to England in
October, and since he had earlier been charged with acquiring a Galilean text
for Newcastle, this seems a plausible explanation.

But where did Hobbes acquire his copy? The traditional assumption is that
he got it from Mersenne.[66] But one wonders why Mersenne would have furnished Hobbes with a manuscript transcription of the original Italian text
rather than with a copy of the French version he had so carefully prepared and
published only a few months before Hobbes's first arrival in Paris. Mersenne
was in intermittent contact with Galileo and his associates and could, presumably, have acquired a manuscript copy from him, should he have required one;
but there is no reason to imagine that multiple copies of the Italian text were
circulating in Paris in 1636. Another possible source for Hobbes's manuscript
of this unpublished early work of Galileo's was perhaps the author himself,
whom Hobbes probably met on the Italian leg of his journey.[67]

The notion that Hobbes met Galileo on this journey has the warrant of
one of Hobbes's biographers, his close friend, John Aubrey (who is followed
by Richard Blackburne); but it lacks the endorsement of Hobbes himself,
who doesn't mention any such meeting in either of his autobiographies.[68] It
is widely, though not universally, believed that Hobbes is referred to when,

64   Lenoble R., *Mersenne ou la naissance du mécanisme* (Paris: 1943) 38.

65   British Library, MS Harley 6796, fol. 317r.

66   Jacquot J. – Jones H.W. (eds.) Thomas Hobbes, *Critique du 'De mundo' de Thomas White*,
        (Paris: 1973) 14.

67   He left Paris for Italy in August 1635; we hear nothing more of him until the spring of 1636,
        when he writes from Florence and speaks of a recent visit to Rome.

68   Aubrey, *Brief Lives*, I, 366; Molesworth W. (ed.), Thomas Hobbes, *Opera latina*, 5 vols
        (London: 1839) I, xxviii.

writing on 1 December 1635, Galileo informs a correspondent (probably the Venetian Friar, Fulgenzio Micanzio) that, 'Over the last few days I have received many visitors from beyond the alps, among whom was a notable English gentlemen, who told me that my unfortunate *Dialogo* has been translated into that language'.[69]

The tradition of glossing this 'Signor principale Inglese' as Hobbes, who was at this time a mere travelling tutor, seems on the face of it historically insensitive; nor does the application of the term to Hobbes's charge, the twenty year-old Earl of Devonshire, entirely solve the puzzle (why not 'giovane', 'nobile'?); but it is colourable.[70] And we must set against such perplexities the fact that Galileo's informant knew about the Webbe translation of the *Dialogo*, one of the keynotes of which was, we have noted, its privacy. It is unlikely that someone who was *not* a familiar of Cavendish and his circle would have known of it; and what other intimate of Welbeck might reasonably be supposed to have visited Galileo, or even to have been in Tuscany, in late November 1635?

In addition to the possibility that Hobbes returned to England in 1636 with a copy of *Le meccaniche*, it is also possible that he was involved in the provision, sometime before the end of the English year 1635 (therefore, by the end of March 1636) of the copy of Castelli's *Della misura dell'acque correnti* used by Payne for his 1635 translation. Hobbes had left Paris for Italy in late summer 1635 and was in Florence, whence he had recently arrived from Rome, in April 1636. He would have arrived in Italy before the onset of winter and would, therefore, have just had time to acquire a copy of Castelli's work and send it back to England before the year's end. In Rome, he would have had the opportunity not only to purchase the volume but also to meet its author. There is, then, some evidence to support the view that Hobbes brought to Welbeck not only the possibility of a mechanical philosophy but also, perhaps, the Galilean texts that precipitated the Cavendish-sponsored quest for it.

The third contribution Hobbes made to the Welbeck effort was to provide criticism that may have had some effect on the abandonment of alternative

---

69   Galileo, *Le Opere*, XVI, 355: 'Ho hauto li giorni passati molte visite di oltramonti, tra'quali un Signor principale Inglese, il quale mi dice, il mio sfortunato Dialogo essere stato trasportato in quella lingua'.

70   It also seems odd that, if Devonshire were indeed in the party, Galileo did not mention the fact to Micanzio, who had written a regular newsletter to his father during the period 1615–25, letters moreover, which Hobbes had translated. Even so, perhaps this isn't quite as absurd as it might seem. There is no reason Galileo should have known of Micanzio's correspondence, and no reason why Micanzio would have advertised the fact that he was sending a regular newsletter to a foreign dignitary.

attempts to develop a mechanical philosophy under Cavendish's auspices. In letters from Paris of August 1635 and August 1636 Hobbes criticised both Walter Warner and Claude Mydorge for presenting their theories on optics as demonstrations rather than mere opinions.[71] In the former letter he also dismissed Warner's researches into the passions ('For the soule I knowe he has nothinge to giue your Lordship any satisfaction'), adding the self-promoting rider: 'I would he could giue [a deleted] good reasons for the facultyes & passions of the soule, such as may be expressed in playne English. [I do *deleted*] if he can, he is the first (that I euer heard [>of) could] speake sense in that subiect. if he can not I hope to be the first.'[72] Such criticisms reflected Hobbes's absorption of the scepticism of the Mersenne circle about the limits of demonstrability in most areas of physical knowledge. They also, no doubt, registered some personal anxiety about the advancing researches of his fellow clients and rivals for Cavendish's attention and philosophical prestige at a time when his own investigations appear to have been making slow progress, if any.[73]

We cannot be certain that Hobbes's criticisms had a direct effect on the efforts of Warner or Payne to develop a mechanical philosophy, but we do find evidence that Cavendish took on board Hobbes's repeated distinction between certainty and opinion and heeded his caution that 'the greatest part of Naturall Philosophy' is not demonstrable, as 'dependinge vpon the motion of bodies so subtile as they are inuisible'.[74] In his play, *Wits Triumvirate* (dated 1635), Cavendish appears to echo Hobbes on the prevalence of opinion over knowledge and on the limited scope of demonstration, which he restricts, in a thoroughly Hobbesian manner, to arithmetic and geometry: 'We have no demonstrations else, or very few'.[75] In the 1650s he subjected Hobbes's own division of the sciences in chapter IX of *Leviathan* to a slightly critical analysis on the basis of the certainty of principles; to Cavendish even poetry and rhetoric were demonstrable, 'suposinge the Passions vnderstoode'.[76] In 1663 we find him

---

71   Hobbes, *Correspondence*, I, 28–29, 33–34.

72   Hobbes, *Correspondence*, I, 29.

73   'Opinion' and 'demonstration' (and the distinction between supposition and certainty they imply) are central terms and concepts in Hobbes's letters to Cavendish from Paris during the period 1634–1636; *Correspondence*, I, 22–23, 28–29, 33–34. For Hobbes's impact on the Mersenne circle in this regard, see Malcolm N., "Hobbes and Roberval", in *Aspects of Hobbes*, 156–99 (178–80). On Hobbes's difficulties in expounding his philosophy at this time, see Hobbes, *Opera latina*, I, lxxxix.

74   Hobbes, *Correspondence*, I, 33; cp. Also I, 22–23.

75   Nelson, *Wits Triumvirate*, II, 197.

76   NUL, Pw1 666. On this document, see Hobbes, *Leviathan*, Malcolm N. (ed.), 3 vols. (Oxford: 2013) I, 145.

insisting that the whole of natural philosophy is undemonstrable.[77] There can, in sum, be little doubt that Cavendish's ideal of demonstration and his sense of its limited applicability outside the realm of pure mathematics derived from instruction by Hobbes during the middle 1630s.

Finally, whatever his precise contribution to the Welbeck effort, Hobbes's greatest contribution to the development of the mechanical philosophy in England was, of course, not his provision of the germinal idea, nor his supply of seminal texts, nor even his provision of critical commentary on the efforts of rival clients. Rather, his greatest contribution was his own painstaking effort to elaborate an entire physics and metaphysics on the basis of his insight into the primacy of motion. The first draft of this system appeared in *The Elements of Law, Natural and Politic*, which Hobbes presented to Cavendish on 9 May 1640. That this work set down in writing, at Cavendish's command and in English, ideas Hobbes had previously adumbrated orally to him, allows us to regard it as the crowning glory of Cavendish's patronage of mechanical philosophy during the 1630s.[78] It was for Hobbes, of course, only the first draft of an effort that would cost him enormous pains and consume a large part of his working life. But even had he never written *Leviathan*, *De cive*, or *De corpore*, the *Elements* would still stand as a significant monument to the effort—sponsored by Cavendish though largely conceived by Hobbes—to develop a mechanical explanation of human nature and to deduce from it the consequences for civil life.

Selective Bibliography

Cavendish Margaret, Duchess of Newcastle, *The Life of William Cavendish, Duke of Newcastle*, (ed.) Firth C.H. (London: 1906).

Feingold M., "A Friend of Hobbes and an Early Translator of Galileo: Robert Payne of Oxford", in North J.D. – Roche J.J. (eds.), *The Light of Nature* (Dordrecht: 1985).

Hall M.B., "Galileo's influence on seventeenth-century English scientists", in McMullin E. (ed.), *Galileo, Man of Science* (New York & London: 1967).

Hobbes Thomas, *The Correspondence*, 2 vols., (ed.) Malcolm N. (Oxford: 1994).

Jacquot J., "Sir Charles Cavendish and his Learned Friends", *Annals of Science* 8 (1952).

Raylor T., "Thomas Hobbes and 'The Mathematical Demonstration of the Sword'", *The Seventeenth Century*, 15 (2000) 175–98.

---

77   Cavendish Margaret, *Philosophical and Physical Opinions* (London: 1663) 464; Raylor, "Hobbes and 'The Mathematical Demonstration'", 178–79.

78   Thomas Hobbes, *The Elements of Law, Natural and Politic* (ed.), Tönnies F. (London: 1984) xvi.

Raylor T., "Newcastle's Ghosts: Robert Payne, Ben Jonson, and the 'Cavendish Circle'", in Summers C.J. – Pebworth T.-L. (eds.), *Literary Circles and Cultural Communities in Renaissance England* (Columbia & London: 2000).

Raylor T., "Hobbes, Payne, and *A short tract on first principle*", *The Historical Journal* 44 (2001).

Van Beneden B. – de Poorter N. (eds.), *Royalist Refugees: William and Margaret Cavendish in the Rubens House 1648–1660* (Antwerp: 2006).

Walker E., *'To Amaze the People with Pleasure and Delight': The Horsemanship Manuals of William Cavendish, Duke of Newcastle* (London: 2010).

CHAPTER 8

The Role of Honour in the Life of William Cavendish and the Philosophy of Thomas Hobbes

Lisa T. Sarasohn

Samuel Pepys, in 1668, dismissed the biography Margaret Cavendish had written of her husband, William Cavendish, the Duke of Newcastle, with words insulting both to the nobleman and his wife. Yesterday, the diarist writes, I 'stayed at home reading the ridiculous history of my Lord Newcastle wrote by his wife, which shews her to be a mad, conceited, ridiculous woman, and he an asse to suffer her to write what she writes to him and of him'.[1] Apparently, the Cavendishes warrant two 'ridiculouses', with Margaret as the out-of-control wife and William the powerless husband. Here is a living example of the shrew and the buffoon so familiar in English literature from Shakespeare to Dryden, which does little justice either to the marriage or achievements of the duke and duchess, but reveals how far the noble pair had fallen in the eyes of the fashionable world.

How did Cavendish, one of the most pre-eminent nobles in England before and during the First English Civil War, merit such casual disdain near the end of his long life? In this essay, I will explore some of the reasons for the decline of Cavendish's reputation in the context of changing notions of honour in the later part of the seventeenth century, particularly as developed in the thought of Cavendish's friend and client, Thomas Hobbes. Cavendish and Hobbes were generational peers, both were born during the reign of Elizabeth and died in the 1670s. Cavendish was a nobleman and Hobbes was often dependent on the support of noble patrons and employers, including Cavendish's relatives, the Earls of Devonshire, who resided at Hardwick.[2] Thus, both were familiar with the intricate meaning of honour at the beginning of this period. Honour in the sixteenth century included elements of medieval chivalric codes of martial behaviour, Aristotelian concepts of internal virtue and excellence, and the

---

1 Latham R. – Williams M. (eds.), *The Diary of Samuel Pepys* 9 (Berkeley: 1974) 123–24.
2 Hardwick rather than Chatsworth remained the main family seat until the end of the seventeenth century.

© KONINKLIJKE BRILL NV, LEIDEN, 2017 | DOI 10.1163/9789004326217_010

courtly etiquette of Italian humanism.[3] Honour was also associated with lineage and place in the social hierarchy. The conditions and the attributes that defined an honourable man, however, had changed by the end of the seventeenth century. Cavendish and Hobbes realized that honour would become an attribute attached to the favour of the ruler, without necessarily reflecting the excellence of the honoured. Although Cavendish sometimes relied on the earlier definitions of honour, he and Hobbes acknowledged that the approbation of the monarch was the essential and necessary condition for the recognition of a nobleman or a gentleman as an honourable man.[4] In doing so, they anticipated what would become increasingly the norm in royal courts.

The meaning of 'honour' in early modern England was complex and malleable. It could be either 'horizontal', that is, among peers or 'vertical': a high nobleman's recognition of a lower-level aristocrat. Richard Cust summarizes how multifold the notion of honour could be during early modern times:

> As social historians and anthropologists have demonstrated, an individual's reputation within a society is the result of a complex amalgam of judgements and evaluations. These might relate to office and recognition by the ruler, but equally they can depend on such matters as hospitality, personal display, family integrity and sexual reputation ... This broadens considerably the range of topics appropriate to a discussion of honour and politics, and again points up the need to look at how sexual metaphors and conventions, and issues relating to gender, helped to shape political culture.[5]

In other words, to be considered honourable, or worthy of honour, one might either be respected by one's peers or possess honours: tangible and material benefits bestowed by a higher authority.

Cavendish's career was emblematic of these many diverse characteristics of honour. He benefited greatly from the favour of princes early in his career

---

3   On honour, see Cust R., "Honour and Politics in early Stuart England: the Case of Beaumont *v.* Hastings", *Past & Present* 149 (1995); James M.E., *Society, Politics and Culture: Studies in Early Modern England* (Cambridge: 1988); Peltonen M., *The Duel in Early Modern England: Civility, Politeness and Honour* (Cambridge: 2003); and Thomas K., *The Ends of Life: Roads to Fulfilment in Early Modern Europe* (Oxford: 2009).

4   James argues that the state was increasingly defining what and who was worthy of honour, 310–412.

5   Cust, "Honour and Politics", 61, http://go.galegroup.com.ezproxy.proxy.oregonstate.edu, accessed 5 February 2014.

when he was made Governor to Prince Charles and Privy Councillor in 1638, and in his elevation to marquis in 1643.[6] He gained a reputation for grandiose hospitality in 1633 and 1634 when he entertained Charles I with two extravagant masques, written by Ben Jonson, during the king's two processions through the North. The second event at Bolsover cost between £14,000 and £15,000 and prompted the first of Edward Hyde's many swipes at Cavendish: 'a more stupendous entertainment, which (God be thanked), though possibly it might too much whet the appetites of others to excess, no man ever after in those days imitated'.[7] His homes were lavishly decorated, even by the standards of the day, and murals at Bolsover celebrated his sexual prowess, another aspect of his reputation which was well known.[8] Cavendish understood the mechanics of the honour society, although his problematic career as a courtier, campaigner and husband undermined his manipulation of its various aspects. There is some irony in the advice he directed at the young Prince Charles in 1638, when he argued that it is irrelevant whether a ruler is truly honourable, as long as he creates the *persona* of honourability. According to Cavendish, certainly influenced by his reading of Machiavelli, 'authority doth what it list, I mean power thats the stronger, though sometimes it shifts sides, therefore the King must know at what time to play the King, and when to qualifie it, but never put it of[f]; for in all triumphs whatsoever or publick shewing your self,! you cannot put upon you too much King'.[9] This is a lesson Charles did not learn well, but Cavendish's friend and client, Thomas Hobbes, enshrined it in the development of his political philosophy between 1640 and 1651.

In Hobbes's first political work, the *Elements of* Law (1640), dedicated to Cavendish, honour is described in horizontal terms, as either inborn or as the esteem of others for the virtues and talents of the honourable gentleman. Thus, 'beauty of person, consisting in a lively aspect of the countenance, and other signs of natural heat, are honourable, being signs precedent of power generative, also, general reputation amongst those of the other sex, because

6 Although Charles II bestowed a dukedom on Cavendish in 1663, he did so partly to wipe out the debts he owed him and partly as a 'consolation prize' for his refusal to offer him a government post and the accrued honour that it would have brought Cavendish.

7 Quoted in Trease G., *Portrait of a Cavalier: William Cavendish, First Duke of Newcastle* (London: 1979) 70. Trease describes these events and other efforts Cavendish made to secure his political career in his detailed biography of the duke.

8 Raylor T., "'Pleasure Reconciled to Virtue': William Cavendish, Ben Jonson, and the Decorative Scheme of Bolsover Castle", *Renaissance Quarterly* 52, ii (1999) 402–439.

9 "The Earl of Newcastle's Letter of Instruction to Prince Charles for His Studies, Conduct, and Behaviour", in Ellis H. (ed.), *Original Letters, Illustrative of English History* 3 (London: 1824) 288.

signs consequent of the same. And, actions proceeding from strength of body and open force, are honourable, as signs consequent of power motive, such as victory in battle or duel; *et á avoir tué son homme'*.[10] Arguing from his psychological and physical principles, Hobbes in this work also concluded that there is a natural equality between men in the state of nature which inevitably leads to a state of war. One of the primary reasons for this disorder is that one man does not give to another the honour he thinks is due him:

> On the other side, considering the great difference there is in men, from the diversity of their passions, how some are vainly glorious, and hope for precedency and superiority above their fellows, not only when they are equal in power, but also when they are inferior; we must needs acknowledge that it must necessarily follow, that those men who are moderate, and look for no more but equality of nature, shall be obnoxious to the force of others, that will attempt to subdue them. And from hence shall proceed a general diffidence in mankind, and mutual fear one of another.[11]

The only solution to this problem is to establish a superior to determine the honour due each individual: 'nevertheless, by the diversity of judgments and passions in so many men contending naturally for honour and advantage one above another: it is impossible, not only that their consent to aid each other against an enemy, but also that the peace should last between themselves, without some mutual and common fear to rule them."[12]

Thus, the vertical nature of an honour was part of Hobbes's philosophy from the beginning of his political writings, and this theme became an increasingly important element in his philosophy in the 1640s. By the time of the publication of *Leviathan* in 1651, Hobbes included natural excellence as a source of honour, but emphasized that honour was an adjunct of power, 'Honourable is whatsoever possession, action, or quality, is an argument and signe of Power'.[13] In both works, however, Hobbes argued that the competition for honour or honours was one of the major causes for war in the state of nature. In Chapter 11 of *Leviathan*, he wrote, 'Competition of Riches, Honour, Command, or other power enclineth to Contention, Enmity, and War'. And, in Chapter 13, in his

---

10   Hobbes Thomas, *The Elements of Law Natural and Politic* (Virginia: Electronic Text Center), http://etext.lib.virginia.edu/toc/modeng/public/Hob2Ele.html, accessed 1 May 2013.

11   Hobbes, *Elements of Law*, Chapter 14.

12   Hobbes, *Elements of Law*, Chapter 19.

13   Tuck R. (ed.), Thomas Hobbes, *Leviathan* (Cambridge: 1991), 65.

famous description of the war of all against all, Hobbes argued that men will fight 'for trifles, as a word, a smile, a different opinion, and any other signe of undervalue'.[14] The only way to curb such basic passions, once the state emerges from this honour-bred chaos, is to give the sovereign the monopoly on honour and power: 'To the Soveraign therefore it belongeth also to give titles of Honour; and to appoint what Order of place, and dignity, each man shall hold; and what signes of respect, in publique or private meetings, they shall give to one another'.[15]

Hobbes's Early Relationship with William Cavendish

When Hobbes wrote about honour and power, he clearly could have had a nobleman he knew well in mind—William Cavendish—and the state of nature in which that nobleman operated: the royal court during the turmoil before and during the civil war and at the court-in-exile in Paris. The qualities associated with Cavendish, at least by his sometime friend and later critic, Edward Hyde, the Earl of Clarendon, exactly fit the parameters of Hobbes's definition in *Elements of Law* although the statesman and historian did not necessarily view them as honourable. He described Cavendish's honour and loyalty to the king in his *History of the Civil War*, but after blaming him for the defeat of the royalist army in 1644 at the Battle of Marston Moor, he added,

> And it was a greater wonder that he sustained the vexation and fatigue of it [the battle] so long, than that he broke from it with so little circumspection. He was a very fine gentleman, active and full of courage, and most accomplished in those qualities of horsemanship, dancing, and fencing, which accompany a good breeding; in which his delight was. Besides that, he was amorous in poetry and music; to which he indulged the greatest part of his time; and nothing could have tempted him out of those paths of pleasure which he enjoyed in a full and ample fortune, but honour and ambition to serve the king when he saw him in distress."[16]

Cavendish was famous for enjoying the luxuries his great wealth provided. Years later, Margaret Cavendish described her husband's character: 'I know him

---

14   Hobbes, *Leviathan*, 70; 88.
15   Ibid., *Leviathan*, 126.
16   Hyde, Edward Hyde, Duke of Clarendon, *History of the Civil War Volume III* (Oxford: 1826) 374–75.

not addicted to any manner of vice, except that he has been a great lover and admirer of the female sex; which, whether it be so great a crime as to condemn him for it, I'le leave it to the judgment of young gallants and beautiful ladies'.[17] Cavendish loved the ladies, but more significantly, he was a patron of poets and philosophers, although he was not a scholar himself. Hence, his relationship with Thomas Hobbes should be viewed in the context of Cavendish's 'paths of pleasure'. The pleasure he took in the company of Thomas Hobbes began in the 1630s, when Hobbes was member of the household of the Hardwick branch of the Cavendish family, serving as tutor and advisor to the 2nd. and 3rd. Earls of Devonshire. While Hobbes always remained in a dependent relationship with Devonshire Cavendishes, he and the Welbeck William Cavendish had a more nuanced relationship, particularly when it came to intellectual activities; the two performed scientific experiments together, Hobbes executed commissions for Cavendish and, ultimately, the thinker dedicated the *Elements of Law* to him.[18] During this period of intellectual partnership, Cavendish's chaplain, Robert Payne, in a tract originally credited to Hobbes, wrote *Considerations touching the facility or Difficulty of the Motions of a Horse on straight lines, & Circular*, which reflects Cavendish's interest in the *manège* and anticipates his later mathematical approach to the subject.[19] By 1636, in a curious reversal of traditional hierarchy dynamics, Hobbes wrote to Cavendish, 'I am sorry your Lordship finds not so good dealing in the world as you deserve. But my Lord, he that will venture to sea must resolve to endure all weather, but for my part I love to keepe a'land'.[20] While this advice sounds trite, it indicates that Hobbes knew about Cavendish's aspirations at first hand, and that the scholar was fashioning himself as the earl's philosophic confidant. In another letter, written several months earlier, Hobbes thanked Cavendish for a gift of money, but added, 'let me tell your Lordship once for all, that though I honour you as my Lord, yet my love to you is just of the same nature that it is to Mr. Payne, bred out of private talke, without respect to your purse'.[21] The vertical aspect of

---

17   Cavendish Margaret, *The Life of the (1st) Duke of Newcastle & Other Writings by Margaret Duchess* (London: 1916) 140.

18   On Hobbes's relationships with the Cavendish cousins, see my article, "Was *Leviathan* a Patronage Artifact?", *History of Political Thought* 21 iv (2000) 606–631.

19   On this work, see Raylor T., "Hobbes, Payne, and 'A Short Tract on First Principles'", *The Historical Journal* 44 (2001) 29–58 and Malcolm N., *Aspects of Hobbes* (Oxford: 2002) 80–145.

20   Thomas Hobbes to the Earl of Newcastle, 29 July–8 August, 1636, HMC, "Portland MSS". II 129.

21   Thomas Hobbes to the Earl of Newcastle, 25 August, 1635, HMC, "Portland MSS" II, 125.

honour is clear, but Hobbes certainly was trying to establish a horizontal bond of mutual esteem.

By 1638, Cavendish's star was on the ascendant; he was at last successful in procuring a position at court as the governor to Prince Charles. According to Margaret Cavendish, 'His Majesty called him up to Court, and thought him the fittest person whom he might intrust with the government of his son Charles ... and made him withal a member of the Lords His Majesties most honourable Privy Council; which as it was a great honour and trust, he spared no care and industry to discharge his duties accordingly'.[22] As Hobbes writes in the *Elements of Law*, 'But the signs of honour from the superior to the inferior, are such as these: to praise or prefer him before his concurrent, to hear him more willingly, to speak to him more familiarly, to admit him nearer; to employ him rather; to ask his advice rather, to like his opinions'.[23] Cavendish had, indeed, become an honourable man, at least according to the criteria for honour that Hobbes enumerated here.

But, Cavendish's success was short-lived, due to other enemies he had in Parliament. He had yoked his career to that of Thomas Wentworth, Earl of Strafford, and when that great noble fell from power, so did he. During his retirement at Welbeck, he received Hobbes's *Elements of Law*, which although not printed until 1651, was in wide circulation by 1640. In the dedication to Cavendish, Hobbes argued that he has discovered the certain principles of 'justice and polity ... which I have heretofor acquainted your Lordship withal in private discourse; and which, by your command, I have put into method'. During this same period, Cavendish was writing his 'Letter of Instruction' to Prince Charles. It is intriguing to imagine the newly-marginalized earl and his old friend discussing the nature of court politics, honour and disgrace, which the patron then commanded his client to put into method. Like Hobbes, Cavendish knew that the human desire for honour is one of the motivating factors for competition in all societies—natural or courtly—and therefore the prince should use the awarding of honours to supplement his power and thus flatter all people into supporting him: 'the putting off of your hat and making a leg pleases more then reward or preservation, so much doth it take all kind of people'.[24]

---

22   Cavendish M., *Life of William Cavendish*, 25.

23   Hobbes, Chapter 8, *Elements of Law*, http://etext.lib.virginia.edu/etcbin/toccer-new2?
        id=Hob2Ele.sgm&images=images/modeng&data=/texts/english/modeng/parsed&tag=p
        ublic&part=8&division=div2, accessed 10 May 2013.

24   "The Earl of Newcastle's Letter of Instruction to Prince Charles", 288–91.

But before Wentworth's fall, the characteristics Hobbes had identified as leading to war in the state of nature were undermining Cavendish's success. The Scots had risen against the king in 1638 and Cavendish gathered a troop of '120 knights and gentlemen of quality' to fight the invaders. When his company which 'had the honour to march with the Prince's colours' was not given the precedence in the order of march Cavendish thought they deserved, he 'immediately commanded his cornet to take off the Princes colour's from his staff, and so marched in the place appointed, choosing rather to march without his colours flying, then to lessen his master's dignity by the command of any subject'. The slight ultimately resulted in Cavendish challenging the Earl of Holland, the other commander, to a duel, because 'their design had been discovered to the King by some of his opposite's friends, who presently caused them both to be confined until he had made their peace'.[25] This was dishonour indeed, especially if others believed as Hobbes did, that the signs of honour in part consisted of 'victory in battle or duel; *et à avoir tué son homme*'. It also vividly demonstrated that when it came to honour, the king ultimately was in control.

If Hobbes hoped that the congeniality of ideas he shared with Cavendish, and the latter's patronage, might protect his work and give him added status, he soon recognized that he had chosen the wrong protector. Quentin Skinner suggests that one of the reasons Hobbes became 'the first of all that fled' was because he feared that because of Cavendish's loss of power at court, the nobleman would no longer be able to protect his client.[26] Four years later, Cavendish, who had been honoured with a marquisate on account of his efforts and monies on the king's behalf, also fled to France after the defeat at Marston Moor. He was never again to regain either the honour or influence he felt was due to him and from this time on, and Hobbes's relationship with him became increasingly complex.

Cavendish and Hobbes in Exile

The relationship between Hobbes and Cavendish continued during the 1640s when both men were in Paris. Hobbes's prestige on the continent was much higher than it had been in England, particularly with the group of thinkers who were patronized by Father Marin Mersenne. Mersenne was the great facilitator of the French intellectual community, which included René Descartes and Pierre Gassendi, the rehabilitator of Epicurean atomism. Hobbes was taken into this circle, as was Sir Charles Cavendish, Cavendish's brother and

---

25   Cavendish M., *Life of William Cavendish*, 26–7.
26   Skinner Q., *Reason and Rhetoric in the Philosophy of Hobbes* (Cambridge: 1997) 229.

a respected amateur mathematician. In what may be an apocryphal story, Cavendish hosted Hobbes, Descartes and Gassendi at a dinner party in 1647 or 1648 during which Gassendi and Descartes were reconciled after a philosophical feud.[27]

It may be that Cavendish was seeking to recapture the honour he had jeopardized because of his military loss in England by becoming a Maecenas of philosophy. In fact, in the dedication to Cavendish at the beginning of the unpublished *Optiques* (1646), Hobbes wrote to the marquis, 'your Lordship, after having performed so noble and honourable acts for defense of your countrie, may think it no dishonour in this unfortunate leasure to have employed some thoughts in the speculation of the noblest of the senses, Vision'.[28] In this reversal of roles, Hobbes was honouring and thus raising the status of the nobleman. The reversal was completed in 1648, when the impecunious lord was forced to borrow 106 pistoles from Hobbes to help pay off his creditors so he could leave Paris to join the prince on his first campaign; he gave Hobbes his telescopes and microscopes as surety for the loan.[29] In the *Elements of Law*, Hobbes had written that one of the signs of honour of a superior to an inferior is giving 'him any gift rather than money, or if money, so much as may not imply his need of a little: for need of little is greater poverty than need of much'.[30] The small loan might also be taken to imply the dishonour of the debtor.

Another incident indicates how close intellectually Cavendish and Hobbes had become. In 1645, Cavendish instigated and moderated a debate between Hobbes and John Bramhall, the Bishop of Derry, even deciding that Hobbes and Bramhall would discuss the nature of free will and determinism. The by now infamous philosopher claimed that he had written down his argument only because 'the many obligations wherein I was obliged to [Cavendish], prevailed with me to write this answer', even though he knew, 'there were some reasons for which I thought it might be inconvenient to let my answer go abroad'. The theological questions debated were certainly explosive and when this debate was finally published in 1654, it led to a bitter feud between the two contenders. However, at the time of the debate, according to Hobbes, 'the Bishop was

27   Sarasohn L., "Thomas Hobbes and the Duke of Newcastle: A Study in the Mutuality of Patronage before the establishment of the Royal Society", *Isis* 90 iv (1999) 715–57; 728.

28   Hobbes Thomas, *A minute of first Draught of the Optiques* (1646): http://www.bl.uk/manuscripts/Viewer.aspx?ref=harley_ms_3360_fs001r, accessed 5 February 2014.

29   Concerning the loan, see NUL, Pw1 406 (MS Cavendish Misc. 43); and Malcolm N. (ed.), *Thomas Hobbes: The Correspondence* 1 (1994) liv–lv.

30   Hobbes, *Elements of Law*, Chapter Nine: http://etext.lib.virginia.edu/toc/modeng/public/Hob2Ele.htm, accessed 5 February 5, 2014.

not then in passion, or suppressed his passion, being then in the presence of my Lord of Newcastle'.[31]

In the world of philosophic and scientific discourse, Cavendish commanded and Hobbes possessed the esteem and honour they expected. And, by the end of the 1640s, both he and Hobbes experienced some success at the court-in-exile where Cavendish regained his position as a privy counsellor and Hobbes was hired to teach the young prince mathematics. Nevertheless, by 1651, Cavendish's had lost out to others in the competition between factions at court, and Hobbes was barred from the now king's presence because of Queen Henrietta Maria's fear of his pernicious philosophy.

The court-in-exile itself was a treacherous mess, with different nobles allying themselves with and against the Presbyterian Scottish nobles, who themselves were split into different factions. Cavendish advocated a policy of accommodation with the Scottish Engagers after the execution of Charles I in 1649, in opposition to the anti-Scottish feelings of Edward Hyde and Secretary Nicholas. The marquis wanted to accompany the uncrowned Charles II on a campaign into Scotland, but had sufficiently alienated some members of the Scottish contingent who, according to Margaret Cavendish, 'would not suffer him to come, or be in any part of that kingdom'.[32] Ultimately, Cavendish did not accompany Charles to Scotland in an enterprise which almost led to the young king being captured and to the crippling of the royalist cause until the Restoration. Not surprisingly, Cavendish never regained any power at court after this fiasco. He retired to Antwerp, where he had established a household and a riding centre in the residence of the late painter, Peter Paul Rubens. In 1651, Hobbes also returned to England after he had published *Leviathan*, alienating among others, Edward Hyde, who years later accused him of trying to win Cromwell's favour.[33] Cavendish continued to try to serve his lord and master, as Madeline Dewhurst argues in this collection, but he never again was a political player.

Cavendish, Margaret Cavendish and Hobbes

In 1653, Margaret Cavendish discussed the nature of courts in the first book she wrote, *The Worlds Olio*, which clearly reflected her husband's experiences:

31   Newcastle's role in this controversy is explained in Thomas Hobbes, "Of Liberties and Necessitie", in Molesworth W. (ed.) Hobbes, *English Works* Volume V (London: 1839–45) 2.

32   Cavendish M., *Life of William Cavendish*, 74–75.

33   Sarasohn, "Thomas Hobbes and the Duke of Newcastle", 731. I discuss Hobbes's reasons for returning to England in Sarasohn S., "Was *Leviathan* a Patronage Artifact?", *History of Political Thought*, 21 iv (2000) 606–631.

Courts should be a patern and an example of vertue to all the rest of the kingdom, being the ruler and chief head, to direct the body of state; but most commonly instead of clemency, justice, modesty, friendship, temperance, humility, and unity, there is faction, pride, ambition, luxury, covetousnesse, hate, envy, slander, treachery, flattery, impudence, and many the like; yet they are oft-times covered with a vaile of smooth professions and protestations, which glisters like gold, when it is a copper'd tinsel: but to study Court-ship, is rather to study dissembling formality, then noble reality.[34]

Cavendish's actions as a general and courtier had alienated members of the court; Hyde wrote to Secretary Nicholas in 1650 that the marquis was 'a very lamentable man and as fit to be a gen[era]ll as a B[isho]pp'.[35] Nevertheless, Hyde joined Cavendish in urging Sir Charles Cavendish to go to London to try to recoup his own losses. He was accompanied by Margaret Cavendish, who made a vain attempt to access some monies from her husband's confiscated estates.

While in London, Margaret Cavendish encountered Hobbes. In spite of Cavendish's long relationship with the philosopher, it perhaps comes as no surprise that he declined her invitation to dinner: 'I told him as truly I was very glad to see him, and asked him if he would please to do me that honour to stay at dinner, but he with great civility refused me, as having some businesse, which I suppose required his absence'.[36] It seems that the now notorious thinker did not want to acknowledge his prior friendship with the great lord—or his wife—who had fallen into dishonour, at least in Hobbesian terms, not only for his defeat at Marston Moor and subsequent flight but also because of his unsuccessful role at the court-in-exile in Paris. If Hobbes, as Hyde would later charge, really wanted to ingratiate himself with the Cromwellian government, he might have avoided contact with the family of his old patron, whom the Commonwealth government had named, according to Margaret, 'the greatest Traitor to the State'.[37] He might also have been reacting to Margaret Cavendish

---

34   Cavendish Margaret, *The Worlds Olio* (London, J. Martin & J. Allestrye: 1655) 48.

35   Quoted in Mendelson S.H., *The Mental World of Stuart Women: Three Studies* (Amherst: 1987) 27. I wish to thank Dr. Mendelson for all of her help with this essay.

36   Cavendish Margaret, *Philosophical and Physical Opinions* (London, William Wilson: 1663), B3r.

37   Cavendish Margaret, "A True Relation of my Birth, Breeding, and Life (1656)", in Bowerbank S. – Mendelson S. (eds.) *Paper Bodies: A Margaret Cavendish Reader*, (Peterborough ON: 2000) 51.

herself, who although she had not yet published any of her unusual works, was eccentric in her appearance and behaviour. As she described herself, she was 'so afraid to <u>dishonour</u> my Friends and Family by my indiscreet actions, that I rather chose to be accounted a Fool, than to be thought rude or wanton'.[38] After her works began to appear in 1653, she would be regarded as both a fool and a wanton, and therefore bring yet more dishonour on her husband.

Cavendish's efforts to gain restitution were futile and in 1653 she joined her husband on the continent. As might be expected, Cavendish did not abandon his efforts on Charles's behalf, leading the exiled English community in Antwerp and, as Dewhurst has argued, even acting as a factor in gaining support for Charles's restoration among foreign powers and through his contacts in the north of England. During this period, he also wrote a *Letter of Advice* to Charles II, which blamed the turmoil of the rebellion on the failure of former kings to 'cherish' the traditional nobles and instead to 'make much of mean men' who 'only lived off the king'. Dancing and kowtowing courtiers had undermined the royal authority and caused faction, Cavendish warned, which could only be avoided, 'Sire, [by keeping] up your Nobility, and Gentry to all their just rights and Dignities'.[39] Cavendish apparently realized that allowing the ruler to monopolize the bestowing of honour and office—as Hobbes had advocated—could undermine the traditional place of the nobility and allow unworthy men to succeed at court at their expense. Cavendish, here, was filling the role of elder statesman, as Dewhurst argues, but the history of the reign of Charles II shows that however much the king might have respected his old governor and counsellor, he did not listen to him and thus Cavendish's honour was in question. The old horse master was about to be put out to pasture.

Cavendish and Horsemanship

It is at this point that Cavendish determined to do something to reclaim his lost honour by capitalizing on an ability beyond the reach of any rebel or courtier. He was one of the finest horsemen in Europe and particularly

---

38   Cavendish, "A True Relation", 46.

39   Cavendish, William, "A Letter of Advice to Charles II on the Eve of the Restoration", in Slaughter T.P. (ed.), *Ideology and Politics on the Eve of the Restoration: Newcastle's Advice to Charles II* (Philadelphia: 1984) 211–12. I have modernized the spelling in this quote. The dating of this document is in dispute. Slaughter argues that it was written shortly before the Restoration, while Gloria Anzilotti argues that it was written as early as 1651, which Dewhurst accepts as the probable date of composition (Dewhurst, page 246, fn. 44).

versed in the skills of the *manège*, which he demonstrated at a riding academy attached to the Rubenshaus. He had learned the method of deductive reasoning from Hobbes and he now decided to put this method to work in a manual on the art of horsemanship. Cavendish was betting his honour and position on a book, not a battle. He would become a philosopher of equestrian science and would be honoured by all who could appreciate his knowledge.[40] The frontispiece to his treatise, published in 1658, proclaims that it contains *"La Méthode Nouvelle Invention extraordinaire de dresser les Chevaux les travailler selon la nature, et parfaire la nature par la subtilité de 'art; la quelle n'a jamais été treuvée que Par Le tres-noble et puissant Prince Guillaume Marquis et Comte de Newcastle".*[41] Cavendish, now self-styled a prince, is the first to have discovered the true and natural art of the *manège*. This claim should be compared with Hobbes's description of his work at the beginning of his 1656 work, *Elements of Philosophy*, 'A little Book, but full; and great enough, if men count well for great; and to an attentive Reader versed in the Demonstrations of Mathematicians . . . clear and easy to understand; and almost new throughout, without any offensive novelty'.[42]

While the subjects of Cavendish's and Hobbes's works may have differed, their styles did not. Each man thought himself the discoverer of his respective science, and each suggested that any failure to understand his method was the fault of the reader, not the author or his ideas. Both men reflected the desire to find demonstrative truth evident in many philosophical works of the seventeenth century. Both employed geometric demonstration to show how nature or animals move. Both rejected the notion that animals are automatons, as Descartes had argued. During the controversy with Bishop Bramhall on free will and determinism, Hobbes had written to Cavendish, 'And first your Lordship's own experience furnishes you with proof enough, that horses, dogs, and other brute beasts, do demur on the way they are to take'.[43] In fact, in *La Méthode Nouvelle*, Cavendish takes the question of animal rationality even further than Hobbes was willing to go, arguing, 'Altho' horses do not form their reasonings from the A B C, which, as that admirable and most excellent

---

40   For further information on Cavendish's public displays of the *manège* at Antwerp, see Peter Edwards's essay in this collection.

41   This volume was translated into English in 1743, with engraved illustration appended: Cavendish William, *A General System of Horsemanship* (North Pomfret Vermont; 2000).

42   Hobbes Thomas, *Elements of Philosophy, the First Section, Concerning Body: Written in Latin by Thomas Hobbes of Malmesbury, and Now Translated into English* (London, A. Crooke: 1656) vii.

43   Hobbes, "Of Liberties and Necessitie", 244.

philosopher master Hobbs says, is no language, but the marks and representation of things, he must notwithstanding give me leave to think, that they draw their reasonings from things themselves'. (1743V: 12) In other words, Cavendish felt able to critique Hobbesian nominalism—as well as Cartesian dualism—with his own experience of equine epistemology and reason. In some sense, the former patron and client had become equal in their abilities and presumably equally worthy of honour.

Cavendish's claims were based on his own extensive experiences with horses. When he served as governor to Prince Charles, he had taught his charge the art of horsemanship and had hitherto unsuccessfully sought the title of Master of the Horse.[44] In his exile, aristocrats from all over the continent, including Queen Christina of Sweden and Don Juan of Austria, came to admire his skills, and perhaps even take lessons in the *manège*, an art which he defended against accusations that it was without utility: 'Some wagg perhaps will ask, what is a horse good for that can do nothing but dance and play tricks? ... People of that character (who from a wrong turn and for want of judgment) are good for nothing themselves, and laugh at all the world, and at every thing'. (1743V: 14) While ignorant people might be laughing at his dancing stallions, Cavendish felt they brought honour and glory to the rider, and that the skills of horsemanship were particularly important for a king. In the "Letter of Advice", Cavendish proclaimed, 'Certainly there is nothing keeps up a king more than ceremony and order which makes distance, and those bring respect and duty and those obedience which is all'.[45] And, in his *La Méthode Nouvelle* he emphasized this point:

> I presume those great wits (the sneering gentlemen) will give Kings, Princes, and persons of quality leave to love pleasure-horses, as being an exercise that is very noble, and that which makes them appear most graceful when they shew themselves to their subjects, or at the head of an army, to animate it; so that the pleasure in this case is as useful as any thing else, besides the glory and satisfaction that attends it. (1743V: 14)

Thus, being able to ride gracefully brings honour and establishes authority and power not only for a king but also for 'persons of quality'. A poem by Cavendish precedes the text and begins, 'If you seek to attain the Art of Kings, Practice

---

44   Walker E., *'To Amaze the People with Pleasure and Delight': The Horsemanship Manuals of William Cavendish, Duke of Newcastle* (London: 2010) 12–13.

45   Cavendish, "Letter of Advice", 211.

these lessons in order to equip yourself'.[46] He included a series of engravings in this volume which graphically illustrate the honour brought to a commander in front of an army and his similarity to a king. In her discussion of Cavendish's horsemanship, Elaine Walker argues that the then marquis used the engravings to refashion his status and to reclaim his public role, 'Plate 1 presents Newcastle in his glory: a leader of men, acknowledged and approved of by heaven'. (1743V: 143, 172) This engraving depicts him leading victorious troops in the early years of the English Civil War, before his defeat at Marston Moor: (Fig. 8.1)

Cavendish emphasized that great noblemen are worthy of honour because of their own intrinsic worth and he emphasized this claim graphically in *La Methode Nouvelle* by depicting horses worshipping him: (Fig. 8.2) The text of the inscription on the engraving repeats Cavendish's claim to honour both as a general and a philosopher:

> Newcastle, the power of your genius
> Which makes you triumph over other horseman;
> Who to the furious encounter for the love of glory,
> In combat carries off the victory.
> Inside your circles, you do nothing but conjure,
> When you mount, you Philosophise;
> And then you tame the fiery and the wise
> And altogether they pay you homage.[47]

The horses worship Cavendish and serve him, according to the epigram under another engraving, 'With humility, submission and servility, Adore him like God and the author of their skill'. In this art, Cavendish shares the power of kings, 'And that all Horses are subject to his law; Then that they obey him as they would their King'. This kingly horse-master's method is so good 'all the world admires'. Or, as Cavendish might like it: all the world honours.

But, his excellence at horsemanship did not win Cavendish the honour and position he believed he deserved. In a last ditch attempt to regain his honour immediately before the Restoration, he offered Edward Hyde a horse. Writing to Secretary Nicholas, he exclaimed, 'My service to my Lord Chancellor, and tell him that now I hope to wait on him to Westminster to see him take possession of the Chancery, and upon one of my horses of manage, which will be the quietest, safest, and surest he or any man can have'.[48] Whether Hyde rode

---

46   Quoted in Walker, '*To Amaze the People*', 195.
47   Translation is by Walker, '*To Amaze the People*', 197.
48   Newcastle to Nicholas, 13 May, 1659, in Ellis, *Letters*, 208.

FIGURE 8.1 *"La Bataille Gagnée". From William Cavendish, La Méthode Nouvelle, plate 1.*
COPYRIGHT ELAINE WALKER.

FIGURE 8.2 *Horses worshipping Cavendish. From William Cavendish,* La Méthode Nouvelle, *plate 3.*
COPYRIGHT ELAINE WALKER.

into Westminster on Cavendish's horse is unknown, but he certainly did not favour the latter's return to power. The erstwhile general and counsellor was rebuked by Hyde and the king after he and his wife publically questioned the king's decision not to include him in an embassy to England to prepare for the Restoration. According to Hyde, Charles II had 'real kindness for him, rather pitying his weakness than forgetting his inadvertency'.[49]

It is never good when a ruler considers oneself to be weak, as Hobbes and Cavendish knew. Cavendish acknowledged the tenuousness of his position and blamed the 'woeful people' surrounding the king, adding 'the next generation of lords they tell me are fools. It will be a brave Upper House! Pray present my humble service to my Lord Chancellor...I write with so much freedom to you that I pray burn this'.[50] The old courtier, it appears was a favourite neither with the new nor old powers at court, although Charles did reward him with a dukedom in 1663 in lieu of paying back money he owed him. During his farewell interview with the king, Cavendish protested, 'I am not ignorant, that many believe I am discontented; and 'tis probable they'l say, I retire through discontent: But I take God to witness, that I am in no kind or ways displeased; for I am so joyed at your Majesties happy restauration, that I cannot be sad or troubled for any concern to my own particular'.[51]

And so, Cavendish returned to his country estates, leaving the perils and rewards of kings behind him. He appears to have been resigned to his fate, but his wife certainly was not. 'I observe', Margaret states in her biography of her husband, 'That spleen and malice, especially in this age, is grown to that height, that none will endure the praise of any body besides themselves; nay, they'l rather praise the wicked then the good; the coward rather then the valiant; the miserable then the generous, the traytor, then the loyal: which makes wise men meddle as little with the affairs of the world as ever they can'.[52]

Clearly, by the time Margaret Cavendish published her biography, her husband was powerless, having been vanquished by his dishonourable enemies. But neither of them were yet willing to give up on their own reputation in the world. In fact, Margaret's biography, *The Life of The Thrice Noble, High and Puissant Prince William Cavendishe*, was part of a two-book strategy by husband and wife to reclaim Cavendish's honour, which included another treatise on horsemanship in 1667, *A New and Extraordinary Method to Dress Horses*. Despite the similarities in name with *La Methode Nouvelle*, the two works were

---

49   Quoted in Mendelson, *Stuart Women*, 39–40.
50   Newcastle to Nicholas, 23 June 1659, in Ellis, *Letters Illustrative*, 207.
51   Cavendish M., *Life of William Cavendish*, 90.
52   Ibid., 177.

not the same textually, though, as Peter Edwards argues elsewhere in this volume, this was partly due to differences in the readerships of the two books. The motive, re-establishing Cavendish's honour remained the same. Indeed, he is even more insistent in this book about the uniqueness of his extraordinary method for training horses: 'But my Book is stolen out of no Book, nor any mans Practice but my own, and it is as True as it is New; and if any Man do not like it, it is a greate Signe he understands it not: for there is no way of Dressing *Horses* like it; If it be not Good, I am sure it is the Best that hath been Writ yet'. (1667: 4)

The strategy did not work, as Cavendish himself acknowledged. In the *Life*, his wife recounts that she had told him that great princes 'glory and splendor proceeded rather from the ceremony which they received from their subjects. To which, My Lord answered, that subjects were so far from giving splendor to their princes, that all the honours and titles, in which consists the chief splendor of a subject, were principally derived from them; for, said he, were there no princes, there would be none to confer honours and titles upon them'.[53] Cavendish clearly recognized that all of his efforts to regain his honour by appealing to his fellow horsemen and noble peers were nothing without the honour only the king could confer. At its core, honour was vertical, not horizontal; it could not be earned—it could only be given. Cavendish had returned to the place he and Hobbes had arrived at long before. Perhaps Cavendish composed his own epitaph in the poem he wrote for his wife's 1666 work, *Observations upon Experimental Philosophy*,

> This Book is Book of Books, and onely fits
> Great searching Brains, and Quintessence of Wits;
> For this will give you an Eternal Fame,
> And last to all Posterity your Name:
> You conquer Death, in a perpetual Life;
> And make me famous too in such a Wife.

Cavendish did achieve fame for having such a wife, but it was not the kind of glory which brings honour to the possessor. It rather made him ridiculous, at least in the eyes of Samuel Pepys and probably in the eyes of others at court.[54] In *Leviathan*, Hobbes wrote about man in the state of nature, 'men have no pleasure, (but on the contrary a great deale of griefe) in keeping company,

---

53   Ibid., 168.

54   See Trease, 194 on the reaction to Margaret Cavendish, and Sarasohn L.T., *Reason and Fancy during the Scientific Revolution: The Natural Philosophy of Margaret Cavendish* (Baltimore: 2010) 15–33.

where there is no power able to over-awe them all. For every man looketh that his companion should value him, at the same rate he sets upon himself'.[55] Cavendish had attempted to achieve honour throughout his long life, first at court, then on the battlefield, in exile and in print. But the search for honour, and the power which honour brings, ultimately eluded him. Margaret Cavendish tells a story in her biography of her husband: 'My Lord being in banishment, I told him, that he was happy in his misfortunes, for he was not subject to any state or prince. To which he jestingly answered, that as he was subject to no prince, so he was prince of no subjects'.[56] Essentially, Cavendish's failure to keep his position and power disenfranchised him, putting him in a kind of Hobbesian state of nature where his worth was known only by his horses and his wife.

Selective Bibliography

Cavendish Margaret, *The Life of the (1st) Duke of Newcastle & Other Writings* (London: A. Maxwell: 1667; reprint, London: 1916). Hereafter cited as *Life*.

Cavendish Margaret, "A True Relation of my Birth, Breeding, and Life (1656)", in Bowerbank S. – Mendelson S. (eds.), *Paper Bodies: A Margaret Cavendish Reader* (Ontario: 2000).

Cavendish William, "The Earl of Newcastle's Letter of Instruction to Prince Charles for His Studies, Conduct and Behaviour", in Ellis, H. (ed.), *Original Letters, Illustrative of English History Volume 3* (London: 1824).

Cavendish William, *A General System of Horsemanship* (London: J. Brindley: 1743; facsimile reproduction, North Pomfret, Vermont: 2000).

Cust R., "Honour and Politics in early Stuart England: the Case of Beaumont v. Hastings", *Past and Present* 149 (1995): 57–94.

Hobbes Thomas, *The Elements of Law Natural and Politic* [1640; Virginia: Electronic Text Center), http://etext.lib.virginia.edu/toc/modeng/public/Hob2Ele.html.

Hobbes Thomas, *Leviathan*, Tuck, R. (ed.) (1651; Cambridge: 1991).

Mendelson S., *The Mental World of Stuart Women: Three Studies* (Amherst: 1987).

Sarasohn L.T., "Thomas Hobbes and the Duke of Newcastle: A Study in the Mutuality of Patronage before the Establishment of the Royal Society", *Isis* 90 iv (1999): 715–57.

Walker E., *'To amaze the people with pleasure and delight': the horsemanship manuals of William Cavendish, Duke of Newcastle* (London: 2010).

---

55   Hobbes, *Leviathan*, 88.

56   Cavendish M., *Life of William Cavendish*, 167.

CHAPTER 9

William Cavendish as a Military Commander

Andrew Hopper

William Cavendish was the foremost of Charles I's 'grandee' commanders, those generals appointed in 1642–3 because of their wealth and status rather than their military experience. The king believed their example would stimulate patronage networks into the royalist camp, yet historians have long considered their military record to be dismal.[1] However, P.R. Newman's detailed work on northern royalism has defended his reputation, lamenting that no other royalist grandee had been 'so consistently denigrated by historians as he'. He pointed out that Cavendish was general of the largest royalist army of the First Civil War. He also stressed the wisdom of his choices of subordinate commanders, remarking that no other grandee commander had a greater capacity or potential to deliver a decisive royalist victory.[2] Indeed, for a while during late summer, 1643, Cavendish's military success appeared to suggest that a decisive royalist victory was close at hand.[3] Despite the historical emphasis that has been placed on Parliament's advantages in wealth and resources, we have recently been reminded that military leadership was no small influence on the outcome of the wars.[4] Therefore, a fresh understanding of Cavendish's generalship is timely and worthwhile.

Newman's admiration of Cavendish was a reaction to a negative tradition that stretched back to the royalist historian, Edward Hyde, Earl of Clarendon. Cavendish had refused to assist Clarendon in writing his history, which helps to explain the censure of him that followed.[5] Clarendon considered Cavendish personally courageous, but ill-suited to generalship and the rigours of field campaigning. He claimed that he was negligent of the king's orders and hostile

---

1 Gentles I., "The Civil Wars in England", in Kenyon J. – Ohlmeyer J. (eds.), *The Civil Wars: A Military History of England, Scotland and Ireland, 1638–1660* (Oxford: 1998) 108.

2 Newman P.R., *The Old Service: Royalist Regimental Colonels and the Civil War, 1642–1646* (Manchester: 1993) 79–80.

3 Scott D., "Rethinking Royalist Politics, 1642–1649", in Adamson J. (ed.), *The English Civil War: Conflict and Contexts, 1640–1649* (Basingstoke: 2009) 46.

4 Wanklyn M., *The Warrior Generals: Winning the British Civil Wars, 1642–1652* (London: 2010).

5 Binns J. (ed.), "The Memoirs and Memorials of Sir Hugh Cholmley of Whitby, 1600–1657", *Yorkshire Archaeological Society, Record Series*, 153 (2000) 123.

© KONINKLIJKE BRILL NV, LEIDEN, 2017 | DOI 10.1163/9789004326217_011

to peace negotiations, a man estranged from the court, unacquainted with and distrustful of the Privy Council. Supposedly, Cavendish was diverted from command by 'delightful company, music' and 'softer pleasures', so that he would not consult his principal commanders 'from whence many inconveniences fell out'.[6] His detractors have long highlighted his military inexperience. Sir Philip Warwick, having served on Cavendish's staff, praised his 'grandeur, generosity, loyalty, and steady and forward courage', but reflected 'he had the tincture of a romantic spirit, and had the misfortune to have something of the poet in him'.[7] It seems that several contemporaries unfairly used Cavendish's literary and artistic interests to undermine his military reputation.

Such contemporary criticism was reinforced by Victorian historians, such as the editor of the *Fairfax Correspondence*, who jibed that Cavendish was a better horseman than a musician, a better musician than a poet, and a better poet than a general.[8] Sir Charles Firth concluded that his campaigns against the weaker northern parliamentarians 'can hardly be considered very creditable to his military talents'.[9] Often criticized for being over-cautious, during 1642–43 he took three attempts to dislodge and defeat a weaker enemy. Consequently, his military attributes continue to be compared unfavourably with his parliamentarian rival, Sir Thomas Fairfax.[10]

Recently, Malcolm Wanklyn has pointed out the problems of attempting to 'audit' the performance of Civil War generals. He argues that many historians have been beguiled by Clarendon's ascribing of blame for the king's defeat, overlooking how this was shaped by Clarendon's personal animosities.[11] Rather than apportioning praise or blame according to previous historical judgments, a fresh analysis of Cavendish's generalship should encompass the multiple roles fulfilled by Civil War commanders in pursuit of military success in Civil War England. Therefore, this chapter will consider Cavendish's importance in the mobilization and maintenance of the royalist war effort, as well as evaluating the success of his strategy and tactics.

---

6   Seaward P. (ed.), *Edward Hyde, Earl of Clarendon: The History of the Rebellion. A New Selection* (Oxford: 2009) 215.

7   Warwick Sir Philip, *Memoires of the Reigne of King Charles I with a Continuation to the Happy Restauration of King Charles II* (London: Richard Chiswell: 1701) 235.

8   Bell R. (ed.), *The Fairfax Correspondence: Memorials of the Civil Wars* (London: 1849) I, 243.

9   Firth, (ed.), *Life of William Cavendish*, ix.

10   Wanklyn, *Warrior Generals*, 48.

11   Ibid., 228–9.

Cavendish and the Royalist War Effort

Clarendon harboured a nostalgic, rose-tinted view of the noble-driven nature of royalist mobilization in 1642. In this, he happily praised Cavendish's mustering of the northern army 'purely by his own interest, and the concurrence of his numerous allies in those northern parts'.[12] To accomplish this, Cavendish was invested with unique powers and the largest territorial base of any royalist commander, encompassing authority over thirty-two garrisons across the North. He demonstrated his vice-regal status by dubbing twelve knights, coining money and raising taxes.[13] By late 1643 he was appointed general for all counties north of the Trent, as well as Nottinghamshire, Lincolnshire, Rutland, Huntingdon, Cambridgeshire and Norfolk.[14] His unique position was underlined by the separate orders the king published for governing his army. Any soldier who drew his sword in Cavendish's presence meaning harm was to lose his hand. Any individual corresponding or treating with the enemy without Cavendish's leave could be executed.[15] The extraordinary powers invested in him reflected his importance to royalist strategy. With the queen gathering officers, arms and munitions in the Netherlands for a projected landing in north-east England, Walter Strickland, the parliamentarian envoy at The Hague, informed John Pym in November 1642: 'they hope to make Cavendish able to command Yorkshire, and be a seed plot for greater hopes'.[16]

Royalists tended to stress personal loyalty over service to a cause, so with the king distant in Oxford, Cavendish's person became an important focus for northern royalism. His wife's claim that he raised 100,000 men for the king, 'and those most upon his own Interest, and without any other considerable help or

---

12   Clarendon, *History of the Rebellion*, 214.

13   Roy I. – Macadam J., "Why did Prince Rupert Fight at Marston Moor?", *Journal of the Society for Army Historical Research* 86 (2008) 236.

14   Wanklyn, *Warrior Generals*, 45; Hulse L., "William Cavendish, first duke of Newcastle-upon-Tyne (*bap.* 1593, *d.* 1676), *writer, patron, and royalist army officer*", *ODNB*, /4946.

15   This anxiety may have reflected uncertainty over the allegiance of those Yorkshire royalist gentry who had negotiated a short-lived local peace with the Fairfaxes in September 1642: BL, Thomason, E127(23), *Orders and Institutions of War, made and ordained by His Majesty, and by him delivered to his Generall His Excellence the Earle of Newcastle. With the said Earles speech to the army at the delivery and publishing the said orders prefix* (1642), 4–6; Woolrych A., "Yorkshire's Treaty of Neutrality", *History Today* 6 (1956) 696–704.

16   Beinecke Rare Book and Manuscript Library, Yale University, Osborn Shelves fb94, folder 23.

assistance', is clearly wildly inflated.[17] Yet, even his enemies ceded the centrality of his person to the northern royalist efforts. Lucy Hutchinson praised his excellent hospitality and long residence in the North, remarking that he was 'a lord once so much beloved in his country', and that 'no man was a greater prince than he in all that northerne quarter'.[18] In 1641 his rents supposedly brought him £22,393 per annum, making him one of the wealthiest peers in England. His estates stretched across Northumberland, Yorkshire, Nottinghamshire, Lincolnshire, Derbyshire, Staffordshire, Somerset and Gloucestershire. His army recruited many soldiers from all these counties save the last two, in addition to Cumberland, Durham, Lancashire and Westmorland. Men from Durham and the Tees valley were heavily recruited.[19] He issued so many commissions that Sir Philip Warwick considered the cohesion of his army compromised by under-recruited units, and Newman conceded that Cavendish was 'consciously creating an army which would reflect upon his own grandeur'.[20] Whilst this method of building an army might not have resulted in the most militarily effective end product, it was undoubtedly an efficient way of mobilizing royalist sympathies among the landowning élites. Around a third of these commissions went to Catholic officers, and, as the Catholic gentry tended to have a closer relationship with their tenants, it has been suggested that they were better able to mobilize their tenantry than their Protestant counterparts.[21]

Although some of Cavendish's infantry originated as trained band units, most were regiments mustered by their own colonels, as, for example, the foot levied through the Commission of Array by Sir Marmaduke Langdale in the East Riding in March 1643 and armed out of the munitions brought by the queen. Sir Henry Slingsby received his commission to raise a regiment of volunteers on 13 December 1642. He beat his drum in and around York, enlisting 200 men and billeting them on his tenants. Like most Civil War armies, on occasion Cavendish had to resort to impressment to recruit his infantry, particularly in response to the Scottish invasion.[22]

---

17   Firth, (ed.), *Life of William Cavendish*, 109.

18   Keeble N.H. (ed.), *Memoirs of the Life of Colonel Hutchinson* (London: 1995) 84.

19   Firth, (ed.), *Life of William Cavendish*, 99–100; Newman P.R., "The Royalist Army in Northern England, 1642–1645" (D.Phil. thesis, University of York, 1978) I, 11, 94, 256.

20   Warwick, *Memoires of the Reigne of King Charles I*, 236–7; Newman, "Royalist Army" I, 106; Newman, *Old Service*, 263.

21   Malcolm J., "A King in Search of Soldiers: Charles I in 1642", *Historical Journal* 21 (1978) 271.

22   Parsons D. (ed.), *Sir Henry Slingsby: The Diary of Sir Henry Slingsby of Scriven, Bart.* (London: 1836) 87, 93; Newman, "Royalist Army", I, 24, 28–9, 62, 239–40, 282.

Having coordinated the mustering of such large numbers of men, their training was no doubt improved by the numerous professional officers who landed with the queen at Bridlington in February 1643. Cavendish not only successfully armed these recruits, but established his own Ordnance Office. Peter Edwards has shown how his army drew from private armouries and some northern manufactures, such as York's saddle-makers, but was mainly supplied by imports from the Netherlands, landed on the north-eastern coast by privateer merchants such as the Fleming, Jan van Haesdonck. On top of equipping his own forces, the king expected him to send convoys to Oxford, writing to Cavendish: 'I have no greater want then of Armes nor means to supply my selfe than from you'.[23]

Cavendish was also effective in gathering intelligence and acting upon it. Unlike many other royalist commanders, he employed a Scoutmaster-General and was careful to use codes to convey sensitive information. He has recently been credited with establishing 'a sound base of intelligence-gathering', aided by a broad base of popular sympathizers across the North. Successes included the early interception in 1643 of Sir Thomas Fairfax's letters to his father. Cavendish's acting upon useful and timely intelligence reports led directly to the victory at Seacroft Moor.[24]

Cavendish's arrival in Yorkshire was intended to resuscitate the floundering royalist war effort there, and was in response to the 'the earnest Sollicitation and Intreaty of the Prime Nobility and Gentry of *Yorkeshire*'.[25] He forced his army's passage across the River Tees at Piercebridge on 1 December and arrived in York two days later. Pledging to avoid plundering civilians, he aimed to maintain his army through three means: loans, taxation and the sequestration of enemy estates. Firstly, he invited the Yorkshire gentry to lend him money for the king's war effort.[26] The means by which he raised loans became formalized with the Yorkshire Engagement, a document popularly known as the Yorkshire Magna Charta. Lenders were promised reimbursement from the Engagement's signatories, who pledged to repay loans according to their estates' size. As a result, over 100 people subscribed and £19,445 was raised very quickly. Many

---

23   Edwards P., *Dealing in Death: The Arms Trade and the British Civil Wars, 1638–1652* (Stroud: 2000) 31, 50, 171, 203, 227.

24   Ellis J., *To Walk in the Dark: Military Intelligence during the English Civil War, 1642–1646* (Stroud: 2011) 40, 55, 58, 97, 102–4, 112–3, 124, 207.

25   Wing / N875A, *An Answer of the Right Honourable Earle of Newcastle, His Excellency &c. to the six groundless aspersions cast upon him by the Lord Fairefax in his late warrant* (*here inserted*) *bearing date Feb. 2, 1642 by the Earl himselfe* (Oxford, 1643) 5.

26   Binns J., *Yorkshire in the Civil Wars: Origins, Impact and Outcome* (Pickering: 2004) 57.

were forced to make contributions or sign the Engagement against their will, under threat of plundering, or to procure their release from imprisonment.[27] Despite the Scots' invasion, the scheme remained in operation in February 1644.[28] Cavendish also donated large sums of his own money to the royalist war effort; Margaret, his wife, later calculated the losses he suffered during the wars as £941,303.[29]

Secondly, from April 1643 Cavendish imposed upon Yorkshire what became known as the 'Great Sesse', a scheme which emulated the assessments placed upon territories under parliamentarian control. It was designed to raise £30,000 per month to support his army. Subdivided into the county's Ridings and Wapentakes, it was collected by parish constables. Its surviving documentation is fragmented, but its collection continued until Cavendish's flight into York in April 1644.[30] So, rather than maintaining his forces by plunder and free quarter, as claimed by parliamentarian propaganda, Cavendish developed several financial mechanisms to support his forces on a long-term basis. Given the size of his army, reported by Sir George Goring to be 18,000 men on 22 April 1643, this was no mean achievement.[31]

In the war of words that accompanied his mobilization, Cavendish proved himself an effective propagandist, despite his subsequent maxim that 'it is a great Error in a State to have all affairs put into Gazettes, (for it over-heats the peoples brains'.[32] In March 1642 the king had established Stephen Bulkley's royalist press at York, which printed at least 74 different tracts that year alone. Cavendish later used this facility to propagate print that explained his actions, reinvigorated his supporters and perhaps also won over converts.[33] Upon his southward march into Yorkshire, he circulated 500 copies of a manifesto explaining his actions to the people of Durham and Northumberland, to keep

27   TNA, State Papers (hereafter SP) 19/8/248–52, 353–4; SP 19/10/ 308; SP 19/119/2, 25, 46, 48, 61; SP 19/120/72, 76, 84, 111, 120.

28   TNA, SP 19/122/70.

29   Firth, (ed.), *Life of William Cavendish*, 102.

30   Bennett M., *The Civil Wars in Britain and Ireland, 1638–1651* (Oxford: 1997) 179, 208; see Page W. (ed.), *The Victoria History of the County of York, North Riding* (London: 1923) II, 137–8, 214–6, 282–6, 309–14, 383–5.

31   Warburton E. (ed.), *Memoirs of Prince Rupert and the Cavaliers* (London: 1849) II, 182.

32   Firth, (ed.), *Life of William Cavendish*, 173.

33   Hanson L., "The King's Printer at York and Shrewsbury 1642–3", *The Library* 23 (1943) 129–31; Sessions W.K., *Stephen Bulkley: Peripatetic Royalist* Printer *of London* – York – Newcastle – Gateshead – Newcastle – York, *who died in 1680, and his son John Bulkley who died in 1695* (York: 1997).

them from thinking he was deserting them.[34] His wife later credited him with winning over the parliamentarian, Sir Hugh Cholmley, by making 'rational and convincible Arguments'.[35] Cavendish's efforts were in response to personal attacks upon him in the London press that branded him as 'the Atheisticall Marquess' or a 'Semi papian' on account of the Roman Catholic nature of his forces.[36] This reflected the fear his army inspired among parliamentarians, but also of the Catholic presence within his officer corps. Initially, the second article of the king's martial code sent to govern Cavendish's forces commanded 'No Papist of what degree or quality soever shall be admitted to serve in our Army'.[37] Yet, when the king wrote to him on 23 September 1642, he commanded him to 'make use of all my loving subjects' services, without examining their consciences'. Thereafter, many Catholics were commissioned into Cavendish's forces: about thirty-six per cent of his officers and forty per cent of his colonels.[38] Some, such as Lords Belasyse and Widdrington, were in positions of high command. Consequently, parliamentarian propaganda played on popular anti-Catholic prejudice, blaming Cavendish's forces for their rape and 'barbarous usage' of civilians, fusing this with xenophobia by highlighting the foreign and French component of his army.[39] As David Scott has recently argued, the purpose of much of this was to convince the Scots that the royalists were a threat to the Protestant religion not just in England but throughout the three kingdoms.[40]

Yet, unlike some royalists, Cavendish appreciated the power of print. Allegiance was to be negotiated, not commanded, and he did not let parliamentarian propaganda go unanswered. Needled by enemy declarations about his employment of Papists, he published three personal declarations both to

34   Trease G., *Portrait of a Cavalier: William Cavendish, First Duke of Newcastle* (London: 1979) 98.

35   Firth, (ed.), *Life of William Cavendish*, 24.

36   BL, Thomason E252(22), *A Perfect Diurnal of Some Passages in Parliament*, 19–26 February (London, 1644) 242; BL, Thomason E267(2), *A New Discovery of Hidden Secrets: In Severall Letters, Propositions, Articles, and Other Writings concerning the Earle of Newcastle, Captaine John Hotham, and many other Malignant Gentry of the Northerne Counties*, 3 November (London, 1645) 2.

37   BL, Thomason, E127(23), *Orders and Institutions of War*, 3.

38   Newman, *Old Service*, 87, 212–4, 266; P.R. Newman, "Catholic Royalists of Northern England, 1642–5", *Northern History* 15 (1979) 91.

39   Hopper A., "The Popish Army of the North: Anti-Catholicism and Parliamentarian Allegiance in Yorkshire, 1642–46", *Recusant History* 25 (2000) 12–28; BL, Thomason E104(13), *A Miraculous Victory obtained by the Right Honorable, Ferdinando Lord Fairfax* (London, 1643) 5.

40   Scott D., *Politics and War in the Three Stuart Kingdoms, 1637–49* (Basingstoke: 2004) 42.

vindicate his own honour and to chastise the enemy.[41] These included a brave personal defence of his Catholic soldiers that he ordered to be published in all churches and chapels within the county of York: 'That I have in mine Army some of the Romish Communion I do not deny . . . These I admitted for their Loyalty and Abilities, not for their Religion'. He claimed that Parliament's armies included foreigners who were Roman Catholic, against whom no exception had been made. Then he contrasted the loyalty of his Catholic supporters with the rebellion of Fairfax's 'Sectaries, Brownists, Anabaptists, Familists'. He depicted the parliamentarians as deceivers of their own followers, insurgents who did 'prostitute the Ordinance of God to the rebellious designes of ambitious men'.[42] Then, in a move calculated to appeal to the gentry's nightmarish memories of Tudor popular uprisings, he also accused the Fairfaxes' men of being sacrilegious iconoclasts with a levelling and anarchic design against the honour and property of the landed élite:

> They have spared no places, The Churches of Christians which the Heathens durst not violate, are by them prophaned: Their Ornaments have been made either the supply of their necessities, or the subject of their scurrilities, their Chalices, or Communion Cups . . . have become the objects of their Sacriledge, the Badges and Monuments of ancient Gentry in Windows, and Pedigrees have been by them defaced; Old Evidences, the Records of private Families, the Pledges of Possessions, the boundaries of Mens Properties have been by them burned, torn in Pieces, and the Seals trampled under their Feet. Ceilings and Wainscot have been broken in Pieces, Walls demolished . . . And all this by a Company of Men crept now at last out of the Bottom of Pandora's Box.[43]

---

41   BL, Thomason, E83(1), *A Declaration made by the Earl of Nevv-Castle, Governour of the town and county of New-Castle: and Generall of all His Majesties forces raised in the Northern Parts of this Kingdom, for the defence of the same. For his resolution of marching into Yorkshire. As also, a just vindication of himself from that unjust aspersion laid upon him, for entertaining some popish recusants in his forces* (London: 1642); Wing / N875A, *An Answer of the Right Honourable Earle of Newcastle, His Excellency &c. to the Six Groundless Aspersions cast upon him by the Lord Fairefax in his Late Warrant (here inserted) bearing date Feb. 2, 1642 by the Earl himselfe* (Oxford: 1643); Wing (2nd ed.) / N874A, *The Answer of His Excellency the Earle of Newcastle, to a late declaration of the Lord Fairefax dated the 8. of June, 1643* (York: 1643).

42   Wing / N875A, *Answer of the Earle of Newcastle*, 1, 3, 5, 7; BL, Thomason, E83(1), *Declaration made by the Earl of Nevv-Castle*, 5.

43   Wing / N875A, *An Answer of the Earle of Newcastle*, 9.

In a similar vein, Cavendish had earlier compared Fairfax's men to the German peasants of the 1520s and the Anabaptist commune at Munster. These insurgents would 'attempt the cutting of Throats of all Landlords and Magistrates, and will maintain, That it is against the Law of God for any Man to hold an Estate by Law or Birthright, but only according to Merit and Worth'.[44]

On 8 June 1643 Cavendish personally responded to another of Fairfax's declarations, admonishing Fairfax for having 'perfidiously broken' the peace treaty at Rothwell and thereby causing an unnecessary armed conflict in Yorkshire. He refuted Fairfax's accusation that the parliamentarian prisoners captured at Seacroft Moor had been unlawfully and tyrannically imprisoned and maltreated, with hundreds sick and dying, despite having quarter promised them. As well as denying that such a promise had been made, he also declared that the wounded prisoners had been treated by the royalist surgeons and given medicine by the queen's own physicians. Far from seeking their destruction, Cavendish sought to keep them from harm and reform them into good subjects. Charitable collections for the prisoners and visits from their female relatives had been permitted. Instead, he diverted blame for deaths in his custody onto Lord Fairfax himself, who had led them into rebellion, and who denied them their liberty when he had the means to exchange them and fair offers to do so.[45] Cavendish was also at pains to point out that Fairfax's army was illegal and therefore incapable of treating: 'neither hee nor any of his pretended Captains in this Warr, can challenge any Interest in the Law of Arms'.[46]

Strategy and Tactics

Cavendish's success as a military commander was not underpinned by the formal military education experienced on the continent by so many other Civil War commanders. His first commission was as captain of the Prince of Wales's troop during the First Bishops' War, commanding knights and gentlemen, whom he had done much to raise himself. Although he appears to have seen no action during the Bishops' Wars, he did challenge his commanding officer, Henry Rich, Earl of Holland to a duel for affronting him by deploying the prince's troop in the army's rearguard. The affair suggests that, like many other aristocratic commanders, Cavendish had difficulty reconciling his self-regard to service to a broader cause. The king intervened to prevent bloodshed

---

44   BL, Thomason, E83(1), *Declaration made by the Earl of Nevv-Castle*, 8.

45   Wing (2nd ed.) / N874A, *Answer of the Earle of Newcastle*, 6–13.

46   Ibid., 16.

yet this episode may have enhanced Cavendish's standing when Holland fell into royal disfavour in 1641–2.[47]

In January 1642, soon after the king failed to arrest his leading parliamentary opponents, Charles urged Cavendish to gain for him the vast arms magazine stored in Hull for use against the Scots. He secretly appointed Cavendish governor of the town on 11 January 1642, but the earl was rebuffed and refused entry on 15 January. Lacking the military means to coerce them, and anxious about provoking armed hostilities, he explained to the king: 'the town will not admit me by any means, so I am very flat and out of countenance here'.[48] Instead, John Hotham, MP for Scarborough, talked his way into Hull, backed by companies from his father's regiment of trained bands.[49] Yet, Cavendish experienced more success further north when he secured Newcastle-upon-Tyne for the king without a fight on 17 June, garrisoning Tynemouth Castle and fortifying Shields harbour soon after.[50] His immediate strategic objective was to mobilize the North-east for the king and control enough of the coastline to allow the queen to land safely with munitions from Europe. With this in mind, he was ill-inclined to co-ordinate with other royalist armies, despite Charles ordering him south in November and December 1642, and again in April and May 1643.[51] Predictably, as Cavendish's army increased, rival royalist leaders grew jealous of its size and his autonomy of command. Indeed, because he did not deplete his field force by establishing too many garrisons, it soon swelled to rival the Oxford army in size.

By December 1642 Cavendish controlled Northumberland, Durham, Cumberland and Westmorland, almost without a fight. Establishing himself at York, he spilt the local parliamentarians in two, won the support of the county's royalists and made an example of double-dealers and fence-sitters such as Thomas, Lord Savile. In January 1643, the king's secretary, Sir Edward Nicholas, gave Cavendish 'great thanks for his discovery of the Lord Saviles Treacherie saying that the said service was no lesse acceptable to him then if hee had wonne a battle'.[52] Nowhere in England had such territorial success been

47   Clarendon, *History of the Rebellion*, 37.

48   Ryder I.E., "The Seizure of Hull and its Magazine, January 1642", *Yorkshire Archaeological Journal* 61 (1989) 141.

49   Hopper A. (ed.), "The Papers of the Hothams: Governors of Hull during the Civil War", *Camden Society*, 5th series, 39 (2011) 11–12.

50   Woolrych A., *Britain in Revolution, 1625–1660* (Oxford: 2002) 228.

51   Wanklyn, *Warrior Generals*, 45, 77, 243.

52   BL, Harleian MS 164, fo. 281r. For the substance of Cavendish's charges against Savile see Bodleian Library, MS Clarendon 22, fos. 53–60.

replicated, while his foresight in planting garrisons at Pontefract and Newark would later prove very costly to Parliament's war effort.[53] On 15 December 1642 the king wrote to Cavendish stating that he 'would always look upon you as a principal instrument in keeping the crown on my head. The business of Yorkshire I account almost done'.[54] Nonetheless, from the queen's landing at Bridlington in February until her departure in June 1643 Cavendish's strategy was constrained by having to play the courtier and provide her escort southward. As a considerable proportion of the arms required for the royalist war effort were imported through north-eastern ports and conducted southward in such convoys, it was imperative for Cavendish to ensure they were strongly protected. By June he had assembled 4,000 men for a convoy which delivered the queen to her husband safely and boosted the supply of arms to the royalist forces further south.[55]

Despite this success, given his superior manpower and resources, Cavendish has been blamed for not subduing all the North for the king. However, his freedom of action was limited by the elusiveness of the enemy and by the composition of his own forces. Firstly, he understood that his Yorkshire enemies were geographically and politically divided, between the Hothams in Hull and the Fairfaxes in the West Riding. Their mutual loathing afforded him the opportunity to negotiate a secret treaty with the Hothams in order to concentrate his efforts against the Fairfaxes. Of the elder Hotham, Sir Henry Slingsby fondly recalled that Cavendish 'knew how to work upon his distemper when he once found his pulse'.[56] This was a shrewd move and it spared the queen from military confrontation in her passage from Bridlington to York.[57] In the West Riding, no such accommodation was possible and the army commanded by Ferdinando, Lord Fairfax, proved difficult to engage. As it was numerically inferior and weak in cavalry, it therefore inclined to urban battlefields, hoping to win small, incremental engagements through speed and surprise to buy time and boost morale. The military theorist, Stanley Carpenter, has called this a 'Fabian strategy', or 'attrition by strategic defensive'.[58] Whether this indicates,

---

53   Newman, *Old Service*, 82, 263, 266, 278.

54   Trease, *Portrait of a Cavalier*, 101.

55   Wanklyn, *Warrior Generals*, 60; Newman, *Old Service*, 137, 265; Cromwell estimated the size of the queen's retinue as 3,000 foot and 1,200 horse: "Lowndes MS", HMC, 7th Report, Appendix, Part 1 (London: 1879) 551–2.

56   *Diary of Sir Henry Slingsby*, 92.

57   Binns, *Sir Hugh Cholmley*, 127; Hopper, *Hothams*, 19, 73–82.

58   Carpenter S.D.M., *Military Leadership in the British Civil Wars, 1642–1651: 'The Genius of this Age'* (London: 2005) 59, 63.

as Carpenter argues, that Fairfax's strategic vision was superior remains debatable, but Fairfax's guile certainly frustrated Cavendish. A sign of this is glimpsed in his challenge to Fairfax to name a time and place to fight him in the open, according 'to the Examples of our Heroick Ancestors, who used not to spend their Time in scratching one another out of Holes, but in pitched Fields determined their Doubts'.[59] Cavendish's desire for trial by battle reflected his attachment to chivalric concepts of honour, but also his confidence that in a set-piece battlefield encounter, his substantial advantage in cavalry would prove decisive. This posturing was intended to present himself in a more honourable light and no doubt antagonized the Fairfaxes, but Lord Fairfax's reply, quoting Ben Jonson to the playwright's old patron, that he had no regard for 'knights of the Sun or Amadis de Gauls', must have irked Cavendish further.[60]

So, Cavendish was compelled to develop a patient strategy for rooting the Fairfaxes out of their hole, firstly by isolating them, secondly by disrupting the cloth trade, food supply and provisions upon which their Pennine hinterlands depended and finally by striking at their support base with overwhelming force. After the queen's landing, Cavendish welcomed the defection of Sir Hugh Cholmley, the parliamentarian governor of Scarborough, and neutralized the Hothams in Hull through secret negotiations. Then, he turned on the West Riding parliamentarians, routing their rearguard on Seacroft Moor on 30 March 1643 after they had abandoned their defensive positions at Selby. Thereupon, Cavendish triggered panic at Westminster when it was reported that he was besieging Lord Fairfax in Leeds with 10,000 foot and 30 troops of horse.[61] Whilst the queen and Sir George Goring favoured assaulting Leeds that April, Cavendish exercised greater caution with his men's lives. Appreciating the heavy losses a major assault on a large town might inflict, he favoured the advice of General King and his professional officers who recommended a temporary withdrawal.[62] Given the performance of Fairfax's army in urban encounters thus far at Tadcaster and Leeds, this was sound advice, and significantly came at a time when Cavendish was mourning the death of his first wife at Bolsover on 17 April.[63]

---

59   Wing/N875A, *An Answer of the Earle of Newcastle*, 11.

60   Adamson J., "Chivalry and Political Culture in Caroline England", in Sharpe K. – Lake P. (eds.), *Culture and Politics in Early Stuart England* (Basingstoke: 1994) 183.

61   BL, Harleian MS 164, fo. 364v.

62   Trease, *Cavalier*, 115; Green M.A.E. (ed.), *The Letters of Queen Henrietta Maria including her Private Correspondence with Charles the First* (London: 1857) 184, 189.

63   Trease, *Cavalier*, 113.

Thereafter, the queen's letters grew impatient and undermined him, despite his army's successes in capturing Rotherham and Sheffield in early May. In a letter to the king on 18 May, she called him 'fantastic and inconstant'. On 27 May she advocated renewing the siege of Leeds, adding that if she went south she would be 'enraged to go away without having beaten these rascals ... and if I go away I am afraid that they will not be beaten'.[64] The queen's censure seems to have caused Cavendish some unease. For instance, in his secret correspondence with John Hotham, the latter played upon his concerns, assuring him that Lady Cornwallis had mocked him at court, saying, 'that you were a sweet general, lay in bed until eleven a clock and com'd till 12, then came to see the Queen, and so the work was done, and that General King did all the business'. Hotham went on: 'My Lord you can expect nothing at court but tricks. The women rule all ... You have now done great service that will be forgot when they think they can shift without you'.[65] Such rumour reawakened Cavendish's debilitating anxieties about his status at court, which he had nursed since his days as governor of the Prince of Wales. His worries were heightened by the distance of his removal from Oxford, so much that the king and queen felt it necessary to reassure him on several occasions that his reputation remained untarnished.[66]

Cavendish was also constrained by the conditional nature of his Yorkshire forces' allegiance. The county's royalist gentry had invited him into Yorkshire, and because of this they considered his command over the Yorkshire portion of the army to be 'nominal and by agreement'.[67] At his council of war at Pontefract on 4 June 1643, Cavendish acknowledged in the queen's presence that when he had arrived in Yorkshire he had promised that he would not march south until the county was pacified.[68] This could only be accomplished by forcing the Fairfaxes out of their urban strongholds to give battle: Lord Fairfax from Leeds and Sir Thomas from Bradford. As early as 17 April Sir George Goring had highlighted the means to achieve this: 'wherefore if you can get between Bradford and Leeds, you will so annoy, divert and separate them in all their Designs ... This will so bare them'.[69] Cavendish's eventual

64   Green, ed., *Letters of Queen Henrietta Maria*, 205, 212; BL, Harleian MS 7379.

65   Hull History Centre: Hotham MS, U DDHO/1/12; Hopper, *Hothams*, 93.

66   Roy – Macadam, "Marston Moor", 238.

67   Newman, *Old Service*, 263.

68   Wanklyn, *Warrior Generals*, 77.

69   Wing (2nd ed.) / F121B, *A Miraculous Victory obtained by the Right Honorable, Ferdinando Lord Fairfax, against the army under the Command of the Earl of Newcastle at Wakefield in York-shire* (London: 1643) 8.

pursuit of this strategy paid off, obliging the Fairfaxes to gamble on a desperate surprise attack that backfired, crowning Cavendish with a crushing victory at Adwalton Moor on 30 June that reduced the Fairfaxes to the status of virtual fugitives. This was the largest battle since Edgehill, and with the exception of Lostwithiel, arguably the royalists' greatest victory of the war.

For his personal role in the victory, Newman applauded Cavendish as a 'general of perception and capacity', who personally turned the tide of battle.[70] Yet Malcolm Wanklyn has recently contradicted him, arguing that the victory 'owed little' to Cavendish or General King, accusing them of giving battle without a tactical plan and on ground that favoured the enemy.[71] Newman's evidence was a report of Cavendish's valour in *Mercurius Aulicus* on 3 July, which held that the earl had steadied the wavering royalist line as it was giving ground:

> he presently alighted from his Horse, went himselfe to his Foot, and taking a Pike into his hand, bid them follow him assuring them, not a man should goe further than he himself would lead them, bidding them now shew themselves for King Charles and their Countrey, and by the help of God they would not leave one Rebel in the North.[72]

The tract claimed that Cavendish's personal intervention so infused his soldiers with his noble courage that the tide of battle turned, the rebels fleeing in astonishment at the royalists' bravery. Such reports constructed cults of personality around officers because the need to demonstrate bravery in battle remained an important facet of command. A narrative with a similar purpose, yet conflicting in detail, was published in 1667 by Margaret Cavendish as the prologue to the patent that created her husband a marquis. This stated that his army was on the point of fleeing until he personally intervened in the battle at the head of two troops of horse, and that he "by his Wisdom, Virtue and his own Hand, brought death and flight to the Rebels".[73]

Another tract, *An Expresse Relation*, published in Oxford soon after the battle and possibly Cavendish's own account, did not mention personal heroics. Instead it exaggerated the size of Fairfax's army to underline the victory's importance. Fairfax's infantry were said to outnumber the royalist foot and to consist almost entirely of musketeers, while the cavalry were inflated from

---

70   Newman, *Old Service*, 79, 137, 262.

71   Wanklyn, *Warrior Generals*, 60.

72   BL, Thomason, E60(18), *Mercurius Aulicus*, 27th week (Oxford: 1643) 350.

73   Firth, (ed.), *Life of William Cavendish*, 126.

thirteen to twenty troops. This tract also credited the royalist artillery with precipitating the enemy's collapse.[74] Sir Henry Slingsby ascribed the victory to General King, and Sir Thomas Fairfax's later memoirs blamed one Colonel Skirton as intervening at the critical moment: "A wild & Desperate man", who "Desired his Gen: to let him Charge".[75]

Whatever the reasons for the victory, there was embarrassment among royalists that the battle had been so hard fought and that Fairfax's smaller army had proved so difficult to beat. Following the example of *An Expresse Relation*, both Margaret and Jane Cavendish exaggerated the size of Fairfax's army. The latter's poem, 'On the 30th of June: to God', implausibly referred to her father's army as a 'little flock'.[76] In his thanksgiving sermon for Adwalton Moor, John Bramhall, bishop of Derry, praised Cavendish's generalship, saying God had favoured his forces at '*Seecroft, Tankersley, Yarum, Atherton, &c'.* He claimed that the victory was especially providential by insinuating that the rebels held the advantage of numbers, ground and wind. In explaining Cavendish's previous setbacks at the hands of the Fairfaxes, Bramhall blamed being taken by surprise, and 'the negligence of Scouts'.[77] The victory raised Cavendish's stock in Oxford, where it was celebrated with a public thanksgiving, bonfires and bells in all the city's churches.[78]

Samuel Rawson Gardiner, Charles Firth and Cavendish's wife, Margaret, have all agreed that he might have ended the war on the back of this success, had he marched south to join the king.[79] There was no immediate obstacle to this. Bradford and Leeds fell to him within days of the battle. Remaining parliamentarians were driven from the West Riding and royalist garrisons were established in the clothing towns. Yet Cavendish's failure to capture the Fairfaxes and their senior officers allowed his enemies to escape and rebuild a

---

74   Wing / E3893, *An Expresse Relation of the Passages and Proceedings of His Majesties Armie vnder the command of His Excellence the Earle of Newcastle: against the rebels, under the command of the Lord Fairfax and his Adherents* (Oxford: 1643), 2.

75   *Diary of Sir Henry Slingsby*, 96; Bodleian Library, MS Fairfax 36, fo. 8v.

76   Beinecke Rare Book and Manuscript Library, Osborn Shelves, b233, fo. 38.

77   BL, Wing / B4233, John Bramhall, *A Sermon Preached in the Cathedrall Church of York before Hi[s] Excellence the Earle of Newcastle and many of the prime nobility and gentry of the northerne covnties: at the publick thanksgiving to Almighty God for the late great victory upon Fryday, June 30, 1643, and the reducement of the west parts of Yorkeshire to obedience* (York: 1643), epistle dedicatory and 23.

78   BL, Thomason, E60(18), *Mercurius Aulicus*, 350.

79   Johnson D., *Adwalton Moor, 1643: The Battle that Changed a War* (Pickering: 2003) xv.

new army behind Hull's formidable fortifications.[80] With the West Riding pacified, Cavendish did eventually move southward. Recapturing Gainsborough on 30 July and reaching Lincoln on 4 August 1643, his army forced the parliamentarians south-eastwards, causing panic in East Anglia. Yet at Lincoln, came news that Fairfax was overrunning the East Riding and threatening the estates of Yorkshire's royalists. Therefore, Cavendish had to inform the king that he was duty bound to return to besiege Fairfax in Hull.[81] In many respects this decision had been forced upon him; the Yorkshire gentry refused to march further and Sir Marmaduke Langdale warned Cavendish that if he forced the issue, 'they should say he had betrayed them'.[82] Despite this, Sir Philip Warwick considered that Cavendish's vanity was to blame because if he marched south, he would have to relinquish personal command and his status as the war's decisive general might be called into question. Yet Warwick's lament smacks of the retrospective apportioning of blame that became so common among royalist writers, signifying more about the nature of internecine royalist politics than the reality of the strategic situation.[83]

This has not prevented other historians echoing Warwick's criticism. Ian Gentles suspected Cavendish was 'hampered by the same dilettante attitude as the other royalist peers', and that he was 'deficient in strategic consciousness'.[84] Even Newman acknowledged that Cavendish's geographical immobility brought about his final defeat.[85] His failure to march south may have pushed the king into the fateful siege of Gloucester to occupy his forces until Cavendish's army arrived.[86] The subsequent failure to capture Hull, either by force or treachery, owed much to parliamentarian vigilance, naval support and the formidable strength of Hull's defences. Having procrastinated too long, Sir John Hotham and his son were arrested before they could change sides, undermining Cavendish's patient strategy of converting them.[87] Thereafter, between August and December 1643, Cavendish switched his attentions to Nottingham Castle, where he offered large sums to the governor, Colonel John Hutchinson, and his officers. They were warned that the king held keeping a

---

80   Hopper A., 'Black Tom': Sir Thomas Fairfax and the English Revolution (Manchester: 2007) 46.

81   Wanklyn, Warrior Generals, 78.

82   Bodleian Library, MS Clarendon 23, fo. 229v.

83   Beinecke Rare Book and Manuscript Library, Osborn Shelves, fb87, fo. 8ov; Warwick, Memoires of the Reigne of King Charles I, 244–5.

84   Gentles, "Civil Wars in England", 123.

85   Newman, Old Service, 262.

86   Wanklyn, Warrior Generals, 63, 76–7.

87   Hopper, Hothams, 21–24, 73–99.

castle against him as more treasonous than service in Essex's army. Yet, the strategy backfired.[88] In such futile efforts against parliamentarian strongholds, Cavendish's strength was dissipated for the remainder of 1643. With hindsight, he lost the initiative in 1643 due to poor strategic decisions, but in mitigation it must be recognized that his freedom of action was constrained.

From January 1644, the long-negotiated invasion of northern England in Parliament's favour by the Scottish Army of the Covenant, commanded by Alexander Leslie, Earl of Leven, threw Cavendish onto the defensive. On 27 October 1643 the king had rewarded him with the title of marquis, reminding him with the acclamation: 'he who defends the Borders, should be created by Us Governour, or Marquis of the Borderers'.[89] Cavendish's strategy was to impede and delay the invaders, and it was pursued with limited success. Despite being heavily outnumbered, he checked the Scots at Corbridge on 19 February, Boldon Hills on 7–8 March and Hilton on 24–25 March. Edward Furgol has considered these successes were due to Cavendish's 'cool head and devoted, veteran troops'.[90] With their inferior cavalry mounts, the Scots were also anxious about Cavendish utilizing his dangerous cavalry in open country. Leven's progress was slowed as he kept his army in terrain that was difficult for the royalist cavalry. Therefore, it was not Cavendish's faulty strategy but the Fairfaxes' defeat of Sir John Belasyse's Yorkshire portion of Cavendish's army at Selby that forced the latter's return southward to garrison York.[91]

Cavendish proved himself an effective garrison commander in York, dispatching his cavalry southward and enduring a ten-week siege from 23 April to 1 July. The city was well supplied with provisions. He imposed an oath against treachery upon the inhabitants and strung out negotiations with the besiegers in the expectation of relief.[92] Margaret Cavendish later claimed that her husband advised Rupert not to fight at Marston Moor, believing that relations between the Scots and English parliamentarians would deteriorate and that the allied army would divide itself.[93] This smacks of hindsight, but the decision

88   John Hutchinson publicized that Cavendish offered him a barony and £10,000 to deliver the castle: Hutchinson, *Memoirs of the Life of Colonel Hutchinson*, 121–26; BL, Harleian MS 165, fo. 258r; Bodleian Library, MS Tanner 62, fo. 467; BL, E79(30), *A Discovery of the Trecherous Attempts of the Cavaliers, to have Procured the Betraying of Nottingham Castle into their Hands* (London: 1643), A2v, A3v.

89   Newman, "Royalist Army in Northern England", II, 158.

90   Furgol E., "The Civil Wars in Scotland", in Kenyon – Ohlmeyer, *Civil Wars*, 51.

91   Newman P.R., "The Defeat of John Belasyse: Civil War in Yorkshire: January–April, 1644", *Yorkshire Archaeological Journal* 52 (1980) 123–33.

92   Wenham P., *The Siege of York, 1644* (York: 1994 edn.) 15–17, 48–55.

93   Firth, (ed.), *Life of William Cavendish*, 46–7.

to give battle was very much Rupert's, acting on the king's orders. Driven on by fear of underhand courtly treachery against him, Rupert hoped to find a kindred spirit and ally in Cavendish, a nobleman who flattered him in letters and shared his suspicion of the court.[94]

As a consequence of being overruled, Cavendish appears to have abdicated command once his army's late arrival prevented Rupert from exploiting the unpreparedness of the allied armies. Whether his inertia extended to a 'malign' influence, as suggested by some, seems too harsh.[95] Ill-discipline among the soldiery rather than the outright hostility of Cavendish and General King seems the better explanation for the late arrival of Cavendish's infantry on the scene.[96] Yet his late arrival in a coach rather than on horseback suggests his disinclination to force an engagement. Owing to the enemy's surprise attack, Cavendish exercised no tactical role and his status in the chain of command beneath Rupert remains unclear. His battlefield heroism as described by his wife reflects more the role of a cavalry captain than a commanding general.[97]

Had he chosen to fight on foot as he was claimed to have done at Adwalton Moor, he would have been fortunate to come away alive. His famous infantry regiment, the Whitecoats, were refused quarter. Killed where they stood, fewer than 30 were left alive. In all, between 4,000 and 6,000 royalists were slaughtered in just ninety minutes, making this encounter the bloodiest engagement of the Civil Wars in England.[98] Cavendish seems to have remained on the field longer than many other royalist commanders. Yet, many of the dead were his own infantry, as 'good foote as were in the world' as he had boasted.[99] From their perspective, there can be no questioning his failure of leadership, as ultimately he abandoned them to escape on horseback. The psychological blow wrought by their massacre made this too painful an episode for him to reflect upon in writing. Instead, his wife later excused his defeats as having occurred in his absence through 'Jugling, Treachery, and Falshood' amongst his subordinates.[100] This is unpersuasive; rather than admit to their mistakes or shortcomings, bewailing treachery and blaming others to deflect responsibility

---

94 Roy – Macadam, "Marston Moor", 245, 256; Warburton, *Memoirs of Prince Rupert*, II, 275, 309.

95 Barratt J., *The Battle of Marston Moor, 1644* (Stroud: 2008), 150.

96 Roy – Macadam, "Marston Moor", 239–40, 251.

97 Wanklyn, *Warrior Generals*, 107.

98 Newman P.R. – Roberts P.R., *Marston Moor, 1644: The Battle of the Five Armies* (Pickering: 2003) 124.

99 Wanklyn, *Warrior Generals*, 90; Binns, *Sir Hugh Cholmley*, 136.

100 Firth, (ed.), *Life of William Cavendish*, 21, 50, 118.

was a common response of Civil War commanders trying to come to terms with defeat.[101] In this way, Cavendish's admirer, Sir Hugh Cholmley, along with Sir Philip Monckton, voiced rumours that the side-changer, Sir John Urry, betrayed Rupert's cavalry at Marston Moor.[102]

Supposedly unwilling to 'endure the laughter of the court', Cavendish considered that his reputation would not survive the disaster. Indeed, Gavin Robinson suggests he was 'running away from the court as much as from Parliament'.[103] Cavendish would have shared Rupert's embarrassment that their armies had been ordered to stand down immediately prior to the enemy attack.[104] Cavendish rode to Scarborough and took ship for Hamburg. According to Sir Hugh Cholmley, if Cavendish had remained, it would have done much to rally royalist support; but, persuaded by General King that all hope was lost, he set a corrupting example by his passage to Hamburg. Seventy peers and gentlemen accompanied him in two ships from Scarborough.[105] In response other royalist officers laid down arms and went home. York was left with little hope of relief.

Cavendish's injured honour and fear of ridicule had massive consequences far beyond his personal allegiance: ultimately, it brought about the decapitation of the royalist cause in the North. Cavendish hoped that his past services would outweigh the disservice of his flight. In this, he lacked the resilience of the Fairfaxes, who responded to their defeat at Adwalton Moor very differently. Cavendish was ill-equipped to emulate them, as Eliot Warburton observed, 'the weary and disheartening prospect of recommencing an almost hopeless strife ... was too undelightful for his temperament'.[106] In adversity, Cavendish's brittle honour and overriding concern for his status was an important military weakness. He had tried to resign his commission as early as March 1644, but the king rejected this and responded: 'All courage is not in fighting; constancy to a good cause beeinge the chiefe, and the dispysing of slanderous tongues and pennes being not the least ingredient'.[107] Cholmley perceived that Cavendish's retirement from command had been brewing for months before the battle, and

101   Hopper A., *Turncoats and Renegadoes: Changing Sides during the English Civil Wars* (Oxford: 2012) 134–8.

102   Bodleian Library, MS Clarendon 23, fo. 153v; BL, Lansdowne MS 988, fo. 328r; Wanklyn, *Warrior Generals*, 107; Binns, *Sir Hugh Cholmley*, 137.

103   Firth, (ed.), *Life of William Cavendish*, 41n; Robinson G., *Horses, People and Parliament in the English Civil War: Extracting Resources and Constructing Allegiance* (Farnham: 2012) 210.

104   Newman and Roberts, *Marston Moor*, 74.

105   Binns, *Sir Hugh Cholmley*, 139.

106   Warburton, *Prince Rupert*, II, 467.

107   Barratt, *Battle of Marston Moor*, 32; Trease, *Cavalier*, 127.

later considered that even if the royalists had won Marston Moor, Cavendish had intended to resign his commission.[108]

Conclusion

In conclusion, recent assessments of Cavendish's generalship remain mixed. Despite his admiration for Cavendish and his achievements, including the manner in which he 'so successfully out-generalled the Fairfaxes', Newman concluded that the successes of his army 'did nothing whatsoever for the king further south, in the Midlands and the West'. His final verdict was that the 'single long-term contribution that Cavendish made to the war may have been the ultimate embroilment of Parliament with the Scots'.[109] Similar conclusions have been reached more recently by David Scott and David Johnson: Cavendish's success as a general widened the conflict and raised the stakes, forcing Parliament to procure an alliance with the Scottish Covenanters and the king to recall more of the English army in Ireland.[110]

Although far from being a great general, Cavendish was certainly foremost among the king's 'grandees'. Despite being blamed unfairly by many for the failure of the king's 1643 campaign, he remained the most successful royalist commander of that year. Exceeding his initial objectives, he did much to raise, maintain and protect the largest royalist army of the First Civil War. In this he was a great coalition builder, sustaining a large multi-confessional armed force for two years. He proved an effective figurehead, organiser and propagandist, although perhaps a poor reader of the terrain. His personal courage and loyalty go unquestioned. On occasion, he showed himself a successful tactician, overcoming his lack of pre-war military experience.[111] Dependent on professional advice, he took it, choosing talented and experienced subordinates such as James King, Sir Thomas Glemham and Sir Marmaduke Langdale. His army's series of victories at Piercebridge, Tadcaster, Seacroft Moor and Adwalton Moor raised the possibility of an outright royalist victory.

Yet, Cavendish was unable to capitalize on his military successes. Lacking in ruthlessness and tenacity, his failure to finish the Fairfaxes cost the royalists dearly. Had he ordered his Yorkshire regiments to garrison the North and contain Hull, allowing him to march south with his other forces, he may have

---

108   Binns, *Sir Hugh Cholmley*, 138.
109   Newman, "Royalist Army in Northern England", 1, 26; Newman, *Old Service*, 262, 264.
110   Johnson, *Adwalton Moor*, 119; Scott, *Politics and War in the Three Stuart Kingdoms*, 49.
111   Wanklyn, *Warrior Generals*, 7.

panicked Parliament into peace negotiations. If so, the outcome of the Civil Wars may have proved different. Even though this argument is highly speculative and driven by hindsight, it did not prevent his fellow royalists from voicing it when explaining their defeat. It must be remembered that their criticisms of Cavendish had a personal edge and remain far removed from dispassionate objectivity. However, as a battlefield commander it seems that Cavendish was fundamentally flawed. Indeed, he seems to have recognized this by wisely leaving tactics to others. Whilst his concern for his reputation and status did much to inaugurate his armed royalism, these considerations ultimately undermined his resilience once his army was decisively defeated in the field.

Selective Bibliography

Binns J., *Yorkshire in the Civil Wars: Origins, Impact and Outcome* (Pickering: 2004).

Binns J. (ed.), "The Memoirs and Memorials of Sir Hugh Cholmley of Whitby, 1600–1657", *Yorkshire Archaeological Society, Record Series*, 153 (2000).

Carpenter S.D.M., *Military Leadership in the British Civil Wars, 1642–1651: 'The Genius of this Age'* (London: 2005).

Hopper A., *Turncoats and Renegadoes: Changing Sides during the English Civil Wars* (Oxford: 2012).

Hopper A. (ed.), "The Papers of the Hothams: Governors of Hull during the Civil War", *Camden Society*, 5th series, 39 (2011).

Hopper A., *'Black Tom': Sir Thomas Fairfax and the English Revolution* (Manchester: 2007).

Johnson D., *Adwalton Moor, 1643: The Battle that Changed a War* (Pickering: 2003).

Newman P.R. – Roberts P.R., *Marston Moor, 1644: The Battle of the Five Armies* (Pickering: 2003).

Newman P.R., *The Old Service: Royalist Regimental Colonels and the Civil War, 1642–1646* (Manchester: 1993).

Newman P.R., "The Royalist Army in Northern England, 1642–1645" (D.Phil. thesis, University of York, 1978), 2 vols.

Parsons D. (ed.), *Sir Henry Slingsby: The Diary of Sir Henry Slingsby of Scriven, Bart.* (London: 1836).

Trease G., *Portrait of a Cavalier: William Cavendish, First Duke of Newcastle* (London: 1979).

Wankyln M., *The Warrior Generals: Winning the British Civil Wars, 1642–1652* (London: 2010).

CHAPTER 10

The Double Edged Sword: William Cavendish's Political Career 1644–1660

Madeline Dewhurst

In 'The Truth off the Sorde', a manuscript treatise written by William Cavendish, Marquis of Newcastle, during his exile from England, he declared: 'that moste of mankinde knowes that whatt I had or am is all [sacrificed] to your ma*j*estie servise—In my longe exsile sinse the publike sorde for thatt time was layde bye I thaughte howe I might advanse the truth off the private sorde ... Ande truth had neede In these dayes off falsehood'.[1] For an aristocrat whose identity was defined by his relationship with his monarch, abandoning his king for a life of seclusion would have been unthinkable. Previous scholars have made a strong case for Cavendish's retirement, based on Edward Hyde's account that he retired after defeat to pursue a life of pleasure, but this view should not be taken at face value.[2] Neither should we accept uncritically the claims made by Margaret Cavendish in her biography of her husband, which emphasise his 'retirement' to Antwerp.[3] What can be overlooked here is that Cavendish is drawing on the poetics of retirement used so frequently in royalist poetry; the retreat of 'those who are defeated but who need not surrender'.[4] Where she may insist upon Cavendish's life of *otium*, this article will argue that he was still involved in the *vita activa*. His 'was no withdrawal, but a *negotium ex otio*; the performance of public duty by other routes'.[5] That is the private, rather than the public sword.

The period 1644 to 1660 was one of constant flux for the royalists: hopes of re-establishing the monarchy rose and fell, positions shifted and alliances

---

1   BL Harley 4206, inserted leaf.
2   Hyde E., *The history of the rebellion and civil wars in England* (Oxford: 1958) VIII. 86, 38; *The Life of Edward Earl of Clarendon, Lord High Chancellor of England, and Chancellor of the University of Oxford: in which is included a continuation of his history of the grand rebellion / written by himself* (Oxford: 1857) 249.
3   Cavendish M., *Life of William Cavendish*, sig. Rv, 62.
4   Miner E., *The Cavalier Mode from Jonson to Cotton* (Princeton: 1971) 179.
5   Loxley J., *Royalism and Poetry in the English Civil Wars: The Drawn Sword* (Basingstoke: 1997), 203.

© KONINKLIJKE BRILL NV, LEIDEN, 2017 | DOI 10.1163/9789004326217_012

were made and broken. Toby Osborne has written about the complexity of exile as both 'a state and a process', noting that 'exile was reversible,...and did not necessarily imply the end of a public career or alternatively total isolation from a home state. Lines of communication could remain open...states and sovereigns themselves could employ exiles to maintain informal diplomatic channels with other states'.[6] Where people found themselves placed after the Restoration was not necessarily an indication of how they were favoured during the Interregnum. Certainly, there was a great deal of infighting and jockeying for position among the English exiles and Cavendish had his fair share of enemies; his popularity, like theirs, waxed and waned. This fluidity makes a definitive interpretation of his position difficult. While Hyde and Margaret Cavendish's works are invaluable as sources of information they are also deeply compromised. As Ronald Hutton has pointed out, Hyde's historical writing is often vengeful and deceptive.[7] Hyde, a staunch Anglican, disapproved of Cavendish's attitude to religion and to politics, especially when it came to negotiations with the Scots, something that may have influenced his appraisal of him. Neither is Margaret Cavendish's biography impartial.[8] Dedicated to Charles II, the book is also to some extent a petition for reparations. Throughout, she is at pains to prove the extent to which the king's 'most loyal subject' lost out financially, losses that she claims forced him into retirement.

If Cavendish may not have been the most savvy or successful of political players, as a marquis he was one of the highest ranking aristocrats among the English refugees, and this alone would have been sufficient to accord him a level of prestige. A member of the exiled Privy Council from 1650 to at least 1653, he was seen as a stabilising and authoritative figure within the expatriate community in Antwerp. The evidence also suggests that he worked hard to maintain a presence in the political and cultural life of both royalist exiles and European élites. As an English aristocrat whose love for the king was apparently 'above the love he bore to his Wife, Children, and all his Posterity, nay to his own life',[9] to relinquish his participation in the royalist cause and his faith in a royalist victory would surely have been a form of self-annihilation.

---

6   Osborne T., "'Chimeres, monopoles and stratagems': French Exiles in the Spanish Netherlands during the Thirty Years' War", *The Seventeenth Century*, Vol. 15, (Autumn 2000), 149–173 (155).

7   Hutton R., *Debates in Stuart History* (Basingstoke: 2004), 11.

8   See also Sarasohn L., "Margaret Cavendish, William Newcastle, and Political Marginalisation", *English Studies* Vol. 92, No. 7 (November 2011) 806–817.

9   Cavendish M., *Life of William Cavendish*, sig. Zz2r, 179.

The Public Sword

After his hasty departure from England, Cavendish went first to Hamburg and then to Rotterdam, where he was met by the English Resident Agent for the United Provinces, Sir William Boswell. Cavendish's brother, Charles, 'found [Boswell] to be that which I supposed him formerlie to be a discrete civill gentleman'.[10] From Rotterdam Cavendish may well have made the short journey to The Hague for he was evidently keen to establish and maintain good relations with the House of Orange.[11] Before leaving Rotterdam in March 1645 he wrote a gracious letter to Jehan Polyander van de Kerckhoven, Lord of Heenvliet, and superintendent to Mary Stuart's court: 'You have shewn me so much affection that I should be both ungrateful and uncivil if I left this town without thanking you in these lines. The favour which the Princess Royal has done me of writing by me to the Queen, and the favourable construction which the Prince of Orange has made of my ill fortune, are the results of their kindness, which your courtesy and that of Madame Stanhope, whose hands I kiss, have procured for me'.[12]

Cavendish did not travel directly to the queen, however, visiting Antwerp, Mechelen, Brussels, Valenciennes, Cambrai and Peronne before finally arriving at the French capital in late April 1645. It is possible that he was pursuing a diplomatic mission. Perhaps after his communications with the Stuarts at The Hague and with Boswell in Rotterdam, he had been entrusted with gaining support for the royalist cause from Spain's representatives in the Spanish Netherlands. In Brussels, the archducal capital and the 'true heart of seventeenth century espionage',[13] Cavendish received visits from Manuel de Moura y Corte-Real, Marquis of Castel-Rodrigo, Adjunct-Governor of the Spanish Netherlands; Charles IV, Duke of Lorraine; and the Austrian general, Octavio Piccolomini, Duke of Amalfi and Count of the Habsburg Empire. 'An

---

10   BL Add. MS 4278, fo. 203r.

11   This may have been facilitated by Newcastle's cousin, Utricia Ogle. The Anglo-Dutch Utricia was a lady-in-waiting to the Princess Royal and a good friend of the Princess's companion, Catherine, Lady Stanhope who carried considerable influence at Mary's court. Utricia would therefore have been perfectly placed to introduce Newcastle into that circle.

12   *HMC*, "13th Report, appendix", part 2, The Manuscripts of His Grace the Duke of Portland Preserved at Welbeck Abbey, (London: 1893) 134. The original copy of this letter should be included in BL Add. MS 70499, but appears to have been lost when the letters were compiled and given to the British Museum.

13   Osborne quoting Alcalá-Zamora y Quiepo de Llano, 'Chimeres, monopoles and stratagems' (150).

experienced military entrepreneur, rich in cash, capable in command, but free from territorial ties,' the Duke of Lorraine 'could provide military muscle and financial assistance to any prospective employer'.[14] And that is exactly what Henrietta Maria attempted to become from 1644 to 1645, hoping that the duke, driven into exile by the French, would provide assistance to her husband. In return, Lorraine sought her help at the French Court. According to English parliamentarian propaganda: 'the very Duke of Lorraine himself is Treated with to come over and Conduct his Army in person, consisting of Ten thousand men: And where can a more desperate and Jesuited Prince, or a more declared Enemy to Protestants be found out?'[15]

Cavendish's encounter with Lorraine during his trip to Brussels may have involved negotiations on behalf of Henrietta Maria. The marquis was an old favourite of the queen's, who had written to him after his defeat, assuring him 'of the continuance of [her] esteem for [him], not being so unjust as to forget past services upon a present misfortune'.[16] Indeed, there had been occasions when she placed his judgement above that of her husband. In 1643 she had written to Cavendish: 'The king ... had written to me to send you word to go into Suffolk, Norfolk, or Huntingdonshire. I answered him that you were a better judge than he of that, and that I should not do it'.[17] As a commander noted for his employment of Catholic soldiers (his army during the Civil Wars was frequently referred to as the 'Popish army'), Cavendish may have been considered just the man to negotiate with the 'Jesuited' Lorraine.

In May 1645 Randal MacDonnell, Marquis of Antrim, signed a contract with Castel-Rodrigo, receiving two frigates in exchange for the promise to recruit 2,000 men from his Irish estates to fight for the Spanish. Since Cavendish met Castel-Rodrigo in April, he was in a position to oversee this contract. Indeed, in May 1645 Henry Jermyn wrote to Lord Digby from Paris, regarding the transportation of a body of horse to accompany troops raised in Ireland for an invasion of England, noting that the queen approved of the plan: 'If the Marquis of Newcastle should be thought fit to have the charge of any troops appointed to join with those the Colonel [Fitz-Williams] shall bring, he [Fitz-Williams] is well content all should fall under the Marquis's command and himself to com-

---

14   Ó Siochrú M., "The Duke of Lorraine and the International Struggle for Ireland, 1649–
      1653", *The Historical Journal*, Vol. 48, issue 4, (December 2005), 905–932 (1).
15   *The Lord George Digby's Cabinet And Dr Goff's Negotiations* ... (London, Edward Husband,
      Printer to the Honourable House of Commons, March 26. 1646), sig A4v, 8.
16   BL Harley MS 7003, fo. 11v.
17   BL Harley MS. 6988, fo. 177.

mand under him, but if any other the Colonel must have the chief command'.[18] In the Spring of 1645 then, Cavendish is still held in such high regard that not only is he being considered as a commander of royalist troops, he is also the only man whom Colonel FitzWilliam, a person highly esteemed by the king and queen, is willing to serve under.[19]

Later that year Cavendish would undermine his relationship with the queen by marrying one of her ladies-in-waiting without her approval. It is possible that Henrietta Maria had been planning to arrange a match herself for her old favourite. Given Cavendish's family associations and his tolerance towards Roman Catholics the devout Henrietta Maria may have hoped to marry him to a Catholic. His union with Margaret Lucas was certainly not approved of at court, as is shown in Margaret's letters to him. When she wrote to him just before their wedding, she expressed her hope that she and the queen were friends again.[20] Margaret is pragmatic about the fluctuations in royal preferment, however, reassuring him that: 'for the King and qeenes favour my lord j think you will never be in danger of loosing it for j never hard that any body perfectly had it'.[21] This wise advice was borne out by later events for the queen appears to have been reconciled to the couple, writing affectionate letters to Cavendish in which she assured him of her continued gratitude and friendship.[22]

In 1646 Prince Charles arrived at the palace of St. Germain-en-Laye, just outside Paris, 'the biggest single rendezvous point for royalist exiles'.[23] It is possible that Cavendish was temporarily reinstated to his old position as groom of the bedchamber to Prince Charles, since Charles reverted to the same household structure he had had before the civil war.[24] As Neil Reynolds suggests: 'Charles clearly surrounded himself within his bedchamber with those with whom he had been familiar. . . . There was no groom of the stool listed; it is impossible to discover whether this post was left vacant, or whether the first titular holder of the office of first gentleman to the prince, the marquis of Newcastle played some part'.[25]

---

18   *CSPD 1644–1645*, 465–66.

19   Carte T. (ed.), *A Collection of Letters* (London, J.J. & P. Knapton: 1735) III, 416.

20   BL Add. MS 70499, fo. 295r.

21   Ibid.

22   BL Harley MS. 7003, fos.13–15.

23   Hutton R., *Charles the Second King of England, Scotland and Ireland* (Oxford: 1989) 21–22.

24   Newcastle is not included in the 1649 pay list of servants in Charles' retinue, but the list is not complete. *HMC*, "Pepys MSS" (London: 1911) 255.

25   Reynolds N., "The Stuart Court and Courtiers in Exile" (Unpublished Ph.D. thesis, Cambridge University, 1996), 92.

Although Cavendish has never been placed within any of the factions which existed at St. Germain, his support for making a pact with the Scots would suggest that at this time he fell within the 'Louvre Group' headed by Henrietta Maria, her advisor Henry Jermyn and John Colepepper (Lord Culpepper). Cavendish can also be connected to Jermyn through the Army Plot of 1641, in which the two men were implicated. Both Jermyn and Cavendish patronised the poet, William Davenant, who had served as Lieutenant-General of the Ordnance under Cavendish and was now employed as a messenger and spy by Jermyn. Davenant was evidently still closely connected to Cavendish, sending him the preface to *Gondibert* in 1650.[26] Margaret did not approve of Jermyn and warned Cavendish against him.[27] Her admonishments appear to have had little effect however for, during their engagement, Cavendish had confided in Jermyn against Margaret's wishes.

The Second Civil War saw Cavendish eager to wield his public sword once more. According to a letter to the Earl of Lanark (24 June 1648), he was pressing for a commission: 'My Lord Newcastle has prest mouch for his dispach, and a comission for the North. It is delaied; he is mede believe a great part of the caus is from Scotland.' On 1 July an anonymous letter recorded: 'My Lord Newcastell is discontent that hei getes no commision for his contrie. It is believed that som parte of the caus is from Scotland. Hei is thoght to be a great friend to that nation, and a dar say he is, and pertecolarly to your family. He is to goe presently into his contrie, where you will have a more free correspondence with him'.[28]

From these letters it would seem that Cavendish was planning to return to England to head another military campaign. Despite his support for an alliance with the Scots, the latter were no doubt wary of allowing the commander with the greatest power base on the English side of their borders into Scotland. This is also likely to have been the reason why he was refused permission to travel to Scotland with Charles II in 1650. The Scots wanted Charles under their control; Cavendish, who may still have been able to raise an independent army in the north of England, would have threatened this.

In June 1648 the queen's trust in Cavendish was again demonstrated by her request that he follow Prince Charles to Holland, where the latter was making arrangements for war. Indeed, Henrietta Maria was so eager for Cavendish to

26   BL Add. MS. 4278, fo. 295r.

27   BL Add. MS. 70499, fos. 259r–v; 267r.

28   Gardiner S.R. (ed.), 'The Hamilton Papers: being selections from original letter in the possession of His Grace the Duke of Hamilton and Brandon, relating to the years 1638–1650", *Camden Society* (1880) 220, 226.

join her son that she had her Controller, Sir Henry Wood, and Treasurer, Sir Richard Foster, bound over for the debts Cavendish had accumulated.[29] The Cavendish household hurried to Rotterdam after the prince only to discover he had already set sail for England. They were not the only ones to be left behind, however, for in a letter to Secretary Nicholas a disgruntled Lord Hatton complained that Culpeper and Lord Hopton had deliberately delayed the arrival of Charles' counsellors whilst urging the prince not to wait for them.[30]

In August there were evidently renewed plans for Cavendish to be part of an invading army. According to 'a Catalogue of Letters taken at Worcester' on 14 August 1648 a Commission was issued for Lord Henry Wilmot to be made Lieutenant-General under the Marquis of Newcastle.[31] Charles's voyage proved fruitless, however, and he returned to The Hague on 4 September. His invitation to travel to Scotland was rescinded two weeks later, after the Duke of Hamilton was defeated in Lancashire by Oliver Cromwell. As the royalists were to suffer one disappointment after another, Cavendish was spending money he didn't possess entertaining soldiers and commanders in the belief that they would soon be aiding Charles I. In September 1648 Cavendish and his household moved to Antwerp.

The year 1650 saw Cavendish once more actively engaged in politics. His support for accommodation with the Scots, when in St. Germain, now paid off, as the Louvre group came to dominate policy. In January the Privy Council voted unanimously to invite the Scottish Covenanters to negotiate at Breda. Cavendish was awarded the Order of the Garter, a ceremony not only rarely performed in exile, but one that had held great importance to Charles I. Cavendish was also given 'full power and Authority' to raise and command forces in the Northern counties of England.[32] On April 6 he was furthermore appointed to the newly enlarged Privy Council, along with Hamilton and Buckingham, who, like Cavendish, favoured making concessions to the Covenanters.

Hyde, who was appalled by the proposed treaty and the exclusion of his allies, wrote to Nicholas from his post in Madrid: 'You have a very precious junto to determine concerning three kingdoms; you will find the Marquis of Newcastle a very lamentable man, and as fit to be a general as a bishop'.[33] This is another of Hyde's summations that has been widely quoted to Cavendish's

---

29   Cavendish M., *Life of William Cavendish*, sig. Qr, 58.

30   Warner G.F. (ed.) "*The Nicholas Papers*, correspondence of Sir Edward Nicholas", Camden Society (1886) 92.

31   HMC, "Pepys MSS" (London: 1911) 283.

32   BL Harley MS 6852, fos. 335–350.

33   *Calendar of the Clarendon State Papers* (hereafter *CCSP*) iii, 20.

disadvantage, but it should be remembered that Hyde considered the concessions a betrayal of the royalist cause on religious grounds. It was unlikely
that Cavendish, whose 'Advice' to Charles II was so evidently influenced by
Machiavelli, had any such scruples. Margaret Cavendish points out that 'his
Highness the Prince of *Orange*, and my Lord, agreed in one opinion, *viz.*, that
they could perceive no other and better way at that present for his Majesty,
but to make an agreement with his subjects of *Scotland*'.[34] In fact, Frederik
Hendrik, Prince of Orange, and Cavendish have been described in similar
terms as far as religion is concerned. According to Jonathan Israel, 'Frederick
Hendrick was, and remained, a *politique* through and through. If religious
conviction influenced his politics it was hard to discern where. The Venetian
ambassador, Contarini, believed the new Prince of Orange had no religion
other than 'ragion di stato'.'[35] Similarly, Cavendish's indifference to religion was
common knowledge.[36]

Charles, however, was hedging his bets. Whilst continuing to support the
Marquis of Ormond's campaign in Ireland, he had also given the Marquis of
Montrose permission to proceed with an invasion of Scotland. Instead of waiting to see if Montrose's expedition was successful Charles went ahead with
negotiations with the Covenanters. 'A competent leader', according to James
N.M. Maclean, would have 'given priority to Montrose by committing every
available resource to the invasion of Scotland. There were not enough arms,
supplies or money for one campaign, let alone two.'[37] This estimation is significant because it appears to have been shared by Cavendish. Montrose had
sought his advice in Antwerp before setting out on his disastrous 1650 Scottish
expedition, enquiring of him whether he was also going to England. Cavendish
responded that, had his king commanded him to go alone before a whole army,
he would have done it. But he would not venture the lives of those friends
who might follow him when he had no funds to resource such a campaign,
because to undertake such an action would be to send them to their deaths
with no benefit to his majesty. Cavendish counsels Montrose that, 'if he had
no Provision nor Ammunition, Armes ... he would likely ... suffer for his rash

---

34   Cavendish M., *Life of William Cavendish*, sig. S2v, 68.
35   Israel J.I. *The Dutch Republic: It's Rise, Its Greatness, and Fall 1477–1806* (Oxford: 1995) 491.
36   BL Add. MS 15391: fo. 241v.
37   Maclean J., "Montrose's Preparations for the Invasion of Scotland", in Hatton R. – Anderson
       M.S. (eds.) *Studies in Diplomatic History*, (London: 1970) 7–31 (16).

undertaking'.[38] He was quite right; by 21 May Montrose was swinging from a gibbet thirty feet above Edinburgh.

By the end of April Charles had won over the Covenanters and was formally invited to Scotland. Despite this, Cavendish was in the minority of royalists who encouraged Charles in his negotiations with the Kirk party. Various courtiers from the different factions at St. Germain: Henrietta Maria, the 'Old Royalists': Hopton, Hyde, Nicholas and Cottington, and Rupert's 'Swordsmen', were united in their disgust at the demands made by the Covenanters and the humiliating concessions agreed by Charles. Cavendish was, no doubt, one of those who urged the king to make concessions and then break them as soon as it was expedient to do so. It would seem that he had little faith in Ormond's ability to raise an army in Ireland since, according to Margaret Cavendish, he saw no probability of raising an army anywhere but in Scotland. She also claims that the Scots 'were so unreasonable in their treaty that his Majesty had hardly patience to hear them', although it was Cavendish who was reprimanded by the Earl of Cassilis for his bad language.[39] It is testimony to Cavendish's loyalty that it was due to Scottish demands for the king to disown Montrose and Ormond that caused him to lose his temper.[40] As with many other of Charles's courtiers, the Scots would not allow Cavendish to accompany the king into Scotland. In fact Henry Wilmot, known to be sympathetic to Presbyterianism, was one of the few royalists allowed to remain with Charles in Scotland. Given Cavendish's reputation for impiety and the fact that he had led campaigns against them at the beginning of the first Civil War, it is hardly surprising the Scots refused him admission, notwithstanding his support for the treaty.

At this time, according to David Underdown, Cavendish was preparing for an uprising in Yorkshire. A plan was underway to seize Hull and Scarborough as entry points for the forces he was attempting to procure in Germany. Cavendish was apparently liaising with Sir Hugh Cholmley, the Governor of Scarborough, who was rumoured to be sympathetic, as were some of the local Presbyterians.[41] The initial invading force would, however, land in Dover. The parliamentarian agent, George Bishop, wrote to his master, Thomas Scot: 'Mrs. Hamlin... is gone to the Earl of Newcastle: she shall have their names there. I have a copy of their letter and the figure. They write that all things

---

38 Cavendish M., *Life of William Cavendish*, sig. Ll2v, p. 132. Cavendish is of course keen to emphasise Newcastle's lack of financial resources.

39 *CCSP*, II, 53–54.

40 Trease G., *Portrait of a Cavalier: William Cavendish, First Duke of Newcastle* (London: 1979) 167.

41 Underdown D., *Royalist Conspiracy in England 1649–1660* (New Haven: 1960) 39.

are readie (except their Commissions.) It seemes Dover is designed, and upon that surprize 4000 Dutch and English are to land in Kent, under the command (as wee thinke) of Newcastle (for wee have a letter under his hand to the Kinge wherein hee begs it)'.[42] By January 1651 Bishop was informing Cromwell that 'Four thousand Germans and English, which Newcastle, and Lieutenant General Carpe, negotiates (whose letters to the Kinge of Scotts and Buckingham concerning that I have, and from Ancram, &c.) are to land in Kent'.[43]

Letters to Cavendish from William Kerr, Earl of Lothian, and Henry Wilmot also attest to the authority and respect he still enjoyed in northern quarters. Cavendish was evidently still hoping to take up a prominent role once more, following a successful invasion of England, as Lothian's letter from Perth on 15 January 1651 demonstrates.

> My Lord I tooke your remembrance of me for a greate Honor and Favor, and I beseach your Lordship beleave that noe man hath more respect to your person then myself, nor can desire more the occasion to doe you service. I earnestly therefore desire you wilbe pleased to lay some commands on me. . . . Your Lordship, when you sett yourself to act in what wee are about, wilbe—as you have beane always formerly—very usefull and instrumental and I should be exceedingly glade to see you where I might in person offer you my service.[44]

Five days later, also from Perth, Wilmot wrote the following to Cavendish:

> My Lord Withrinton will informe your Lordship of all things heere boath as what concerns the publicke and your lordships owne particular, I shall . . . entreat you to doe mee the honor to let mee heare from your lordship whether I shall continue all here according to your former commands to me, incase wee should bee soe happie as to bee able to greet upon english ground, or wheither you will thinke it fitte to give mee any new commands which shall bee most punctually obayed.[45]

---

42   Nickolls J. (ed.), *Original Letters and Papers of State, Addressed to Oliver Cromwell: Concerning the Affairs of Great Britain. From the Year MDCXLIX to MDCLVIII* (London, William Bowyer: 1743) sig. L2r, 39.

43   Ibid., sig. Ov, 50; sig. Xr, 77.

44   BL Add. MS. 70499, fos. 321r–v.

45   BL Add. MS. 70499, fo. 323r. Richard Ward, the editor of the *HMC* volume, dates these letters as being written in January 1652. However, events in January 1652 do not corroborate

It is clear from these letters that both Lothian and Wilmot are relying on instructions from Cavendish, whom they hold to be in a position of trust and influence.

Meanwhile, Cavendish had been sent as ambassador extraordinary to Frederick III of Denmark to seek help for the invasion of England. This was considered newsworthy in England, where the parliamentarian propagandist, Marchamont Nedham, used Cavendish's reputation as a poet and playwright against him: 'As for *Newcastle*, he is to Act a Comedy in hope of supplies from his Majesty of *Denmark*; his Lordship is a good *Poet*, and a few begging Rythms may doe much when the *Dane* is in his Cups, of which he may chance to send a dozen or two to his Cousin *Stewart*'.[46]

Cavendish was also negotiating with the Elector of Brandenburg, and appears to have been more successful than Montrose, who had also attempted to borrow money from him. On 7 September 1651 Count Johan Arndt von Gottstein informed Cavendish that the elector would supply 6000 infantry and 4000 cavalry, while soliciting ships from Denmark. The seriousness, with which this offer was made, is indicated by the fact that Gottstein asks 'In what harbour of Scotland or England are the troops to land?' On 11 September the elector wrote to Cavendish congratulating him 'upon the success of the King of Great Britain' and offering to enter into a treaty for the employment of his troops in the king's service.[47] Evidently, the elector had not yet heard about the destruction of the king's forces at the Battle of Worcester on the 3 September. Nor did he know that the king was at that date hiding in Staffordshire disguised as a farmer's son. What might have been a diplomatic coup for Cavendish was rendered void by the temporary defeat of royalism in the British Isles.

The Private Sword

Although, prior to 1656, the Cavendishes were in the minority of English exiles choosing to live in the Spanish Netherlands, Antwerp was, as Ursula Härting has noted, 'conveniently located for political negotiations conducted in

---

this, as Wilmot, for example, was by then in Germany. The date, therefore, must be 1651. *Vide HMC*, "Portland MSS", II, 138–139.

46   Nedham M., *A rope for Pol, or, A hue and cry after Marchemont Nedham, the late scurrulous news-writer being a collection of his horrid blasphemies and revilings against the king's majesty, his person, his cause, and his friends, published in his weekly Politicus.* (1660).

47   *CCSP*, II, 106.

exile'.[48] Antwerp may not have been as vital a centre for Stuart exiles as Paris or The Hague, but it was a convenient stopping place on the route between the two and so enjoyed a steady stream of important visitors. Whenever the Cavendishes wanted or needed to visit the Stuart courts they could travel by barge, or ride to Brussels in one day and The Hague in three. Antwerp was also very close to the English coast, facilitating travel and news between the two countries.

It has generally been accepted that Cavendish retired from politics, settling in Antwerp because he was out of favour at the Stuart Court and could not afford to live elsewhere. However, there are several factors that suggest this was not the case. Inhabited by a rising class of wealthy merchants, Antwerp was not a cheap backwater, but an expensive, multilingual metropolis renowned for its artworks and its production of luxury goods. When the Cavendishes settled there Antwerp was still the richest city in the Southern Netherlands, with a reputation for being 'an unequalled world centre with an internationally oriented nightlife'.[49] Indeed, Edward Nicholas, who went to stay in Antwerp with Hyde in 1651, was forced to cut his visit short, writing to the Marquis of Ormond that Antwerp was more expensive than The Hague and that he would be constrained 'to seek some cheaper and more private corner to reside in ... some more retired place'.[50] During its 'Golden Age' Antwerp had been one of the most important cultural and commercial centres in Europe. Although the city had declined after its reincorporation into the Habsburg territories in 1585 and the subsequent Dutch blockade, it enjoyed what has been called an 'Indian summer' during the first half of the seventeenth century. While it did not return to its former eminence, it remained a pivotal financial centre, hosting its own stock exchange and acting as an intermediary between the Protestant North and the Catholic South. Its art market remained active until the 1660s, with a higher turnover than that of Paris.[51] For example, the Duke of Buckingham

---

48 Härting U., "Inhabitants of Antwerp", in Van Beneden B. – de Poorte N. (eds.), *Royalist Refugees, William and Margaret in the Rubens House 1648–1660"* (Antwerp: 2006) 64, 63–69.

49 Soly H., "Social Relations in Antwerp in the Sixteenth and Seventeenth Centuries" and Pleij H., "Antwerp Described", in Van der Stock J. (ed.), *Antwerp: Story of a Metropolis* (Ghent: 1993), 37–47 (43); 79–85 (84).

50 Carte, *A Collection*, sig. D6r, 43.

51 Despite the blockade the Scheldt was still open to inland vessels and even retained access to the open sea, although regulated by the North. Voet, L. "Antwerp, the Metropolis and its History", in Van der Stock J. (ed.). In 1650 as many as forty to eighty vessels a day were arriving in Antwerp from the United Provinces. As a domain of the Spanish Netherlands Antwerp also benefited from trade with the Iberian Peninsula. *Vide* Sukyens F. *et al.* (eds.), *Antwerp A Port for all Seasons* (Antwerp: 1986).

was able to maintain himself as one of the wealthiest English exiles, having smuggled sixteen chests of paintings out of England, sending them first to Amsterdam and then to Antwerp on the advice of Dr. Stephen Goff, advisor to Henrietta Maria, who explained, 'without question Antwerp will afford many chapmen, and the Archduke's good success in Flanders will make him prodigal in these curiosities.'[52] Antwerp was certainly not the place for economising, especially for a former patron of the arts. Nor was it an isolated location; the Cavendishes continued to receive well-connected guests, both English and European.

Margaret Cavendish's biography informs her readers that her husband spent some time in Antwerp looking for the right house. The one that he eventually did choose, Peter Paul Ruben's former home, sent out a clear message that he was a man, not only of cultural importance but also one with royal connections. As David Norbrook points out, in addition to being the 'foremost exponent of northern Counter-Reformation art, Rubens had also been a champion of the Stuarts'.[53] An important international diplomat, who had been knighted by Charles I for his part in bringing about the Anglo-Spanish Peace of Madrid in 1630, it was Rubens who had 'fashioned a royal image for Charles'.[54] And it was the Rubenshuis that would form part of the image Cavendish wished to fashion for himself in Antwerp. Furthermore, by 1656 Antwerp's profile was raised among the English refugees as a result of the establishment of Charles II's court in nearby Bruges. Indeed, Antwerp was now a significant enough location for an English intelligence gatherer, John Watts, to take up residence there. Watts reported that Wilmot, now Lord Rochester, and Ormond were both in Antwerp and were not just seeking financial relief, but had 'disines to make frinds in Ingland; thay have all desines upon sum townes'.[55]

Cavendish was also visited by many members of the European nobility; indeed his riding-school seems to have become something of a tourist attraction. Among these illustrious visitors were Don Luis de Benavides, Marquess of Caracena, the Prince of Condé, the Duke of Guise, the Duke of Oldenburg, George II, the Landgrave of Hesse-Darmstadt and the Prince of East Friesland. Charles II, whom Cavendish had taught to ride, also visited the riding stables. Cavendish recorded 'the Joy I had then, to see, That His Majesty made my Horse goe better, than any Italian , or French-Riders (who had often Rid

---

52   Stoye J. *English Travellers Abroad 1604–1667* (London: 1989) 220–225.

53   Norbrook D. "Women, the republic of letters, and the public sphere in the mid-seventeenth century", *Criticism* 46, No. 2,(Spring 2004) 223–240 (27).

54   Brotton J. *The Sale of the Late King's Goods* (London: 2006) 152.

55   TNA, SP 77/31, fo. 405r.

them) could do'.[56] Another illustrious visitor was Queen Christina of Sweden. Cavendish, although not very impressed by her horses, recorded 'I had the Honour to Wait on the Queen of *Sweden* when she was at *Antwerp*, and she used me very *Graciously*, and *Civilly*; and an *Extraordinary Lady*, I assure you, she is in All things'.[57]

It was no doubt useful for Charles II to have a trusted elder statesman in residence in Antwerp as a representative of the English exiles. As one of the highest ranking aristocrats in exile, Cavendish could use his status to restrain the anti-social behaviour of some of the younger English royalists in the city. The duelling and drinking of royalists was a public relations problem both at home in England and on the Continent. Hyde, acting on behalf of the king, wrote to Cavendish, to tell him that the duellists, 'the Earle of Oxford and Colonell Slinger...must acknowledge that your Lordship as a Privy Counceller hath Authority over them'.[58] The king permits Cavendish to use his name in any way necessary. If the duellists refuse to obey him, the king will conclude that they would not obey him either, implying that Cavendish's authority over the English in Antwerp is second to none. It is clear from this letter that Cavendish was still a respected member of the Privy Council in December 1652.

Cavendish's position of authority is again attested to in the 'very odd' case of Lady Page.[59] In 1653 Lady Page had made a pressing representation to Hyde on behalf of her husband, Sir Richard Page, who, like all the exiles, was living in penury. The king, however, was unable to help. Whether this had any bearing on her later actions, apparently motivated by revenge against her former lover, William Murray, Earl of Dysart, cannot be determined. Dysart and Page were both in Antwerp in 1654, when Lady Page claimed to have found two letters in Dysart's chamber. She called for a servant of Cavendish, a Mr. Watson, (possibly Ned Watson, an old retainer of the Cavendishes) and asked him to read an unsealed letter to her. Seeing that the letter concerned Dysart, Watson refused to read it. The next day Lady Page brought the letters to Cavendish, who told her they were of 'dangerous consequence', and returned them to her. However, wishing to be discharged of the letters, she waited again the next day on Cavendish, who asked her to remain until he could find a convenient oppor-

---

56   'It would fill a Volume, to repeat all the Commendations that were given to Horses, and
     to Horsemanship, by several worthy Gentlemen, of all Nations, High and Low-Dutch,
     Italians, English, French, Spaniards, Polacks, and Swedes, in my own private Riding-House
     at Antwerp'. Cavendish, *A New Method*, sig. (c)2v.

57   Ibid., sig. U2v, 76.

58   BL, Add. MS. 70499, fo. 327v.

59   *CCSP*, II, 311.

tunity to send them to the king. Instead, she sent a copy of the letter, a forgery implicating Sir Robert Moray and the Earl of Dysart in a plot to kill the king, to her husband in The Hague. Moray was briefly imprisoned while the matter was investigated, but by 1655 he had been fully cleared and had returned to Paris.[60]

Whether Cavendish delayed in acting upon the letters because he realised they were fakes, cannot be known. What is clear is that he was the authority in Antwerp to whom English exiles referred and also the means of communicating with the Crown. This is again evident in a letter Cavendish wrote on 1 May 1659 to Secretary Nicholas. Lord Wentworth and Cecil Howard had come to tell him that they had been informed, via a chain of Chinese whispers, of a plot to kill the king. However, having heard the previous day from Nicholas, Cavendish was able to reassure them that there was no cause for alarm. 'God Ever preserve my Gratius Master from all knaves fooles & bludye Rascalls' he exclaims, though whether he is referring to his mistaken informants or those who might actually attempt an assassination is a moot point.[61] Cavendish's life in Antwerp evidently encompassed more than just his horses. He continued to fulfil the responsibilities of his rank, networking with local dignitaries and foreign aristocrats, and acting as a restraining and reassuring presence among the English refugees.

It may have been during the early 1650s that Cavendish felt so confident, not only of his position with the king but also of his future restoration, that he decided to write his manual of advice to Charles II. While this document has previously been dated as written on or just after the Restoration, Gloria Anzilotti convincingly dates it to Margaret's sojourn in London.[62] Certainly it would make sense that Cavendish would divert himself with a suitably serious occupation in his wife's absence. What is more, this *vade mecum* suggests that he still considered his old role of governor as valid and, rightly or wrongly, that the young king was still in need of and receptive towards his advice. In

---

60   *Nicholas Papers*, 56–58; Martin D.C. "Sir Robert Moray, F.R.S. (1608?–1673)", *Notes and Records of the Royal Society of London*, 15, (July 1960) 239–250.

61   BL Egerton MS. 2536, fo. 370r.

62   'As regards the genesis of the work, Madan's claim that it dates from the second half of 1660 or the first half of 1661 is not corroborated by what Newcastle's wife, Margaret, says in the biography of her husband, where she explicitly states that he wrote and sent the King a <little book> when they were in banishment. Furthermore if we consider an unobtrusive addendum preceding the Earl of Dorset's name at the start of the subchapter <For the Civil Law>, we may, with a sufficient degree of accuracy assert that the present treatise was written during Margaret's eighteen month stay in England, which began in November 1651: Anzilotti, G., *An English Prince, Newcastle's Machiavellian Political Guide to Charles II* (Pisa: 1988) 12.

the introduction to his edition of the 'Advice' Thomas Slaughter insists upon its important legacy in Restoration policy: 'What can be established, however, is that claims that Charles 'did not take' Newcastle's advice are misleading. In large measure, many actions in which Charles engaged on his own initiative and that clearly represented his personal preferences were remarkably similar to Newcastle's vision of a wise government'.[63] This would certainly suggest that Charles respected Cavendish enough to read and absorb the 'Advice' he had written for him; even if he did not consider the elderly grandee suitable for a post in government after the Restoration.

In 1654 Cavendish was certainly anticipating Charles's return to the throne as he wrote to Secretary Nicholas to 'Remind his Majesty to renew to me those offices and places that his late father gave me, that others may not pass them, his Majesty not knowing of it'.[64] In September Charles II replied to Cavendish, assuring him that he would 'not be less kind to him than his father and grandfather were, and gives his word that the person Newcastle apprehends, shall never get before him; no importunity or money shall remove him from that resolution'.[65]

The Lifestyle of the Cavendishes in Exile

What is most striking about the exile of the Cavendishes is that, despite their letters of complaint, they appeared to live in so much more luxury than any of their compatriots. In June 1653 Hyde wrote to Nicholas about the extreme poverty of the king and his courtiers, who existed on one meal a day together for a pistole a week but had owed even for that for many weeks. Meanwhile, Cavendish was negotiating over the purchasing of pearls for his wife and looking for a translator for his opulent book on horsemanship. A parliamentarian agent noted from Brussels on the 9/19 July 1656 that 'The Marquis of Newcastle was lately here to take the air. The rest of the English through poverty and little hopes of amendment are so scattered and retired that they are scarce visible'.[66] Margaret Cavendish herself pays tribute to the generosity of their creditors in *'France, Holland, Brabant* and *Germany'*, who 'showed so much love, respect, and honour to my Lord, a stranger to their Nation; and notwithstanding his

---

63   Slaughter T.P. (transcribed), *Ideology and Politics on the Eve of Restoration: Newcastle's Advice to Charles II*, The American Philosophical Society (1984) xii.

64   *CSPD, 1654*, 288.

65   *CCSP*, vol. II, 288.

66   *CSPD, 1656–7* .

ruined Condition, and the small appearance of recovering his own, credited him wheresoever he lived'.[67] She cites several instances where her husband's creditors demanded payment only to be won over by his charm and promises of future reimbursement. His position among the *émigrés* must have been such that these creditors believed their loans were secure. Cavendish certainly made sure that the citizens of Antwerp saw him as a useful ally, one with close connections to the Stuart court. As late as April 1659 he was writing to Nicholas for information about the peace between Spain and France: 'The reson is the Bourgamasters & Governors off this towne desierde ^mee^ to lett them knowe iff I coulde the sertentye off itt, I tolde them thatt my Kinges principall Secretarye was my verye Noble freinde & I woulde write unto him thus by your favors I shall ingratiate my selfe verye much to this towne'.[68] When asked by Don Juan Jose of Austria, the Governor-General of the Spanish Netherlands from 1656 to 1660, whether he wanted anything and whether he lived 'peaceably and without molestation or disturbance', Cavendish replied that 'he lived as much to his own contentment as a banish'd man could do; and that he received more respect and civility from that City than he could have expected'.[69]

Antwerp was a place where, despite the constant appeasing of creditors, Cavendish could exist to some degree as he had been accustomed in England, playing the liberal host and the chivalric knight. The Cavendishes evidently enjoyed a sociably and artistically fulfilling lifestyle in Antwerp, living in Ruben's former residence, attending musical soirees, writing and, in William's case, buying and training horses. In his artistic endeavours, theatrical and musical, Cavendish continued to assert a royalist aesthetic. According to James Knowles, 'Among the wide range of patronage activities that William Cavendish employed while in exile in Antwerp was a series of dramatic entertainments'.[70] One of these was organised to commemorate the awarding of the Order of the Garter to Jean Gaspard-Ferdinand de Marsin, Comte de Graville, presented by Cavendish and the Earl of Bristol on 16 February 1658. It is significant that Antwerp should have been chosen as the location for this ceremony and that the Cavendishes' finances and popularity were such that they were able to host a ball to celebrate this event, one attended by Charles II, his brothers, James and Henry, and his sister, Mary, Princess of Orange, in addition to other aristocrats and local dignitaries. As Knowles points out, 'the guest-list

---

67   Cavendish M., *Life of William Cavendish*, Sig. U2r, p. 75.

68   BL Egerton MS. 2536, fo. 361r.

69   Cavendish M., *Life of William Cavendish*, sig. Xv, 78.

70   Knowles J., "'We've lost, should we lose too our harmless mirth?'", in *Royalist Refugees*, 70–77 (70).

illustrates the prestige that Cavendish retained.'[71] The ball was obviously something of a talking point as the letters describing it testify. Sir Gilbert Talbot, for instance, wrote to his father that '(the enterlude) the next day was performed with all circumstances of greatness in a little volume, and embellished with my Lady's owne poetry.'[72]

Unfortunately, the entertainment was not the only thing being talked about. The king's messenger, Thomas Ross, wrote to Nicholas a few days after the ball, complaining that Cavendish had been told about an expedition undertaken by Ormond to promote a royalist insurrection in England. Cavendish was so vociferous in his opposition to Ormond's mission that Hyde and, through him, the king, got to hear of it. Ross blamed Margaret for Cavendish's attitude and the '*Duke of York's* people' for telling him. The king, despite being offended by Cavendish's criticisms, was also unwilling to hold him personally responsible. Ross explained in a letter to Nicholas written from Brussels on 1/11 March:

> They checked *Newcastle* gently, but were severer on his intelligencers, *Elliot* and honest *Will Love*; but *Newcastle* and the *King* parted kindly, the *King* having real kindness for him, rather pitying his weakness than forgetting his inadvertency, and the malice of those who informed him, who are great decriers of this business, and in that satisfy the humours of *Newcastle* and of his wife, who swears that the affair cannot and shall not be effected without her husband.[73]

Evidently, the king was still fond of his old governor, who was perhaps something of a father figure to him, one whose advice was adopted even after his pupil had outgrown his authority.[74] According to Slaughter, 'Charles seemed ever the *protégé* of Newcastle, never a son of the obnoxiously pious Charles I'.[75] The king's mother also still saw Cavendish as an ally worth courting, writing in November 1658 to thank him for a book he had sent her. 'I am very glad to see that you still remember me', Henrietta Maria told him, 'I pray you to believe

71   Knowles, 77.

72   TNA, SP 77/32, fo. 32.

73   *CSPD 1657–8*, 311.

74   Newcastle's dismay at Ormond's mission turned out to be well founded as Ormond, poorly disguised, was pursued around London by Cromwell's men, before escaping back to the Continent. Hutton, *Charles the Second*, 111.

75   Slaughter, xxix. Anna Keay also describes Cavendish as 'probably the single most influential figure in the prince's upbringing'. *The Magnificent Monarch: Charles II and the Ceremonies of Power* (London: 2008) 21.

that I shall never forget you but that I shall seek all opportunity of testifying the continuance of my esteem for you'.[76]

Conclusion

Cavendish had done his best to fight for his position during his exile, maintaining his political profile and his royal connections, including access to the king, who visited him in Antwerp on several occasions. Up until 1651 he clearly maintained hopes of leading a military force into England. He continued to exert his influence in royalist affairs, sitting on the Privy Council from 1650 until at least 1653. He was a key player in the negotiations at Breda and although banned from accompanying the king to Scotland, he retained a position of command, as the letters from Lothian and Wilmot testify. After Charles' defeat at the Battle of Worcester Cavendish focused on his role as an elder statesman among the *émigré* community in Antwerp, using this position to his advantage among the native inhabitants as well. Even as late as 1658 he was popular enough to be fêting the royal family in his home. By this time he was no longer being included in royalist conspiracies; at sixty-five (an advanced age for the seventeenth century) he was probably considered too old, but this did not stop his desire for involvement. Cavendish may have overestimated his importance and he had his detractors, but he should not be dismissed as a figure of ridicule; he was still held in high esteem by many at court. It is telling that a report from the Herald's Office on 7 August 1660 stated: 'Yesterday there passed some hot and high words in the Lords House betwixt the Duke of Buckingham and the Earl of Bristol by reason the Earl of Bristol did set a higher value on the Marquis of Newcastle's actings and sufferings for the King than of the Duke's'.[77]

Since the 'publicke sorde' had denied him 'that hapines I labored ffor with untouch loyaltye' Cavendish instead dedicated his private sword to 'the only Master thatt ever I had'.[78] Whether, after the Restoration, his loyalty was rewarded as he and his wife thought fit is another matter.

---

76   BL Harley MS. 7003, fo. 13v.
77   *HMC*, "5th Report" (London: 1876), 177.
78   BL Harley MS 4206, fo. 93v.

Selective Bibliography

Gardiner S.R. (ed.), *The Hamilton Papers: being selections from original letter in the possession of His Grace the Duke of Hamilton and Brandon, relating to the years 1638–1650, Camden Society* (1880) 220, 226.

Härting U., "Inhabitants of Antwerp", in Van Beneden B. – de Poorte N. (eds.), *Royalist Refugees, William and Margaret in the Rubens House 1648–1660* (Antwerp: 2006) 63–69.

Hutton R., *Charles the Second King of England, Scotland and Ireland* (Oxford: 1989).

Hutton R., *Debates in Stuart History* (Basingstoke: 2004).

Hyde E., *The history of the rebellion and civil wars in England* (Oxford: 1958).

Israel J.I., *The Dutch Republic: It's Rise, Its Greatness, and Fall 1477–1806* (Oxford: 1995).

Loxley J., *Royalism and Poetry in the English Civil Wars: The Drawn Sword* (Basingstoke: 1997).

Maclean J., "Montrose's Preparations for the Invasion of Scotland", in Hatton R. – Anderson M.S. (eds.), *Studies in Diplomatic History*, (London: 1970) 7–31 (16).

Norbrook D., "Women, the republic of letters, and the public sphere in the mid-seventeenth century", *Criticism* 46, No. 2, (Spring 2004) 223–240 (27).

Pleij H., "Antwerp Described", in Van der Stock J. (ed.), *Antwerp: Story of a Metropolis* (Ghent: 1993), 37–47 (43).

Reynolds N., "The Stuart Court and Courtiers in Exile" (Unpublished Ph.D. thesis, Cambridge University, 1996).

Sarasohn L., "Margaret Cavendish, William Newcastle, and Political Marginalisation", *English Studies* Vol. 92, No. 7 (November 2011) 806–817.

Slaughter T.P. (ed.), *Ideology and Politics on the Eve of Restoration: Newcastle's Advice to Charles II*, The American Philosophical Society (1984) xii.

Soly H. "Social Relations in Antwerp in the Sixteenth and Seventeenth Centuries" in Van der Stock, 'Antwerp', 79–85 (84).

Underdown D., *Royalist Conspiracy in England 1649–1660* (New Haven: 1960).

Warner G.F. (ed.), *"The Nicholas Papers, correspondence of Sir Edward Nicholas"*, *Camden Society* (1886).

iii. Horsemanship, Authority and Identity

∴

'The Epitome of Horsemanship': William Cavendish's Method 'Anatomized'

Elaine Walker

The first cause of Absurd conclusions I ascribe to a want of Method.
THOMAS HOBBES, *Leviathan*

∴

William Cavendish's 'New Method' horsemanship manuals of 1658 and 1667 are complicated at many levels with the added confusion of different languages and a shared title. But they are entirely separate texts and each has its own complex agenda, linked to the time of publication, the desired readership and its relationship with texts by other authors. The commentaries, with Cavendish's philosophies and conversational anecdotes, offer insights into his political motivation and character and these are inevitably more readable, and probably of more interest to a non-rider, than the technical material. However, the manuals are key texts in the development of classical horsemanship and the only seminal works on the subject by an English writer. Their prime focus is training a horse 'according to his Nature, Disposition, and Strength' (1667: 349), an aim with complex motivations in itself. Any metaphoric or idealistic agenda they serve can only be effective if they fulfil their role as training guides. But, far from undermining readings of deeper motivation and symbolic significance, a consideration of their practicality not only illuminates all other aspects of the texts but also offers important insights into Cavendish's character.

Cavendish's skill with horses helped clarify many of the tensions of his life and the manuals offer insight into a complex man with a strong urge for self-expression. While they are significant in the development of horsemanship literature, they include a biographical subtext found as much in the training method as in the underlying philosophy. To appreciate fully the value of Cavendish's manuals involves an understanding that the symbolic importance of horsemanship was rooted in the needs of a practical skill requiring a high level of knowledge. Therefore, the method and its execution are bound to the

© KONINKLIJKE BRILL NV, LEIDEN, 2017 | DOI 10.1163/9789004326217_013

political and philosophical ideas from which they were born and neither can
be fully understood without reference to the other.

Horsemanship as an art had begun to develop in Renaissance Italy, where
Frederigo Grisone published *Gli Ordini di cavalcare* in Naples in 1550. Grisone
was one of an élite company of riders and established his own riding academy, probably in the 1530s.[1] His manual was the first important horsemanship
text to be of interest primarily to the élite, rather than the military, horseman,
although a great many readers would have been both. Grisone also set the
precedent for the riding manual itself as a feature of the master's work, and
a huge array of manuals followed. As many were derivative, or translations of
Grisone's work 'improved' upon by others, locating ownership of the material
becomes difficult, especially as not all who were influential published their
methods. Pignatelli, for example, trained under Cesare Fiaschi, then joined
Grisone's academy in Naples to become the most celebrated instructor of his
time, but he did not publish his own manual. His influence, then, could only be
interpreted through oral tradition, constantly filtered through the experience
of those who followed him. To a certain extent this is also true of the manuals of
Antoine de Pluvinel, the next seminal author and a pupil of Pignatelli, possibly
alongside Monsieur St. Antoine, Cavendish's own riding tutor.[2] Pluvinel's manuals were published posthumously and prepared by his student, Rene Menou,
partly from rough notes and fragments of writing. Large tracts of the material
in Pluvinel's manuals appeared in Menou's own text of 1612, so it becomes difficult to separate the student from the master.[3]

In this respect, Cavendish's manuals are straightforward but his political
and personal agenda complicate the motivation behind each manual, adding
a further complex dimension. For Grisone and Pluvinel to set down their ideas
for future riders was a way of recording the ephemeral, one of the functions of
the published text. Cavendish's reasons for doing this are not simply related
to being a great horseman but also reflect the situation of his life at the time
when each manual was written.

One of the primary features of Grisone's work is the acceptance that extreme
brutality should be used to counter any resistance from the horse. Pluvinel

---

1   For a discussion of Grisone's work and importance, see Elizabeth Tobey's essay, "The Legacy
    of Frederico Grisone", in *The Horse as Cultural Icon*, 143–171.

2   While Roy Strong refers to St. Antoine as a pupil of Pluvinel in *Henry, Prince of Wales and
    England's lost Renassiance* (London: 2000) 41–42, Cavendish says he trained alongside
    Pluvinel under Pignatelli (1667: 3).

3   Nelson H. (trans.), *La Maneige Royal* (London: 1989); for a consideration of the relationship
    between Pluvinel's texts and Menou's, *La Pratique du Cavalier* (Paris: 1612) see v–vi. All subse-
    quent references to Pluvinel's work will be to Nelson's translation.

advocates a more humane approach and his manual, the next significant text, took horse training into a new area of refinement. He sets his manual entirely within the confines of the riding house, whereas Grisone's uses ploughed fields, ditches and other outdoor locations in the training. Cavendish's method adds further refinement and his claims of innovation are justified, although he also includes developments from earlier practices. This is inevitable as, while methods may change and develop, the ways in which the rider influences his mount, namely, by his weight and position on the horse's back, are bound by the anatomy of both. The use of these fixed physical features, however, is where the development in both understanding and method is seen. This sense of progression in the horsemanship text can be traced further by considering the way in which Cavendish influenced later masters, including the most famous, François Robichon de la Guérinière, Director of the Académie des Tuileries in Paris, who held him in high esteem.[4] Cavendish stands alone as the first—and still the only—English author whose work was not derivative of early Continental texts and who became acclaimed as a primary influence by later generations of horsemen. Nevertheless, rather than attempting to see him as he saw himself, in splendid isolation, a more accurate perspective is gained by seeing him in the lineage of great horsemen, each with an individual contribution to make.

The moral purpose of horsemanship was in contention from the Renaissance onwards and Cavendish contributes to the debate in characteristically emphatic style in 1667 with a chapter entitled, 'That it is a very Impertinent Error, and of Great prejudice, to think the Mannage Useless'. He also comments resignedly that 'There are great Disputes amongst Cavaliers about this Business' when it comes to choosing the best horse 'Either for the War, or for Single-Combat, or for Any Thing Else'. With his usual wry insight, he notes 'how Difficult a thing it is to have a Good Horse in any Kind, for Any thing'. His conclusion that 'a Knowing Horseman is not so Happy for Horses, as a citizen of London, that knows Nothing' illustrates again his ironic acceptance that knowledge is not always a help, because divided opinion then complicates the matter (1667: 5, 77, 81). A tension is apparent as riding moves from the battlefield to the riding house, largely, it seems, due to attempts, as made by Cavendish himself, to retain the links between the two.

The movements of the riding house were originally based on the behaviour of stallions in the wild, either displaying to mares or fighting rivals. The aggressive kicking or striking nature of many of these movements serves well the male display involved in the art. Cavendish believed strongly that the

---

4 Boucher T. (trans.), *School of Horsemanship*, (London: 1994) 78, 87. De la Guérinière's *Ecole de Cavalerie*, was published in four parts in 1729–31, then in a single volume edition in 1733, and remains the core text for the work of the Spanish Riding School of Vienna.

horseman should 'do nothing against Nature; for Art is but to set Nature in Order' (1667: 271), giving a masculine imperative of control within the context of shaping nature to man's purpose. However, these natural skills were refined and defined until little remained that truly resembled wild natural movement. In theory at least, the fighting movements could transfer usefully to the battle-field but there seems to have been a gradual move to separate the riding house horse and the warhorse, which may be traced through the manuals.[5]

In translating Grisone, Sir Thomas Blundeville distinguishes between the warhorse and the horse of pleasure so that the latter should learn additional skills more suited for ceremony and display.[6] In *La Maneige Royale*, Louis XIII's comment to Pluvinel that certain airs 'are not necessarily the best for war' implies a doubtful anticipation that the training could lead to the battle-field. Interestingly, Pluvinel's only reply is that some modified exercises may be useful 'when one fights in a duel or in battle'. It may be that this token mention of the matter is a cautious recognition of it as a controversial subject.[7] Primary source evidence suggests that the art in its advanced form had little or no place on the battlefield in Cavendish's time. No mention at all of any of the school airs appears in *The young Horseman or The honest plain-dealing Cavalier*, written in 1644 by John Vernon, which is aimed very much at the ordinary mounted soldier.[8] Vernon's schooling focuses on exercises that supple the horse to ensure speed and agility, which seem both practicable and capable of implementation:

> you must use him often to ride the Ring, and the figure eight, first in a greater compass and afterwards in a lesser by degrees: first in his pace, then on his trot and so to his gallop. And lastly in full careere, you may teach him this by using your hand, legge and voice, for the using him unto your hand you must observe not to use your arms at all, but your rist only, this is excellent for facings, as if you would turn him to the left, a little motion of the left little finger and a touch of the left leg not using the spur doth it.[9]

---

5 See Treva Tucker's discussion of the impact of changing military roles on the French noble-man in her essay, "Early Modern French Noble Identity", in Raber K. – Tucker T.J. (eds.), The *Culture of the Horse: Status, Discipline and Identity in the Early Modern World* (Basingstoke: 2005) 273–309.

6 Blundeville Thomas, *A new booke, containing the Arte of Ryding and breaking greate Horses* (London: Willyam Seres, 1560) Aiiii. (Hereafter, Blundeville).

7 Pluvinel, 89–90.

8 Tincey J. (ed.) *The Young Horse-man, or honest plain-dealing Cavalier*, (London: 1993) 11.

9 Ibid., 43.

This has much in common with Cavendish's basic training methods for teaching suppleness and mobility through circle work, with his refined use of the hands on the reins to encourage lightness and a swift response. These techniques would be sufficient, as it seems very unlikely that in battle there would be time to focus on the execution of elaborate caprioles and curvets, which aside from seeming to lack practical military purpose, would also expose the horse's belly to attack. Also, while the drama of the capriole, with the horse leaping forward high above the ground, may in theory threaten the head of any man below, even in the refined atmosphere of a riding house, it is a difficult and specialized movement.

An additional key consideration when judging the suitability of the airs of the riding house for the battlefield, must be the time and cost involved in producing the horse and rider combination capable of performing such moves. As Cavendish expounds at great length on the cost and difficulty of obtaining and importing a good Spanish horse (1667: 51–52), it seems unlikely that this would be the horse to risk in battle, in spite of, or perhaps because of, his skill. To produce even one horse who could perform the most modest of airs would take many months, with two or three handlers involved in the training.[10] Then, the number of horses who had the skill and physique to perform the great leaps would be limited, and these would be highly expensive animals. Cavendish states that, 'It is a Hard thing to find Fit Horses for the Mannage, either upon the Ground, or in Ayres' and stresses the need to work with the horse's natural aptitude in the airs (1667: 79, 271). Nicholas Morgan argues against teaching the high airs at all, due to them 'tending altogether towards [the horse's] destruction' and being 'a matter rather of delight than good use'.[11]

A theatrical and active general, such as Cavendish, might wish to inspire his army in the moments before the battle as a figurehead on his superbly trained horse. But, unless that horse could then lead a charge under fire, such a display

---

10   Cavendish claims he can 'dress' a tractable horse in three months, but adds that the horse must have 'spirits and vigour, a quick disposition, judgment and memory' and be 'without faults' and then 'practice must make him perfect' (1743: 18). This does not necessarily include the high airs, as not all horses would be suited to them and they would be advanced, not basic training. Perhaps most significantly, a horse 'without faults' might be a challenge to find in the first place. As I have used the original 1743 edition rather than the modern facsimile versions, there is no need to distinguish between the London and Vermont publications.

11   Morgan Nicholas, *The Horseman's Honour: or the Beautie of Horsemanship* (London, John Marriott: 1620) 207. Displays today by the Spanish Riding School of Vienna and the Cadre Noir at Saumur have only a few horses performing these movements, due to the rigorous training required and immense physical strain they put upon them.

would be undermined and it seems unlikely that more than a few riders would possess such mounts. Cavendish may have had a number of horses with him on the battlefield to allow for casualties, which could have included school horses to inspire his men and warhorses to lead a charge. The question remains as to why critics, who disparaged the value of the riding house in war training, irritate him, as he appears to accept that the high art of the riding house has no place there. His advice on choosing a horse 'For the War, or for Single-Combat' (1667: 77), does not specify a Spanish horse, which is always his first choice for the riding house, despite his personal preference for the Barb (1743: 21). For war, he is interested more in size and attitude, claiming that 'the Midling or Less Horses is Best' (1667: 78). It is unthinkable that the 'all-rounder' he describes would be one of his expensive imported pure-bred Spanish horses. It seems most likely that he means a versatile cross-bred, perhaps with some Spanish blood, as he believes the Spanish stallion is 'Absolutely the best Stallion in the world' to add quality to any breeding programme (1667: 50–51). Another clue that such a horse is not a *manège* horse is his preference for geldings rather than stallions, due to their more placid behaviour; a true *manège* horse would always be a stallion for its fire and presence.

While he advocates his basic method for all horses, the training he suggests for a warhorse does not include any advanced school airs, but rather that, 'You should teach him To Leap Hedge, Ditch and Rail [...] also to swim' (1667: 311–312). However, being offended by those who disparage his managed horses, he argues that they too are versatile without suggesting that the airs of the riding house are transferable to the battlefield:

> If those gentlemen were to fight a duel or go to the wars, they would find their error; for these horses perform a journey, as well as they do the high airs; and the long marches occasionally make them soon forget those airs, which are calculated merely for pleasure; moreover, they are much fitter for galloping, trotting, wheeling, or any thing else which is necessary (1743: 14).

This is the true value of the riding house horse in war: his excellent and solid training which makes him skilful and, above all, responsive, even in the face of danger so that 'I will run him on Fire, Water, or Sword, and he shall Obey me'. (1667: 6). His ability to perform a capriole may or may not be an added bonus, but his swift obedience and dexterity makes him invaluable. Cavendish's irritation, therefore, appears, as elsewhere, to be rooted in the common lack of understanding of the art rather than the need for blind devotion to it. Thus, the art of the *manège* was useful as part of the general education of the officer class for its discipline and overall skill rather than for specific techniques.

Riding displays before an audience of his peers allowed the noble rider to demonstrate the skills of control, presence and leadership he could bring to the
battlefield. The deeply rooted messages about power and control implicit in
the skilful riding of a horse were made very clear in the execution of high airs
and beautifully balanced paces.

Cavendish's annoyance with those who could not see the intrinsic value of
the work, alongside its beauty as an art form and political importance as a
means of display, becomes understandable. It also gives him the motivation to
add his theories on this art, justifiable entirely in its own right, to those already
well-known and to fix them in print as his own. His manuals and the complex
issues surrounding the riding house illustrate the combined practical, philosophical and personal concerns involved when he came to write. The art of
horsemanship was a yardstick for aristocratic self-awareness against which
Cavendish measured his own life and society. For him to set his ideas down
precisely and with great attention to detail offers as much insight into his character as any of the more widely known aspects of his history.

As stated above, the relationship between his two manuals is complex, and
the 1667 publication is not a translation or even an adaptation of the 1658
French-language text. It is a new work based on the same ideas, later on their
development.[12] However, the essential purpose of training a horse remains the
same, so Cavendish advises the use of both his manuals together and directly
refers his readers to the plates from the first manual. As he points out, 'There
is in my French Book, Circles and the Prints of Horses Shooes, to shew how his
Leggs should Go; there is also exact figures of all Postures, and of all Actions,
both of Man and Horse, and more cannot be' (1667: B2v, 43, 93, 112).

To ride the horse so that he can display his beauty is a highly skilled activity,
as the rider must not hinder his freedom of movement. The power in a horse
comes from the haunches and the further back the centre of balance, the more
weight they will carry. This frees the front legs to manoeuvre and move with
lightness, thereby making efficient use of the horse's energy, and 'is our main
Business and Work' (1667: 334). It is also essential for the advanced movements
towards which Cavendish worked his horses. Much of the modern understanding of the movement of horses comes from the advent of photography, which
has enabled close analysis of each stage of a step. That Cavendish had begun to
uncover this depth of knowledge is evident from the technical accuracy of his
descriptions, and also of the plates, which can only have resulted from many
hours of detailed discussion with the artist. Both manuals also contain very

---

12   The relationship between the two manuals is discussed in detail in Walker E., 'To
      Amaze the People with Pleasure and Delight' (Virginia: 2015), in particular, 34–65; 91–120.
      (Hereafter Walker, 'To Amaze the People').

similar versions of a lengthy discussion on the positioning on the horse's feet, perhaps inspired by the work of Robert Payne[13] (1658: 36–37; 1667: 145–155; 1743L: 30–34, 36–37). All of these details indicate the level of precision and artistry the manuals set out for example and training.

Cavendish divides his comprehensive 'New Method' into four progressive sections. These start with choosing parents to produce a suitable horse for the riding house. They then move on through care from birth, to early handling and backing, before addressing the various levels of training. He includes more detail on preparation prior to riding than earlier authors due to his understanding that the raw material is highly important. His first innovation is his complete rejection of the idea that the early rides will involve taming wildness.[14] He also uses short varied lessons on the principle of never allowing the horse to grow too tired to retain what he has learned (1743: 28). This is in deliberate contrast to earlier methods that rely on exhaustion in the horse to achieve compliance.[15] Before the training under saddle can begin in earnest, the rider must understand the workings of Cavendish's great technical innovation, the cavesson noseband of his own design, illustrated in plate 13 and throughout the training plates. Surprisingly, this vital piece of equipment is introduced casually and without any of the self-congratulation which is a feature of Cavendish's style. It is, however, repeatedly emphasised in both manuals as essential 'to Stay, to Raise and to make the Horse Leight; to Teach him to Turn, to Stop, to Firm his Neck, to Assure and Adjust his head, and his Croup, without Offending His Mouth' (1667: 156). The focus on lightness and protection of the horse's mouth are the key points, for the reasons discussed above. Similarly, his belief that avoiding the use of a bit at all in the early stages of training and introducing it alongside the cavesson 'to manage his head by degrees' (1743: 27) illustrates that his method aimed at results through subtlety and patience.

The use of the cavesson noseband with ropes attached to a pillar had a long history by the seventeenth century but Cavendish's method is a considerable refinement. In using a rope tied to a fixed point, the horse learned that his movement was restricted but without injury to the mouth or a handler. Over time, at least in theory, the horse would learn to refine his movements to avoid working against the rope. Cavendish takes this idea and, instead of using fixed points, puts reins on the cavesson, passing them through rings on

---

13   Possible links with the work of Robert Payne are discussed in Walker, 'To Amaze the People', 37–40; 98–99.

14   Including Pluvinel, 21; 32, 39; Blundeville, A8v–A810v.

15   Cf. 1743: 27 and Blundeville, C7i–D1v.

the noseband and the saddle, into the rider's hands. This means that the horse cannot tear the reins away but the rider can give and take on them to allow the horse gradually to grow used to lateral flexion. The rider's control of the reins has much more potential sensitivity and Cavendish does not introduce this until later in the training than the pillar method. He is also developing flexibility, rather than simply restricting forward movement, to teach response to pressure. By the time this stage is reached using his method, the horse has already learnt to respond to pressure from the years of regular early handling and initial lessons using only a halter (1743: 27). Cavendish claims that 'I have greater command over him with two fingers in this method than with both hands in the common method' (1743: 35), a point which any thinking rider can understand. Any method of training that diffuses the horse's greater strength and encourages co-operation, rather than unwilling submission, will be more effective in the long term. This device is not the same as draw-reins, which pull the horse's head down towards his chest vertically, using equal pressure on both reins on the bit. Cavendish is emphatic that forcing the horse into position through what he calls the 'Perpendicular-Line' is a mistake and says plainly, 'This I never use' because, rather than engaging the hind-quarters, it puts horses 'horribly upon their shoulders, though their Heads be down' (1667: 175, 265–266).

Once riding has begun, the progressive approach continues and Cavendish advocates steady steps over a period of days rather than intensive training. He devotes considerable detail to explaining how, by the use of a firm but sensitive hand and circling exercises, the desired position of the head will be achieved. The use of exercises 'upon Large Circles', which are reduced as the horse becomes more supple, ensures that the hind legs must reach further under the horse's body. The horse will move towards the ideal of lightness and elegance by bearing more weight on the haunches and giving relative freedom to the forehand. With a light hand on the rein, in time the horse's head will lower as his back rounds. The rider should 'give him no other lesson than this, until he be very Supple on the Shoulders upon his Trot' because all the early training is to ensure that 'the Foundation of all things in the Mannage' is secure and well-established (1667: 208–209).

The use of the cavesson noseband in the exercises that follow have the effect of flexing the horse's neck so that his head is turned toward the shoulder. Changing sides regularly ensures that muscle is developed equally. The cavesson teaches the horse to flex laterally with mobility between the jaw and neck rather than the jack-knife flexion between the shoulder and the lower-neck. The purpose of this is to create a finished, that is, fully trained animal, who is supple through his neck and shoulder and ultimately through his back.

This is very difficult for the horse due to the construction of his spine, which because it has to support the heavy contents of the body, is a fairly rigid structure. If the spine were more flexible, it would not be possible to ride the horse, but training works towards the maximum flexibility possible. Most of the spinal movement is in the neck and tail areas and the apparent bending of a horse upon a circle is due to the mobility between the cervical vertebrae, the movement of the rib-cage and the freedom of movement available to the front legs, which can adduct and abduct in relation to the body. This is best observed by watching a horse attempt to reach around to scratch his own back, which illustrates just how little flexibility there is between the shoulders and the croup. No other author prior to Cavendish uses a method such as this, and it suggests a close understanding of the way the horse's spine works.

The training plates (numbers 14–29; 36–37) in the first manual[16] follow the text, illustrating in accurate technical detail the points that Cavendish makes. They demonstrate the practical application of the method in a way that is helpful to the inexperienced, as well as the already confident rider, illustrating key points in the progressive training method. Marginal notes in the text in the first manual direct the reader to the correct plates and some of the plates have a page reference. By following the training method in the text with reference to the plates, both their technical accuracy and the way Cavendish uses them to support the text becomes clear. His method is based on his understanding of the horse's mind and behaviour, which can only have come from long observation: he was evidently not the sort of horseman who visited his stables only to mount a horse readied for him by a groom.[17]

The horse is a herd animal, needing the security offered by confident leadership and his natural place in his social group. This is a need that Cavendish frequently demonstrated himself, especially in his relationship with his monarch, suggesting that his affinity with horses had its foundation in his own character.[18] When the herd leader is replaced by a human handler, the horse still needs that sense of security and while modern equine psychology has defined this relationship, it has long been used instinctively by the perceptive horse handler.

---

16   Brindley's translation and the several facsimile editions produced since, including by Allen J.A. (London: 2000), retain the plates from the first manual, though they are not in the same relationship to the text as in the 1658 original.

17   *Vide* Walker, *'To Amaze the People'*, 120–139.

18   Ibid., 33–64.

In the highly competitive early modern world, the nobleman on horse-back displayed the essentials of his own nature in the way he handled a horse. Cavendish's method establishes leadership through his firm but non-aggressive insistence that 'the Horse follow my Wayes and Obey me', rather than the cruder methods of earlier practitioners such as 'Fire, Hedge-Hoggs, Nailes, and I know not what' (1667: 181) that relied on pain and fear. Observers, readers or riders, able to appreciate the difference revealed—indeed still reveal—something about themselves too. 'I have never yet seen that force and passion have prevailed the least upon the horse', he says, as, 'his passion is so much the stronger, which makes him always get the better of the horseman, and shews that violent methods will not do' (1743: 105). He advocates swift 'but Seldome' use of the spurs 'upon Just Occasion' if a horse persistently resists, followed by equally swift reward for acceptance, 'that he may see you have Mercy as well as Justice, and that you can Reward, as well as Punish' (1667: 184–185). His approach is based largely on the calm assertion of his will upon them, which he describes as 'Force' and in response 'they Obey willingly, for the most part; and however, all Yeeld, and Render themselves at last' (1667: 42). This reflects an understanding of a horse's acceptance of confident leadership that is part of his nature as a herd animal and commonly understood today. In practice, it relies on a channelling of the horse's energy through the use of firm, con-sistent, but not aggressive, positioning and movement of the rider's body. For Cavendish, however, it represented a point of departure from other writers and he therefore feels justified in claiming total originality, regardless of his place in the lineage of riders that went back to Grisone.

Relaxed ease and clear focus in the riding position will transmit that calm leadership to the horse, which will be more responsive as a result. As the horse is influenced by every movement, even the most experienced rider must address his contribution to the working partnership with a sensitive animal that responds to pressure, both physical and psychological. So Cavendish's ini-tial concern is that the rider's position should not hinder the horse's training but, instead, help create common centres of gravity as if 'they had but one Body, and one Mind, like a Centaur' (1667: 13). This, of course, is best illustrated by an image of the perfect horseman, Cavendish himself, in plate 14 (Fig. 11.1): alongside the technical accuracy in the plates, there is the constant reminder of whose expertise this is all based on.

Not only the rider's but the horse's position must be precise. Cavendish devotes considerable detail to discussing the position of the horse's feet and in the first manual uses diagrams to illustrate the tracks made by the hooves. This illustrates the level of horsemanship to which he is aspiring. A rider who

FIGURE 11.1   *The Perfect horseman. From William Cavendish,* La Méthode Nouvelle, *plate 14.*
ALL IMAGES IN THIS CHAPTER ARE COPYRIGHT ELAINE WALKER.

can feel where each hoof is on the ground at any given moment can achieve much greater precision. To develop that feel, the rider must understand what is happening beneath him and Cavendish's use of floor patterns, which are also shown in the plates, and the accompanying complex discussions are his attempts to translate feeling into text in a very new way.

Well-fitting and appropriate tack is also a key factor. Cavendish stresses that severe bits do not put a horse upon his haunches, wherein the power lies, but on the forehand or behind the bit, meaning that he will tuck his head in to avoid contact at all. Here, he illustrates his awareness of the horse's anatomy, which is in direct opposition to those who 'shew themselves full of Ignorance ... to imagine, That a piece of Iron in a Horse's Mouth can bring him Knowledge' (1667: p. 343). He also seems to be making a direct reference to early Italian manuals that devote a large proportion of the text to bits, frequently severe in their action, while the sheer number of choices points to a problem area. This indicates that use of the hind legs and back to achieve head carriage was not fully understood, even though the use of circles in training was already established. Cavendish argues that a good rider will not need remedial methods. He favours relatively simple bits and aims always for self-carriage. This means that while there is a relationship between the bit and the rider's hand along the rein (which he calls 'appuy', meaning 'support'), the horse is balanced rather than leaning or pulling on the bit.

Once the young horse is at ease moving forward with a rider, the next stage is 'to Supple his Shoulders [...] for that is the Foundation of all things in the Mannage' (1667: 209), to develop confidence, flexibility and self-carriage. Cavendish explains the use his cavesson to ensure the greatest benefit, then details a series of lessons with great precision. His plates, while beautiful in themselves, are a crucial part of the instructions, as plate 15 (figures 11.2 and 11.3) illustrating the exercise, 'Trot a Droite', makes particularly clear. The horse has a bit in his mouth but is being ridden from Cavendish's cavesson. Captain Mazin, directed by Cavendish, holds the cavesson reins, using the subtlest flexing of his hands to influence the horse's movements. Although the back of Mazin's hand is towards the reader, it can be seen turning slightly so that the fingernails are upwards. This brings the rein under a different tension than if the hand is straight but without shortening its length, while encouraging the horse to round his body through pressure on the cavesson via the rein. This is also clear in plate 15, where the horse is driving forward from the haunches, with the different paces illustrated to show the progression of the exercise. The slight rotation of the hand adds more subtlety of movement than a direct lift: to flex the horse laterally at the neck, encourage suppleness throughout the body and prevent the horse from falling onto his forehand. (Figs. 2–3) This difference has a considerable effect on the ability of the horse to move elegantly and efficiently.

The rider's legs are positioned to help the horse curve through the body and prevent the hindquarters drifting outwards, which is easier but less effective. The instruction to a rider of a horse working the circle to 'bring in your outward Shoulder moderately' (1667: 177) reinforces the importance of the body as an aid, as the turn inward would influence the rider's weight and pelvis position, and with it the horse's response. A change in the rider's position will urge the horse to maintain the unit in balance and adjust position accordingly for his physical and psychological comfort. With an accomplished rider and relaxed attentive horse, there is potential for great subtlety and refinement.

Plate 16 (Fig. 11.4) moves the horse to the next level, working away from the circle, though still using the cavesson reins. The images in this plate are particularly helpful in showing the progression through one exercise at the trot and *galop* (collected canter). This illustrates one of Cavendish's main methods of progression, namely to bring the horse to a place where he is 'so Leight, as he offers to gallop of himself' (1667: p. 209), that he is ready to move to the next natural gait without any additional pressure being put upon him.

If the images in plate 16 are viewed from the centre to the outside in both phases of the exercise, it becomes clear that Captain Mazin is preparing the

FIGURE 11.2   *Using the cavesson to develop suppleness in the horse. From William Cavendish,*
                La Méthode Nouvelle, plate 15.

FIGURE 11.3
*Detail of plate 15, showing
rotation of the rider's wrist.*

horse to turn and go in the opposite direction. His weight is further back in the images to the outside edges of the plate and, as he prepares to turn his body, he encourages the horse to take more weight on the haunches and pivot, allowing the forehand freedom to change direction. Also, the hand holding the flexed position of the head has moved higher and closer to his body by a few inches. The hand to the outside of the turn is on the reins attached to the bit, and will use them to support the horse's neck and shoulder through the turn. These images are a highly technical and accurate depiction of the exact nature of the horse and rider relationship to accomplish a complicated exercise.

Cavendish is aiming to enable the horse to free up this motion through a range of specific exercises. These start by using the wall of the riding house as a barrier to prevent forward movement and is less restrictive than if the barrier were provided by the bit, via the rider's hand. This illustrates that the lessons for working the horse's croup encourage the horse to move the hind legs later-ally, as well as forward and back, enhancing his athletic ability. The capacity to cross the hind legs when travelling directly sideways or on a circle, makes a great difference to the range of movement of the horse, but takes a consider-able amount of practice. The plates illustrate the exercises from both sides and then progress to working away from the wall around a pillar. While working towards the wall, the horse is required to cross his legs directly to the side. In the exercises around the pillar, the legs also move on a circle but as the move-ment is much more difficult, it is introduced once the horse understands the task. Cavendish focuses on making the desired movement easy and any other difficult to enable success.

The detail in the plates not only illustrates the precision of Cavendish's method but provides a reference point for his readers in training their own horses. In plate 17 (Fig. 11.5) Captain Mazin's position demonstrates how the weight and body alignment of the rider assist the horse by turning in the direc-tion the horse is moving. In 'Au pas a sa Longeur a Droite', the crossing of the left hind foot in front of the right hind may be seen very clearly. The floor pat-terns show that the horse is turning in a small circle around a fixed notional centre. The pillar is used in much the same way as the wall, so that each time the horse encounters the pillar, to avoid it he will correct his position, sup-ported by the rider's aids. The rider must use the 'Inward Reyn, and Outward Legg' (1667: 222), effectively balancing the horse between the rein and the leg. He advises that the rider should 'not help every time, but (in Musical time),[19]

---

19   Elisabeth LeGuin discusses the importance of physical and musical harmony to early
      modern thinking in her essay, "Man and horse in harmony", in Raber – Tucker, *Culture of
      the Horse*, 175–196.

FIGURE 11.4   *Progression away from the circle: one exercise at the trot and 'galop'. From William Cavendish,* La Méthode Nouvelle, *plate 16.*

according to the time of the horse'. (1667: 291) This advocacy of intermittent stimuli is more effective than constant pressure, which the horse's brain would eventually ignore, 'for then he will not Care for them no more than a Stone or a Block' (1667: 185).

Establishing these initial foundations under saddle is essential, as the horse needs to understand and make instinctive connections between the aids and the movements. Once this is established, the lessons can progress and Cavendish proceeds comparatively quickly through the fourth and fifth divisions of lessons. As the horse is much more advanced in his training, Cavendish is now moving towards riding off the long-shanked bit, which operates on the basis of leverage on the horse's poll and jaw. In light hands, use of the shanked bit is a refined and precise method, while in untrained hands, it is capable of putting the horse's head in a counterproductive restriction, causing distress and even injury. The length of rein in Cavendish's plates illustrate that the weight of the rein on the branches of the bit should be sufficient contact.

FIGURE 11.5   *Directing the horse using the rider's weight and body alignment. From William*
Cavendish, La Méthode Nouvelle, *plate 17.*

Throughout the first manual, the plates underpin the riding method but also impart messages about status and role. In the early plates, Captain Mazin rides the horse, while Cavendish actively directs the lesson, either standing or seated in a throne-like chair. By plate 20 (Figs. 11.6–11.7), when the horse moves in to the advanced stages of training, Cavendish takes over the riding. His own status is further reinforced by the passive position of Mazin, who stands quietly in the centre of the school watching. There are several indirect references to Pluvinel's manual in the text and plates, and as a very noticeable difference in status of the two masters, Cavendish, unlike Pluvinel, never carries his own hat.[20]

Plate 20 is another that is particularly useful in exemplifying the accuracy of the illustrations. Cavendish is in the saddle and uses his body position to direct the horse, looking over his shoulder, thus putting weight on the seat bone in the direction of movement. This acts as a brake without him touching the

20   This is discussed further in Walker, *'To Amaze the People',* 80–85.

FIGURE 11.6   *Cavendish uses his body position to put the horse on the haunches. From William*
Cavendish, La Méthode Nouvelle, *plate 20.*

FIGURE 11.7
Detail of plate 20, showing
use of rider's focus to
influence the horse's centre
of balance.

horse's mouth, so that his mount is effectively rocked back on the haunches without hindering self-carriage.

Once more, the plates illuminate the method and underline all the personal and politic imagery by presenting Cavendish as a man of skill and authority. The final lessons in this advanced groundwork include the 'demy-airs', in which two legs remain upon the ground, as opposed to the airs-above-the ground in which all four feet leave it. As this first challenging and complicated stage of the training draws to a close Cavendish points out that 'it requires more paper to write these lessons, and more time to read them, than to put them into practice' (1743: 67). In preparing for the highly advanced moves, not suitable for all horses, Cavendish stresses that the rider must 'in all Ayres follow the Strength, Spirit and Disposition of the Horse and do nothing against Nature' (1667: 271). Choosing the air for which the horse has a ready aptitude is emphasised many times in both manuals and this illustrates why, in performance, a number of horses are used in turn, each displaying special skills 'unto which Nature hath most Fitted him' (1667: 272).

For the advanced training, he returns to working the horse in hand, this time around the pillar. Experience and observation are always the basis for his arguments and he believes that one pillar, rather than the earlier tradition of two, allows the novice horse support without restriction, thus encouraging athleticism. This is illustrated in Plate 24, where the horse is prepared for the curvet, the foundation upon which the airs above the ground are built. Training for this movement begins in hand so that the horse can learn without the weight of the rider, prompted by a short stick tipped with an iron point to simulate the aids given by the spur once the rider is in place. A second handler taps the horse on either side of the shoulders with a switch to shift his weight backwards and raise the forehand. The groom holding the rope tied to the pillar has it looped around twice so it can be released quickly but not be pulled through the groom's hands. This is yet another illustration of good working practice in the plates.

Once the foundation of the curvet is established, the high airs, although exceptionally difficult to perform well, are built one after the other with relatively little additional information, being designed for the advanced horse. However, it is also likely that Cavendish chooses to withhold his most important secrets to maintain his uniqueness, 'for, to make them go in Perfection in all Ayres as I can, were too much and too great a Miracle' (1667: p. 48). As an experienced trainer, he is aware that riders, like their horses, may try to take the easy way out, so explains why following his method without fully understanding or taking the time needed for precision will not work. His indignation comes through strongly at 'many presumptuous Fellows, as Ignorant as they are Presumptuous that Laughing, say, They will make any horse a Leaping-Horse' (1667: 317).

Both the detailed explanation of Cavendish's 'new method' and the remarkable precision of the plates in the first manual are innovative. The attention to the finer points of each exercise suggests preparation for publication that involved the artist, writer, horse and rider in detailed experimentation. While the two are different in many respects, the 'new method' remains the same in both manuals, showing an ongoing process of development in the intervening years as befitted a system used on a daily basis. That they were written in very different stages in his life is reflected in several of the plates in the 1658 manual and the introductory discussion in 1667, as well as the overall layout, but this does not impact upon the way in which he explains his method.

This practicality is a significant departure from earlier manuals whose failure to explain the training process to his satisfaction set Cavendish on his own journey, because 'there was something not Found out, which They and their Books Mist' (1667: 42). Regardless of the self-promotion in his view of other manuals, his point about their usability is fair. Many of the methods put forward in Blundeville's adaptation of Grisone, for example, are impractical and dangerous. Cavendish underlines this by saying, 'my Method is True', which 'cannot better be Demonstrated, than by Experience, which will clearly show, That Mine never misses its End' (1667: 41). He invites the reader to put him to the test, for he believes there is 'no other Philosophy but trying' (1667: 28).

He promotes élite understanding as both the evidence and natural quality of nobility and his lexis presupposes that the notional reader is an experienced rider. By implication then, his readers achieve a certain confirmation of refinement if they have the ability to understand his philosophy and methods. His conviction as to the unique truth of his ideas goes with the need to be seen as an indispensable authority and current practitioner during times when the work of what he disparagingly calls 'old authors' (1667: 27) was given more value than any living rider.[21]

Each manual offers Cavendish's current thoughts on training alongside a retrospective of his life. The 1658 manual, published during his exile, reminds his Continental readership of the years before the Civil War through the plates of his lands and property in their full glory. The 1667 manual, published after his return home, ensures that his countrymen are aware of the success and acclaim he received from Continental horsemen. His manuals fix ownership of his ideas and assert his position as a recognised expert during times in his

---

21   For a detailed comparison between Cavendish and other key horsemanship authors, see Walker, 'To Amaze the People', Chapter 3, 34–65.

life when his position at court had been undermined. By publishing, he also disseminated his ideas to a wider audience, thereby widening his own reputation, and standing up for the art he believed offered a model for noble behaviour. In 1658, he set out to disparage ideas that it was a frivolous art (1743: 14). By 1667, he was particularly concerned that 'the Noblest' and 'Healthfullest Exercise in the World' was in decline, due to interest in pastimes that had 'no Use at all, meerly Pleasure' (1667: 14). However, far from democratising the process by publishing, his manuals frequently underline the great expense and difficulty of the art, stressing that, 'a Spanish Horse is Dear Ware' (1667: p. 52) and that 'I am afraid the charge will be too much for a private person' (1743: 26).

As a committed royalist, the riding house offered a glorious model for all he held dear. That he should desire to locate both himself and his method at the forefront of developments in the art by publishing was entirely in keeping with his character. Like the building projects that occupied him throughout his life, the horsemanship manuals offered a potential legacy, not only on paper but on horseback, in those who followed him. The technical precision of the manuals therefore functions as a means of expressing and fixing the value of the art—and indeed himself—during times of change and uncertainty and for the future.

Stephen Greenblatt says that Renaissance figures 'understand that in our culture to abandon self-fashioning is to abandon the craving for freedom, and to let go of one's stubborn hold upon selfhood, even selfhood conceived as fiction, is to die'.[22] Cavendish typifies this awareness in his self-conscious and deeply held instinct to make a place for himself, regardless of the circumstances. The manuals create a personal location, fixed in print, which the winds of change could not influence. In this too, he is unique. No other significant horsemanship author in the early modern period published during a time of enforced exile or in circumstances where his personal emotional survival was so evidently linked to his method of horse-training.

Yet this never compromises their practical application, which reinforces the purpose of the manuals not only as beautiful and philosophical reminders of an élite way of life, but as genuine 'hands-on' ways of living that life through skill, hard work and dedication. Cavendish's reiteration of values, such as noble display and the loving fear for the superior, illustrates the way in which writing the riding house enables him to write himself, so that in using the method he reinforces his life. The great sense of indignation that comes through in both manuals reveals perhaps a secret fear that the value of beauty for its own sake is lost or become worthless. His long list of noblemen who support his views

---

22   Greenblatt S., *Renaissance Self-Fashioning: From More to Shakespeare* (Chicago: 1980) 257.

sounds anxious and while he states 'I leave every one to his own Wayes, and his own Delights, desiring they will do the like by Me', the very act of writing and publishing reveals a need to persuade. For a man acutely aware of the role of host, patron and aristocrat the manuals become the idealised performance of his life. No earlier or subsequent horsemanship author attempts such an enterprise and in the successful combination of art, technique and propaganda, Cavendish's work is significant in ways that travel far beyond the metaphors of a courtly art.

Selective Bibliography

Blundeville, Thomas, *A Newe booke, containing the Arte of Ryding and breaking greate Horses* (London: 1560).

Cavendish, William, *A New Method, and Extraordinary Invention, to Dress Horses* (London, Thomas Milbourn: 1667).

Cavendish, William, *A General System of Horsemanship*, John Brindley's 1743 English translation of William Cavendish's *La Méthode Nouvelle et Invention Extraordinaire de Dresser les Chevaux* (Antwerp, Jacques van Meurs: 1658), 1 (London: 1743).

Cavendish, William, *Le Methode Nouvelle et Invention Extraordinaire de Dresser les Chevaux* (Antwerp, Jacques van Meurs: 1658).

Edwards P., Enenkel K.A.E., Graham E. (eds.), *The Horse as Cultural Icon: the Real and the Symbolic horse in the Early Modern World* (Leiden: 2011).

Greenblatt S., *Renaissance Self-Fashioning: From More to Shakespeare* (Chicago: 1980).

Gueriniere, François Robichon De La, *School of Horsemanship*, trans. Boucher, T. (London: 1994).

Hobbes, Thomas, *Leviathan*, ed. Minogue, K. (London: 1994).

Morgan, Nicholas, *The Horse-man's Honour: Or the Beautie of Horsemanship* (London, Widow Helme & Marriott, J.: 1620).

Pluvinel, Antoine De, *The Maneige Royal*, trans. Nelson, H. (London: 1989).

Raber K. – Tucker T.J. (eds.), *The Culture of the Horse: status, discipline and identity in the early modern world* (New York: 2005).

Strong, R., *Henry, Prince of Wales and Englands's lost Renassiance* (London: 2000).

Vernon, John, *The Young Horse-man, or honest plain-dealing Cavalier*, ed. Tincey, J. (Leigh-on-Sea: 1993).

Walker E., '*To Amaze the People with Pleasure and Delight*': the horsemanship manuals of William Cavendish, Duke of Newcastle (Virginia: 2015).

CHAPTER 12

Embodying *'Bonne Homme à Cheval'*: William Cavendish and the Politics of the Centaur

Monica Mattfeld

In 1667 William Cavendish, first Duke of Newcastle, outlined his approach to the practice of horsemanship in his manual, *A New Method, and Extraordinary Invention, to Dress Horses.* 'As for Pleasure and State', Cavendish posited,

> What can be more Comely or Pleasing, than to see Horses go in all their several Ayres? and to see so Excellent a Creature, with so much Spirit, and Strength, to be so Obedient to his Rider, as if having no Will but His, they had but one Body, and one Mind, like a Centaur?.... Thus it is Proved, That there is nothing of more Use than A Horse of Mannage; nor any thing of more State, Manliness, or Pleasure, than Rideing. (1667: 13)

While it was debatable whether the 'Mannage' had much practical cross-over value outside the ring, for Cavendish it was the perfect art, the most profitable science, the method of ensuring a stately bodily grace and the pastime that was essential for gentlemen to perfect.[1] Horsemanship, he claimed, was an exercise not to be ignored, and it certainly was not a pastime that could withstand imperfect dabbling. Instead, horses and horsemanship needed time, effort and practice to perfect. But why? What was meant to be like a Centaur? Why should a gentleman spend so much time, effort and money in riding? What was it about horses that could be so beneficial? These and other questions relating to Cavendish's practice of horsemanship are the focus of this essay, and while the answers are necessarily somewhat general in scope, they can provide a glimpse into the complicated, technical, competitive and highly political world of seventeenth-century horsemanship.

Today, most scholars of horses and horsemanship agree that the embodied act of riding a horse was inherently political during the seventeenth and

---

1 The *manège* was never fully accepted within England as a useful pastime. Some considered it to be a practice that produced horses who were capable of nothing better than dancing and prancing, while others thought it dangerous as it taught horses to perform tricks that would hinder their duty to protect their riders during battle. (1743L: 15–16).

eighteenth centuries. However, the intricacies of this relationship and its performativity still require clarification. This is also the case for Cavendish, that most studied of horsemen, even though Karen Raber has taken up the reins, so to speak, and has examined Cavendish's politics in relation to horsemanship. She argues that Cavendish, while he may have appeared to follow royalist philosophies, was harbouring political leanings that diverged from older beliefs in absolute monarchy and which fell more in line with the emerging republican philosophies popular in the post-civil wars era.[2] However, while horsemanship that was more republican in form may have been an unintended result of Cavendish's theories, when his horsemanship is approached through an alternative governmental model, the cooperation between man and horse and the hard-won hierarchy between species take on more traditional absolutist overtones than previously thought. As such, while exploring Cavendish's multi-layered discussion on the importance of horsemanship detailed above, I look to Cavendish's relationships with his horses alongside his frequent entanglement with Thomas Hobbes's theories of government and the implicit hierarchy between man and animal inherent therein. In this essay, I briefly explore the Hobbesian overtones of Cavendish's theories of horse-human relationships and argue Hobbesian political theory was an embodied, trans-species experience for Cavendish. It was an experience that created absolute sovereignty over man and animal through fearful obedience, and it was an experience that in turn generated power and honour for the useful display of the horseman's political animality.

The Material-Discursive Leviathan

According to Hobbes, there was a distinct process to the creation of a commonwealth that took man from a state of insecurity and incivility to one of prosperity and contented security under a sovereign. To summarise: for Hobbes, prior to the development of a political administration, man is essentially by nature in a state of violent and competitive being. Mankind displayed 'a generall inclination' for 'a perpetuall and restlesse desire of Power after power, that ceaseth onely in Death'.[3] Searching for bodily comfort, wealth, honour and status, mankind for Hobbes was in a state of incivility and war when in his natural state, but paradoxically continually searching for peace as a means of ensuring his

---

2   Raber, K., "'Reasonable Creatures': William Cavendish and the Art of Dressage", in Fumerton, P. – Hunt, S. (eds.), *Renaissance Culture and the Everyday*, (Philadelphia: 2005) 50–58.

3   Hobbes Thomas., *Leviathan*, Macpherson C.B. (ed.), (London: 1968), 161. Hereafter cited as *Leviathan*.

security and safety. Only available through the creation of a sovereign body that would regulate man's continual quest for power, this peace was obtained through the giving up of some of man's natural freedoms, such as the freedom of independent movement or resistance to a stronger body than oneself. The relinquishing of some of these freedoms or natural rights to a sovereign, or the indication of the will (desire) to relinquish them, was done through a 'PACT or COVENANT' that created 'subjects' of the natural persons under one ruler. As Hobbes argued:

> THE finall Cause, End, or Designe of men, (who naturally love Liberty, and Dominion over others,) in the introduction of that restraint upon themselves, (in which wee see them live in Common-wealths,) is the foresight of their own preservation, and of a more contented life thereby; that is to say, of getting themselves out from that miserable condition of Warre, which is neccessarily consequent ... the naturall Passions of men, when there is no visible Power to keep them in awe, and tye them by feare of punishment to the performance of their Covenants.[4]

Covenants created a three-tiered being for Hobbes, where in the first instance covenanting, in effect, served to 'reduce' the people's 'Wills, by plurality of voices, unto one Will'. This resulted in a situation where the 'reall Unitie of them all' brought into being and was represented 'in one and the same Person', or the sovereign. This '*Soveraignty*' was, in turn, the being upon which the artificial animal, Leviathan, depended, as without it there would be no life, since the sovereign 'is an Artificiall *Soul*, as giving life and motion to the whole body.'[5] The resulting 'great LEVIATHAN called a COMMON-WEALTH, or STATE, (in Latin CIVITAS) which is but an Artificiall Man; though of greature stature and strength than the Naturall', was imagined as an artificial human body; a body composed of a sovereign head and a multitude of persons upon which it rested.[6] Wonderfully hybrid in its creation, Hobbes theorised an ideal commonwealth as a being at once mechanical (Cartesian), artificial and alive. His commonwealth was monstrous in its form and consisted of a body and soul brought together through education and skill as art.[7]

Jacques Derrida has analyzed Hobbes's formulation of the great Leviathan in his examination of sovereignty and sovereign power. For him, and for many

---

4   *Leviathan*, 223.

5   Ibid. 81.

6   Ibid. 81.

7   Derrida J., *The Beast and the Sovereign*, (transl.) Bennington G. (London: 2009) I, 27–28. Hereafter cited as Derrida, *Beast*.

previous philosophers, political man is always a political animal (or *zōon poli-tikon*, to use Aristotle's famous phrase) and, as such, is a 'double and contradictory figuration' of being. Building upon western epistemological ties to Biblical teachings that mandate man's domination over animal life as a natural right (a 'right of nature' for Hobbes), Derrida argues that political man is *'on the one hand* superior, in his very sovereignty, to the beast that he masters, enslaves, dominates, domesticates or kills, so that his sovereignty consists in raising himself above the animal and appropriating it, having its life at his disposal'.[8] This natural right at once placed man in a superior position above animals (along with many humans, such as women, children, slaves and those of less social power), while also situating the sovereign in a position of the semi-divine. In an imitation of God's creation of mankind, political man artificially creates the beast Leviathan through art and law.[9] This ongoing divine domination and creation of animal life within the Leviathan in turn necessitated Derrida's other half of man as political animal. As Derrida argues: there was *'on the other hand* (contradictorily) a figuration of the political man, and especially of the sovereign state *as animality*, or even as bestiality . . ., either a normal bestiality or a monstrous bestiality itself mythological or fabulous.'[10] Frequently figured as wolfish by political theorists, for Derrida political man was at once always superior to animality and animal life, but was also animal himself. The creation and maintenance of sovereignty was by necessity a violent process that was only marginally removed from the continuous state of war that the sovereign lifted the people out of through domination and covenants. Sovereign power was a fragile thing, and was maintained through absolute actions of men, who appeared not much different from the animals in spite of their evident distinguishing attribute of rationality.[11]

In this formulation, political man as a potentially ravenous political animal was a contradictory figuration of man as superior to animals on the species hierarchy (animals were there to be dominated by man) and of political man as artificially constructed animality close to the divine. A remarkably apt figuration of both Leviathan and of Cavendish's Centaur, Derrida's construction of political man as animalistic sovereign was determined by discourse, was figurative in form and could theoretically include live animals in its formation. As a result, he calls for a 'restructur[ing of] the whole problematic' of critical examinations of the past; however, even though he does so, Derrida remains oddly silent about live animals in his wolfish tracking of sovereignty

8   Derrida, *Beast*, 26; *Leviathan*, 28.

9   Derrida, *Beast*, 26–27.

10   Ibid. 26.

11   Ibid. 55.

as dualistic animality.[12] Nonetheless, neither Hobbes nor Derrida, in his deconstruction of Hobbes's theories, explore the role of live animals within the formation of covenants or sovereign states. As such, this essay begins the process of restructuring our understanding of the beast and the sovereign by taking seriously the constitutive role of animals within the animalised sovereignty of Cavendish and his horses.

What we see when we take animals seriously is a reorientation of focus that looks to the 'relationships' between all 'intra-acting' material-discursive elements.[13] In this instance, there is a negation of a conceptualisation that understands either party as pre-existing the other. Instead, it is through those relationships that Cavendish and his horses co-create each other. As Karen Barad argues, 'Humans' [and other 'animals'] are neither pure cause nor pure effect but part of the world in its open-ended becoming'. There are no horses and there are no riders prior to their ongoing and ever-evolving relationships together; they co-create each other through iterative intra-actions, and through each other performatively generate a physical gendered body. In other words, '*All bodies, not merely "human" bodies, come to matter through* the world's iterative intra-activity: its performativity'.[14] Therefore, when we move beyond figurative animality or beastiality, when a material, live animal is added to the equation of sovereignty, what we see is not only a mythological representation of animality wrapped up in discourses and acts of power in the Derridian sense, but also a lived becoming and a way of being in the world. A becoming that was but one body and one mind in a co-mingling of beast and human. It created a very real hybrid body of man and animal as a living, breathing commonwealth: a live, intra-active, Centauric Leviathan.

Government and Horsemanship

That being said, Hobbes would have disagreed with Barad and her theories of animal and human together generating each other performatively, because creating covenants was only possible between natural persons; creating covenants was not possible with animals. For Hobbes, a sometimes dubious Cartesian, who disallowed animals the ability of speech and response,

---

12   Ibid. 55.

13   Birke L. – Bryld M. – Lykke N., "Animal Performances: An exploration of intersections between feminist science studies and studies of human/animal relationships", *Feminist Theory* 5 ii (2004) 177.

14   Barad K., "Posthumanist Performativity: Toward an Understanding of How Matter Comes to Matter", *Signs: Journal of Women in Culture and Society* 28 iii (2003) 3821; 823.

a covenant required the indication of the will, so '[T]o make Covenant with bruit Beasts, is impossible'. This was 'because not understanding our speech, they understand not, nor accept of any translation of Right; nor can translate any Right to another: and without mutuall acceptation, there is no Covenant.' Man (in this instance in the role of sovereign) was not intelligible to the animal (the multitude), and because the animal could not think abstractly or speak he was unintelligible to man. As a result, a horse was incapable of making his desire to covenant clear, to add his own interests to that of his sovereign, of understanding his natural rights to man or of understanding man's conditions of right when presented to him.[15] However, while Cavendish's frequent political musings closely mirror Hobbes's theorising of the animal Leviathan, when it came to creating covenants with animals he radically disagreed with Hobbes's theories. As Raber has argued, for Cavendish horses were rational beings capable of understanding and (admittedly limited and dumb) communication with their riders.[16] For him, 'Altho' horses do not form their reasonings from the ABC, which, as that admirable and most excellent philosopher master HOBBS says, is no language, but the marks and representation of things, he must notwithstanding give me leave to think, that they draw their reasonings from things themselves. (1743L: 12)[17] Horses could think, they had will, were capable of indicating it, and the art of horsemanship was the medium through which their Othered addresses came to be understood.

A complex process generated through years of concentrated effort and practice, horsemanship was founded upon the perfection of intra-active bodily communication. Just as Donna Haraway's companion species are 'co-constitutive' today, so also horsemen for Cavendish were fashioned through the willed kinesthetics of their horses and their horses were formed through the rational domination of the rider in a reciprocal relationship that, if implemented correctly, could produce embodied human-animal 'symbiogenesis'.[18] Ann Game further explains this process. By coming to know the other's 'culture' man and horse learn the language of riding, of communication, and over time come to inhabit the other. Horsemanship, for her, 'is the bringing to life of *the* relation between horse and rider, involving a mutual calling up of horse and rider in each other. What horse and rider entrain with is the relation,

---

15   *Leviathan*, 197; Skinner Q., *Hobbes and Republican Liberty* (Cambridge: 2003) 46.
16   Raber, "Reasonable Creatures".
17   For an analysis of this passage, see also Graham E., "The Duke of Newcastle's 'Love [...]' for Good Horses': An Exploration of Meanings", *The Horse as Cultural Icon* (Leiden: 2012) 64–68.
18   Haraway D., *The Companion Species Manifesto: Dogs, People, and Significant Otherness* (Chicago: 2003) 32.

the rhythm between, the transporting flow, the *riding*.[19] While too egalitarian for Cavendish's hierarchical and absolutist horsemanship methodologies, the theory of horse-human relationships Game proposes, highlights the coming together, the continual intra-active process of creation that occurred during riding. In this formulation, over time and through concentrated effort with the help of skilled riding techniques, the rider learns the art of riding and the horse in turn comes to learn true obedience to his sovereign master's instructions.

It was this obedience that was the ultimate indicator of sovereign status, the indicator of absolute perfection in horsemanship and the means of creating the Centaur. As such, as Cavendish explained, 'A horse must be wrought upon more by proper and frequent lessons, than by the heels, that he may know, and even think upon what he ought to do'. (1743L: 12) Horsemanship consisted of more than taking a 'gallop from St. Alban's to London, or to make a horse trample with a snaffle and martingal the old English way'. As many authors argue in this volume, it took years of concentrated effort under a master of horsemanship for ease on horseback to develop, and those 'are mistaken vastly, who think themselves great masters, because they have learned to ride a month or two, and have not been thrown'. (1743L: 82)[20] A horseman needed to move with his horse in everything that he did, he needed to flow from movement to movement while remaining strong, courageous and masterful. Learning the rhythm and harmony of riding, or the mechanics of horse-human communication, so agreeable and profitable an enterprise for Cavendish, was essential for horsemanship. (1743L: 12) It is this intra-active moving together that ensures the Centauric becoming, communication and performativity. It was through dedicated and intensive effort on the part of both horse and rider that they became together able to communicate, or understand, the other, and hence came to create a covenant.

Horses were not easily brought to obedience, however. As Cavendish argued: 'The horse being, after man, the most noble of all animals (for he is as much superior to all other creatures as man is to him, and therefore holds a sort of middle place between man and the rest of creation) he is wise and subtile'. As a result, it was because of this middle ground, this superior-beast status, that 'man ought carefully to preserve his empire over him, knowing how nearly that wisdom and subtilty approaches his own'. (1743L: 44) Because horses could think for themselves, they had to be persuaded through communication to covenant.[21] A sovereign horseman, through his excellent horsemanship ability,

---

19   Game A., "Riding: Embodying the Centaur", *Body & Society* 1 (2001) 5.

20   Gailhard J., *The Compleat Gentleman* (London, John Starkey: 1678) 'Book II', 50.

21   Karen Raber has shown that this language of love and friendship had a long history, and was common in manuals by the time Cavendish was writing. What was new was the connection of this discourse to Hobbesian political theory. Raber K., "From Sheep to Meat,

was required to educate them in their rights and the rights of the sovereign by generating 'love' in, or becoming 'friends' with, his mount. Cavendish's whole goal of horsemanship 'therefore is to make the horseman and his horse friends, and bring them to will the same thing', that is to be 'Obedient to his Rider' as sovereign. (1743L: 105; 1667: 13) Once this was done, there would be a Centaur. As Cavendish explained: a sovereign, as an 'expert Rider' on a perfectly *manèged* horse, would have 'small use of a Rod, or any other help, but to keep his true, just, and perfect seat, because his Horse, by the least token of Bridle or Spur, will do all things in such time and measure, as the Beholders will judge the Man and Horse to be but one Body, one Mind, one Will'.[22]

However, the process of persuading horses to love their riders was one of frequent mishaps and one grounded upon sometimes violent physical persuasion. Horsemanship was a covenant through conquest; full of setbacks, to ride a horse took iron control and the carefully measured use of rewards and punishments.[23] As Cavendish argued, 'Hope of *Reward*, and Fear of *Punnishment*, Governs this whole World; not only Men, but Horses: And thus they will Chuse the *Reward*, and Shun the *Punnishment*'. (1667: 198)[24] The same process of monarchical government espoused by Hobbes, ruling a horse as sovereign took careful judgement, time and was ultimately based on fear. In a theory of horse and human control that was the result of the 'Counsel of a Friend' (who was more than likely Hobbes), Cavendish argues cherishing was only to be given in moderation, while 'Fear' of possible punishment 'doth Much', and 'Love' from the rider, or excessive leniency and cherishing, 'doth . . . Little.' It was useful to a certain degree, but it was still 'Impossible to Dress any Horse, but first he must Know, and Acknowledge me to be his Master, by Obeying me', Cavendish argued. 'That is, He must *Fear* me, and out of that *Fear, Love* me, and so *Obey* me . . . For it is *Fear* that makes every

---

From Pets to People: Animal Domestication 1600–1800", in Senior M. (ed.), *A Cultural History of Animals in the Age of Enlightenment* (Oxford & New York: 2007) 76.

22   Blagrave J., *The Epitome of the Whole Art of Husbandry* (London: 1667), 227; also verbatim in A.S., *The Gentleman's Compleat Jockey: with the Perfect Horseman, and Experience'd Farrier* (London: 1696) 37.

23   Many scholars have pointed out Cavendish's more 'humane' and caring methods of training over those of his contemporaries, and while there is a distinct change in the treatment of animals in his manuals (along with a concerted effort to differentiate his methods from those that were deemed 'cruel'), he frequently advocated, for example, the use of sharpened spurs over blunt ones. (1667: 185)

24   Seventeenth-century horsemanship manuals continually espoused the necessity of 'cherishing' their mounts. See for example Landry D., *Noble Brutes: How Eastern Horses Transformed English Culture* (London: 2009) 30–33.

Body *Obey*, both Man and Beast'. (1667: 196; 1743L: 138–39)[25] It is 'Fear' that creates the desire for covenants, ensures obedience from a horseman's inferiors, either man or animal, and it is 'Fear' that ensures a natural hierarchy of animal to man. 'It was impossible to dress a horse before he obeys his rider,' Cavendish explained, 'and by that obedience acknowledges him to be his master'. Indeed, as Cavendish emphatically summarised: 'Fear commands obedience, and the practice of obedience makes a horse well dressed. Believe me, for I tell it you as a friend, it is truth.' (1743L: 138–39)

This 'Fear', as Elisabeth LeGuin argues, did not suggest being afraid of something or someone as the more familiar designation of the word means today. Instead, Cavendish's 'Fear' was patriarchal in tone and defined as the command 'Fear God' or 'the physical enactment of respect' towards a father figure.[26] Indeed, Cavendish's truth about government stipulated horses and humans 'all doe love thee, yett we feare they rodd, / Nott love for feare, butt feare for love, like Godd'.[27] A horseman was to 'chastise him [horse or man] like a kind of divinity superior to him', a sovereign capable of carrying out the artificial, patriarchal, God-like, action of creation; of iteratively creating the artificial being called Leviathan or Centaur.[28] A horseman was to be a benevolent but masterful rider who enacted his hard-won governance, and become semi-divine himself ('for the Holly writt sayes, wee have Calld you Godds'), with his horse as all ideal sovereigns were to do.[29] For Cavendish and Hobbes, 'Sovereignty causes fear, and fear makes the sovereign'; it was the basis for law and governance, the method behind creating 'the best of kings', and one experience did not exist without the other.[30]

---

25 *Leviathan*, 188. Cavendish also advised Charles II to 'Governe by both Love and feare mixte together as ocation serves', as quoted in Walker E., *'To Amaze the People with Pleasure and Delight': The Horsemanship Manuals of William Cavendish, First Duke of Newcastle* (Geneva: 2010) 129.

26 LeGuin E., "Man and Horse in Harmony", in Raber K. – Tucker T. (eds.), *The Culture of the Horse: Status, Discipline, and Identity in the Early Modern World* (New York: 1995) 181.

27 Cavendish W., unpublished poem 'On the best of kings', as quoted in Walker, *To Amaze the People*, 131.

28 Derrida, *Beast*, 26–27; Tribe K., *Land, Labour and Economic Discourse* (London: 1978) 38.

29 Newcastle's Advice to Charles II, 45; Pocock J., *The Machiavellian Moment: Florentine Political Thought and the Atlantic Republican Tradition* (Princeton & Oxford: 1975) 352–353.

30 Derrida, *Beast*, 40–41; Cavendish, "On the best of kings", as quoted in Walker, 131. For details on the connections between sovereignty and law see Menely T., "Animal Signs and Ethical Significance: Expressive Creations in the British Georgic", *Mosaic* 39 iv (December: 2006) 567–569.

Cavendish's ideal of figurative and embodied sovereign horseman-as-animal-God was most clearly illustrated in plate four of *A General System of Horsemanship*. (Fig. 12.1) Depicted on horseback with the horse 'flying' in a *capriole* as '*Perseus* upon *Pegasus*', Cavendish is shown to be a divine being who has managed the submission and humility of his own passions and social inferiors as only elite and properly sovereign horsemen were able to do. Above him are clouds, on which the pantheon of Greek gods are artfully arranged, and who are 'brought to ecstasy' because of the sight of his 'delightful wonders' (Et par ses merveilles ravit en extases les Dieux). Because of his exceptional reining, his 'Fear' inducing combination of punishment and love, Cavendish has not only impressed the gods and received honours in return, but has himself crossed over into the realm of the divine. He has become greater than the legendary Bellerophon (the tamer of Pegasus, who was thrown when he attempted to fly), and has managed to touch 'the seat of the Heavens' (Il monte si haut qu'il touche de sa teste les Cieux) because of his intra-active covenants with brute being. Cavendish illustrated himself as 'the most absolute and only Master' of horsemanship; he was a Master, and all previous authors on the subject, along with current noble horsemen, were his 'Pupils', while his manuals of horsemanship were the means of sharing his teachings.[31] For example, the Vice-Chancellor and Senate members of the University of Cambridge found:

> both Kings and Princes resorting to your [Cavendish's] Palace, conde-scending to sit at your Feet,' like the horses at Cavendish's feet are shown to be doing, 'and intreating you as their Oracle to declare unto them, first where and of what Race to chuse a Horse for the Mannage, and then how to Feed, and Order, and Mount, and to Work, and Raise, and Stay, and Ride in all Voltoes, and Corvetts, Forward, Backward, Side-ways, on both hands, just as the Rider directs.' Cavendish, for them, was the only one fit to teach; he was 'the only Governour, and Dictator, and Umpire, and such a Master of Horse, as can (when you please) infuse sense, and reason not only into Men, but also into Brutes.[32]

---

31   See also Graham's essay in this volume for an interpretation of this illustration and the following "centaur" image.

32   The Vice-Chancellor and the whole Senate of the University of Cambridge, 'Letter to the Most Eminent Prince, March 13, 1667,' in Cavendish Margaret (ed.), *A Collection of Letters and Poems: Written by several Persons of Honour and Learning, Upon divers Important Subjects, to the Late Duke and Dutchess OF NEW CASTLE* (Langly Curtis, London: 1678) 51–52.

FIGURE 12.1   *Cavendish riding Pegasus. From William Cavendish,* La Méthode Nouvelle, *plate 4.*
COPYRIGHT ELAINE WALKER.

While wrapped up in excessive flattery, such comments illustrate that Cavendish had become, through his political horsemanship, a figure worthy and able of supporting the commonwealth and improving its governors through the spectacle and ceremony of his own horse-man and Centauric greatness, and the application of his divine art.

This argument is further expressed through the image's symbolism. As Elaine Walker argues, eleven horses are bowing down to Cavendish, which could represent the eleven disciples minus Judas, a common iconographic element in early modern art; and if we count Pegasus as the twelfth, Cavendish may be subtly shown as a Christ—or God-figure over human and animal life. While Cavendish was in no way trying to offend his readers, and this image can seem to negotiate a fine line between shameless self-promotion and heresy, Cavendish represented himself as a Hobbesian god, as 'a secular God' secure in his governance.[33] Cavendish is shown to embody all of the qualities necessary for Hobbes's sovereign person, the one who could covenant at will, and who represented the most influential men in society. What is certain about

---

33   Walker, *'To Amaze the People'*, 123–124.

the print is that Cavendish is depicted as a man who, through his skill in discursive horsemanship with rational horses, has become more than a noble of the realm, more than human, more than his peers; he has become his ideal masculine governor and virtuous gentleman, who is worthy of being honoured by his subordinates. He has left the earth through his divine horsemanship and become a sovereign god himself who is worshiped as a right reigner (reiner) by his mounts who are arranged in homage around him and 'Worship him as God and author of the their skill' (L'adorer comme Dieu et auteur de leur adresse). (1743L: Plate 4)

Power and Ceremony

According to Thomas Slaughter, 'Both Hobbes and Newcastle emphasized that the basis of regal authority was power, that the important consideration was not who the sovereign was but whether or not he could maintain order among his subjects and retain his throne'.[34] Because of the horse-human body as Leviathan, the ongoing intra-action of both man and animal provided not only the practice necessary for the maintenance of a strong commonwealth, it also evidenced those who were worthy of doing so and those who evidently were not. For Cavendish and Hobbes all men were by nature equal, and it was only through the display of power, or honour, that hierarchy and sovereignty was established. Only true horsemen, those who could rationally govern themselves and their mounts through labour and perseverance under the guidance of a Master, as Cavendish had done, were able to maintain the social, rational and species hierarchy thought necessary for the establishment of a strong commonwealth. And, only those who participated in public displays of this honourable activity could perform his power and fitness to rule.

Especially beneficial on the jousting field, the performance of a man's equestrian skills was a tried and true method of reinforcing the ultimate power of a sovereign before his subjects. As such, Cavendish, in his advice letter, recommended to Charles II that he should 'ride' his 'Horses of manege, twice a weeke, which will Incourage Noble men, to Doe the Like, to wayte of' him and to 'To make matches, with the Noble men, So many of aside, to rune Att the Ringe, for a supper, & a play, or Some Litle Juell'. Upon Charles's coronation day, Cavendish wrote that it would be beneficial to his power and the security of the commonwealth if the king was 'to have, a Tilting by your young Lordes,

---

34   *Newcastle's Advice to Charles II*, xviii.

& other Great persons'.[35] Such virtuous exercises were no longer performed at Charles II's masque-loving court, a change Timothy Raylor shows was due to Charles's desire to be viewed as the focus, rather than the jousting baronage, for all court entertainment. In a tournament, Raylor argues, the focus was on the horsemen, not the king (unless he personally participated in the tourney, an activity Charles had not learnt), who become spectacles to further their own honour. In a masque, by contrast, the representation of the monarch is not that of a ruler, who depends on his nobles for prestige, but as one upon whom the nobles depend.[36] However, even in light of these changes at court Cavendish still felt, incorrectly perhaps, that tournaments were necessary to entice other nobles to the activity and to make visible to 'the Lordes And the Ladeies' the honour, power and sovereign horsemanship of the participants and the English monarchy.[37]

Jousting and running at the ring, however, were decidedly archaic practices by the time Cavendish recommended them to the king. Betraying nostalgia for pre-Civil Wars government (especially that of Queen Elizabeth), a common sentiment among many ageing courtiers of Charles II's court was that jousting, regardless of its outmoded practice, remained useful because the activity was ideally ceremonial.[38] Ceremony was the means of ensuring obedience from man and horse through 'a habitual acceptance of status which is affirmed . . . in ritualistic display'.[39] And, while Cavendish was careful to avoid advocating the sport to Charles directly, for fear of possible injury to the kingly body, he still intimated it was eminently useful and essentially important for the king to know, much like riding in the *manège*. To run at the tilt was to perform martial masculinity as an ideally covenanted man and horse within a Centauric commonwealth. It was pomp and ceremony at its best. As Cavendish rhetorically asked Charles II, 'what preserves you kings more than ceremony'?[40] The trappings of ceremonial practice, the practice itself and the reverential distance that it engendered were all absolutely essential for the performance of power

---

35   Ibid. 61.

36   Raylor T., "A Manuscript Poem on the Royal Progress of 1634: An Edition and Translation of John Westwood's 'Carmen Basileauporion'", *The Seventeenth Century*, 9 no. 2 (Autumn 1994), *Special Issue: The Cavendish Circle* 175.

37   *Newcastle's Advice to Charles II*, 61.

38   *Newcastle's Advice to Charles II*, xii.

39   Condren C., "Casuistry to Newcastle: 'The Prince in the World of the Book'", in Skinner Phillipson N. – Skinner Q (eds.), *Political Discourse in Early Modern Britain* (Cambridge: 1993) 175.

40   *Newcastle's Advice to Charles II*, xxvi.

as sovereign, and hence for the continued survival of the monarch as secure in his leadership of the commonwealth. In other words,

> The cloth of estates, the distance people are with you, great officers, heralds, drums, trumpeters, rich coaches, rich furniture for horses, guards, martialls men making room, disorders to be labored by their staff of office, and cry "now the king comes" resulted in 'even the wisest though he knew it and not accustomed to it, shall shake of his wisdom and shake for fear of it.[41]

The display of sovereignty on horseback as a live Centauric commonwealth, where the horse has covenanted with his rider through fear, in turn creates fear and awe of the horseman as sovereign over his covenanted people. It was the creation of fear that created covenants with the sovereign, and it was the maintenance of it through glorious performances of kingly power that helped secure the hierarchy of servant and sovereign within the commonwealth. Cavendish summarised this phenomenon further in his advice to Charles II. Mirroring the iconography in Plate 4 of his *General System of Horsemanship* discussed earlier, Cavendish argued,

> your Majestie will bee pleased to keepe itt [ceremony] upp strickly, in your owne, person, & Courte, to bee a presedent to the reste of your Nobles, & not to make your selfe to Cheape, by to much Familiarety, which as the proverb sayes, breedes Contempte But when you appeare, to shew your Selfe Gloryously, to your People; Like a God, ... & when the people sees you thus, they will Downe of their knees, which is worshipp, & pray for you with trembling Feare, & Love.[42]

Through ceremony the appropriate distance was maintained between sovereign and servant, and hence the appropriate level of fear and love necessary for the health and security of the commonwealth. 'Seremoney, & order' was everything for Cavendish: 'Seremoney though itt is nothing in itt Selfe, yett it doth Every thing'.[43] Sovereign performances maintained kingship, the church, law, the army and the commonwealth, and without them hierarchy would disintegrate and all would fall to ruin.

---

41   Ibid. xxvi.
42   *Newcastle's Advice to Charles II*, 45.
43   Ibid. 44–45.

Cavendish had witnessed the result of a lack of ceremony before. According to Lynn Hulse, Cavendish 'believed that Charles I's failure to maintain ceremony and degrees of honour had ultimately weakened the nobility and brought them into contempt', eventually resulting in the destabilisation or full destruction of the people's covenants with their sovereign.[44] When this occurred, for both Cavendish and Hobbes, man degenerated back into a state of nature, a process that both men had experienced in the English Civil Wars. Horsemanship, therefore, as the ultimate form of ceremonial display available to a monarch (at least according to Cavendish), was absolutely essential to the continuation of a strong commonwealth.

For Cavendish and for Hobbes, unlike the increasingly vocal, Parliamentarian proponents of mixed government, sovereignty was indivisible. There must only be one legislator, one governor in war and peace; a 'government' which has power shared between the commons, lords and king 'is not government, but division of the Common-wealth into three Factions'. Thus, for Hobbes republicanism, mixed government or 'a Kingdome divided in it selfe cannot stand.'[45] Similarly for Cavendish, 'Monarchy is the Government In cheefe of the whole body Politick, In all its partes, & Capaseties by one person only So that if eyther the whole Body Poleticke bee under Any pretennce overned in cheef by more then one severally Itt is no monarchy.'[46] As for horsemanship, the physical embodiment and enactment of a commonwealth as 'an Artificial Animal', if a ruler or horseman failed to display or maintain his sovereignty over his social inferiors, both horses and humans, through balanced reward and punishment, his power to rule would be completely lost and society thrown into chaos.[47] Without checks and rewards in place, or a balance between love and fear, the monarch's inferiors (and Cavendish's) would be allowed to run riot; they would gain power over their legitimate governors, causing civil unrest, or at worst another 'horid rebellion'.[48] Those who are not horsemen, those who do not 'study', 'understand', communicate or govern correctly would again, Cavendish feared, spend their time 'medeling' in state affairs, which in turn would 'much disorder the Comon wealth, for their perticuler Gayne'.[49] The non-horsemen

44   Hulse L., "'The King's Entertainment' by the Duke of Newcastle", *Viator* 26 (1995) 378.

45   *Leviathan*, 236; Skinner, *Hobbes and Republican Liberty*, 105–106.

46   *Newcastle's Advice to Charles II*, 12.

47   Skinner, *Hobbes and Republican Liberty*, 73–75.

48   *Newcastle's Advice to Charles II*, 35; Condren, "Casuistry to Newcastle", 169, 180.

49   *Newcastle's Advice to Charles II*, 56.

of the world would 'breed' 'confution, & the king, & the Comonwealth' would be 'ill served'.[50]

Therefore, the public display of ceremony, and ceremony, coupled with the performance of secure sovereignty with a horse, was essential to maintaining a civil society. 'To be seen to have power was to have power', and as such horsemanship was 'an exercise that is very noble'. It makes 'Kings, Princes, and persons of quality' 'appear most graceful when they shew themselves to their subjects, or at the head of an army, to animate it'. Indeed, the 'pleasure' of the manège was 'as useful as any thing else, besides the glory and satisfaction that attends it'. (1743L: 14) This advice was well known by early-modern monarchs, men for whom right reining of all mounts was theoretically the most important. Charles II, for example, boasted that he followed Cavendish's advice and 'rid every day', while James I wrote to his son Henry (Cavendish's fellow horseman) that 'It becometh a Prince better than any other man to be a fair and good horseman'. This was because, Cavendish believed, it was only those who had resigned themselves to 'study horsemanship', those who intimately had intra-actively communicated with horses, and who had gained the skill and experience needed for correct decisions on the duties of their social inferiors, who could protect the kingdom from further rebellion and social unrest, while preserving their social position as powerful sovereigns.[51]

Centaurs

While Cavendish's love of chivalrous tilts, jousts and Hobbesian political theory was not continued into the eighteenth century, rulers continued to cherish horses, horsemen continued to strive for Centaur status, and horsemanship continued to be practised by military men in gendered, material-discursive spectacles of power. For sovereigns within the body politic, truly communicative horsemanship as Centaurs visibly distinguished the social and political élite from those who were not capable or worthy of their honours. Certainly, 'for the dignity and order of the Common wealth there ought to be degrees of Honour [and horsemanship], Lest the Common people and the nobility, private men and magistrates … a King and a Captain should be all of one

---

50   Ibid. 57.

51   Charles II as quoted in Keay A., *The Magnificent Monarch Charles II and the Ceremonies of Power* (London: 2008) 22; James I as quoted in Edwards P., *Horse and Man in Early Modern England* (London: 2007) 27.

Accompt'.[52] A man was continually required to 'frame' himself to others in such a way that displayed his power. Horsemanship, as it consisted of 'vertuous exercises' of the mind and body, resulted in individual glory, in the increase of power and in benefits for the entire kingdom of England.[53] As a result, 'the noblest act of vertue' in seventeenth—and early eighteenth-century England was not conducting oneself with virtuous restraint in public, of providing hospitality to others, or being well spoken, but the development and practice of horsemanship.[54] To own or breed 'Great Horses,' and to be able to train and ride the same with tempered managing of the passions and physical skill, was a 'chiefe' avenue of not only social advancement and distinction, but of powerful honour. As Nicholas Morgan argued:

> what scrutiny can finde a Beaste more behouefull to the greatnesse of persons of Estate, and necessary to men of inferior condition then the Horse, which besides (his serviceable obedience) is beautified with a chiefe Excellency of comely shape and couragious boldenesse.... Hence it is, that Antiquity, named them *Jumenta*, as the chiefe Adivméta or helpes of humane nature, that by the very name, the noblenesse, necessary use and profite of them might be knowen, and the division betwixt the Noble and Worthy, Base and Unworthy, manifested in fit difference.[55]

Power and honour for the seventeenth-century man was one of '*The principall markes whereat every mans endeuour in* this life aimeth,' for himself and the commonwealth, and horsemanship was an essential avenue for its development, maintenance and propagation.[56] Thus, learning to ride, to govern a horse/multitude as absolute sovereign, and performing one's hard-won skills before other horsemen not only made visible a man's power, it also evidenced the capability of the horseman to create and maintain power as sovereign over a happily covenanted multitude. To see a horse performing obediently within the horse-human relationship was to see the security of the commonwealth

---

52   Quoted from Ashley, Robert, *Of Honour* in Foyster E., *Manhood in Early Modern England: Honour, Sex and Marriage* (New York: 1999) 33.

53   Blundeville Thomas, *The fower chiefyst offices belongyng to Horsemanshippe* (London: 1609). Dedication.

54   Markham Gervase, *Cauelarice* (London: 1607) Dedication to Book II.

55   Morgan Nicholas, *The Perfection of Horse-manship, drawne from nature; arte, and practise* (London: 1609) Dedication.

56   Segar Sir William, *Honor Military, and Ciuil, contained in foure Bookes* (London: 1602) Dedication.

within a live body politic, and to see that body politic disintegrate through fraction and discord was to see the loss of sovereign power, honour and the resulting destabilisation of the entire commonwealth. To return to Cavendish's rhetorical questioning of the usefulness of the *manège* with which we started this exploration of Hobbesian horsemanship, there could be nothing more glorious than ceremonially performing and living the material-discursive Centaur. There could not be more benefit to kings and princes to run at the tilt or to joust, and nothing could be 'of more Use than A Horse of Mannage; nor any thing of more State, Manliness, or Pleasure, than Rideing'.

Selective Bibliography

A.S., *The Gentleman's Compleat Jockey: with the Perfect Horseman, and Experience'd Farrier* (London: 1696).

Ashley R., *Of Honour* in Foyster E., *Manhood in Early Modern England: Honour, Sex and Marriage* (New York: 1999).

Barad K., "Posthumanist Performativity: Toward an Understanding of How Matter Comes to Matter", *Signs: Journal of Women in Culture and Society* 28 iii (2003).

Birke L. – Bryld M. – Lykke N., "Animal Performances: An exploration of intersections between feminist science studies and studies of human/animal relationships", *Feminist Theory* 5 ii (2004).

Blagrave J., *The Epitome of the Whole Art of Husbandry* (London: 1667).

Blundeville Thomas, *The fower chiefyst offices belongyng to Horsemanshippe* (Company of Stationers, London: 1609).

Cavendish Margaret (ed.), *A Collection of Letters and Poems: Written by several Persons of Honour and Learning, Upon divers Important Subjects, to the Late Duke and Dutchess OF NEW CASTLE* (Langly Curtis, London: 1678).

Cavendish William, *A new method, and extraordinary invention, to dress horses, and work them according to nature* (Printed by Thomas Milbourn, London: 1667).

Cavendish William, *A General System of Horsemanship* (London: 1743).

Cavendish William, "A Letter of Advice to Charles II on the Eve of the Restoration", in Slaughter T.P. (ed.) *Ideology and Politics on the Eve of Restoration: Newcastle's Advice to Charles II* (Philadelphia: 1984).

Condran C., "Casuistry to Newcastle: 'The Prince' in the World of the Book", in Phillipson N. – Skinner Q. (eds.), *Political Discourse in Early Modern Britain* (Cambridge: 1993).

Derrida J., *The Beast and the Sovereign*, Bennington G. (transl.), (London: 2009).

Edwards P., *Horse and Man in Early Modern England* (London: 2007).

Game A., "Riding: Embodying the Centaur", *Body & Society* 1 (2001).

Graham E., "The Duke of Newcastle's 'Love [...] for Good Horses': An Exploration of Meanings", in Edwards P. – Enenkel K. – Graham E., (eds.) *The Horse as Cultural Icon* (Leiden: 2012).

Haraway D., *The Companion Species Manifesto: Dogs, People, and Significant Otherness* (Chicago: 2003).

Hobbes Thomas, *Leviathan*, Macpherson C.B. (ed.), (London: 1968).

Hulse L., "'The King's Entertainment' by the Duke of Newcastle", *Viator* 26 (1995).

Keay A., *The Magnificent Monarch Charles II and the Ceremonies of Power* (London: 2008).

Landry D., *Noble Brutes: How Eastern Horses Transformed English Culture* (London: 2009).

Leguin E., "Man and Horse in Harmony", in Raber K. – Tucker T. (eds.), *The Culture of the Horse: Status, Discipline, and Identity in the Early Modern World* (New York: 1995).

Markham Gervase, *Cauelarice* (London: 1607).

Menely T., "Animal Signs and Ethical Significance: Expressive Creations in the British Georgic", *Mosaic* 39 iv (December 2006).

Morgan Nicholas, *The Perfection of Horse-manship, drawne from nature; arte, and practise* (Edward White, London: 1609).

Raber K., "'Reasonable Creatures': William Cavendish and the Art of Dressage", in Fumerton, P. – Hunt, S. (eds.), *Renaissance Culture and the Everyday* (Philadelphia: 2005).

Raber K., "From Sheep to Meat, From Pets to People: Animal Domestication 1600–1800", in Senior M. (ed.), *A Cultural History of Animals in the Age of Enlightenment* (Oxford & New York: 2007).

Raylor T., "A Manuscript Poem on the Royal Progress of 1634: An Edition and Translation of John Westwood's 'Carmen Basileauporion'", *The Seventeenth Century*, 9 no. 2 (Autumn 1994), Special Issue: *The Cavendish Circle*.

Segar Sir William, *Honor Military, and Ciuil, contained in foure Bookes* (London: 1602).

Tribe K., *Land, Labour and Economic Discourse* (London, Henley & Boston: 1978).

Walker E., *'To Amaze the People with Pleasure and Delight': The Horsemanship Manuals of William Cavendish, First Duke of Newcastle* (Geneva: 2010).

CHAPTER 13

'Manèging' to Survive: Horsemanship and the Rehabilitation of the Exiled William Cavendish, Marquis of Newcastle

Peter Edwards

On 2 July 1644 the royalists suffered the calamitous defeat of Marston Moor, which shattered Charles I's northern army and at a stroke lost him the North with its supplies of money, men and provisions from home and abroad. If the impetuous Prince Rupert had 'bounced' the more cautious Cavendish into giving battle that day—and many blamed him for it—the latter still took the disaster very badly, feeling that he had let the king down.[1] How would Cavendish react? According to the later account of his wife, Margaret, he was faced with three options: 'to quit the Kingdom, or submit to the Enemy, or die'.[2] In spite of Rupert's attempts to dissuade him, he chose exile.[3] The next day his party, some seventy strong and comprising his sons, associates (including General King, his second-in-command), Captain Mazin (his Master of the Horse) and a number of servants, made its way to Scarborough, thence by ship to Hamburg.[4] As his ship weighed anchor and sailed away from his homeland, Cavendish surely felt he had lost everything he held dear: his power and influence; his status and wealth; his reputation and self-esteem; and his possessions, including his beloved horses.[5] If his experience in exile was less bumpy and fraught with difficulties than it was for the majority of royalist *émigrés*, that did not mean that he felt his losses less acutely.

Nonetheless, Cavendish took with him one intangible asset of vital importance to a member of the landed élite, namely, expert knowledge of and experience in horsemanship, a skill that virtually defined a gentleman. Even better,

---

1 Marshall A., *Oliver Cromwell Soldier: the Military Life of a Revolutionary at War* (London: 2004) 118; Worsley L., *Cavalier: a Tale of Chivalry, Passion and Great Houses* (London: 2007) 168. (Hereafter cited as Worsley).

2 *Life of William Cavendish*, 52.

3 Worsley, 167.

4 Worsley, 167; Trease G., *Portrait of a Cavalier: William Cavendish, First Duke of Newcastle* (London: 1979) 141–42.

5 Graham E., "The Duke of Newcastle's 'Love [...] for Good Horses': an Exploration of Meanings", in *The Horse as Cultural Icon*, 43–44. (Hereafter cited as Graham, "Good horses").

he had acquired an enviable reputation as a master of the *manège*, a system of refined exercises that demonstrated the complete control of the rider over his mount. Alongside Princes Henry and Charles and a number of youthful companions, Cavendish had learnt these skills from Monsr. de St. Antoine, whom the French king, Henri IV, had sent over to England.[6] In turn, Cavendish, as the governor of the future Charles II, passed on his expertise to his royal charge. Fortunately, interest in the *manège* was much stronger on the Continent than in England so Cavendish's skills were appreciated to a far greater extent there. His public displays, therefore, regularly attracted sizeable numbers of élite onlookers.[7] His influence continued to be felt even after he had left because during his stay at Antwerp (1648–60) he had set down his method in a manual on horsemanship, entitled *La méthode nouvelle et invention extraordinaire de dresser les chevaux*. He subsequently published an English version, *A new method, and extraordinary invention, to dress horses* on his return home.[8] The publication of the two versions cemented his reputation as a horseman at home and abroad and as they continued to be read after his death they ensured that his methods continued to influence horsemanship practices for generations.

Consequences of Cavendish's Flight

Cavendish's flight laid him open to charges of disloyalty and cowardice and, naturally, his enemies seized on the opportunity to blacken his name. In a virulent anti-royalist pamphlet, dated 26 April 1645, the anonymous author described him as 'a silken Generall, that ran away beyond Sea in a Sayler's Canvas'.[9] Malicious gossip also circulated at court.[10] To some, his marriage at fifty-three to the twenty year old Margaret Lucas in December 1645 suggested that he had abandoned the struggle, opting for a life of domesticity instead. If it confirmed his reputation as an old *roué*, Cavendish had a pressing reason for marrying a young, presumably fertile, woman. A year earlier, while *en route* to Hamburg, his sons, Charles and Henry, had become dangerously ill

---

6   Edwards P., *Horse and Man in Early Modern England* (London: 2007) 82–83.
7   See below, Page 311–13.
8   See list of abbreviations for publication details.
9   Thomason Tracts, TT E.279(6), "The Character of an Oxford-Incendiary" (London: 26 April 1645) 7.
10   Trease, 143; Dewhurst M., "'And Make Me Famous Too in Such a Wife': How Margaret and William Cavendish Negotiated the Interregnum", Ph.D. thesis, Queen Mary College, London University (2009) 27–29, 33–34; Worsley, 134.

and this had made him sharply aware of the fragility of the family's succession. This conflict of interests could have influenced Hyde's assessment, made in his account of the rebellion, that he was a lightweight, preferring the pursuit of pleasure to the hardships of campaigning.[11] In her admittedly biased biography of her husband, Margaret indirectly refuted this assertion in her account of the events of Spring 1648 when a revolt in the parliamentarian navy raised the hopes of a royalist revival. Her husband, she recalled, had eagerly welcomed 'excellent' soldiers and 'noted' commanders to the open house they kept at Rotterdam, 'still hoping that some occasion would happen to invite those worthy Persons into England, or doing His Majesty any service in that kind.'[12] Cavendish would have found innuendoes about his commitment to the cause hurtful because in spite of his limitations as a military commander, he had displayed courage in battle and an unwavering devotion to the king.[13] Specifically, these jibes questioned his notion of honour, which governed his conduct in public affairs. Of course, by leaving the country, Cavendish also lost the basis upon which he could display honour, namely, the influence that his rank and ownership of a large estate gave him. This depressed him, though his status as one of the highest ranking *émigrés* accorded him respect in the claustrophobic, faction-ridden world of royalist politics. Unfortunately, it did not always put him at the centre of affairs. While throughout his exile he did participate in various projects and intrigues to bring about the restoration, he sometimes found himself on the wrong side, out of favour and ignored.[14]

In addition, Cavendish lost the material benefits derived from the income of a large estate. When preparing to leave the country, his steward reputedly informed him that he had but £90 left.[15] In exile, he received some money from the queen and from his friends, relatives and associates, among whom his brother, Sir Charles Cavendish, was prominent. Having compounded for his own estate *in absentia* in 1649, Sir Charles had to return to England two years later to redeem it again.[16] Margaret accompanied him, but her own petition for an allowance was summarily dismissed on the grounds that her husband was the greatest traitor in the country and that she had known this when she married him. Cavendish's daughter, Jane, on the other hand, successfully

11   Dewhurst, thesis, 27, 37; *Life of William Cavendish*, 53.

12   *Life of William Cavendish*, 62; Whitaker K, *Mad Madge, Margaret Cavendish, Duchess of Newcastle, Royalist, Writer and Romantic* (London: 2003) 105–106. (Hereafter cited as Whitaker).

13   See above, Chapter 9.

14   Dewhurst, thesis, 26; Sarasohn L., see above 203-205.

15   *Life of William Cavendish*, 52.

16   Whitaker, 135–36.

petitioned for one-fifth of the income of her father's Welbeck estate. In February 1652 Parliament's Treason Trustees began to sell off his vast estate, which Sir Charles was powerless to save because he did not gain control of his own lands until June 1652. Thereafter, he was able to help his brother. He even bought back Bolsover Castle (at an inflated price) and provided for his brother's children. After Sir Charles's death in 1654, Cavendish gained access to his brother's somewhat diminished estate, which, together with the credit his sons obtained in England, gave him (by Margaret's account) a yearly income of about £2,400. This money he distributed among his creditors.[17] Yet, it was not enough to underwrite a lifestyle that was far more comfortable than that of other exiled royalists. Even the king remarked on it. The key to his success was his ability to gain credit wherever he was residing. If his status engendered confidence among creditors, his wife also attributed it to his charm and persuasiveness. This support, at odds with his treatment at the hands of his countrymen at home, helped to lift Cavendish's spirits.[18]

Probably the greatest loss that Cavendish suffered as a result of the defeat was his self-confidence. For all his haughty aristocratic bearing and assurance within his own sphere of influence, he seems to have harboured feelings of insecurity in situations beyond his control. His failure to obtain the coveted post of Master of the Horse in spite of the lavish entertainments he put on for the king at Welbeck (1633) and Bolsover (1634) shook his confidence and made him doubt his beloved monarch's favour. Why had the king not granted him the honour he felt he deserved? His private letters reflected his uncertainty and insecurity.[19] Ironically, on realizing his ambition with his appointment as governor of Prince Charles in 1638, he found life at court distasteful. Lacking 'the subtleties and guile of the seasoned courtier', his plain speaking and prickly manner caused friction and hostility.[20] It manifested itself in his uneasy relationship with the dashing Prince Rupert, the king's nephew, especially in their capacity as military commanders in the First Civil War. At the fateful moment in York on 2 July 1644 their clash over the course of action they should take against the retreating parliamentarian army had fatal consequences. In this context, his purported reason for abandoning the cause, to avoid 'the laughter

---

17   *Life of William Cavendish*, 71, 80, 82–83, 90; Whitaker, 131, 138, 141, 151–52.

18   *Life of William Cavendish*, 56, 59, 75, 80.

19   Dewhurst, thesis, 31–33; Walker E., *'To Amaze the People with Pleasure and Delight': the Horsemanship Manuals of William Cavendish, Duke of Newcastle* (London: 2010) 137. (Hereafter cited as Walker, *'To Amaze the People'*); Worsley, 85, 120.

20   Worsley, Cavalier, 134.

of the Court', even if apocryphal, contains a grain of truth in it.[21] Had Cavendish not acted so precipitously, he might have reviewed his decision. Yet, his abrupt departure does serve to underline the depth of his despair, a feeling that persisted throughout his years of exile. In a letter he wrote to an unknown foreign nobleman in October 1649 he contrasted his generosity with the indifference he had encountered from his English friends. He also despaired of a restoration of the king. Assessing his own state of mind, he admitted that,

> Trewlye…I am so astonishte diseye, & amasde with misfortune, as I knowe nott wether I am awake or no or wether I am alive for I am paste thinking I have no roume lefte mee for that I am travelde beyond hopes sum days Jurneye towards dispayre butt I thanke God am nott yet arivde ther & thats all Wee are fit nowe for God for nothinge butt a miracle can restore use…[22]

The Landed élite and Their Horses

Integral to Cavendish's aristocratic identity was the possession of a string of top quality horses, ones which transcended their functional value. Naturally, the bulk of the horse-owning population employed the animals for purely utilitarian purposes: to ride on or as beasts of draught or burden. So did the landed élite, even if some of the functions were exclusive to their class: hunting and hawking, racing and pulling private coaches. Nonetheless, they maintained larger stables of horses, of better quality and used for more specific tasks. Appearance was also important, that is, in terms of conformation, size, gait and even colour. Such horses had iconic appeal too. For the ruling class the image of a rider mounted on a fine horse in public demonstrated to the general population its members' fitness to rule. The same symbolism is reflected in the vogue for equestrian portraits.[23] Advocating the benefits of the *manège*, Cavendish asked rhetorically,

> What can be more comely or Pleasing, than to see Horses go in all their several Ayres? And to see so Excellent a Creature, with so much spirit, and Strength, to be so Obedient to his Rider, as if having no Will but His,

21   Trease, 141; Worsley, 167, quoting Warburton Eliot, *Memoirs and Correspondence of Prince Rupert and the Cavaliers* (London: 1849) ii, 468.

22   NUL, Portland MSS, Pw1/537.

23   Edwards, *Horse and Man*, 1–5, 27–30.

they had but one Body, and one Mind, like a Centaur? But above all What sets Off a King more, than to be on a Beautiful Horse at the Head of his Army? (1667: 13)

In terms of horsemanship, the key symbol here is that of the centaur, a creature with a human brain and a horse's body, with both elements working as one. However, in the actual relationship between horse and rider, Cavendish told his readers to consider both minds, emphasizing the point that a horse possessed reason and understanding and that the rider could only achieve real harmony with his mount if he worked with rather than against him.[24]

By the time that Cavendish was growing up and developing an interest in horses, the country's stock was improving and becoming more diverse. This was largely due to the importation of horses from abroad, a development initiated by the Crown but taken up enthusiastically by the landed élite.[25] As Cavendish observed, 'English horses are the Best Horses in the whole World for all Uses whatsoever, from the Cart to the Mannage; and some are as beautiful Horses as can be any where, for they are Bred out of Horses of all Nations. (1667: 58–59) Cavendish's stud, one of the finest in the country, certainly contained horses with foreign blood in their veins. On 14 January 1631, William Cecil, 2nd Earl of Exeter, wrote to him, enquiring about the horses his 'youths' were bringing from France, almost certainly north African Barbs imported through Marseilles.[26] While hoping that they met his expectations, he declared that 'your Lordship will finde asmuch contentment in your owne stable and race, as they can bringe you out of France and on this constant opinion I will rest'. (1667: 54–56) In 1649 the eleven horses, named Newcastle, at the royal stud at Tutbury would undoubtedly have possessed a good deal of Barb blood.[27]

Members of the élite regularly acquired horses off each other, often as gifts as a means of acquiring or dispensing honour and favour. They also loaned out their stallions to serve each others' mares. As Cavendish later reminisced, 'I have bestowed many thousands of Pounds in Horses, & have given many away'. (1667: C2r) On 22 January 1631, for instance, Philip Herbert, 4th earl of Pembroke, thanked him for his 'noble favour in sending mee so fine a horse'. A shared interest in horses and an attachment to the code of honour might throw up some apparently strange alliances. On 24 January 1634 Thomas,

---

24   Walker, 'To Amaze the People', 126–127, 132–133.
25   Edwards, *Horse and Man*, 10–14.
26   BL, Add. MS 70499/133.
27   BL Add MS, 70499/135; Prior M., *The Royal Studs of the Sixteenth and Seventeenth Centuries* (London: 1935) 56–60.

1st Baron Fairfax, grandfather of the parliamentarian commander in the Civil War, and, like Cavendish, a keen horse-breeder, offered the latter, his social superior, the choice of some fine colts. As he explained, he had heard that Cavendish was concerned that his stable was 'not so complete as it hathe beene', a situation which he likened to the king of Spain, as Lord of the Indies, worrying about a shortage of money. Fairfax then enquired about some colts he had sent him, the progeny of his mare by Cavendish's Barbary stallion.[28]

Ironically, when Cavendish faced his grandson on the battlefield the horses they and their troops were mounted on surely included some drawn from a common gene pool. Sir Thomas II rode a Barb, perhaps with Cavendish-owned Barb blood in his veins.[29] Incidentally, the conflict offered Cavendish the opportunity to test his theory that horses schooled in the *manège* were good for more than merely performing tricks. He argued that a well-trained horse, obedient to hands and heels, responded more quickly and more nimbly to his rider's prompting, of considerable value in the confusion of the battlefield. Thus, he concluded,

> ... a Good Horse-man, upon such a Horse, would have too much Advantage ... of him that Talks against it, either in a single Combat, or in the Warrs; for a Ready-Horse will Run, Stop, Turn, go Back; and if he Rise, he knows how to come Down again, and so is Well on the Hand, as you cannot pull him Over with both your Hands; and so Obedient, That I will Run him on Fire, Water, or Sword, and he shall Obey me: and all This cannot Be done but by the Art of Rideing, and that in the Mannage. (1667: 6)

Given the effort that Cavendish had put into breeding and training his horses, abandoning them in the aftermath of the battle was probably one of the hardest things he had to do. Predictably, as soon as he could, he started buying replacements. Even so, for an aristocrat of the old school, one who deemed it effeminate to ride in a coach, his first purchases somewhat surprisingly comprised a coach and nine Holsteiners, costing £160 the set. Shortage of money had previously forced him to ride in a wagon, a common mode of conveying people, if less luxurious and comfortable, and the need to create the correct image would have prompted his action. He had chosen well for Margaret noted that at Paris he was offered a hundred pistols for one of them. Typically, he refused the money, presenting seven of them to Henrietta Maria, Charles I's queen, and keeping the other two for his own use. When he resolved to move

---

28   BL, Add MS 70499, fos. 143, 170.
29   Brereton J.M., *The Horse in War* (Newton Abbot: 1976) 43.

in Paris in February 1645 his *cortège* included a coach, a smaller chariot and two wagons. On his departure, again funded by borrowed money, he and his party travelled with a new coach, a chariot, three wagons and a number of servants on horseback.[30]

Cavendish's first bought 'Great Horses', that is, imposing horses for the *manège* or for ceremonial occasions, in 1647, having secured more credit. With it, he could afford to leave his lodgings and move his family into a rented house, which he furnished. More settled and with time on his hands, he indulged his passion by acquiring two Barbs, one costing 200 pistols and the other, belonging to Lord Crofts, £100. At least, Crofts agreed to wait for payment until Cavendish returned to England. When both of these horses died, one shortly after the other, his immediate reaction was to replace them, although 'he wanted present means'.[31] By degrees, he bought others: eight, according to Margaret, though he listed four Barbs and five Spanish horses, apart from many Dutch horses, 'all the most Excellent Horses that could be'. (1667: C1v) He also received gifts of horses. The Duke of Oldenburg gave him two horses of his excellent breed, 'as Fine Horses as ever I saw, & One was the Hopefullest that could be seen'; The Prince of East Friesland (1667: 67) sent him another very fine horse.[32] After one public display of the art of the *manège* the absent Don John of Austria, the governor of the Spanish Netherlands, subsequently asked an onlooker if his horses 'was as Rare, as their Reputation was Great'. In reply, the man claimed that the 'horses were such, that they wanted nothing of Reasonable Creatures, but Speaking'. (1667: B2r) That Cavendish managed to acquire horses of such exceptional quality not only reflects his ability to obtain credit but also his reputation as a horseman and as a connoisseur of horseflesh.

Having painstakingly acquired several great horses, it is no wonder that Cavendish was loath to part with them. In spite of his constant worry about money, his wife observed that he would sooner sell anything else rather than lose them. In explanation, she added, 'I have hear'd him say, that good Horses are so rare, as not to be valued for Mony and that He who would buy him out of his Pleasure (meaning his Horses) must pay dear for it'. And, because of the reputation of his horses, he did receive offers. When a stranger sought to buy Cavendish's favourite mount, a Spanish horse, he was told that the price that day was £1,000 and would increase by £1,000 every day. On another occasion, a gentleman in Paris commended a grey leaping horse of Cavendish's to the Duke of Guise, a great lover of horses. Guise offered to pay 600 pistoles for

30   Edwards, *Horse and Man*, 214–17; *Life of William Cavendish*, 53, 58.
31   Cavendish M., *Life of William Cavendish*, 57, 65.
32   Ibid., 76.

the horse and asked the man to relay the information to Cavendish. However, as Margaret noted, her husband was 'so far from selling that Horse that he was displeased to hear that any Price should be offer'd for him: So great a Love hath my Lord for good Horses'.[33]

Cavendish tended to use Barbs and Spanish horses for the *manège*. In the English version of his manual, he declared that Spanish horses were the noblest in the world, princes among horses, and the best from which to breed mounts for the saddle, whether for the *manège* ring, hunting field, battleground, race-track or country road. He did admit that because of their intelligence, they were not easily trained for the *manège* and therefore required expert handling. In the earlier, French version he distinguished between different Spanish breeds, the lighter Ginetes and the larger Andalusians. He must have deployed the latter in the *manège* as he rated them the highest, especially those bred at the king's stud at Cordoba. (1667: 49–51; 1743: 21) Cavendish considered Barbs, the 'Gentlemen' of horses, as next in wisdom to Spanish horses. Perversely, this made them easier to train, which perhaps explains why in the French version he confessed that Barbs were his favourites. They possessed 'a good disposition, excellent Apprehension, Judgment, and Memory' and, if roused, 'no Horse in the World goes better in the Mannage, in all Ayres whatsoever, and Rarely upon the Ground in all Kinds'. (1667: B2r, 53–4; 1743: 21) When the marquis of Caracena, the governor of the Spanish Netherlands, saw him perform at Antwerp, Cavendish rode on three horses: two Spanish horses and a Barb. The first, Le Superbe, a light bay Spanish horse, 'was a beautiful Horse; and though Hard to be Rid, yet when he was Hitt Right, he was the Readiest Horse in the World'. Then he mounted Le Gentry, a brown bay Spanish horse, and 'the finest Shap'd Horse that ever I saw, and the neatest'. He rounded off the display by putting a Barb through his paces, which included performing the *Metz-air*, very high, both forward and upon his *voltoes*, and *terra a terra*. (1667: B2v–C1r)

Nonetheless, Cavendish found suitable horses in other breeds, one consequence of the admixture of foreign blood. For instance, many German princes possessed studs of fine horses, using Neapolitan coursers, Spanish horses, Turcomans and Barbs as stallions. He recalled owning a grey 'leaping' German horse, sired by a Neapolitan courser, which no Neapolitan in the world could match for Shape, Stature, Colour, Strength, Agility, and Good Nature'. He executed thirty-two *capriols*, the highest and 'justest' he had ever seen, without any help at all, and was equally adept performing on the ground, galloping and changing, and going *terra a terra*. (1667: 66–67). For English readers, Cavendish recommended that breeders of *manège* horses should use a well-shaped

---

33   Cavendish M., *Life of William Cavendish*, 65.

Spanish horse as a stallion, one with great spirit and strength but also docile, good natured and with an excellent disposition. English Neapolitans he thought too gross, while Barbs, as stallions, were 'too Slender, and too Lady-like', though they were the best in the world to perform the movements. For mares, English horses were ideal, if well-chosen, though he also recommended putting a little, finely shaped Dutch mare to a Spanish stallion. For his Continental readers he had recommended a well-shaped Spanish mare or a Neapolitan. (1667: 87–90; 1743: 23)

Cavendish's Public Displays of the manège

In England, Cavendish's public demonstrations of the *manège* would have excited less interest among his peers than they did abroad, though it did have its *aficionados*. Prince Henry, for instance, had commissioned one of the first custom-built riding houses in the country. As the prince's erstwhile fellow-student, one can only speculate how much better the young Cavendish's fortunes would have been, had Prince Henry not died in 1612. By then, however, interest in the *manège* had peaked and Cavendish was just the latest in a succession of authors who complained about the poor quality of his countrymen's horsemanship. Clearly, gentlemen had to be competent horsemen, if only because they enjoyed hunting but for most of them that was the limit of their ambitions.[34] As Gervase Markham remarked in his *Countrey Contentments*, first published in 1615, '... our English gentrie from a sloath in their industrie ayme for the most part at no more skill then the riding of a ridden and perfect Horse, which is but onelie the setting foorth of an other mans virtue, and thereby making themselves richer in discourse then action'.[35] Cavendish believed that their reluctance was due to ignorance and to a fear that they would not be able to control and direct a great horse. Inevitably so, he claimed, since they lacked the patience and determination to master the complex system of exercises. They excused their indolence by claiming that it was demeaning for a gentleman to do anything well. (1667: 6–7) For Cavendish, such an attitude perverted the principles on which the élite based their conduct of affairs, first expounded by Baldessare Castiglione in *The Book of the Courtier* [1508–28]. Actions, he stated, had to appear both graceful [*grazia*] and natural/effortless [*sprezzatura*], a perspective that underpinned all of Cavendish's

---

34   Edwards, *Horse and Man*, 83–84.
35   Markham Gervase, *Countrey Contentments* (London: 1615) 35.

advice on horsemanship.[36] However, as he knew, this entailed long hours of hard work: 'He that will take Pains for Nothing shall never do any thing Well; for arts, Sciences, and good Qualities, come not by Instinct, but are got by great Labour, Study, and Practice'. (1667: 9)

It was different on the Continent. When John Evelyn went into self-imposed exile in 1643, he observed riders exercising their skills throughout Europe, specifically referring to Geneva, Florence, Naples, Rome, Vicenza and Paris.[37] In France, he claimed, hardly any town of note lacked one or two academies devoted to the art, and some taught so many pupils that they required 100 horses. This, he concluded, explained French superiority in horsemanship.[38] Indeed, by then France had replaced Italy as the centre for the *manège*. In the sixteenth century the French aristocrats, who had travelled to Italy to learn from masters of the art such as Grisone, brought their knowledge back with them and often opened academies to pass on the skills.[39] This development coincided with a change of ethos within the ranks of the French nobility, which transformed the concept of *vertu* (that is, 'manliness') from a military virtue to a courtly one. As mastery of the art could not be lightly achieved, practitioners could demonstrate *vertu* because riding, training and controlling the powerful Great Horse required similar qualities: courage, strength, judgement, initiative and determination, for example.[40] When Cavendish arrived in Paris in 1645, he could watch young noblemen being taught to ride the Great Horse at numerous academies, including those belonging to Monsieurs du Plessis and de Veaux, which Evelyn had attended the previous year.[41] In this environment it is not surprising that he 'picked up the reins' again.

If Cavendish was pleased with the opportunity to observe the training methods being employed in establishments in the then leading centre of equitation, it did not overwhelm him or lead him to change his own views. On the contrary, seeing the methods of French masters like Pluvinel being put into practice may have convinced him (or reinforced an existing intention) to write

---

36   Castiglione Baldesar, *The Book of the Courtier*, Bull G., transl. (Harmondsworth: 1967) 65–68.

37   de Beer E.S., ed., *The Diary of John Evelyn*, 6 vols. (Oxford: 1955) II, 134; 195; 232; 327; 330; 484; 526.

38   Ibid., I, 88.

39   Edwards, *Horse and Man*, 82–83.

40   Tucker T.J., "Early Modern French noble identity and the Equestrian 'Airs above Ground'", in Raber K. – Tucker T.J. (eds.), The *Culture of the Horse: Status, Discipline and Identity in the Early Modern World* (Basingstoke: 2005) 273–282.

41   Evelyn, II, 134.

a manual of his own, one that would supersede everything that had been written before it.[42] Setting out his credentials in the English version of the book he wrote on his return home, he proclaimed,

> I have Practised, and Studied Horse-manship ever since I was Ten years old; Have Rid with the Best Masters of all Nations, heard them Discourse at Large, and Tryed their several Wayes: Have Read all their Italian, French, and English Books, and some Latin ones; and in a Word, All that hath been Writ upon this Subject, Good and Bad.' (1667: 41)

His purchase of two *manège* horses in 1647, whilst at Paris, is indicative of his intentions. Unfortunately for the local horsemen, they did not have long to appreciate and then implement his methods, for in September 1648 he moved to Antwerp. There, by good fortune and the support of his creditors he had the opportunity, the means and the space to perfect his method and to demonstrate to a knowledgeable audience its superiority over other systems. Cavendish quite rightly acknowledged his debt to the city, the stage for the displays of horsemanship that cemented his fame as the leading horseman in Europe. (1667: B1r–v)

At the Rubens House, which he rented from the painter's widow, he had the perfect setting. The house formed three sides of an open courtyard, with Cavendish's double-height riding house, established in Rubens's old studio, standing to the south of it.[43] Although large, Cavendish observed that the crowds were often so closely packed that his equerry, Captain Mazin, hardly had room to ride. For one display, Cavendish counted over twenty coaches (Margaret saw seventeen) bringing the whole of Don John's court to the Ruben's House, where they joined Flemish nobles like the Duke of Aerschot, along with other spectators. (1667: B1v, C2v) As an international *entrepôt*, many people came to or passed through Antwerp and almost all the persons of quality who stayed there visited the Rubens House to watch Cavendish at work in the *manège*.[44] Friedrich, the Landgrave of Hessen-Eschwege, hearing of his reputation, travelled specifically to see him exercise his horses, and wrote an

---

42   Raber K., "A Horse of a Different Colour: Nation and Race in Early Modern Horsemanship Treatises", in Raber & Tucker, 225–43 (Hereafter cited as Raber, "Nation and Race"); Walker E., "'The Author of their Skill': Human and Equine Understanding in the Duke of Newcastle's 'New Method'", in *The Horse as Cultural Icon*, 329. (Hereafter cited as Walker, "Author").

43   Worsley, 169–170, 172.

44   Cavendish M., *Life of William Cavendish*, 76.

appreciative letter to him when he returned home. Had he not died in battle shortly afterwards, he would have sent him two promised horses from his own breed. (1667: C1v) Among the nations represented in his audiences, Cavendish noted High and Low Dutch, Italians, English, French, Spaniards, Poles and Swedes. Among the Englishmen who supported him were the Earl of Bristol and the Marquis of Ormonde, the latter often attending his displays. (167: C1v, C2v)

The reference to Captain Mazin on horseback reveals that Cavendish's roles were normally those of trainer and ring-master rather than rider. Having trained his equerry in his own method, he declared him to be the best horseman he had ever met. (1667: 5) Of course, Cavendish could be tempted into the saddle if a very high ranking nobleman asked him. When Don John's court decamped to the Rubens House, he felt that the honour warranted a personal appearance 'which otherwise he never did but for his own exercise and delight'. On another occasion, the Marquis of Caracena persuaded him to ride in spite of his protests that an illness had kept him from exercising his horses for up to two months.[45] He rode the two Spanish horses and a Barb, while Mazin put five horses through their paces. (1667: C1r) Cavendish found it an exhilarating experience, especially on the back of Le Gentry, the brown bay Spanish horse. He recounted that the horse performed the pirouette in his length so precisely and so quickly that 'the Standers by could hardly see the Rider's Face when he went; And truly, when he had done, I was so Dizzey, that I could hardly Sit in the Saddle'. Much to his delight, the marquis congratulated him on the performance. The Spanish who accompanied him in his entourage were even more gushing, crossing themselves and crying *Miraculo*. (1667: B2v, C1r)

Among the visitors Cavendish wanted to impress two parties stand out. One, comprising the Prince of Condé, with a group of French nobles and officers, twice visited the riding house. As the French thought that, 'all the Horsemanship in the World is in France', he probably expected them to find fault with the performance. This made their praise all the more welcoming. One of the onlookers, 'a very great Man in his Country', told him that it was a bold person who mounted a horse in front of him. Another exclaimed that there could not be such a lord as him left in England. (1667: C1r) Cavendish also entertained Charles II, the Princess Royal and the Dukes of York and Gloucester at the Rubens House. Not only did the king see Cavendish ride but he also displayed his own skill in the *manège*, 'he being an Excellent Master of that Art'.[46] Cavendish treasured a particular comment that the king made, namely,

---

45   Ibid., 77; 79.
46   Cavendish M., *Life of William Cavendish*, 79.

'That there are very few that Know Horses'. How true, he thought, 'it being very certain, That all Men undertake to Ride them, but very few Know them, or can tell what they are good for'. (1667: C2r)

Basking in the praise of a knowledgeable and appreciative audience of his peers, it was evidently the moment to set down his method in print for wider circulation and influence. He published the French version for the Continental market in general and the French one in particular. Opulently produced, with forty-two double page plates engraved by Petr Clouvet from etchings supplied by Abraham van Diepenbeke, a pupil of Rubens, it was designed to impress as well as educate. He reckoned that it would cost over £1,300 to print.[47] With its recitation of Cavendish's titles in the illustrated title-page and the depiction of the author against a backdrop of his properties in many of the plates, the manual clearly had a self-publicizing purpose. (1743: frontispiece, various plates) Remarkably, one of the engravings depicts the apotheosis of Cavendish, the master horseman, while another portrays him crowned and seated in a chaise drawn by two centaurs within a circle of horses paying homage to him (1743: plate 1): no self-doubt or lack of ambition here then![48] In 1667, back in England, he published an English version 'for the more particular Satisfaction of my Country-men'. In a veiled rebuke to the king for the perceived dishonour of not offering him the role in government that he felt his sacrifices had warranted, he told Charles II he had been able to produce the book because he had had 'much leisure, in my solitary Country Life, to recollect my Thoughts and try new Experiments about that Art'. (1667: B1r–v) The two versions cover much of the same ground but are distinct and can be read as separate entities, though preferably viewed together. Although Cavendish wrote the two versions of the horsemanship manual for an *élite* market, there is a discernible difference of emphasis in the text.[49] In the first one he presumed a receptive readership, whereas in the English edition he was hoping to revive an interest in the *manège* among his peers. In both versions, however, he was seeking to establish his credentials with the target audience, boldly asserting the primacy of his innovative, scientific approach over all other systems, whether the one written by recently deceased Pluvinel's abroad or that of the long dead Blundeville's at home.[50] He must have felt vindicated, therefore, when at an audience with Don John, the latter asked him (and several times afterwards) for a copy of the book, then only available in manuscript form.

---

47 Trease, 176; Walker, "Author", 329.
48 Graham, "Good Horses", 63–68.
49 Walker, "Author", 329–30; Walker, 'To Amaze the People', 6, 138–139.
50 Raber, "Nation and Race", 225–43 *passim*; Walker, "Author", 329–330.

When Cavendish eventually presented one to him, he proudly recorded that Don John received it 'with great Satisfaction'. (1667: B1v)

Conclusion

Obviously, it is far too simplistic to claim that once Cavendish had bought a couple of Great Horses and had found a space to train them, he initiated and brought to fruition a programme of personal rehabilitation, based on his love for the *manège*. Not only was he unable to overcome his feelings of loss, failure and despair completely, but other factors intruded too. Nonetheless, his work with horses was therapeutic and it did help. In the immediate aftermath of the Marston Moor disaster Cavendish was shattered psychologically as well as militarily. If it prompted his flight from the country, it seemed to confirm the view held by a section of the political nation, friend and foe, that he lacked conviction and mental stamina, that he was a dilettante, a womaniser and an ineffectual aesthete, who was more interested in the pleasures of life than the rigours of campaigning. This is unfair. Neither a soldier by inclination or training, events pitchforked him into a position of command that his status, wealth and devotion to the king demanded. Yet, without hesitation he pledged his support, put his vast income at the disposal of his monarch and showed a complete disregard for his own safety on the battlefield. Surveying the scene of carnage on Marston Moor, strewn with the corpses of his Whitecoats, he felt personally responsible for their deaths and that, as he considered himself incapable of redeeming the situation, honour demanded that it was time to retire from the fray. As Worsley suggests, shame and despair rather than injured pride forced him out.[51]

For a person, whose identity was closely connected with his estate, the residences he had helped to design and his patriarchal authority there, exile was not an easy option, especially after his sons rejoined his daughters in England in 1647. Between 1644 and 1648 he led a peripatetic existence, moving from Hamburg to Antwerp via Paris and Rotterdam, which, if it was comparatively comfortable, always depended upon hand-outs and loans from friends, relations and associates, and credit from money lenders. Only at Antwerp did he find a proper home, one where he felt he might put down roots, albeit reluctantly, should his exile prove to be permanent. Antwerp, with its cosmopolitan atmosphere, its trading and cultural links with other European centres and its vibrant arts scene, was the perfect place for a person with Cavendish's literary

---

51   Graham, "Good Horses", 43–4; Worsley, 168.

and artistic interests to live.[52] He even rented Rubens's House. While it could never fully compensate for the desperate feeling of loss that he felt throughout his years of exile, his time in Antwerp did aid his rehabilitation. In her account, Margaret constantly expressed the gratitude that she and her husband felt for the kindness and hospitality they found there, more so than they had received from their fellow-countrymen.[53] It still rankled, but at Antwerp 'my Lord lived there with as much content as a man of his condition could do'.[54]

Apart from the generosity of strangers, Margaret attributed an improvement in Cavendish's peace of mind to his renewed involvement in the *manège*, 'his chief pastime and divertisement' at Antwerp.[55] Here, in the riding house, Cavendish was in control, confident in his ability and in harmony with his horses. Exercising his mounts, he was no dilettante, having honed his skill over many years of riding, as well as thinking and reading about the subject. Here, he showed his true worth: among his peers good horsemanship, especially expertise in the refined skills of the *manège*, served as a metaphor for one's capacity as a ruler of men. In England, courtiers had scorned him and he had failed his monarch, leaving him feeling insecure and ashamed. In exile, on the other hand, foreigners, among whom he counted princes, viceroys and governors, came to watch his displays and fêted him for his skill. Arguably, the acclaim he received for these performances helped Cavendish re-establish his status and reputation in his own eyes and thereby improve his sense of self-worth. As Raber points out, participating in such an aristocratic pastime, 'soothed his sense of loss and displacement', whilst emphasizing his status and allowing him to show off his skills to a discerning audience.[56] By the time he returned to England he had enhanced his already impressive reputation across Europe as a horseman, and in his manual he had provided *manège* riders with a guide to what he considered to be best practice. If he still harboured a grievance on his trip home, he travelled in a far better frame of mind than he had been on his hurried departure sixteen years earlier.

Selective Bibliography

Cavendish Margaret, *The Life of the Thrice Noble, High and Puissant Prince William Cavendishe, Duke, Marquess and Earl of Newcastle* (London, A.Maxwell: 1667).

---

52 Worsley, 179–180.
53 *Life of William Cavendish*, 63–65; 72–75; 77–78; 81–82.
54 Ibid., 65.
55 Ibid., 65.
56 Raber, "Nation and Race", 229.

Cavendish William, *A New Method, and Extraordinary Invention, to Dress Horses* (London, Thomas Milbourn: 1667).

Edwards P., *Horse and Man in Early Modern England* (London: 2007).

Raber K., "A horse of a different colour: nation and race in early modern horsemanship treatises", in Raber K. – Tucker T.J. (eds.), *The Culture of the Horse: Status, Discipline and Identity in the Early Modern* World (Basingstoke: 2005).

Trease G., *Portrait of a Cavalier: William Cavendish, First Duke of Newcastle* (London: 1979).

Tucker T.J., "Early Modern French Noble Identity and the Equestrian "'Airs Above Ground'", in Raber K. – Tucker T.J. (eds.), The *Culture of the Horse: Status, Discipline an Identity in the Early Modern World* (Basingstoke: 2005).

Whitaker K., *Mad Madge, Margaret Cavendish, Duchess of Newcastle, royalist, writer and romantic* (London: 2003).

Walker E., *'To Amaze the People with Pleasure and Delight': the Horsemanship Manuals of William Cavendish, Duke of Newcastle* (London: 2010).

Walker E., "'The Author of their Skill': Human and Equine Understanding in the Duke of Newcastle's 'New Method'", in Edwards P. – Enenkel K.A.E. – Graham E. (eds.), *The Horse as Cultural Icon: the Real and the Symbolic Horse in the Early Modern World* (Leiden: 2012).

CHAPTER 14

William Cavendish: Riding School and Race Track

Richard Nash

This chapter poses a fairly straightforward question in the history of agriculture and sport, and offers as an answer a potentially far-reaching set of claims about changing ideas of human-animal relationships in the early modern period. Why did William Cavendish, 1st Duke of Newcastle, not exert a more lasting influence on the sport of horse racing that may be thought of as originating in England during his lifetime?

Tradition has long held that while some form of racing has probably existed as long as humans have ridden horses, the modern sport of thoroughbred horseracing emerged from contests on the heath at Newmarket patronized by Charles II, who sponsored the earliest Royal Plates. These races among older horses, contested under high weight in multiple 4-mile heats, were justified as providing 'encouragement to breed the best horses'.[1] The breed that developed in the following decades, which became known as 'the thoroughbred', descend in the male (sire) line from one of three 'foundation stallions': The Godolphin Arabian (imported before 1730), the Darley Arabian (imported 1704) and the Byerley Turk (believed to be imported sometime around 1687.[2] While the earliest of these imported stallions could not have sired horses until after the death of Charles II, the earliest articles for Plate racing established by that monarch date from 1665, and it is likely that the horses at Newmarket during the Restoration era would have come from the most noted studs of the seventeenth century.[3]

---

1 The phrase is from William Temple's *Essay on the Advancement of Trade in Ireland* (1673), in which he proposes establishing Royal plates on the Newmarket model.

2 For a recent challenge to the longstanding belief that Byerley's charger was imported, see Nash R., "'Beware a Bastard Breed': Notes Towards a Revisionist History of the Thoroughbred Racehorse", in *The Horse as Cultural Icon*, 191–216.

3 All pedigree historians are indebted to the work done on these early studs in the early twentieth century by Prior C.M., particularly in *Early records of the thoroughbred horse: Containing reproductions of some original stud-books, and other papers . . .* (London: 1924) and *The royal studs of the sixteenth and seventeenth centuries: Together with a reproduction of the Second Earl of Godolphin's Stud Book* (London: 1935). For a recent helpful discussion locating early horseracing in a context that extends back before the reign of Charles II, and documents

As one-time governor to that monarch, who taught him to ride and who throughout a long life had assiduously cultivated a reputation as a pre-eminent horseman, one would have expected Cavendish to have played a leading role in the rise of the equestrian sport most closely identified with the Restoration of monarchy as 'the sport of kings'. Yet, while the names of seventeenth-century breeders that are most familiar to pedigree researchers (Darcy, Wyvill, Place, Hutton, Leedes, etc.) are relatively unfamiliar to cultural historians, the name that seems most pre-eminent in equestrian matters from the perspective of cultural history (as this volume attests), that of William Cavendish, plays what must be considered a minor role in both the history of racing and the establishment of the thoroughbred. Indeed, in the early history of the thoroughbred, Cavendish is overshadowed by other branches of his own family. Why is that? Or, to pose that question less succinctly but perhaps more productively, how can we best understand his relationship to an emerging sport and the establishment of a distinct breed; and might such an understanding offer useful insights into the larger cultural history surrounding these origins?

The answer that I propose here may offer useful insights into the current revival of our critical interest in human-animal interactions and how we think about agency in the material world and in human history. For Cavendish, horsemanship was a rich and powerfully significant practice; more than an artistic display, it enacts a distinctly princely artistic performance of proper management and control. As such, it figures emblematically not only the monarch's relation to his subjects but also the state's relation to the monarch: the performance of horsemanship does not just display the attributes of a proper ruler but figuratively performs the state itself. That political work of figuration does not occlude but operates alongside a notion of 'identity' more performative and less essential than is common for his contemporaries.[4] In one sense, of course, Cavendish's ideology of horsemanship is profoundly conservative, aristocratic, royalist and, above all, anthropocentric, positioning man as ruler to the beast over whom he is granted dominion. This is an ideology more backward-looking than forward-looking, one not easily assimilated into our current categories. In another sense, however, just as relevant, the ideal performance Cavendish seeks to realize constitutes a transcendence of conventional forms of identity, for the ideal horseman does not merely control his beast but performs a composite identity in governing partnership with his mount. In terms of the political metaphor, the proper exercise of sovereignty produces an identity that exceeds either sovereign or subject

---

the popularity of a seventeenth century sport that was not well recorded, see Edwards P., "The Racecourse" in *Horse and Man in Early Modern England* (London: 2007) 89–118.

4   Cf. Mattfeld's discussion of Cavendish's performative identity in this volume, pp. 281–99.

in attaining an ideal state. Such a notion may privilege human over horse, just as a monarch rules his subjects; but that privilege is not itself an end but a means to attaining a performative, relational identity that exceeds the limits of discrete identities available to either horse or human. In the context of this particular trans-specific performative ideal—a notion much closer to many current philosophical positions than his explicit political ideology—Cavendish shares relatively little interest with his contemporaries, who were concerned with a multi-generational project of agricultural improvement dedicated to breeding better horses.[5] His interest is, consequently, not so much in the sport of horse racing (which he practised as recreation not as art), and even less in the breeding of racehorses (which he valued very little), but instead focuses on the sport of the *manège*, or dressage, which he does value as art, and which, unlike horse-racing, he considers to be an art of management that may be practised independently of breed identity. While he expresses marked preferences about breeding, those preferences ultimately are subsumed under a commitment to a performance that takes priority over what might be considered desirable essential qualities.

While it is difficult to imagine a time when humans did not race the horses they rode, the sport we know today only began recording events on a regular ongoing basis in the eighteenth century, with regular recording and publication of racing results beginning in 1709 at York and in 1718 at Newmarket. Sporadic, less systematic, reports make clear that the sport of that era, from which today's sport can be directly traced, was itself a continuation of a gentlemen's recreation conducted regularly (even if only occasionally recorded) during the reign of Charles II. Prior to the Restoration of the monarchy in 1660, while private correspondence and journals give clear indication of racing's popularity, public recording of race results is considerably less systematic. References to two very different forms of racing appear from time to time in early literature. An early form of steeplechase racing, privileging stamina, is described by Gervase Markham, under the name of the Wild Goose Chase. This was effectively a cross-country game of follow the leader, in which a brief sprint determined who would be 'the wild goose', and that rider would then set off on a cross country run, with the others required to stay within 240 yards or be distanced. While tactical speed was obviously an advantage here (a quick horse could not only become 'the Wild Goose', he could distance his slower opponents early), the primary focus was on stamina over testing ground, and a chase could—like the hunting it substituted for—last for miles. At the opposite

---

5   While emphasis might vary, for most such breeders 'better' horses were those who combined more effectively speed, stamina, and spirit.

end of the spectrum were the short sprint races, often as short as a quarter of a mile, usually contested by Hobbies and Galloways.[6]

When James I established a hunting lodge in Newmarket, hunting was his preferred recreation, but there is evidence of a few scattered matches that were likely the precursors of the sport established there later in the century. There is a record of Lord Salisbury winning a private match of £100 from the Duke of Buckingham in 1623 and a less precise reference to the king attending a match there in 1619. Few records exist of racing at Newmarket during the reign of Charles I, but it is from that reign that the first Royal Cup is dated: '1633–4 Mar. – Bay Tarrall said to have won first Gold Cup in the reign of Charles I (1625–1649)'.[7] That long-accepted date, however, is open to challenge on several grounds, as the basis seems to be a reference in Shirley's comedy, *Hyde Park* (1637), and a playwright is not obliged to be a historian. Moreover, the letter below from the Earl of Pembroke and Montgomery to Cavendish (dated from Whitehall, 20 May 1631) clearly indicates that a Cup had been run for at Newmarket in that spring, and strongly suggests that Cavendish feels wrongly done in the outcome:

> I confess that you had no great encouragement to return your horses to Newmarket 'vpon so chargeable conditions', I cannot justify the carrying away of the Cup, but if [you] care to favour us with your company when the king comes next to Newmarket, I will take your part and seek 'a reuenche'.[8]

It is no more clear whether Cavendish sought his 'reuenche' than it is why he thought the 'carrying away of the Cup' to be unjustified, but it does seem clear that as early as 1631, gentlemen were racing for a cup at Newmarket when the king visited, and that Cavendish was among those who competed. Decades later, while in exile during the Interregnum, he would write *La methode et invention nouvelle de dresser les chevaux*, followed in 1667 by a distinct English edition of that work in English, *A new method, and extraordinary invention, to dress horses, and work them according to nature*, after his return to England. In this seminal work in the history of dressage, Cavendish alludes to his experience with horse racing, simultaneously applauding his own performance and downplaying the sport itself:

---

6   See Mackay-Smith A., *Speed and the Thoroughbred* (Lanham, MD: 2000) 1–4; and Markham Gervase, *Cauelarice* (London, Edward White: 1607) 10–11. For references to early race meetings see Edwards P., *Horse and Man in Early Modern England* (London: 2007) 89–119.

7   Muir J.B., Ye Olde New-Markitt Calendar (London: 1892) 17.

8   BL, Add MS 70499 fo. 143.

Let me tell you, that Running-Horses are the most easily found, and of the least Use, commonly they run upon *Heaths*, (a Green Carpet) and must there run all upon the Shoulders, which in troublesome Grounds is ready to break one's Neck, and of no Use; Though I love the Sport of a Running-Horse very well, and think I am as good a *Jockey* as any, and have ridden many hundred Matches, and seen the best *Jockeys*, and studied it more than I think they have done. (1667: 80)

It may be important to note here how for Cavendish 'the sport of a Running Horse' is a fundamentally *human* sport, revolving on the role of 'jockey' in the modern sense of 'rider', a role that he claims to know well both by experience and study. While Cavendish is not unique in using 'jockey' in that sense, he does restrict his sense of the term more than was customary at the time. Elsewhere, the primary sense of 'jockey' was understood to be one who owns and/or trains horses, with a special reference to the buying and selling of horses, a connection to vulgar commerce for which Cavendish expresses explicit disdain in his preface: 'I was then too great a *Beggar*, to think to be made Rich by the Sale of a Horse: I have bestow'd many Thousands of Pounds in *Horses*, and have given many; but never was a good *Horse-Courser; Selling* being none of my *Professions*'. (1667: Sig. c2r)

Cavendish's expressed disdain for racing across 'green carpet' heaths, and his own professed expertise as a jockey may be well illustrated in the limited record that remains of his participation in the sport after the restoration of Charles II. We learn in a letter of 1661 of his last known triumph on the turf: 'There was a great horse race on Thursday last [in Nottinghamshire?] between my Lord of Newcastle and Sir Harry Evorett, his Excellency won and ran the other out of distance though Sir Harry's horse led the way for the first 3 miles but being a little nag and the ground very heavy, being but lately ploughed, could not carry it out'.[9] Remarkably, Cavendish was nearing his sixty-ninth birthday at the time. Perhaps he did not exaggerate his prowess as a race-rider or, perhaps, there were more guests than rivals at this event on a course of his own design; perhaps, also, there was more than a little jockeying in the course design itself. The Sparken Hill course laid out by Cavendish was nothing like the green carpet heath he had so little use for, but a testing course intended to privilege stamina over speed. Five years later, in published articles for the annual race at Sparken Hill, we get a clear sense of what a testing course it would have been over uneven ground: 'his Grace is pleased to Declare, That seeing he hath set up this *Course* onely for the Pleasure and Recreation of the

---

9 NUL, MS NeE8.

Gentry, he hopes they will take it in good part, because his Grace hath no other end in it, but theirs and his own contentment'.[10]

The letter describing the 1661 race indicates that there were a number of the gentry present and many fine horses, but they would not run for so small a prize as Cavendish offered. It may well have been, however, that the course he laid out was designed to disadvantage those 'finer horses' or even (as the 1666 articles suggest) that he explicitly prohibited all but horses intended for buck-hunting, a very early version of the hunter plates of the eighteenth century, designed for non-thoroughbreds. Certainly, the effect as described in the letter of 1661 was that Cavendish rode a patient race, while Harry Everett went too fast over the first three miles and wound up distanced by the waiting tactics and superior stamina of Cavendish and his mount.[11]

What scattered records of early racing that survive from the seventeenth century, then, tend to corroborate Cavendish's self-assessment that he was a knowledgeable and effective race rider of considerable experience. Yet, as the sport emerged and rose to social prominence in the reign of Charles II and the last two decades of Cavendish's life, he remained peripheral to its development, becoming in fact rather more critical than supportive of its development. His activities, as well as the doctrines articulated in his crowning work of horsemanship, bespeak a profound scepticism about the virtues that the sport supposedly encouraged. Royal patronage of the sport during the Restoration was rationalized on economic and military grounds, and as necessary to developing a stronger national defence. Sir William Temple, for example, in *An Essay upon the Advancement of Trade in Ireland* (1673) advocates the establishment of horse fairs and plates to be run for in order to facilitate 'the improvement of horses' in Ireland.[12]

This paired emphasis, yoking racing performance to ideas of improvement and a concept of breed identity, has been a signature claim made on behalf of thoroughbred horse racing for the remainder of its history. But, this is a distinctly modern constellation of ideas, one that Cavendish himself actively resisted. Indeed, he has developed something of a paradoxical reputation, and not without reason. In some respects, particularly in his horsemanship, he seems to anticipate ideas strongly held in our own time; in other

---

10   Welbeck Abbey, rules for racing at Sparken Hill 1666.
11   In heat racing, a 'distance post' was established 240 yards before the finish post; any horse who had not reached the first post by the time the winner reached the finish post was deemed 'distanced' and ineligible to compete in subsequent heats.
12   Temple Sir William, *Miscellanea* (London, Edward Gellibrand: 1680) 133–34.

respects he seems to harken back to a time prior to his own. In her essay in this volume and elsewhere, Karen Raber has caught some of the complexity of his attitude toward human-equine relations in noting how the very doctrines that he professed as symbolizing political authority both facilitated a democratizing spread of such symbolic performance and also entailed a more mutually responsive communicative system between human and non-human than his explicit doctrines acknowledged.[13] His politics and principles were undeniably royalist and élitist, and he is unapologetic in his discussions of horsemanship in advocating a fear-based discipline, in which the horse comes to love his rider through the mediation of a just fear. As contrary as such an ideology is to modern democratic impulses, it is one that is thoroughly in accord with monarchical political views that were grounded ultimately in theorizing the sovereign/ subject relationship in accordance with doctrines subjugating human responsibility to divine authority. A clear analogy governs Cavendish's practice: man should fear God and adore him; and the subject must fear, obey and revere his monarch; and the horse should learn to fear his rider, whose discipline will compel the horse's love and obedience. While there may be some today who would advocate a similar set of correspondences, that is certainly a minority viewpoint, yet many, who would part company with Cavendish over politics and religion, find value in his horsemanship, though they tend to emphasize the 'love' more than the 'fear' in his doctrine, which considered those qualities to be tightly linked to one another. It is, I think, worth attending to the degree to which Cavendish's ideological commitment here is deeply counter to modern notions: because the proper love of subject for sovereign is modelled on the proper love of man for his creator; it is a love that is inextricably bound up with fear, awe and reverence. Our own commitments resist the notion that love can be born of fear, but such a notion is deeply woven into Cavendish's understanding of his practice of horsemanship.

What seems more important than the overt ideological resonances between politics, religion and horsemanship in Cavendish's doctrines is the strong empiricist commitment that he shares with his more modern contemporaries like Thomas, Lord Fairfax. Ultimately, perhaps even more than Fairfax himself could claim, Cavendish returns, time and again, to empiricist experiment as the only reliable touchstone for his doctrines:

---

13   Raber K., "'Reasonable Creatures': William Cavendish and the Art of Dressage", in Fumerton P. – Hunt S. (eds.), *Renaissance Culture and the Everyday*. (Philadelphia: 1999) 42–66.

> That TRYING is the only Way to know HORSES
>   I Told you that Marks, Colours, and Elements, are nothing at all to know a *Horse* by; for they are but *Philosophical Mountebanks* that talk of such *Toys*. Nay, Shape is Nothing to know the Goodness of a *Horse*; and therefore the best *Philosophy* is to try him . . . still ride him, and try him; and that is the best *Philosophy* to know him by. (1667: 104)

Moreover, what may resonate so strongly with horsemen when reading Cavendish, as opposed to so many of his contemporaries, is how committed he is to encountering each horse with whom he works on that individual's own terms. Most early modern texts on horsemanship offer prescriptions, as though horses themselves were utterly interchangeable entities without specific variability. Cavendish often reverts, in expounding his doctrines, to specific memories of exemplary moments with individual animals. As familiar as this mode has become, particularly in oral instruction—the teachers we learn from frequently teach us by recalling particular encounters with specific animals—it is virtually unprecedented in the early modern period. Even though Cavendish's doctrines of horsemanship repeatedly function rhetorically to cast himself in the role of sovereign, compelling love and obedience through fear, his narrative exposition of those doctrines tends to personalize moments of experiential, communicative exchange. The resulting tension between a royalist doctrine of political authority and a discursive practice that foregrounds individualized responsive interaction informs Cavendish's writing on, as well as his practice of, horsemanship.

No man was more highly regarded (or more eager to be viewed) as the greatest horseman in Europe than Cavendish. It was a reputation that mattered mightily to him, and one that he cultivated at every opportunity. Moreover, what counted to him was the proper performance of the display of mastery: the ideal horseman (like the ideal ruler) should be able to demonstrate mastery of any horse he rode. At the centre of Cavendish's views on horse breeding, politics, people and probably religion was the doctrine that most was bad and little was good; but the proper role for the horseman, as for an ideal governor, was to bring out the best that was possible by the good government of that which one governed. (1743L: 15–18) In terms of horsemanship, Cavendish focused his interest on how best to manage the horse one had. In terms of breeding, he sought to preserve the *status quo* from the natural deterioration that would be the effect of climate, if not offset by wise management practice. His belief in geohumoralism took a thoroughly orthodox and traditional form, one that led him to argue that the best horse for a stallion in England was a Spanish Ginete, eventually giving that horse the preference even to the similarly hot-blooded

Barb. His favourite stallions were the Ginete and the Barb. If the Spanish stallion were crossed with suitable mares, he believed it could provide good horses for schooling, cavalry, riding, hunting and racing. The Barb was himself a better horse for schooling than the Spaniard since he was less 'wise' or independent, but was not so fit a stallion to breed *manege* horses when crossed with native mares. In the original 1658 work he had stated that he generally preferred the Barb both as a horse and a stallion, but by 1667 the Barb was not so favoured, except as a sire for racehorses. (1743L: 21–23; 1667: 49–58, 62–63)

This version of geohumoralism maintained that in a northern climate all females tend to devolve toward the phlegmatic, and to offset the malign influence that they would exert on their progeny (especially later progeny) they must be constantly re-invigorated with crosses of freshly imported hot southern blood from Spain. Cavendish wanted his English mares served by newly imported Spanish Ginetes but he sought that blend as a way of preserving and perpetuating as long as possible a *status quo* that, while producing more bad than good, was not as thoroughly devolved as would otherwise naturally occur without the benign influence of the breeder's management. This version of geohumoralist breeding theory was entirely in accord with Cavendish's cavalier politics and it stakes out a position inimical to the emergent doctrines of 'breed improvement' that were foundational to the sport of horse racing.

A pointed contrast to Cavendish can be found in his counterpart at Marston Moor, Sir Thomas Fairfax (3rd Lord Fairfax after the death of his father in 1648), who retired from military service soon after the Civil War and bred horses in his retirement at Nun Appleton. Fairfax also subscribes to the reigning doctrine of geohumoralism, but in a version adapted to his own ideological commitments.[14] Where Cavendish's cavalier application of geohumoralism seeks to preserve a precarious *status quo*, always in danger of deterioration, Fairfax adapts the same theory to a model of improvement. In doing so, he seems to be extending and developing a theory of breeding that he learned from his grandfather, the first Lord Fairfax. In a letter to Cavendish in the 1630s, the language of the first lord explicitly alluded to the parable of the talents in asking Cavendish to accept a gift from him—a literal repayment in kind—for the earlier loan of a stallion: 'I have received somme Talents from you and I will

---

14   For an extended consideration of Fairfax's treatise see Nash R., "Gentlemen's Recreation and Georgic Improvement: Lord Fairfax on Horse Breeding", in Hopper A. – Major P. (eds.), *England's Fortress: New Perspectives on Thomas, 3rd Lord Fairfax* (Farnham: 2014); and Major P., "'The Fire of his Eye': Thomas, 3rd Lord Fairfax's 'A Treatise Touching the Breeding of Horses'", *Modern Language Review* 105, i (2010).

be glad that you will take an account how I have employed them. I have not been necligent in improving them'.[15]

An earlier letter to Lord Fairfax from Cavendish (1627/28), while he was still Lord Mansfield, both makes clear the context of the gift that Fairfax is repaying in the elaborate gift exchange of patronage and deference and also offers our first glimpse of the young Thomas Fairfax's involvement in horse breeding, as a *protégé* of his grandfather and the man who will be his opponent at Marston Moor. In a letter redolent with irony Cavendish offers a gift to his esteemed senior, Lord Fairfax, already in his sixties, while at the same time encouraging the development of that man's grandson, perched, aged fifteen, on the brink of manhood. The divisions that will before long mark the fortunes of these two families are not yet anticipated in the polite exchange between two families, united by common interest:

> My staye above [in London] being verye unsertayne dependinge uppon the parliment makes me the bolder to make an offer & renewe an olde acoustemed sute of truckinge the Comodetye of Horsefleshe &c, the rather because I have harde your Lo:s saye thatt you have plenty of mares butt no Horses, & destitude att this time off a Stallion. Therefore Iff itt please your Lo:s to Aceptt off my Baye Barb: Though for no other use butt a Stallion. I hope he will fitt thatt turne to your Lo:s Contentment & the better Iff you please to lett him runn with them. When I returne from London your Lo:s must nott denye me a Jurneye hether to see summ horses though nott worth your Lo:s Trouble to bringe thatt Noble Gentleman your Grand Childe mr Fayrfaxe with you whoe I heare to my great Contentment is mutch adicted to that exsersice.[16]

Beyond the political ironies of this correspondence, we can see in the contrast between Cavendish and the Fairfaxes, a subtle but significant shift. While they share geohumoral notions about breeding, as well as a common interest in a national priority of developing war horses more than sporting horses, they wind up with distinctly different notions when it comes to the possibilities of improvement and the presumption of degeneracy. The younger Fairfax left at his death a manuscript treatise on horse breeding which begins as follows:

---

15   BL, Add MS 70499 fo. 170.

16   Cavendish William, Viscount Mansfield, to Thomas, first Baron Fairfax, dated Welbeck 29 February 1627. Auction Catalogue. *Bonhams Auctioneers: CAVENDISH (WILLIAM, DUKE OF NEWCASTLE)*. https://www.bonhams.com/auctions/16854/lot/79/?page_lots=2. Web. 28 Sept. 2013.

He that would build well must lay a good foundation. He that would reap good Fruits must plant good Trees; for no Man can gather Grapes from Thorns, or Figs from Thistles. So He that would breed good Horses must look to his Stallion and Mares of which he doth breed be perfect; otherwise his Colts will be imperfect, like those from which they do come.[17]

While Fairfax's treatise echoes his grandfather's rhetoric of the parable of the talents, deploying the figurative language of the gospels to promote a notion of breeding for improvement, Cavendish's preference for the superiority of the Spanish horse is pronounced and associated with notions of innate class difference. But, again, he did use Barbs, as is shown in other correspondence with Lord Fairfax. In her life of her husband, Margaret Cavendish wrote that he believed that '*Spanish horses* were like *princes*, and barbs like gentlemen, in *their kind*'.[18] The doctrines of breeding that Cavendish espoused indicate that he sought to approach as nearly as possible to an ideal mean between extremes, 'neither too gross, nor too slender', seeking to preserve innate quality and avoid the degeneration to which all things are prone:

> Why not breed of a *Neapolitan*? They are too gross *Horses*; and we breed too big *Horses* in *England*, by reason both of Air and Ground.
> Why not Breed of a *Barb*? They are too slender, and too Lady like, for the *Mannage*, though themselves the best in the World for it; but their *Off-spring* are commonly loose and weak *Horses*, fitter for *Running-Horses*, than the *Mannage*; so the *Spanish Horse* is in the Middle, (where Vertue lies) neither too gross, nor too slender, and the finest shap'd *Horse* in the World: and therefore have no other Stallion. (1667: 88–89)

Here, Cavendish clearly acknowledges the influence of sire and dam on their offspring but it is important to note that the passage emphasizes the greater significance of both climate ('air and ground') and virtue (which lies 'in the middle' possessed by the Spanish horse). Thus, the notion of inheritance at work is not dynastic or evolutionary but instead is conceived of as a momentary intervention in the present moment, intended to offset the environmental forces that will otherwise accelerate decline. Cavendish identifies innate virtue (possessed in relatively greater degree by the Spanish 'noble horse') as subject to the degenerative influence of climate. Both rider and breeder have responsibility, derived from their superior human agency, to well manage as

---

17   Fairfax, "Treatise", 1–2; York Minster Library MS Add 47.
18   Cavendish M., *Life of William Cavendish*, 67.

best they can what virtue the horse possesses. The goal of the rider is to elicit from the horse the greatest performance of which the horse is capable; the goal of the breeder is to prevent the decay to which the breed is subject in his climate. Cavendish's notion of horsemanship is fundamentally anthropocentric: it is the 'man' at the centre of the notion, who is responsible for preserving innate ability from decay and to elicit from that ability its finest expression; but the performance in neither case is democratic nor in pursuit of improvement.

Such a notion contrasts sharply with that advocated by Fairfax who counsels a practice of managed development over several generations in order to improve the breed, and in so doing reveals ideas very much at odds with the attitudes espoused by Cavendish. Referencing what he considers to have been an excellent multi-generational managed breeding practice in Friesland, he develops the notion of 'three descents', whereby mixtures that may 'not prove well in the first descent', yet if balanced with planned breedings to complement the previous mixture may improve in such a way that 'in the third Descent they will be the most useful Horses in the world... having made your Race thus perfect you may for many Descents breed of the most perfect of them and have better and better Horses'.[19] Where Fairfax writes of 'laying a good foundation', of developing a breed in several descents, Cavendish's ideas are much more oriented toward maintain a balanced midpoint that adheres to the middle way—'where virtue lies'—and warns against the tendency to degeneration that he argues is natural and inevitable:

> I must tell you, that you must never have a *Stallion* of your own Breed, because they are too far removed from the Purity, and Head, of the Fountain, which is a pure *Spanish Horse*: Besides, should the Stallions be of your own Breed, in three or four Generations they would come to be Cart-Horses; so gross, and ill-favoured would they be: or at least, just such *Horses* as are bred in that Country, so soon will they degenerate: Therefore, have still a fresh *Spanish Horse* for the Stallion. (1667: 92–93)

Neither Fairfax nor Cavendish use 'breed' here in quite the sense we use today, but, of the two, Fairfax's concept is much closer to our own than Cavendish's, imagining that the proper mixture of humoral influences may bring about an improvement that in several generations may achieve a 'perfection' that will breed on in future generations. Both work from within a concept that humours and climate have determinate force; when they speak of horses, they do so in terms of national derivation, but the notion of nation is less our modern idea

---

19   Fairfax, "Treatise", 6. See Nash, "Gentlemen's Recreations" for an extended discussion of Fairfax's theories of improvement.

of a political state than of a specific geographically-fixed, climate-determined national character. 'Breed', in this context, refers principally to the work of the man, who selects and matches the individuals of his stud, so one would have horses who might be of 'Fairfax's breed' or 'Cavendish's breed'; and those, in turn, would be either of mixed or pure national derivation, at the judgment of Fairfax and Cavendish respectively. The selection of the stallion here is important for bringing imported hot blood to the females, who belong to the northern climate of England, which is why Cavendish specifies that the Spanish stallion is best 'for our island' ('The best *Stallion* in our Island, is, a well shap'd *Spanish* Horse'): it brings the necessary heat while remaining closest to the middle way that avoids the faults of other climates. And because the mares will always remain cold, that Spanish stallion must not be allowed to cool himself' but be repeatedly replaced with a 'fresh' successor.[20]

This divergence of approaches between these two marks a fundamental divide at the early modern origin of the equestrian sports of horse racing and dressage. While Cavendish's doctrines of horsemanship in the riding school remain influential with riders today, the sport itself is not attached to any one particular breed identity. Horse racing, on the other hand, continues to imagine the athletic competition as testing an ongoing experiment in breed improvement. The two sports articulate complementary versions of animal-human partnership, each of which may be considered either paradoxical or logically inconsistent with itself. In dressage, the performative union of horse and human that Mattfield elsewhere in this volume describes as the centaur identity to which Cavendish aspired, results, at least in Cavendish's doctrines, from a mutual performance of absolute political authority defining the relation of sovereign and subject. In horse racing, frequently designated as 'the sport of kings', the horse is the athlete at the centre of the sport. That horse is simultaneously granted a priority over his human partners and yet is identified as the product of a multi-generational system of human-managed breed improvement. To return to my original question of why Cavendish plays such a minor role in the history of the sport of kings that originates in his lifetime, my answer turns out to be that his ideology of sport is ultimately too monarchical for that sport, which flourished ultimately under the distinctly protestant ideology that unseated doctrines of absolute royalism in favour of a belief in managed improvement. If Cavendish's ideal of *manège* is to perform a seamless centaur identity where human and horse blend in a (anthropocentric) hybrid identity, that ideal ran counter to a complementary antlhropocentric quest for improvement that identified horses as athletic performers and humans as the agents of their improvement.

---

20   Edwards, *Horse and Man*, 112.

Select Bibliography

Cavendish Margaret, *The life of the thrice noble, high and puissant Prince William Cavendishe, Duke, Marquess and Earl of Newcastle* (London, A. Maxwell: 1667).

Cavendish William, *A new method, and extraordinary invention, to dress horses* (London, Thomas Milbourn: 1667).

Edwards P., *Horse and man in early modern England* (London: 2007).

Fairfax, Lord T., "Treatise Touching the Breeding of Horses", York Minster Library MS Add 47.

Mackay-Smith A., *Speed and the Thoroughbred* (Lanham, MD: 2000).

Major P., "'The Fire of his Eye': Thomas, 3rd Lord Fairfax's 'A Treatise Touching the Breeding of Horses'", *Modern Language Review*, 105, i (2010).

Markham G., *Cauelarice* (London, Edward White: 1607).

Muir J.B., *Ye Olde New-Markitt Calendar* (London: 1892).

Nash R., "'Beware a Bastard Breed': Notes Towards a Revisionist History of the Thoroughbred Racehorse", in Edwards P. – Enenkel K.A.E. – Graham E. (eds.), *The Horse as Cultural Icon: the Real and the Symbolic Horse in the Early Modern World* (Leiden: 2012).

Nash R., "Gentlemen's Recreation and Georgic Improvement: Lord Fairfax on Horse Breeding", in Hopper A. – Major P. (eds.), *England's Fortress: New Perspectives on Thomas, 3rd Lord Fairfax* (Farnham: 2014).

Prior C.M., *Early records of the thoroughbred horse: Containing reproductions of some original stud-books, and other papers . . .* (London: 1924).

Prior C.M., *The royal studs of the sixteenth and seventeenth centuries: Together with a reproduction of the Second Earl of Godolphin's Stud Book* (London: 1935).

Raber K., "'Reasonable Creatures': William Cavendish and the Art of Dressage", in Fumerton P. – Hunt S. (eds.), *Renaissance Culture and the Everyday*. (Philadelphia: 1999).

Russell N., *Like Engend'ring Like: Heredity and Animal Breeding in Early Modern England* (Cambridge: 1986).

Temple Sir W., "Essay on the Advancement of Trade in Ireland (1673)", *Miscellanea* (London, Edward Gellibrand: 1680).

CHAPTER 15

William Cavendish's Horsemanship Treatises and Cultural Capital

Karen Raber

In his 1799 *Analysis of Horsemanship*, John Adams 'lament[s] the want of authors in our own language to assist my pursuit'. Adams has heard about the work of William Cavendish, Duke of Newcastle, but he claims to have only ever seen 'a voluminous edition' of it: 'From the number of size of the plates, it must have been too costly a book for general use; and from the superfluous number of prints, and great expence [sic] of the work, his Grace wrote it for his own amusement, and published it for the gratification of his friends only'.[1] Adams trained cavalry in Edinburgh with enough success that he was appointed Riding Master of Angelo Tremamondo's school of horsemanship,[2] and so was likely thinking of the limited access his pupils might have to such works. Is the disappearence of Cavendish's great horsemanship treatises from circulation among readers of less exalted—and moneyed—status a real consequence of their expensive design? Or were they, as Adams also proposes, never really meant for a broad group of horsemen at all, designed instead as a kind of private pleasure, circulated within a noble coterie, to be appreciated for their aesthetic, rather than their practical value? In other words, when Cavendish published *La Méthode Nouvelle* in exile in 1658 and an English version, *A New Method*, in 1667 after his return home, to what end, and for what audience, were they published?[3]

Numerous critics have argued (myself included) that these texts were part of Cavendish's recuperation of reputation and status through his favourite élite

---

1   Adams John, *Analysis of Horsemanship* (Cadell and Davies, 1799) viii.

2   *A series of original sketches and caricature etchings by the late John Kay, with biographical sketches and illustrative anecdotes* (usually simplified as *Kay's Originals*), Vol. 1 (Edinburgh: 1877) 410.

3   When citing Cavendish's 1658 version, *La méthode nouvelle et invention extraordinaire de dresser les chevaux* Antwerp (Antwerp, Jacques van Meurs: 1658), I have used the 2000 facsimile edition of J. Brindley's English version of 1743, entitled *A General System of Horsemanship* (London: 2000) When referring in the text to one or other manual, the page number for information from the 1658 version will be that of the 1743 reprint with the suffix 'L' to denote the particular publication used.

© KONINKLIJKE BRILL NV, LEIDEN, 2017 | DOI 10.1163/9789004326217_017

pursuit, the *manège* training of the horse. Elspeth Graham has beautifully summarized the 'compensatory' function of horsemanship for Cavendish: 'It served to occupy him, to shore up his identity, to mark out a transformed version of his aristocratic role and, it can be argued, provide an arena in which he sought to heal his emotional or psychological wounds'.[4] In his *New Method*, Cavendish describes the many noble and even royal visitors during his exile on the continent, who provided an audience for his accomplishments, naming among them Don John of Austria, the Duke of Aarschot, the Marquis of Cerralvo, the Marquis of Caracena, the Prince of Condé, the Landgrave of Hesse'in short, representatives of England's competitor nations, who are all uniformly amazed at Cavendish's skill, and the achievements of his mounts. Don John specifically requests a copy of Cavendish's book on horsemanship, 'before it was printed' and 'receive[s] it with great Satisfaction' when it is presented to him. (1667: B1v) 'My own private Riding-House' in Antwerp, writes Cavendish, 'though very large, was often so full that my Esquier, Captain Mazin, had hardly room to ride'. (1667: C2v) Horsemanship affirms a noble identity that rises above national boundaries, allowing Cavendish to illustrate his worthiness in 'a sublime reassertion of identity'.[5]

But, to publish texts on horsemanship is a different thing than to practise one's skills, or even to opine on horsemanship privately. Had he wished merely to circulate his thoughts and expertise among his own rank, Cavendish need not have put his ideas in print—coterie circulation was a long-established practice that allowed aristocrats to gain an audience without the taint of commerce. When Don John presses for a copy of *La méthode nouvelle* before its publication, for instance, Cavendish indicates that coterie circulation of the manuscript might well have satisfied his need to redress his humiliation in war and his sufferings in exile. Cavendish had a hand in other published works (having collaborated with Shirley on several plays that eventually appeared in print)[6] and was clearly not morally opposed to publication in all cases, but his incursion into the world of print treatises on horsemanship was a very different kind of cultural event. Publishing not only interjected Cavendish into an

---

4   Graham E., "The Duke of Newcastle's 'Love [...] For Good Horses': And Exploration of
     Meanings", in *The Horse as Cultural Icon*, 43.
5   Ibid., 50.
6   Cavendish's plays include *The Country Captain* (1649) and The *Varietie* (1649), as well as two
     post-war plays and collaborations on the works of his wife, Margaret Cavendish, which were
     also published. Unlike an earlier generation that would have seen publication as impossible
     for nobles, Cavendish's had more tolerance toward print culture, but with limits on acceptable genres.

ongoing print debate over training methods and made him a *teacher* of riding skills, rather than simply or only a great rider and trainer in his own right. The fact that Adams later singles him out by name might suggest that Cavendish belongs, at least in Adams's mind, to the ranks of English riding masters; but such men were often more directly materially compensated for their labour in passing along equestrian skills, something clearly untrue of Cavendish. Moreover, his remarks about the money he turns down for his horses suggests a profit motive would have been anathema to him. In the *New Method*, for instance, he announces 'as poor as I was, in those days, I made shift to buy' many horses; though the Duke of Guise offers 600 pistoles for a talented gray animal, Cavendish claims he would not have sold the horse at any price, not only because it was priceless, but 'besides I was then too great a Beggar, to think to be made Rich by the Sale of a Horse' (1667: C1v–C2r). Placing his transactions well outside the exchange of mere gold coins, Cavendish parlays his 'beggary' in to a sign of his appreciation of the true value of his art.

Horsemanship treatises had once been the preserve of noble authors, but by the late seventeenth century, the makeup of what we might call a European equestrian community had already changed. Texts on riding were being authored by members of the middling classes, those with some claim to an expertise that could inform others usually based on their performance outside the world of print as equerries, riding masters, military instructors of cavalry or just amateur enthusiasts. As an indication of this shift, we might consider two early treatises, one by John Astley, the other by Thomas Blundeville. Blundeville was a widely educated and accomplished writer on several subjects, and although not of noble lineage, had close connections at court and among other humanists in London. His translation and redaction of Federigo Grisone's *Ordine di Cavalcare* in his *The Art of Ryding* (1560) inspires many of Cavendish's opposing opinions in the *New Method*. Astley was a well-connected courtier, who held several positions at the court of Henry VIII; as a Gentleman Pensioner he travelled to the continent and was exposed to the new riding practices of the Italian masters, which informs his work, also called *The Art of Riding* (1584).[7] By contrast, the years at the turn of the sixteenth and seventeenth centuries saw the incursion of non-élite authors into the field. Gervase Markham, for instance, rose only to the rank of captain in the army,

---

7   Astley is mentioned in Roger Ascham's *The Scholemaster* (London, John Daye: 1570) dining at court with William Cecil and other luminaries, 'Of which number, the most part were of hir Maiesties most honourable priuie Counsell, and the reast serving hir in verie good place' (B1r). Astley's fellow Gentleman Pensioner, Thomas Bedingfield, translated Claudio Corte's *Il Cavallerizzo* (1573) also entitled *The Art of Riding* (London, H. Henman: 1584).

and offered his thoughts on horsemanship as part of an authorial canon that was mainly directed at the middling sort. His *A Discourse of Horsemanship* (1593) announces in its title that it is 'a more easie and direct course for the ignorant', while one of the many editions of *Countrey Contentments* (1615) promises to allow its readers to break and ride 'great horses in very short time'. While Markham professes a knowledge of Grisone's writings, he offers little in the way of *manège* instruction, focusing rather on breeding, hunting, racing, farriery and other forms of interactions with horses that are not so exclusive in nature. When David R. Lawrence observes that English horsemanship treatises, although abundant in the early seventeenth century, were by the century's end no longer giving the kind of instruction in training horses for war, what he is registering is the decrease in emphasis on the *manège* skills in works like those by Markham, Michael Baret's *An Hipponomie, or the Vineyard of Horsemanship* (1618), William Browne's *The Arte of Riding the Great Horse* (1625), or others like them.[8]

Cavendish by birth would have been averse to being perceived to circulate in the milieu of authors like Markham, who wrote for a wide popular audience, and clearly would have been loath to be perceived as demystifying or even eliminating the need for the *manège* arts in his own works. And yet he did choose to publish, rather than merely circulate his books among his own class. In this essay I will argue that in fact Cavendish engages with a print culture of riding instruction manuals in order to further a particular agenda, one that involves the creation, preservation and transmission of what we have come, thanks to the work of social anthropologist Pierre Bourdieu, to call 'cultural capital.[9] Further, I will track the unintended consequences of attempts like Cavendish's to intervene in the tradition of publication of horsemanship treatises, consequences evident in the very different place and content of riding texts in the later eighteenth century.

Making the Superior Rider

The idealized goal of nearly all riding manuals can be found in a broad array of early modern literary texts. In *The Countess of Pembroke's Arcadia*, for instance, Philip Sidney offers this description of Musidorus:

---

8   Lawrence D.R., *The Complete Soldier: Military Books and Military Culture in Early Stuart England, 1603–1645* (Leiden: 2009) 279.

9   Bourdieu P., "The Forms of Capital", in Richardson J.G. (ed.), *Handbook of Theory and Research for the Sociology of Education*, (New York: 1986).

But he, as if centaur-like he had been one piece with the horse, was no more moved than one is with the going of his own legs; and in effect so he did command him as his own limbs; for though he had both spurs and wand they seemed rather marks of sovereignty than instruments of punishment, his hand and leg with most pleasing grace commanding without threatening, and rather remembering than chastising... nor the horse did with any change complain of it; he ever going so just with the horse, either forthright or turning, that it seemed as he borrowed the horse's body, so he lent the horse his mind.[10]

Sidney, himself a consummate horseman, educated in the *manège* by the great Italian master Giovan Pietro Pugliano, summarizes the discipline's educated product—a horseman should accomplish the perfect union of rational, 'sovereign' human control, with equine power and grace. Thomas Blundeville translates the ideal into instruction in his *The Art of Riding* (1587): 'And see that you do not onelie sit him boldlie, and without fear, but also conceive with your selfe that he and you do make as it were but one bodie: and that you both have but one sense and one will'.[11] Likewise, John Astley's *Art of Riding* borrows the image of union and harmony: horsemanship allows 'these two severall bodies [to] seem in all their actions and motions to be as it were but one onlie bodie'.[12] In contrast, Edmund Spenser's *Faerie Queene* (1594) gives us Braggadochio, who betrays his cowardice, vanity and weakness when he steals and tries to ride Guyon's mount:

> So to his steed he got, and gan to ride,
> As one vnfit therefore, that all might see
> He had not trayned bene in cheualree.
> Which well that valiant courser did discerne;
> For he despysd to tread in dew degree,
> But chaufd and fom'd, with courage fierce and sterne,
> And to be easd of that base burden still did erne.[13]

Sidney and Spenser confirm that training in 'cheualree' is essential if one wants to produce a recognizably fit rider, and each passage suggests that knowledge

---

10   Sidney Sir Philip, *The Countess of Pembroke's Arcadia*, (ed.) Evans M. (London: 1977) 248.

11   Blundeville Thomas, *The Arte of Rydynge* (London, Willyam Seres: 1561) 5.

12   Astley John, *The Art of Riding* (London, Henry Denham: 1580) 5.

13   Edmund Spenser, *The Faerie Queene*, (ed.) Roche T.P. Jr. (London & New York: 1987) II.iii. 48–54.

of that art cannot be distinguished or extracted from the individual's birth, breeding and innate character, so that Musidorus's nobility manifests in his (learned) skill, while Braggadochio's inherent 'baseness' shows up in his lack of such training. However, 'breeding' is a word that disguises a complex set of ideas, since it refers simultaneously to birth (inborn qualities) and education (superimposed qualities). Naturalizing equestrian skills as an inherently aristocratic quality, inbred and therefore unappropriable, turns out to be difficult, even impossible. Horsemanship treatises, which must confront head-on the gap between origin and education, suggest that the 'one-ness' of horse and rider is the product of physical ability and moral virtue (Blundeville's requirement of 'boldness'), yes, but also necessarily of education.

Horsemanship treatises emphasize the need to access the highest levels of the discipline in order to become a 'natural' rider, something that is implicitly available only to those with extensive funds, ability to travel and *entrée* into the society of continental courts. As Elizabeth Tobey notes, the great Italian masters were numerous, and engaged in a veritable *diaspora* during the sixteenth century (a remarkable twenty-eight emigrated to France alone, with others taking up positions in England, Flanders and Spain).[14] Cavendish's *A New Method* acknowledges the influence of the great Italian, Federigo Grisone, whose establishment at Naples was where 'This Noble Art was first begun': Grisone 'writ like a Horse-man, and a great Master in the Art for those times: Henry the Eight sent for two Italians that were his Schollars, to come to him into England ... and their Schollars fill'd the Kingdom with Horse-men'. (1667: 1–2). Those who did not have local access to a great master of the art travelled to a court that did. Even Nicholas Morgan, although his treatise is not directed primarily at the *manège*, argues that the noblest aspirant to the art must nevertheless submit to the 'direction of a perfect schoolemaister', lest he develop too many bad habits. Discussing the movement called the capriole, Morgan insists 'I would not haue you begin any lesson, but by the direction of a perfect schoolemaister' and ... be sure to be alwaies present at the excercises of the most skilfull Horsemen'. To this sentence, which indicates that the *manège* is best learned directly from the great masters, Morgan adds, 'and ... read the best writers'.[15] In this coda, then, Morgan hints at the complicated role of the horsemanship treatise in preserving, transmitting and confirming the association of *manège* riding with birth and breeding. Like Castiglione's *The Courtier*, which itself makes horsemanship a crucial skill for the nobleman, Morgan's and other authors' horsemanship treatises promise something they

14   Tobey E., "The Legacy of Federigo Grisone", in *The Horse as Cultural Icon*, 147.
15   Morgan Nicholas, *The Perfection of Horse-manship* (London, Edward White: 1609) 209.

are never entirely comfortable delivering: a way for aspirant, and potentially non-élite, riders to study the art. Treatise writers like Cavendish, who want to use the discipline to shore up aristocratic claims to superiority have trouble conceding that anyone other than a nobly born rider could profit from such instruction, since that would defeat the discipline's function of displaying and legitimizing regimes of blood and birth. But, at the same time, a completely closed system, in which one is simply born with horsemanship in one's blood, would not enable equestrian skill to function as a form of circulating wealth, and so would prevent it from acting to compensate someone like Cavendish for the loss of real power and financial status.[16] The balance point of this paradox comes in the all-important concept of 'schooling' as an analogue, but also a substitute, for 'breeding'.

A brief look at instructions aimed at producing the best position in the rider reveal the degree to which what early moderns would call 'breeding' works. Antoine Pluvinel, Cavendish's precursor at the French court, offers this description of the rider's seat and bearing:

> He must sit only in the centre of the saddle, taking care not to touch the cantle out of fear of falling. At all times must he sit straight in the saddle as if he were standing on the ground. His two shoulders must be bent slightly and equally forward, his stomach thrust forward, making a slight hollow at the waist. His two elbows must, at all times, be placed parallel, and without constraint, slightly away from the body. The right fist must be close to the left one, at a distance of about four or five fingers from each other.... The legs must be thrust forward, the end of the foot pressing firmly in the stirrup; the knees must, as always, be squeezed with all one's strength so that, should the horse become animated, he does not throw my ass [*mon âne*], I mean my man, to the ground.[17]

Pluvinel's account is lavish in minute details—the slight hollow at the waist, the five-finger space between hands—that belie the reality of a moving animal beneath this carefully constructed monument of exactitude. The threat of being dumped on the ground testifies to the importance of holding position, since any jot of departure from its strictures results in the physical, and

---

16   Bourdieu notes that while economic capital is 'at the root of all the other types of capital', they 'produce their most specific effects only to the extent that they conceal (not least from their possessors) the fact that economic capital is at their root'; "Forms of Capital", 252.

17   Antoine Pluvinel, *Le Maneige Royal*, transl. Hilda Nelson (London: 1989), 26.

metaphysical, lowering of the rider. Nicholas Morgan describes the 'perfect rider', whose 'noble nature' is conveyed by his imperviousness to pain and fear, and who must wed 'naturall gifts of true valoure, wisdome and temperance' to 'true knowledge and practice'.[18] Once he has achieved this blend of physically inbred *and* learned qualities, the perfect horseman, 'so ballanced ... floats steadfastly in the midst of all tempests'.[19]

We might see in the convergence of physical training, moral values and assumptions about the importance of things like balance, control and upright-ness, a case of what Bourdieu would call '*habitus*', the production of an accom-plished, graceful body by specific social and cultural forces so that it can be said to possess 'capital', or a kind of wealth that is not accounted for in tradi-tional economic criticism: 'This embodied capital, external wealth converted into an integral part of the person, into a *habitus*, cannot be transmitted instantaneously (unlike money, property rights, or even titles of nobility) by gift or bequest, purchase or exchange', because it inheres in the bodily carriage, in specific cultivated postures, in the muscle memory of an individual.[20] But it is no less a demonstration of entitlement and status than rich clothing or other outward signs on the body. Training the horseman's body to perfection involves lengthy practice on horseback, with constant correction, until the movement of the animal is so naturally accounted for that the rider's position does not change unless deliberately made to do so—in other words, the rider 'floats steadfastly in the midst of all tempests' because he has fully internal-ized the nuances and details of Pluvinel's description so that they have become 'natural'.

In *La méthode nouvelle* Cavendish had described exactly the same physi-cal 'seat' for the rider: he 'ought to sit upright upon the twist, and not upon the buttocks ... he ought to advance as much as he can, towards the pommel, leaving a hand's breath between his backside and the arch of the saddle, hold-ing his legs perpendicular ... and his kneed and thighs turned inwards towards the saddle'. (1743L: 29) The description goes on for a page, giving details about everything from eyes to toes. But in the *New Method* he oddly insists, against what he considers the 'ignorant' opinion, that a horseman who is thrown off his horse is not less of a horseman for that. 'For Good Horse-men little think of *Sitting*, and so may be Surprised, their Thoughts being all how to make their Horses go Well, and never doubt Throwing'. (1667: 15). Above and beyond

---

18   *Perfection of* horsemanship, 166.

19   Ibid., 165.

20   Bourdieu, "Forms of Capital", pp. 244–45; see also Pierre Bourdieu, *Distinction: A Social Critique of the Judgement of Taste*, transl. Richard Nice (Cambridge, MA: 1984) 168–220.

previous writers, Cavendish establishes that maintaining the seat while in motion in order to produce better gaits in the horse is a superior goal to merely sitting well on horseback: 'Thus you see, That any Groom, or Tinker, may Sit, and yet be no Horse-man, which is a Greater Business than only Sitting'. (1667: 16) By raising the physical stakes for the 'true' horseman, Cavendish not only increases the cultural capital involved in demonstrations of *habitus*, but neatly locates other treatise authors as inferior to himself because of their emphasis on a static body, and their fear of a fall. Pluvinel's joke about his 'ass' taking a tumble (maintaining a good seat so that 'should the horse become animated, he does not throw my ass ... I mean my man, to the ground') is thus parlayed into a sign of Pluvinel's lower status among riding masters.

Bourdieu outlines his theory of cultural capital in his 1979 *Distinction: A Social Critique of the Judgement of Taste*, and most cogently in his 1986 essay 'The Forms of Capital'. He observes that individuals participate in a game of cultural investment and acquisition that resembles, but is not identical with, economic capitalism. Cultural capital is 'embodied' or manifested through 'dispositions of the mind and body', 'objectified' in cultural goods and 'institutionalized' in a form that has relative autonomy, and thus can redress some of the limits of biology in cultural capital's embodied form.[21] Cultural capital, Bourdieu argues, is part of the apparatus that reproduces class distinctions and, thereby, forms of social domination; cultural capital makes that domination seem inevitable, eternal and transparent. While it is true that Bourdieu's theories, because they involve a historically specific economics, are generally applied to examples from the nineteenth and twentieth centuries, it is, I think, fair to say that the roots of cultural capital are already evident in changes that mark the century in which Cavendish wrote. We should see in his insistence on a network of noble peers, his celebration of his horses' transcendent value, his discussions of embodied character and his participation in the creation of an educational 'system' evidence of something that will later emerge as cultural capital.

When Cavendish engages in his compensatory activity, *manège* riding, while in exile, he ensures that his reputation will circulate among the great and noble of Europe; when he publishes an instructional treatise on riding and training, he enters into a wider social relationship that not only includes all the great riders and riding masters of his era but also any and every reader with an interest in *manège* riding. These efforts are necessary to Cavendish's ability to demonstrate cultural capital. As Bourdieu puts it, 'The reproduction of social capital presupposes an unceasing effort of sociability,

---

21   Bourdieu, "Forms of Capital", 243; see also, Bourdieu, *Distinction*, 11–96.

a continuous series of exchanges in which recognition is endlessly affirmed and reaffirmed'.[22] But, as we will see, the circulation of those exchanges through the medium of print publication significantly changes the consequences of this form of reproduction.

Schools of Thought

For Bourdieu, educational institutions are important and complex participants in the creation and circulation of cultural capital:

> The objectification of cultural capital in the form of academic qualifications is one way of neutralizing some of the properties it derives from the fact that, being embodied, it has the same biological limits as its bearer. This objectification is what makes the difference between the capital of the autodidact, which may be called into question at any time, or even the cultural capital of the courtier, which can yield only ill-defined profits, of fluctuating value, in the market of high-society exchanges, and the cultural capital academically sanctioned by legally guaranteed qualifications, formally independent of the person of their bearer. With the academic qualification, a certificate of cultural competence which confers on its holder a conventional, constant, legally guaranteed value with respect to culture, social alchemy produces a form of cultural capital which has a relative autonomy *vis-à-vis* its bearer and even *vis-à-vis* the cultural capital he effectively possesses at a given moment in time.[23]

The institutions Bourdieu describes are recognizable as belonging to the nineteenth and twentieth centuries; no comparable education system existed for Cavendish's England. Yet Cavendish's horsemanship treatises do imagine a scholarly community, with rules for entrance, exchangeable value in the credentials gained and a capacity to transcend immediate, bodily limits via the persistence of print. The 'ill-defined profits' of the courtier are indeed realized in the individual stories of European riding masters, but those who wrote treatises, while they may not have profited financially from their writing, certainly profited in a manner early moderns prized: in reputation and fame. Education, whether gained within a family during childhood or gained later in pursuit of official qualifications for a profession, plays a significant role in the process

---

22   Bourdieu, "Forms of Capital", 250; as Bourdieu notes, social capital reinforces the limits of
      the group in these exchanges.

23   Ibid., 248.

of institutionalizing cultural capital, taking what is otherwise heavily masked hereditary transmission and objectifying it through 'performative magic', to legitimize the individual's claims to 'culture'.[24] Indeed, here I want to seize on the two words that appear in Cavendish's two treatise titles, and which distinguish them from others in the period: 'method' and 'system', unlike 'art', actually articulate an idea about education and instruction that begins to establish reproducibility, which in turn will eventually make possible the institutionalization of riding instruction.

Cavendish, like other such writers, enters a debate about the best practices of horsemanship, and announces his own text as substantially different from any that had come before. In so doing, he treads a careful path between acknowledging those among his precursors and contemporaries he wishes to claim as his peers, and denigrating their methods. In his first account, *La Méthode Nouvelle*, he refers only to 'several horsemen', who have 'blotted more paper to demonstrate their Natural Philosophy than their art in Horsemanship', lumping them all together as a nameless, indistinguishable group. (1743L: 19) By 1667 he was more specific, singling out two of them, Federigo Grisone and Thomas Blundeville, who had redacted Grisone's *Gli Ordine di Cavalcare*, from among the host of prior authors. We have seen that Cavendish names Grisone for having 'writ like a Horse-man, and a great Master in the Art for those times'. The emphasis, however, is 'for those times', times that Cavendish wants to supersede, and thus Grisone the master becomes 'Old Grisone' later in his work (1667: 17). But, poor Blundeville gets worse treatment: he does not 'understand' curvets, he 'is deceived' about riding in the Turkish fashion, his 'Bitts are very ridiculous' and his comments on marks and 'elements' are 'false and ridiculous lies' (1667: 18–20, 28).[25] Bourdieu points out that disputes over how a sport or an art is practised are almost always translations of social differences into the specific logic of the field.[26] By casting these very few of his competitors as his only precursors, Cavendish erases the contributions of the *hoi polloi* (Markham and his ilk), thereby elevating the art of the *manège* above their relevance. By castigating them as old ridiculous liars, Cavendish ensures that their mastery seems obsolete. But by inserting his 'method' or 'system' into the mix of treatises, Cavendish signals a sea change in what the 'art' of the *manège* is or can be to individual practitioners by emphasizing its reproducibility for any informed (that is, by his writings) rider.

---

24   Bourdieu, "Forms of Capital", 248.

25   Because he was then writing for an English readership it is not surprising that Blundeville, whose manuals were still favoured by his compatriots, was singled out for particular attack.

26   Bourdieu, *Distinction*, 211.

Again joining other authors of horsemanship treatises, Cavendish borrows the language of schools, scholars and schooling to describe the roles of the rider and trainer—and sometimes of the horse as well. The connections between the schooling of human students and the education of the *manège* horse have been abundantly remarked by scholars from diverse fields.[27] The tendency of horsemanship treatise authors to borrow language and imagery from human education speaks to the convergence of ideals and techniques in these two fields. At the same time that Milton, for example, was dismantling and reorganizing the practice and purpose of human education on the premise that previous systems had incorrect goals and counterproductive methods, horsemen like Cavendish were doing the same with the *manège*. To make children fit and 'godly' citizens, Milton advocates doing away with the remnants of Scholasticism:

> And for the usual method of teaching Arts, I deem it to be an old errour of Universities not yet well recover'd from the Scholastick grossness of barbarous ages, that in stead of beginning with Arts most easie, and those be such as are most obvious to the sence, they present their young unmatriculated Novices at first comming with the most intellective abstractions of Logick and Metapysicks: So that they having but newly left those Grammatick flats and shallows where they stuck unreasonably to learn a few words with lamentable construction, and now on the sudden transported under another climate to be tost and turmoil'd with their unballasted wits in fadomless and unquiet deeps of controversie, do for the most part grow into hatred and contempt of Learning, mockt and deluded all this while with ragged Notions.[28]

---

27   Erica Fudge has observed that the overlap of training methods between children's education and the advanced training of the horse challenged the division of species based on the capacity for reason. Although early modern writers insisted that humans at any age were distinct from animals because born with a rational soul, the necessity of training children, even forcing them to feats of rote memorization to inculcate religious and moral responses, could raise the 'dangerous possibility that being born with a rational soul is not enough, that there is something more required than the mere possession of this essence of the human': Fudge E, *Brutal Reasoning: Animals, Rationality, and Humanity in Early Modern England* (Ithaca, NY: 2006) 49. Fudge points out that when Nicholas Morgan compares the young horse to a 'young Scholler', whom the rider instructs in the same order as a 'discreete Schoole-maister, that teacheth Children to write', the potential slippage from horse to human requires that an emphatically a priori distinction be established between species, however suspect or unstable it might prove (p. 138).

28   Milton John, *Of Education* (London, for Thomas Underhill: 1644) 2.

Nicholas Morgan compares the study of horsemanship to an education in the law that progresses sensibly, not unlike Milton's idea of logical building blocks to knowledge: 'If a Gentleman endeavor to be learned in the Laws of this Kingdome, doth he not first come to an Inne of chauncerie, and there continue one year or two to learne the Lawe, French, and to read bookes fit for a young student, and then goe to an Inne of Court, and must painefully study eight or nine yeares before he be called to the bar?'[29] 'How then shall it be possible', continues Morgan, 'for a Gentleman to attain perfection in so honorable and difficult an Arte as Horsemanshippe without many yeares study and practice?'[30]

In a significant elision, Cavendish refers equally to the horse as a scholar, alongside the student/ rider, who learns the art of *manège* riding from his instructor. He criticizes riders who are 'always beating their scholars with the switch or long staff . . . Such behaviour . . . alienates the affections of their scholars'. (1743L: 18). Like Milton, Cavendish invokes medieval scholasticism to denigrate those who opine based on no real experience. He repeatedly contrasts his more rational, forward-thinking, scientific system with 'mere scholasticisim', occasionally using the term to describe what we might call armchair experts, those who form their false theories out of thin air. Many theoretical pretenders, who have written treatises or offered their views at court, are particularly guilty on the subject of the *horse* as scholar, insisting that a jade is a jade from birth, and cannot be reformed by any amount of education:

> What makes scholasticks degrade horses so much, proceeds (I believe) from nothing else than but the small knowledge they have of them, and from a persuasion that they themselves know every thing. They fancy they talk pertinently about them, whereas they know no more than they earn by riding a hackney-horse from the University of London, and back again. If they studied them as horsemen do, they would talk otherwise . . . This puts me in mind of what the great and excellent doctor Earle says in his characters, that a scholar and a horse are very troublesome to one another; and so I leave them, without giving them or myself any farther trouble. (1743L: 13)

Cavendish insists that these 'scholasticks', or armchair experts, are merely 'jealous' of their 'rational empire' (1743: 13), an empire of belief, a school of thought,

---

29   Morgan, *Perfection of Horse-manship*, 43.
30   Morgan, *Perfection of Horse-manship*, 43.

that they defend against innovative practitioners.[31] We might expect the use of a term like 'empire' to apply to the domain of human dominion, gained through the exercise of reason, thus demarcating the proper realm of human control and authority. But, what Cavendish does with it here is a bit different: he uses the word to detach those without practical experience of horses and riding from actual control over both the animals themselves, and over the abstract field of knowledge they seem to defend. In the name of an essentially conservative defence of aristocratic distinction, and in the interests of liberating the equine, as well as the human, scholar from the irrational prejudices of élite (but ignorant) horsemen, Cavendish thus denigrates 'scholasticks' for lacking rightful (human) dominion over the animal kingdom, ruling instead over an empire of airy nothing. His methods are in contrast 'good lessons, well applied to the nature, spirits, and strength of every horse, that the great and subtle science of Horsemanship consists'. (1743L: 27). What Cavendish does with horses and humans is to link them through their capacity to learn. One consequence of this is that the character and education of the man (the rider) can then be discerned through the horse, much as the old centaur imagery suggested. Another consequence, however, is that Cavendish locates his own methods among competing, but unequally informed, 'schools of thought' that can best be distinguished by their results in the action, rather than the theory, of riding. Such a position ought to link Cavendish's treatises to physical, material schools of riding, a problematic move.

Traditions of horsemanship in the sixteenth and seventeenth centuries were more frequently being passed on through the creation of material, even architectural, 'schools' for the practice of the *manège*: the kind of riding academies that the Italian travelling riding masters were being invited to run at courts around Europe. For instance, Grisone, GianBattista Pignatelli and Cesare Fiaschi were founding figures of what is sometimes called the 'Naples School' (both a physical location and a set of practices), and Pignatelli's student, Pluvinel, founded L'Academie d'Equitation in France in 1594, where in addition to horsemanship, accomplishments of noblemen like dancing and fencing were taught. Cavendish himself came as close to running such a riding 'school' as would have been acceptable for a titled aristocrat, both in his riding house at Welbeck and at the one he temporarily inhabited at Antwerp. Whereas the Italian masters and Pluvinel could claim dozens, perhaps hundreds, of students, the only pupils we can now name after Cavendish's lifetime of riding are Charles II and his equerry, Captain Mazin. But, although

---

31   Cavendish is referring to Descartes; in this passage he is rebuking those who think horses cannot reason.

manège riding is clearly associated with noble traits and character, the *instruction* of others in its nuances has more complex associations. One the one hand, Cavendish was riding master and tutor to the young Charles II, roles entirely compatible with his position at the time as Marquis of Newcastle; on the other hand, high office and the education of a prince were a good distance from the daily instruction of assorted riders from various ranks in a practical discipline. The status of the great riding masters is difficult to pin down—Tobey compares them to the famous dancing masters of the time—but whether they were perceived as mere 'gentlemen' or fully 'noble' is sometimes ambiguous. What is less so is the fact that Cavendish stood outside this group by rank alone, even if in exile his economic circumstances might well have been much worse than those of itinerant instructors.

I argue that we should view the ways Cavendish's treatises harp on his method's relationship to scholarly practices of the time, comparing the training of both horse and rider to formal education, as borrowing the cultural and institutional authority of actual schools, and applying it to the imaginary one constituted by his readers. Like nearly all authors in the field, Cavendish must assert that the art of dressage is *not* simply innate and so untrainable in either humans or horses: in other words, Cavendish needs to demystify and denaturalize his art in order to make it a transmissible science. He observes that while a certain degree of talent is desirable in both parties, it is the process of *going to school* that makes the horseman and the horse true examples of the discipline. 'The horse is dress'd in the same manner that children are taught', he says, that is by habit, repetition, and rational understanding of the tasks they are learning (1743: 11). Cavendish scoffs at those who, in contrast to the well-schooled *manège* rider, think that merely riding a lot makes him a true horseman: any 'post-Boy' can ride a hundred miles in a day, and any 'hunts-boy' can jump ditches; above all, he says, 'I have seen many Wenches ride astride and gallop and run their horses that could, I think hardly Ride a Horse Well in the Mannage'. (1667: 46–47) Only a very specific inculcation in the art itself qualifies the master to speak authoritatively on the subject of horsemanship.

Cavendish's strategy is linked not only to his own changed circumstances during exile but also to the sweeping transformation of social and cultural systems that attended the Civil Wars and their aftermath in England. Along with the destruction of estates, woods, pastures and buildings, came the destruction of customs, assumptions and rituals that had defined the pre-war world; the casualties included aristocratic faith in the links between family origin, wealth and virtuous behaviour. Horsemen had to adapt accordingly and to this end horsemanship treatise writers create and promulgate new standards by which to judge *manège* riding. Cavendish is no exception. He argues that it is

no longer enough to travel to a great European master to learn the art: he tells
the tale of a 'Great Master, held the most Excellent *Horse-man* beyond the Sea',
whose nephew, a product of the Master's 'New Method' cannot make a single
one of Cavendish's own horses go forward. (1667: 34–35). Neither will money
or time suffice:

> Are they not, in All *Trades*, bound *Apprentices* Seven and Nine Years; and
> *Many Bunglers* of them too? And, in Higher *Professions*, Twenty and Thirty
> Years is not too much, before they are *Great Masters* in any one of them:
> And though *Horse-manship* be the Hardest of All, yet *Many a Gentleman*
> will Ride the *First Day* as well as the *Greatest Master*; but he is Deceived,
> as well as those that think to *Buy*, with their *Money*, any *Quality*. (1667: 47)

Only the proper use of Cavendish's texts will make available secrets of the mystery of good horsemanship to a select, cultivated discriminating few, who will
attend Cavendish's 'school' of thought. About his method for producing the
'*terre à terre*' in a horse, he quips in a chapter heading, 'This Practice was a kind
of *Terra à Terra Incognita*, till I had attained it by studying'. (1743L: 48)[32]

It is a balancing act, opening the field of the *manège* to the perceptive few,
while guarding against its accessibility to hunts-boys, post-boys, wenches, and
all the great unwashed, who might aspire to it. Cavendish actually gives an
example of who might learn his system best: his own equerry, Captain Mazin,
whom he describes in language that collapses birth with 'breeding', instruction and physical internalization, horses with humans: 'I bred him from an
infant, and he thoroughly understood the manner of dressing horses according to my new method, which he has imbibed from my instruction'. (1743L: 28)
Mazin, who 'constantly attended me in my adversity' becomes the test case for
the transmissibility of Cavendish's method: 'For since I have invented this new
method, I have dressed under me myself, and under my ecuyer Captain Mazin,
very many horses in very little time; and I have never perceived nor seen that
Captain Mazin, by using this method, ever failed with any horses of any sort'.
(1743L: 67). 'Bred' to Cavendish's standards, Mazin is one of the select few with
the qualifications fully to appreciate and implement Cavendish's method. He
'imbibes' knowledge from the master, a term Cavendish uses to bypasses the
whole process of education as an intellectual exercise in favour of one that
privileges the body's natural functions. Though a servant, and therefore not
of Cavendish's noble status, he is superior among servants: 'I never found so
much love, fidelity and honesty in any other' (1667: 28). Captain Mazin or

---

32   More than one chapter includes 'secrets', either masked aids that come from the rider's
      seat (1667: 206), or unique insights Cavendish has acquired (1667: 254).

someone like him must exist for Cavendish's method to be presented as useful and communicable: if it cannot be learned or passed along, it reverts to the type of limiting aristocratic embodiment we saw in Sidney's and Spenser's idealized horsemen. But, the exemplary student cannot simply be everyman or the method fails as a means to reproduce claims to entitlement and privilege. In response to this paradoxical pressure, Cavendish finds the one noble servant, the extraordinary ordinary man, whose ability to reproduce the master's method is more like osmosis than rote learning, who osmotically internalizes a method that is dependent in equal parts on his own character and the system of the master who instructs him.

Appropriating Cultural Capital

Creating schools and methods, and printing manuals of advice to aspiring riders might successfully represent *manège* skills as a kind of cultural capital but they are strategies that make the exchanges involved in learning it a dangerously open, fluid social process, subject to appropriation by non-élite students, and thus a potentially uncontrollable product in changing social and economic conditions. The institutionalized forms of cultural capital are, in Bourdieu's analysis, strongly conservative and fairly static; yet the requirement for transmissibility brings with it some potential fissures: for instance, dispossessing the aristocratic family of its control over power and privilege, and so possibly influencing 'the choice of its legitimate heirs'.[33] As I've noted, making manège riding *something one does, not something one is* puts the conservative role of horsemanship in jeopardy.

And indeed, *manège* training in the century after Cavendish's treatises appear is on a long slow slide down from its pinnacle in the early to mid-seventeenth century. We see evidence of this in the work of the eighteenth century 'masters', among them François Robichon de La Guérinière, whose *L'École de la Cavalerie* (1729–31) references Cavendish as an important forerunner. Despite that tribute, Guérinière actually has very little to say about status or identity. He includes a brief introduction decrying the supposed decline of practice of his art in France, but he makes it clear that his main concern is the role of public taste in distorting its practice:

---

33 Bourdieu, "Forms of Capital", 254. This 'vulnerability' of institutional forms of cultural capital opens it to 'children of different sex and birth rank', thus diminishing a dominant élite's ability to reproduce itself without change, in Bourdieu's example, and to my mind explains the relative flexibility of cultural capital to reinvent itself in new historical moments.

All arts and sciences have principles and rules governing the methods resulting in those discoveries that lead to their perfection. The Cavalry is the only art for which it seems there is only need of practice; however, that only results in a forced and uncertain performance and a false brilliance that fascinates the demi-connoisseurs, who are often amazed by the horse's kindness, rather than by the rider's skill.[34]

Having only imitation to fall back on, aspiring riders either try to produce the brilliance they observe, and fall into the 'habit of continuously moving their hands and legs, which detracts from a rider's grace', and 'causes the horse to assume a false posture'; or else they try to imitate precision and accuracy, and so ruin a bold horse's courage. 'Still others', Guérinère continues, 'swept along by the supposed good taste of the public, whose decisions are not always from the oracles and against whom timid truth dares not revolt, find that after a lengthy and diligent pursuit, their only attainment is the flattering and chimeric satisfaction of thinking themselves more expert than the others'.[35]

Now Guérinère is clearly invested in the same function of horsemanship as cultural capital that Cavendish is, but his emphasis, unlike Cavendish's, is on resisting the role of 'public taste', which suggests that horsemanship is being transformed by influences outside its narrow cadre of masters. While Cavendish attacked scholastics and armchair experts, these were generally of a limited social range; Guérinère's public is a much broader, less defined group. His terminology and association of public display with issues of 'good taste' indicate that he is responding to the evolution of an eighteenth-century 'public sphere' that dictates standards of performance, discourse or accomplishment.[36] In the main, however, Guérinère's own focus is much more narrowly fixed on the techniques of riding and on the understanding of the physiology and treatment of disorders in horses. In other words, his treatise

---

34   de la Guérinère Francois Robichon, *The School of Horsemanship, Part II: The Method of Training Horses According to the Different Ways in Which They Will be Used* (translator unidentified (Cleveland Heights, OH: 1992) 1.

35   Ibid., 1.

36   I am suggesting that this offhand remark in the treatise provides evidence of the shift to a Habermasian public sphere, one which is seen (as for example Samuel Johnson emphatically does in so many of his works) as a source of controversy over what good 'taste' really is. From the language here, de la Guérinère glancingly and sarcastically acknowledges this new source of influence over horsemanship, turning the *manège* into something much more like Astley's later circus performances than Cavendish's showmanship on horseback for his noble visitors. See Habermas J., *The Structural Transformation of the Public Sphere—An Inquiry into a Category of Bourgeois Society*, transl. Thomas Burger (Cambridge, MA: 1991).

actually aids the transformation of horsemanship into mere technical virtuosity, which he perhaps imagines can escape the distortion of fashion. But, once truly turned into a simple, learnable system without the trappings of art and class, horsemanship's role as cultural capital erodes, while its potential function in generating economic capital is facilitated.

If we fast-forward a mere half-century, we meet one of the more colourful figures in the history of horsemanship treatises. In 1768 Philip Astley, formerly sergeant-major with General Elliott's Light Dragoons, exhibited afternoon performances of trick riding in a field at Lambeth as an advertisement for his riding school, which operated in the same location in the mornings. Later, Astley would build a large circular arena for his school and shows, and eventually a building known by his name in which he establishes the first circus. Astley, the son of a cabinetmaker, obtained his education, such as it was, through hands-on cavalry service during the Seven Years War, after which he turned his extraordinary riding skills into a commodity, one no longer linked to birth and status, moral fortitude, merit or even gender: according to one advertisement, his wife also appeared in his performances.[37] In other words, Astley completes the process Cavendish attempted to guard against, wrenching *manège* riding out of its role as cultural capital for an élite and into a new role as full-fledged money-making product. His invention of the circus, the massively public forum for his feats of horsemanship, realizes one implication of Guérinière's remarks above: the exposure of the art to the whims and fancies, to the 'tastes' of an undifferentiated public.

Astley also wrote two treatises on riding, but they seem an afterthought to a long and successful career profiting off his riding talents. His 1776 *The Modern Riding Master* dwells at inordinate length on how to mount the horse.[38] In contrast to Cavendish, who says 'I take it for granted that every one knows how to mount a horse', (1743L: 29), Astley clearly imagines a readership whose basic exposure to riding cannot be so taken for granted. The preface to his later, and longer, treatise, *Astley's System of Equestrian Education* (1802) specifically and exclusively associates good horsemanship with public amusement and entertainment, bragging that 'I have been able to improve the art of horsemanship, thereby furnishing a greater variety of Public Amusement, of higher

---

37   For this information, and a full account of Astley's use of horses on stage in the circus, see Saxon A.H., *Enter Foot and Horse* (New Haven: 1968) 10. Graham also offers an insightful discussion of how the circus relates to Cavendish's treatises, although from a very different perspective than mine: "Duke of Newcastle's 'Love'", 50–56.

38   Astley Philip, *The Modern Riding Master* (Philadelphia: Robert Aitken, 1776) 23–30. My thanks to Monica Mattfeld for pointing out this fact about Astley's earlier work, and for providing it, since it is not widely available.

entertainment and gratification to the Public'. He adds that good riding will
ensure that riders can safely continue to perform in circuses like his. When he
includes a section on the *manège* at the book's conclusion, he makes no effort
to instruct a rider but merely gives pictures and descriptions of the movements
of the airs above the ground, clearly not expecting that anyone would actually be performing these movements themselves. Instead Astley is 'educating'
the reader in how to recognize them, perhaps while attending the circus. Even
the military context of the more difficult *manège* movements has changed
drastically. Describing the croupade, a move in which the horse lifts all its feet
simultaneously in a leap, he offers this illustration of its military usefulness: 'In
patrolling, a soldier sometimes wants a guide, and gentle means often prove
ineffectual to induce a peasant to quit his bed'.[39] To dismount and knock on
the door, Astley notes, would be dangerous, and so, he turns his *manège* skills
to new use: 'I knew my duty, and ere this, my horse knew his. On approaching
the door, I caused him to strike it with his forefeet. And if this did not answer
my purpose ... I faced him about, when with his croup he would break the
door in pieces'.[40]

Astley, in short, is Cavendish's nightmare, someone who has transformed the arts of horsemanship, the title of horseman and the experience
of riding the advanced movements into consumable objects, circulated for
profit. The distinction between economic and cultural capital has collapsed
where the *manège* is concerned. Actual mounted military service, which
Cavendish repeatedly uses as an important defence against charges the
manège is useless, now is reduced and perverted, 'useful' only for the terror-
izing of peasants by breaking their doors with a horse's hooves. Otherwise,
what it does is furnish the technical credentials that allow Astley to charge the
ignorant public to come to see him ride, providing an entertaining spectacle
for an uninformed mass audience. Astley's *manège* is emptied of any inherent
cultural meaning or value, and thus no longer functions as the means to inculcate, transmit or confirm class differences.

Cavendish engaged in the authorship and publication of horsemanship treatises in order to participate in and shape a world in which the art of *manège*
riding could be deployed as cultural capital. But, the very nature of the process
by which this could be accomplished changed the place of the *manège*, opening its practice to those who could successfully master Cavendish's own system, making it more and more clearly a direct means to the accumulation and
circulation of economic capital. By turning an élite and mysterious art, defined
by the essence of a rider, into a transmissible system of instruction, Cavendish

---

39   Astley Philip, *Astley's System of Equestrian Education* (Dublin: Thomas Burnside, 1802) 177.
40   *Astley's System*, 177.

was establishing his own credentials as a worthy and noble practitioner concerned with protecting the prestige and relevance of his favourite pastime. But, because they appear at an important historical juncture, his treatises exemplify instead the unexpected instability of cultural capital's conservative function.

John Adams thought that Cavendish's treatises were printed only for circulation among his peers and became rare over time because of their expense; we might consider instead whether, as Bourdieu's analysis of education's detachment from individuals and biology hints, Cavendish's treatises simply succumbed to the effects of their own translation of *manège* riding into a system, a school, a method. Now unmoored from its origins in mystery and in concepts of noble birth and blood, *manège* riding—now called 'dressage'—withers in relative obscurity. It is divided into two public variations: on the one hand it is often experienced as a performance provided as public entertainment to an uneducated and undifferentiated audience by the riders of Vienna's Spanish Riding School (thus, exactly as Astley used it). Otherwise, it persists in the marginalized equestrian sport of dressage, whose 'cultural capital', if it has any at all, is sorely limited by the paucity of people and countries capable of claiming a significant awareness of the sport's nuances. In recent debates, spurred by the elimination of wrestling from future Summer Olympic games, dressage and equestrian sports were named almost uniformly by critics of the move as sports that merit inclusion far less: the association of dressage, in particular, with excessive expense, arcane costuming, irrelevance to modern athletes and incommunicability of its techniques and goals makes it a top contender for future omission.[41] *Manège* riding, far from Cavendish's dreams for it, now circulates mainly as a sign of economic capital; beyond that, it has ceased to be a useful marker of anything at all.

Selective Bibliography

Adams John, *Analysis of Horsemanship* (London: 1799).
Antoine Pluvinel, *Le Maneige Royal*, transl. Hilda Nelson (London: 1989).
Astley John, *The Art of Riding* (London, Henry Denham: 1580).
Astley Philip, *Astley's System of Equestrian Education* (Dublin: 1802).

---

41   For an example of this discourse, see ESPN's popular blog site: http://espn.go.com/blog/
     olympics/post/_/id/3623/five-olympic-sports-that-should-get-the-boot-before-wrestling;
     the fact that Anne Romney's horse Rafalca, won a slot at the 2012 Olympics only increased
     the sense among the public that the sport was for the 'top 1%' that she and her husband
     Mitt Romney belonged to rather than a sport whose enthusiasts include everyone from
     small children to middle class mums to members of the wealthy leisured class.

Astley Philip, *The Modern Riding Master* (Philadelphia: 1776).

Blundeville Thomas, *The Arte of Rydynge* (London: 1561).

Bourdieu P., "The Forms of Capital", in Richardson J.G. (ed.) *Handbook of Theory and Research for the Sociology.*

Bourdieu P., *Distinction: A Social Critique of the Judgement of Taste*, transl. Richard Nice (Cambridge, MA: 1984).

Bourdieu P., "The Forms of Capital", in Richardson J.G. (ed.), *Handbook of Theory and Research for the Sociology of Education*, (New York: 1986).

Claudio Corte. *Il Cavallerizzo* (1573) also entitled *The Art of Riding* (London, H. Henman: 1584).

De La Guériniere Francois Robichon, *The School of Horsemanship, Part II: The Method of Training Horses According to the Different Ways in Which They Will be Used* (translator unidentified (Cleveland Heights, OH: 1992).

Edmund Spenser, *The Faerie Queene*, ed. Roche T.P. Jr. (London & New York: 1987).

Edwards P. – Enenkel K. – Graham E. (eds.) *The Horse as Cultural Icon: The Real and the Symbolic Horse in the Early Modern World* (Leiden: 2012).

Fudge E., *Brutal Reasoning: Animals, Rationality, and Humanity in Early Modern England* (Ithaca: 2006).

Graham E., "The Duke of Newcastle's 'Love […] For Good Horses': An Exploration of Meanings", in Edwards – Enenkel – Graham E. (eds.) *The Horse as Cultural Icon: The Real and the Symbolic Horse in the Early Modern World* (Leiden: 2012).

Kay John, *A series of original sketches and caricature etchings by the late John Kay, with biographical sketches and illustrative anecdotes* (Edinburgh: 1877).

Lawrence D., *The Complete Soldier: Military Books and Military Culture in Early Stuart England, 1603–1645* (Leiden: 2009).

Milton John, *Of Education* (London, for Thomas Underhill: 1644).

Morgan Nicholas, *The Perfection of Horse-manship* (London, Edward White: 1609) *of Education* (New York: 1986).

Roger Ascham, *The Scholemaster* (London, John Daye: 1570).

Sidney Sir Philip, *The Countess of Pembroke's Arcadia*, ed. Evans M. (London: 1977).

Tobey E., "The Legacy of Federigo Grisone", in Edwards – Enenkel – Graham (eds.), *The Horse as Cultural Icon: The Real and the Symbolic Horse in the Early Modern World* (Leiden: 2012).

Index

Absolutism   3, 32, 133, 135, 142, 145, 282, 284, 287, 297, 329
Adams, John   331, 351
Addyman, Tom   62, 166, 171
Adwalton Moor
    See Battles
Aerschot, Duke of   311
Alchemy   19, 107, 173
Alington House, London   48
Allegiances and alliances   71, 78, 81, 83–84, 99, 107, 151, 153, 202, 218, 228, 235, 237–238, 242 243, 305
    impolitic or strange   84, 305
    See also Diplomacy
Alpers, Svetlana   67
Ancestry   5–6, 166, 197, 227
    See also Breeding
Andrews, Francis   60
Andrewes, Lancelot   132
Anglicanism   57, 238
Animals
    partnership   269, 318, 324, 329
    rationality   174, 208, 342–344
    rule and hierarchy   31–32, 118, 127, 131, 134, 208, 268–269, 282, 284–292, 297, 304, 318
    zōon politikon   284
    See also Horses, Horsemanship
Anne, Queen Consort of England   64
Anthropocentrism   318, 328–329
Anthropomorphism   130
Antwerp   11, 12, 13, 14, 16, 31, 98–99, 166, 205, 207, 237–239, 243, 244, 247–255, 301, 308, 311, 314–315
    diplomacy and politics   31, 99, 247–249
    financial market and trade   153, 248–249, 314
    manège and riding school   205, 208n, 250n, 332, 344
    publishing   137
Anzilotti, Gloria   251
Apotheosis   102–4
Armour and weaponry   18, 97, 101, 141–142, 144n, 151, 187, 225–226
    See also Swordsmanship

Archimedes   184n, 187
Ariosto, Ludovico   70
Army Plot (1641)   11
Architecture   11, 14, 17, 26, 36, 41–59, 59–60, 69, 91–92, 102, 134, 151–172, 344
Aristocracy   3–6, 18–19, 21–29, 32–34, 70, 78, 111–116, 128, 151, 163, 180–181, 197, 207, 237, 303–4, 332–336, 345–347
    beliefs and identity   18, 21, 29–34, 70, 78, 105, 111, 115, 151, 181, 176n, 180–181, 237, 265
    desirable characteristics   18, 32, 151, 181, 278, 310, 336
    duties and obligations   4, 24, 26, 33, 171, 219, 237
    political and economic power   2–3, 21, 32, 137, 338
    social structure and activity   4–5, 21, 24, 27, 111, 163, 207
    writing and publishing   18–20, 35, 98, 111, 116, 128, 332
    See also Patronage
Aristotle   196, 284
Arscot, Duke of   332
Arundel House, London   48
Arundel, Earl of
    See Howard
Ascham, Roger   333n
Ashby, Thomas   58
Ashley, Sir Anthony   166n
Astley, John   333, 335
Astley, Philip   348n, 349–351
Atomism   174, 203
Aubrey, John   163, 174n, 191
Audley End, Essex   159–160, 172
Autobiography   16, 20–21, 28, 140, 190
Authority   3–5, 21, 29–35, 87–88, 129–146, 196–200, 209–210, 250–251, 264–265, 277–278, 281–298, 310, 318–319, 323–324, 329, 344–345
Authorship   16–19, 26–29, 34–35, 116, 133, 186n, 208, 259–260, 331–350
    individual and collaborative   26, 34, 80–81, 100, 123, 332
    plagiarism   26, 117
    See also Publishing

Bacon, Francis   17, 49n
Banqueting House, Whitehall   49, 55, 65,
    99, 171
Barad, Karen   285
Baret, Michael   334
Baroque   12, 19, 99
Barratt John   85
Barton, Anne   77
Battles
    Adwalton Moor   89, 229–230
    Edgehill   229
    Gloucester   231
    Leeds (siege)   227–228, 230
    Lostwithiel   229
    Marston Moor   29–30, 83–108, 121, 168,
        200, 203, 206, 210, 232–235, 300, 314,
        325, 326
    Piercebridge   220, 235
    Seacroft Moor   220, 224, 227, 235
    Tadcaster   227, 235
    Worcester   243, 247, 255
Bedchamber and Chamber
    See Court
Bedingfield, Thomas   333n
Belasyse, Lord John   222, 232
Benavides, Don Luis de, Marquess of
    Caracena   249
Bennett, Alexandra   113, 116
Bennett, Jane   107
Berwick   165
Bishop, George   245–246
Bishops' Wars   224
Blackburne, Richard   191
Blackfriars   48–49
Blickling Hall, Norfolk   155, 157, 159, 172
Blundeville, Thomas   262, 266, 278, 313, 333,
    335–336, 341
Bolsover Castle, Derbyshire   11, 16, 21, 35–36,
    41, 42, 44, 45–59, 60, 61, 69, 73, 75, 76,
    79–80, 92–95, 99–100, 102–107, 121, 127,
    164, 165, 166, 168–173, 198, 227, 303
    building history (1617–1623)   45–51
    building history (1623–1628)   51–53
    building history (1629–1642)   53–58
    decoration and symbolism   58–59,
        60–61, 69, 93, 94, 95, 102, 106, 166, 171,
        198
    estimated expenditure at   41, 76

later additions   171–172
repurchase   303
riding school   118, 168, 172
theatrical performances   75–80, 92, 121,
    122, 127, 164
Bone, Quentin   80
Boothby, Elizabeth   54n
Boswell, Sir William   239
Bothal Castle, Northumberland   42, 55
Bourdieu, Pierre   334, 337–341, 347n, 351
    cultural capital   334, 339–340, 347–351
    habitus   338–339
Bouwnd, Nicholas   131n
Brackley, Lady
    See Cavendish, Elizabeth (1626–1663)
Brackley, Lord
    See Egerton, John
Bramhall, John, Bishop of Derry   204, 208,
    230
Brandenburg, Elector of   247
Breda   243, 255
Breeding   24, 32, 34, 106, 168, 182n, 264, 296,
    297, 306–308, 318–319, 322–329, 334,
    336–337, 46
    Degeneration   326–328
    See also Animals, Ancestry
Bridlington   220, 226
Brindley, John   268n, 180, 331n
Brome, Richard   145
Brown, Cedric C.   76, 79
Browne, Mary   96
Browne, William   334
Bruegel, Pieter   67
Bruges   31, 99, 249
Brussels   239, 240, 248, 252, 254
Buckingham, Duke of
    See Villiers, George
Bulkley, Stephen   221
Burley-on-the-Hill   152
Burroughs, Catherine   113, 117
Butler, James FitzThomas, Marquess of
    Ormond   244, 245, 248, 249, 254, 213

Cabbalism   19
Cadre Noir
    See Riding schools
Cambrai   239
Cambridge   7, 133, 290

Carey, Robert, 1st Earl of Monmouth   55n
Carpenter, Stanley   226–227
Carr-Howard marriage   66, 69, 70, 73
Cary, Elizabeth   126
Cassilis, Earl of   245
Castelli, Benedetto   177–179, 188, 191, 192
Castiglione, Baldessare   18, 309–310, 336
    grazia and *sprezzatura*   27, 151, 309
Castle Ashby   165
Catholicism   45, 57, 219, 222–223, 240–241,
    248
    Cavendish family   45, 241
Cavalier
    drinking games   112
    ideal of the   86
    politics   325
    See also Royalism
Cavendish, Sir Charles (1553–1617)   6, 11, 36,
    41, 42, 43, 44, 45, 49, 63, 69, 112
    death and memorial at Bolsover   36,
    41–42, 45
Cavendish, Sir Charles (1595?–1654)   6, 16,
    54n, 80, 173–175, 188, 203–204, 206,
    302–303
    mathematical and scientific connections
    6, 173, 175, 188, 203
Cavendish, Charles, Viscount Mansfield
    (1620–1659)   112, 301
Cavendish, Christian(a), Countess of
    Devonshire   77–78
Cavendish, Elizabeth (1527?–1608)
    See Hardwick, Elizabeth, Countess of
    Shrewsbury
Cavendish, Elizabeth (1599–1643)
    (née Bassett, previously Howard)   12, 47,
    76, 90
Cavendish, Elizabeth (1626–1663), Countess
    of Bridgewater   12, 26, 34n, 111, 116, 127
    writing (*The Concealed Fancies*)   35,
    111–128
Cavendish, Henry (1630–1691), 2nd Duke of
    Newcastle   112, 301
Cavendish, Jane (1566–1625)   49, 53
Cavendish, Jane (1622–1669), Lady Newhaven
    12, 26, 34, 34–35n, 89, 112–116, 123, 127,
    230, 302
    writing (*The Concealed Fancies*)   34–35,
    111–128

Cavendish, Katherine (née Ogle)   11, 42, 44,
    46, 49, 53
Cavendish, Margaret, Duchess of Newcastle
    1–2, 5, 11, 12, 14–16, 17–28, 30, 33–34, 37,
    41, 62, 69, 89, 90–91, 93–96, 98, 100, 108,
    113, 117, 122, 132–147, 174, 196, 200, 202,
    205–207, 213–215, 221, 229, 230, 232,
    237–238, 241–245, 249–252, 300–303,
    306–308, 311, 315, 327
    biographical summary   14–16
    collaboration with William Cavendish
    332n
    commitment to publication   18–19, 133
    courtship and marriage   16, 90–96, 241,
    301
    critical rediscovery and reputation
    14–15n, 16
    eccentricity   2, 113, 196, 206–207
    encounters with Thomas Hobbes   30,
    206–207
    life in exile   252–255
    on the character of William Cavendish
    200–201
    on authority and patriarchy   132–145
    partiality as biographer   76, 229, 237–238,
    302
    rhetorical devices and modes in writing
    16, 17, 20, 24, 27
    role in *The Concealed Fancies*   113
    selfhood in writing   17, 27–28
    Works:
        Bell In Campo   141
        The Blazing World   144, 145
        The Lady Contemplation   140–141
        Life of William Cavendish   20–22, 24,
        89, 196, 200–201, 213, 215, 237, 249,
        315
        The Matrimoniall Agreement   142
        The Matrimoniall Trouble   143
        *Nature's Daughters, Beauty, Love and
        Wit*   137, 139
        Nature's Pictures   62, 96, 144
        *Observations upon Experimental
        Philosophy*   133, 214
        Orations of Divers Sorts   134
        *Philosophical and Physical
        Opinions*   129, 133 194, 206
        Playes   26, 136–139

Cavendish, Margaret, Duchess of Newcastle
(cont.)

Poems and Fancies   16, 59n, 140
The Several Wits   135
Sociable Letters   134–135, 139, 142, 145
The Unnatural Tragedy   122
The World's Olio   16, 17, 62, 133, 143,
205–206
Cavendish, Mary (1557–1632)   41, 51, 64
Cavendish, Sir William (1508–1557)   6
Cavendish, Sir William, Viscount Mansfield
(1620) and 1st Duke of Newcastle (1628)
Passim
La Méthode Nouvelle/ A New and
Extraordinary Method/A General
System of Horsemanship   5, 7, 13, 27,
31–33, 47n, 51n–59n, 99–107, 137, 170,
186n, 208–214, 259–280, 286–296, 301,
320, 331–350.
The Variety, later The French Dancing
Master   71, 75, 77, 80–81, 117, 124, 136
Witts Triumvirate   26, 107
Cavendish, William, 1st Earl of Devonshire
(1551–1626)   6, 44
Cavendish, William, 2nd Earl of Devonshire
(1590–1628)   53, 201
Cavendish, William, 3rd Earl of Devonshire
(1617–1684)   13, 191–192, 201
Cavendish Harley, Henrietta, Countess of
Oxford   37, 81
Cavendish circle   6, 20
Cavendish family   1–2, 5, 6, 12, 15, 22, 26–27,
29, 35, 41–42, 67–68, 114–117, 122,
127–128, 140n, 206, 241, 307, 318
background and connections   6–7, 35
compared to Herbert and Sidney families
12, 116
Cavendish sisters
See Cavendish, Jane (1622–1669) and
Cavendish, Elizabeth (1626–1663)
Cecil, Robert, 1st Earl of Salisbury, Viscount
Cranborne   165
Cecil, William, 1st Baron Burghley (1520–1598)
333n
Cecil, William, 2nd Earl of Salisbury
(1591–1668)   320
Cecil, William, 2nd Earl of Exeter, Lord
Burghley   305

Centaurs   32–33, 34, 102, 104–107, 129, 131,
140, 269, 281–298, 305, 313, 329, 335, 344
Cerasano, Susan   116, 117
Cerralvo, Marquis of   332
Cervantes, Miguel de   61, 67
Chancery   10, 210
Charles I   1, 9, 13, 30, 36, 42, 48, 51–57, 63–64,
71, 75–76, 79, 84, 86, 88, 92, 99, 107, 111,
123, 163, 165, 198, 200, 203, 205, 216–226,
228, 230–235, 238, 240, 241, 243, 245,
249, 253, 295, 300, 302, 303, 304, 306,
320
defeat and execution   30, 84, 88, 205, 247,
295, 300
piety   57, 254
royal visits and entertainments   36, 42,
48, 52–55, 58, 63–64, 71, 75–77, 79, 92,
94, 107, 164, 171, 198, 303
Charles II   1, 8, 9, 14, 20, 29, 31, 42, 55, 58, 75,
76, 84, 130, 131, 135, 173, 186, 198, 205,
207, 213–214, 224, 238, 241, 242, 244,
249–255, 293–294, 296, 303, 312–314,
317, 319, 321, 322, 344
advised or governed by William
Cavendish   8, 9, 20, 55, 130, 135, 173,
202, 207, 214, 228, 244, 250, 293–294, 301
honours given to or withheld from
William Cavendish   198, 214, 313
horsemanship   135, 209, 293, 296, 344
opinion of William Cavendish   213, 252
Charles IV, Duke of Lorraine   239–240
Charles Emmanuel, Duke of Savoy   9
Chatsworth House   78
Chemistry   173
Cheyne, Charles, 1st Viscount of Newhaven
34, 115
Cheyne, Lady Jane
See Cavendish, Jane (1622–1669)
Chivalry   37, 60, 65–66, 76–77, 79, 81, 171,
196–197, 227, 296
Order of the Bath   9, 37, 62, 64, 84, 164
Order of the Garter   180, 243, 253
Cholmley, Sir Hugh   222, 227, 234–235, 245
Christina, Queen of Sweden   209, 250
Civil Wars   1, 3, 5, 9, 10, 13, 15, 22, 29, 58, 71,
80, 83–89, 100, 111, 112, 140, 176, 196, 200,
210, 216–236, 240, 242, 295, 303, 325, 345
See also Battles

Clarendon, Earl of
  See Hyde, Edward
Cleopatra 116–117, 127
Classical figures
  Andromeda 138
  Anteros 73
  Apollo 59
  Bellerophon 59, 107, 290
  Chimera 107
  Cupid 70, 72, 73
  Cyclops 50, 57
  Eros 73, 80
  Hercules 46, 49, 171
  Hymen 73
  Medusa 106
  Pegasus 59, 102, 102–104, 106, 107, 135, 137, 138, 290–291
  Poseidon 106
  Venus 59, 73, 105–106
  Vulcan 49–50, 57, 59
  See also Centaurs
Clouvet, Petr 100, 313
Coaches and coach-houses 5, 31, 36, 50, 151, 153, 159–161, 163, 165, 171–172, 294, 304, 306-7
  See also Equestrian buildings
Colchester, Essex 15
Colepepper, John 242
Collaboration 26, 45, 57, 100, 123, 161, 332
Collecting 4n, 12, 16–17, 21, 35, 99
  See also connoisseurship
Compton, William, 1st Earl of Northampton 165
Conan Mériadec 6
Condé, Prince Louis of 249, 312, 332
Connoisseurship 4n, 16–17, 18–19, 42, 58, 307, 348
Cornwallis, Lady 228
Corte, Claudio 333n
Cottington, Francis 245
Court 3–4, 7n, 9–11, 13n, 21, 29, 30–31, 33, 35, 47, 60, 64, 71, 74, 80–81, 83–84, 88, 90–91, 96, 99, 117, 137, 142, 151, 163–164, 197, 202–203, 205–207, 213–215, 226, 228, 233–234, 239n, 240–241, 245, 248-9, 253, 255, 279, 293–294, 301, 303–304, 333, 336

courtly values and ideals 18–19, 27, 30–31, 73, 79, 81, 137, 151n, 197, 206, 309–310, 336–337
Stuart court in exile 3, 13, 16, 30, 90–91, 96, 99, 200, 205, 207, 240–241, 245, 248–249, 253
  See also Monarchy
Covenants 283–298
Cranborne, Viscount
  See Cecil, Robert
de Critz, John 161
Crofts, William 307
Cromwell, Oliver 85–86, 205, 243, 246
Cuddy, Neil 10n
Cust, Richard 197

Daniel, Samuel 117n
Davenant, William 242
De Caus, Isaac 161
Derby 36, 54
de Rohan family 3, 6, 14
Derrida, Jacques 283–285
Descartes, René 13, 174–175, 179, 203–204, 344
  Cartesian dualism 209, 283, 286
Determinism and free will debate 204, 208
Devereux, Robert, 3rd Earl of Essex 66, 164, 232
Devonshire, Earl of
  See Cavendish
Dewald, Jonathan 3, 6
Dewhurst, Madeleine 205, 207
Digby, George, 2nd Earl of Bristol 240, 253, 255, 312
Digby, Sir Kenelm 19
Diplomacy 9, 99, 238–239, 247, 249
  See also Allegiances and alliances
Dorset, Earl of
  See Sackville, Richard
Dressage 81, 127, 319–320, 329, 345, 351
  See also Horses, Horsemanship, Manège
Drury, Paul 152–153
Dudley, Robert, 1st Earl of Leicester 55n, 76, 81
Dunster Castle, Somerset 155–156
Durham House, London 63

Edgehill
    See Battles
Editing   313, 320, 331
Edwards, Peter   214, 220
Edwards, Philip   131
Egerton, Elizabeth, Lady Brackley, Countess
    of Bridgewater
    See Cavendish, Elizabeth
Egerton, John, Lord Blackley, 2nd Earl of
    Bridgewater   116
Egerton, Lady Alice   116
Eliot, T. S. (*The Waste Land*)   81
Elites   2–5, 19, 29, 31, 45, 151–2, 219, 223,
    238, 260, 278–279, 290, 297, 300–301,
    304–306, 309, 313, 332
    horsemanship as elite practice   31, 151,
        260, 278, 290, 300, 304–305, 313, 323, 332
    ideal characteristics   309
    pastimes   31
    power and privilege   3–4
    See also Aristocracy
Elizabeth I   55n, 63, 79, 124n, 153, 163, 293
Equestrian buildings   36, 51–52, 151–172, 249,
    268, 305–306
    See also Coaches and coach-houses
Equine behaviour and training   130, 178,
    261–262, 264–268
    See also Horses, Horsemanship, Riding
    Schools
Erbury, William   131–132
Essex, Earl of
    See Devereux, Robert
Estates   3–5, 11, 14, 16, 22, 24, 31, 41, 50, 60,
    68–69, 99–100, 152–153, 166, 206, 219,
    224, 302–303, 314, 338
Euclid   187
Evelyn, John   96, 105, 310
Everett, Sir Harry   322
Exeter, Earl of
    See Cecil, William
Exile   5, 13–14, 16, 29–31, 87–108, 174n,
    203–209, 237–238, 247–248, 252–255,
    279, 300–304, 314–315, 331–332, 345
Ezell, Margaret   114, 115, 124
Exchequer   10
*Expresse Relation of the Passages and
    Proceedings of His Majesties Armie, An*
    229–230

Falkland Palace, Fife   55
Fairfax, Thomas, 1st Lord Fairfax (1560–1640)
    306, 325–326
Fairfax, Thomas, 3rd Lord Fairfax (1612–1671)
    32, 217, 218, 220, 223, 224, 227–235, 323,
    325–329
    debate on horses between Fairfaxes and
        Cavendish   323–329
    military rivalry between Fairfaxes and
        Cavendish   222–235
Fairfax, Ferdinando, 2nd Lord Fairfax
    222–235
Fencing   173n, 178, 179, 182, 187, 200, 344
    See also Swordsmanship
Fiaschi, Cesare   260, 344
Findlay, Alison   112, 114, 122, 124
Fielding, Colonel Richard   83
Firearms
    See Armour and Weaponry
Firth, Sir Charles   217, 230
FitzWilliam, Colonel John   241
Flanders   67, 249, 336
Fletcher, John   120, 127
Fonthill House, Wiltshire   336
Ford, John   122
Foster, Sir Richard   243
Francart, Jacques   52–53
France   6, 13, 14, 16, 67, 84, 88, 112, 191, 203,
    253, 305, 310, 312, 344, 347
Frederick III, King of Denmark and Sweden
    247
Frederik Hendrik   244
    See also Orange, House of
Fudge, Erica   342n
Furgol, Edward   232

Galileo   184–192
Game, Ann   286–287
Gardiner, Samuel Rawson   230
Gassendi, Pierre   13, 174, 203–204
Gayton, Edmund   67
Geohumoralism   32, 324–326
George II, Landgrave of Hesse-Darmstadt
    249, 332
Gender   34, 72, 123, 132, 134, 136–137, 197,
    285, 296
Gentles, Ian   231
Glemham, Sir Thomas   235

Gloucester, Duke of
    See Henry Frederick, Prince of Wales
Goff, Dr Stephen   249
Goodrich, Matthew   161
Goring, Sir George   221, 227, 228
Gothic architecture   37, 46, 60, 81
Governance
    See Authority
Graham, Elspeth   332
Graham, James, 1st Marquess of Montrose
    244–245, 247
Grant, Douglas   80, 98
Greenblatt, Stephen   279
Gresham, Sir Thomas   153
Grey, Charles, 7th Earl of Kent, Lord Ruthyn
    48
Grey, Elizabeth, Countess of Kent   112
Grisone, Federico or Federigo   260–262, 269,
    278, 310
Guérinière, François Robichon de la   261,
    347
Guise, Duke of   249, 333

Haesdonck, Jan van   220
Hague, The   99, 218, 239, 243, 248, 251
Hamburg   13, 88, 234, 239, 300, 301, 314
Hamilton, James, 1st Duke of Hamilton   11n,
    54, 243
Hamilton, William, 3rd Earl of Lanark
    242
Hanson, Craig Ashley   17–18
Haraway, Donna   286
Hardwick, Elizabeth, Countess of Shrewsbury
    6, 11, 42, 43, 52
Hardwick House   36, 60n, 77, 116, 196
Harleian collection   78, 185–186
Harmony, human-animal   102, 103, 137–138,
    142, 273n, 287, 289n, 305, 315, 335
    discord   98
    music of the spheres   137
Härting, Ursula   247
Hatfield House   165
Hatton, Christopher, 1st Lord Hatton   243
Hawking   31, 138, 304
Heal, Felicity   5
Henri IV, King of France   164, 301
Henrietta Maria, Queen Consort   13, 16, 30,
    36, 57, 71, 75, 76, 79, 80, 84, 88, 90–92,

94, 96n, 107, 111, 117, 205, 218–220,
    224–228, 239–242, 245, 249, 254, 302,
    306
catholicism   57
court in exile   16, 84, 88, 90, 242, 245, 249
disapproval of Cavendish-Lucas courtship
    16, 91, 241
distrust of Thomas Hobbes   205
relationship with William Cavendish   80,
    241–242, 254
theatrical entertainments   36, 57, 71,
    75–79, 92, 94, 107, 117
Henry Frederick, Prince of Wales   8–9, 13,
    37, 44, 52, 55n, 62–65, 84, 164, 166,
    309
    chivalry and medievalism   9, 37, 62–65,
        81, 84
Henry VIII   333
Heraldry   5, 43n, 44, 46, 47, 137, 180
Herbert, Mary
    See Sidney Herbert, Mary
Herbert, Philip, 4th Earl of Pembroke   305,
    320
Herbert, William, 3rd Earl of Pembroke   49,
    117
Hierarchy   4–5, 10, 21, 27, 34, 134–137, 141,
    197–200, 201, 282–295
    See also Aristocracy, Absolutism
Hobart, Sir Henry   155
Hobbes, Thomas   12, 13, 27, 30, 33, 37, 94n,
    107, 173–194, 196–216, 259, 282–289, 292,
    295, 296, 298
    Elements of Law   33, 173, 194, 198–202,
        204
    Leviathan   193–194, 199–201, 205, 214–215,
        259, 282–286, 289, 292, 295
    on animals   37, 208–209, 215, 282,
        284–289, 298
    on honour   30, 33, 196–216
    on mathematics and science   37, 107,
        173–194
    on physiology and psychology   37, 107,
        177, 183, 189, 194, 199
    on swords   179–180, 182–183, 189
    political theory   33, 173, 198–200, 214–215,
        282–289, 292, 295–296, 298
    relationship with Margaret
        Cavendish   30, 206–207

Hobbes, Thomas (cont.)
  relationship with William Cavendish   30,
    33, 193–194, 200–205, 207–209,
    288–289, 292
Hoby, Sir Thomas   18n
Holland, Earl
  See Rich, Henry
Holland House   36, 159, 161–163, 172
Holmes, Clive   5
Honour   13, 19, 21, 28, 30, 33, 37, 89, 137,
    196–216, 223, 227, 234, 282, 292–293,
    295, 297–298, 302, 305, 314
  See also Chivalry
Hopton, Ralph, Baron Hopton   243, 245
Horses   5, 24, 30, 31–34, 36, 37, 52–53, 79, 81,
    97, 99, 100–106, 118, 126, 127, 129–146,
    151–172, 175–176, 178–182, 188, 200,
    207–213, 215, 250, 257–351 *passim*
  great horse   127, 151–152, 161, 181, 292, 307,
    309, 310, 314, 334
  images and symbolism   5, 31, 97, 100–106,
    118, 126–127, 130–135, 144, 145, 210–212,
    270, 272, 274, 276, 290–292, 304, 313
  racing   32, 135, 304, 317–329, 334
  stabling and treatment   36, 52–53, 118,
    130, 134, 142, 151–172, 249–250, 260–261
    304–306, 288n
  value and exchange as gifts   133, 151–152,
    210, 304–308, 325–326, 333
  See also Centaurs, Equestrian buildings,
    Equine behaviour and training,
    Manège
Horsemanship   9, 11, 13, 14, 17, 18, 19, 31–34,
    58, 62–63, 79, 81, 84, 91, 99–103, 106–108,
    129–146, 163–166, 168, 175–176, 200,
    207–213, 217, 252, 257–351 *passim*
  and gender authority   34, 126–127,
    129–146, 284
  and political or cultural authority   18–19,
    31–34, 102, 129–146, 209–213, 259–261,
    264–265, 278–280, 281–298, 300,
    304–305, 309–310, 315, 318–319,
    322–323, 328–329, 331–351
  chivalric   62–63, 79, 81, 292–293, 296, 335
  military   18, 100–101, 140, 144, 151, 163, 229,
    260, 262–264, 296–297, 306, 310, 333
  of William Cavendish   9, 11, 13, 17, 31,
    52, 58, 62, 79, 81, 84, 91, 99–100, 102,

    106–108, 129–130, 163–166, 172, 175–176,
    200, 217, 229, 249–250, 257–351 *passim*
Hotham, John, and Hotham family   225–
    228, 231
House of Commons, House of Lords
  See Parliament
Houses
  See Alington House, Arundel House,
    Audley End, Blickling Hall, Bolsover,
    Bothal, Castle Ashby, Chatsworth,
    Dunster Castle, Durham House,
    Falkland, Fonthill, Hardwick, Hatfield,
    Holland House, Kenilworth, Longleat,
    Ludlow Castle, Newcastle House,
    New Place, Northampton House,
    Nottingham Castle, Osterley Park,
    Owlcotes, Pendennis, Penshurst,
    Peover Hall, Petworth, Renishaw
    Hall, Rufford Abbey, Shapwick,
    Sheffield Manor, Somerset House,
    Stirling Castle, Syon House, Welbeck,
    Whitmore Hall, Wilton, Wimborne St
    Giles, Wollaton Hall, Worksop Manor
Households   4–5, 12–13, 20–27, 69, 84, 112,
    116, 122, 141–142, 172, 205, 241
Howard, Aletheia, Lady Arundel   49n
Howard, Elizabeth
  See Cavendish, Elizabeth (1599–1643)
    (née Bassett, previously Howard)
Howard, Frances   66, 71n
  See also Carr-Howard marriage
Howard, Henry (1592–1616)   12, 47, 90
Howard, Henry, Earl of Northampton
    (1540–1616)   47
Howard, Thomas, 1st Earl of Suffolk   12, 159
Howard, Thomas, 14th Earl of Arundel   49
Howard, Sir Cecil   251
Huizinga, Johan   69
Hull   225–228, 231, 235, 245
Hulse, Lynn   75
Humanism   197, 333
Humoralism   92–94, 105, 121
  See also Geohumoralism
Hunting   4, 31, 43, 127, 163, 304, 308, 309, 319,
    320, 322, 325, 334
Huntley, Stuart   183
Hutchinson, Colonel John   231–232
Hutchinson, Lucy   76, 219

Hutton, Ronald   238
Hyde, Edward, 1st Earl of Clarendon   29, 30,
    83, 87–88, 90n, 176 198, 200, 205, 206,
    210–211, 213, 216–217, 218, 225, 237, 238,
    243–245, 248, 250, 252, 254, 302
    criticism of William Cavendish   29, 30,
        87–88, 90n, 176, 198, 216–217, 237, 238,
        243–245, 302

Identity   4–5, 16–18, 21–24, 26–29, 30, 34, 41,
    83–108, 111—127, 237–238, 279–280, 304,
    314–315, 318–319, 329, 331–332
Illiteracy   31
Interregnum   1, 76, 206, 238, 320
Intertextuality   17, 27–28, 35, 120–125
Ireland   73–75, 235, 240, 244–245, 322
Israel, Jonathan   244

James I   9, 10, 32, 42, 47, 48–49, 51, 52, 62–66,
    73–77, 79, 99, 164, 296, 320
James II   312
Jermyn, Henry, Earl of St Albans   96n, 240,
    242
Johnson, David   235
Jones, Inigo   45, 48, 49, 52, 53n, 57, 65, 79, 99,
    159, 161–162, 171
Jonson, Ben   12, 19, 36, 42n, 45–49, 53–57,
    65–67, 69–81, 92–95, 100, 102, 106–107,
    125–126, 174n, 185, 187, 198, 227
    masques at Bolsover and Welbeck   36,
        54–57, 71, 75–80, 92–93, 94–95, 100, 198
Juan José of Austria   209, 253
Jousting   31, 62, 164, 292–293, 296, 298
    See also Chivalry

Karl Eusebius, Prince of Liechenstein   32
Keay, Anna   254n
Keirinex, Alexander   12
Kenilworth Castle, Warwickshire   55, 76
van de Kerckhoven, Jehan Polyander   239
Kerr, William, Earl of Lothian   246–247, 255
Killigrew, Thomas   26n
Kinaesthesis   33, 286–287
King, James, Lord Eythin   235
Kirkby   43–44
Kitson, Elizabeth, Lady Kitson   54n
Knight of the Bath, Knight of the Garter
    See Chivalry

Knight, Lucy   117n
Knowles, James   79, 253–254

Landowners
    See Aristocracy
Langdale, Sir Marmaduke   219, 231, 235
Laud, William, Archbishop of Canterbury
    52n
Law   3, 20, 32, 132, 143, 210, 224, 240, 289–290,
    295, 343
Lawrence, David   334
Ledston   54
LeGuin, Elisabeth   273n, 289
Leicester, Earl of
    See Dudley, Robart
Lennox, Duke of   51, 52n
Leslie, Alexander, Earl of Leven   232
Lincoln   231
Lindley, David   71n, 72n
Lineage
    See Ancestry
Littleton, Adam   116
London   12, 14, 15, 30, 36, 44, 45, 47, 48, 58,
    64, 99, 123, 164, 165, 171, 206, 222, 251,
    254n, 261, 287, 326, 343
    Cavendish property in (Newcastle House)
        11, 36, 57, 58, 165, 171
Longleat House   36
Lostwithiel
    See Battles
Love
    conventions   35, 79–80, 91, 94–95,
        323–324
    in animals   129–133, 288–290, 294–295,
        323–324
    literary writing   35, 67, 70–72, 79–80,
        90–98, 104, 107–108, 121–122
Loyalism and loyalty   1–2, 9, 21, 37, 89, 200,
    213, 217, 218, 233, 238, 245, 255
Ludlow Castle   165
Lukin, Henry   45n
Lucas, Margaret
    See Cavendish, Margaret
Lucas family   15, 91

MacDonnell, Randal, Marquis of Antrim
    240
Machiavelli, Niccolò   198, 244

Maclean, James 244
Malory, Thomas 62
Manège 8, 18, 31–34, 99–102, 129–137, 142–145, 151, 163–165, 168, 176–178, 180–181, 208–209, 264, 281n, 288, 293–298, 301, 304–315, 319, 325, 332–351
See also Horsemanship
Mannerism 55–56, 166, 172
Mansfield 43, 54
Mansfield, Viscount
See Cavendish
Manuscript culture 15, 18–19, 24, 79, 96, 98n, 185–186, 332–333
Markham, Gervase 123, 309, 319, 333–334, 341
Marriage 5, 32, 35, 78, 90, 96, 111–113, 115, 118, 120–122, 125–127, 132, 139–145
de Marsin, Jean Gaspard-Ferdinand, Comte de Graville 253
Marston Moor
See Battles
Mary, Queen of Scots 63, 124
Masculinity 33, 72, 141–142, 151n, 261–262, 281, 292–294, 310
See also Gender
Masques 26, 36, 45, 48, 57, 54–57, 59, 65, 69–80, 92–93, 94–95, 100, 198, 293
Masten, Jeffrey 26
Master of the Horse 11, 36, 51, 54, 75–76, 164, 209, 303
Mathematics 45n, 58, 174–175, 178–179, 182, 187–188, 194, 201, 203–204, 205, 208
Mazin, Captain John 25, 27, 36, 168, 172, 271–275, 300, 311–312, 332, 344, 346–347
Mechanical philosophy 176–194, 283
Mechelen 239
Medievalism 19, 60–65, 80–81, 171, 196, 343
Menou, Rene 260
Mersenne, Marin 94n, 179, 184n, 188, 190, 191, 193, 203
Metamorphosis 129
Micanzio, Fulgenzio 192
Middleton, Richard 131
Middleton, Thomas (*The Changeling*) 121
Milton, John 116, 342–343
Monarchy 3–4, 8–11, 14, 22, 33, 36, 83–84, 198, 237–238, 282, 293–296, 318–319, 323, 329
See also Aristocracy, Court

Moncke, George, 1st Duke of Albemarle 11n
Monckton, Sir Philip 234
Monmouth, Lord
See Carey, Robert
Montrose, Marquess of
See Graham, James
Moray, Sir Robert 251
Morgan, Nicholas 263, 297, 336–337, 338, 342n, 343
Motion, theories of 37, 107, 176–194, 201, 283, 335, 338–339
de Moura y Corte-Real, Manuel, Marquis of Castel-Rodrigo 239
Munster 224
Murray, William, 1st Earl of Dysart 250–251
Mydorge, Claude 193

Naples School
See Riding schools
Natural philosophy
See science
Nedham, Marchamont 247
Neoclassicism 92
Neoplatonism 30, 91, 94–95, 97, 100, 102, 104, 107
Netherlands
See Spanish Netherlands
New Place, Stratford-upon-Avon 117
Newark 226
Newcastle, Duke and Duchess of
See Cavendish
Newcastle House 11, 57
Newcastle, horses named after 305
Newcastle's Lambs 124
Newcastle-upon-Tyne 124, 225
Newhaven, Viscount
See Cheyne, Charles
Newman, Peter 85, 216
Newmarket 165, 317, 319, 320
Nicholas, Sir Edward 30, 205, 206, 210, 225, 243, 248, 251, 252
Nobility
See Aristocracy
Norbrook, David 249
Northampton, Earl of
See Howard, Henry
See Compton, William
Northampton House, London 48

Northern Army 13, 29, 84, 218, 300
Nottingham Castle 11, 57n, 171, 231
Nun Appleton 325

Ogle, Jane, Countess of Shrewsbury
    See Cavendish, Jane (1566–1625)
Ogle, Utricia 239n
Olbricht, Erika Mae 141
Oldenburg, Duke of 249, 307
Optics 173, 175, 183–184, 186, 193
Orange, House of 239, 244, 253
Ormond, Marquess of
    See Butler, James
Osborne, Dorothy 71
Osborne, Toby 238
Osterley Park, Middlesex 152–155, 159, 172
Oxford 15, 88, 218, 220, 225, 228, 229, 230
Oxford, Earl of
    See Vere, Aubrey de
Owlcotes 44

Padua 14, 42, 46, 52n, 184, 185, 186n
Page, Sir Richard, and Lady Page 250–251
Paris 88, 90, 99, 174, 191, 192, 193, 200, 203,
    204, 206, 240, 241, 248, 251, 261, 306,
    307, 310, 311, 314
Parliament 3–4, 42n, 49, 65, 66, 73–74, 202,
    234, 235–236, 295, 303
Parliamentarians 29, 32, 75, 85, 86, 93,
    216–232, 240, 245, 247, 252, 295,
    302–303
Patronage 3–4, 7n, 11–14, 16–17, 21, 27, 36,
    37, 41, 43–44, 52, 57–58, 83–84, 94–95,
    116, 163, 172, 173–179, 194, 196, 201–205,
    209, 216, 227, 242, 249, 253, 280, 322,
    326
    cultural 4, 12–14, 16–17, 36, 37, 41, 43–44,
        84, 94–95, 116, 172, 201, 249, 253
    political 11, 21, 41, 83, 163, 202, 216, 227,
        242, 326
    scientific 173–179, 194, 196, 203
Payne, Robert 12, 27, 172, 177–182, 188–194,
    201, 266
Peacham, Henry 17–18
Peats, Richard 152
Pell, John 175n
Pembroke, Countess of
    See Sidney Herbert, Mary

Pembroke, Earl of
    See Herbert
Pendennis Castle, Cornwall 127
Penshurst Place 12n
Peover Hall, Cheshire 155, 159
Pepys, Samuel 113, 196, 214
Percy, Henry, 9th Earl of Northumberland
    165
Performativity 31, 94, 101, 285–287, 318–319,
    329
Peronne, France 239
Petworth House, Sussex 152, 165
Piccolomini, Octavio 239
Piercebridge
    See Battles
Pignatelli, GianBattista 260, 344
Plays
    See Masques, Theatre
Pluvinel, Antoine 260, 262, 275, 310, 313,
    337–339, 344
Poetry 12, 16–17, 19, 26, 34n, 60, 69, 79n, 80,
    84, 88, 90–93, 96–98, 106, 133, 193, 200,
    201, 217, 242, 247, 254
Politics
    See Court, Monarchy, Aristocracy,
        Parliament, Royalism
Pontefract 54, 226, 228
Power
    See Authority
Presbyterianism 205, 245
Print culture
    See Publishing
Privy Council 3–4, 10, 31, 198, 202, 217, 238,
    243, 250, 255
Property
    See Estates
Prophécies de Merlin, Les 65
Publicity 30–31, 33, 84, 88, 99, 33, 313
Publishing 14–15, 18–20, 27–28, 33–34, 57n,
    96, 133, 175, 259, 278–280, 332–334,
    340–351
Pugliano, Giovan Pietro 335
Puritanism 71, 77
Pym, John 218

Raber, Karen 186n, 282, 323
Racing
    See Horses, racing

Raylor, Timothy   27, 92, 93, 293
Readers and reading practices   5, 20–21, 33,
        34, 61–62, 67, 123–124, 130–132, 135n,
        180–181, 186n, 208, 213–214, 259–260,
        265, 268–273, 278, 292, 305, 309, 313,
        334, 339, 350
Reading, Berkshire   83
Rembrandt   68
Renishaw Hall, Derbyshire   56n, 59n
Republicanism   76, 282, 295–296
Reynolds, Neil   241
Rich, Henry, 1st earl of Holland   11n, 13, 36,
        159–165, 172, 203, 224–225
    rivalry with William Cavendish   13,
        164–165, 203, 224
Rich, Robert, 2nd Earl of Warwick   48
Richmond-upon-Thames   64, 165
Riding
    See Horsemanship
Riding Schools   36, 52, 137, 144, 165–172,
        261–266, 273, 275, 279, 309—310, 329,
        344–345, 351
    Antwerp   11, 133, 166, 249—250, 250n,
        311–312, 325, 332, 344
    Astley's   349–350
    Bolsover   36, 58, 58n, 118, 166–172
    Cadre Noir, Vienna   263n
    L'Academie d'Equitation   344
    Naples   260, 310, 336, 344
    Spanish Riding School, Vienna   261n,
        263n, 350
    Welbeck   36, 53, 166, 167–168, 171–2,
        344
    Wolfeton   166–171
    See also Equestrian buildings
Robinson, Gavin   234
Rolleston, John   20–27, 35n, 69, 89, 185
Roman Catholicism
    See Catholicism
Ross, Thomas   254
Rotherham, Yorkshire   228
Rothwell   224
Rotterdam   16, 239, 243, 302, 314
Rowley, William (*The Changeling*)   121
Royal Society   18, 175
Royalism   1–2, 6, 9, 15, 18–19, 29–30, 33,
        83–84, 86–89, 94, 107, 111–112, 115, 141,
        205, 216–219, 221–222, 231, 237–239,
        241, 244–245, 247, 253–255, 279, 282,
        301–303, 318, 323, 324, 329
    anti-royalism   247, 301
    historiography   1n
Rubens, Peter Paul   16, 98–100, 103, 205, 249,
        311, 313
Rubenshuis   11, 16, 98–100, 102, 208, 249,
        311–312, 315
Rufford Abbey   49n, 60n
Ruthyn, Lord
    See Grey, Charles
Rupert, Count Palatine of the Rhine and
        Duke of Cumberland   11n, 29, 84, 86–87,
        232–234, 245, 300, 303
Russell, Conrad   1, 19

Sackville, Richard, 5th Earl of Dorset   251n
Salisbury, Lord
    See Cecil
Sampson, William   123–124
Sarasohn, Lisa   174, 180
Satire   5, 35, 79, 107, 145
Scarborough   225, 227, 234, 245, 300
Schaffer, Simon   175
Science   6, 13–14, 16–19, 20n, 27, 29, 37, 94,
        173–194, 201, 203–205
Scot, Thomas   245
Scotland   13, 30, 42, 45, 53–55, 64, 76, 79n,
        203, 205, 221–222, 225, 232, 235, 238,
        242–245, 255
Scott, David   222, 235
Scottish Covenanters   164, 232, 235, 243–245
Scottish Engagers   30, 205
Scudéry, Madeleine de   61
Seacroft Moor
    See Battles
Secretary Nicholas
    See Nicholas, Sir Edward
Selby   227, 232
Sensation   173, 178, 183, 188, 190
Servants   4, 10, 21–27, 46, 60, 68, 69–70, 72,
        119, 134, 140n, 142, 250, 294–295, 300,
        307, 346–347
Shadwell, Thomas   61–62, 80, 94
Shakespeare, Susanna   117
Shakespeare, William   62, 117–123, 127,
        135–139, 196
Shapin, Steven   175

Shapwick Manor, Somerset   155, 158, 159
Sheffield   50n, 164n, 228
Sheffield Castle   63
Sheffield Manor   124
Sherwood Forest   43, 77
Shields Harbour   225
Shirley, James   12, 80–81, 122, 320, 332
Sidney, Sir Philip   12, 42, 61, 116, 334–336, 347
Sidney Herbert, Mary, Countess of Pembroke
      12n, 116–117, 126, 334
Skinner, Quentin   203
Skirton, Colonel   230
Slaughter, Thomas   207n, 252, 254, 292
Slingsby, North Yorkshire   54, 56n
Slingsby, Sir Henry   219, 226, 230
Smith, Emily   123
Smithson, Huntingdon   38
Smithson, John   36, 41–58, 105, 165, 168–169
Smithson, Robert   36, 43, 152
Somerset House, London   49n
Spain   138, 239–240, 249, 253, 306, 325, 336
Spanish Netherlands   31, 218, 220, 239–240,
      247–248, 253, 307, 308
Spenser, Edmund   61, 335–336, 347
Sport   11, 32, 317–322, 325–329, 341, 351
Spies   220, 239–240, 242, 249
sprezzatura
      See Castiglione, Baldessare
St Antoine, Monsieur de   164, 260, 301
Stables
      See Equestrian buildings
Stanhope, Lady Catherine   239
Stanton, Kamille Stone   112, 122
van Steenwyck, Hendrick   49, 53
Stirling Castle, Scotland   55
Stoppard, Tom   70
Strickland, Walter   218
Strong, Sir Roy   260n
Stuart, Lady Arbella   51
Stuart Ludovic, Duke of Richmond and
      Lennox, Earl of Newcastle   51n, 52n, 53
Stubbs, John   117
Suckling, Sir John   117
Swann, Marjorie   16–17
Swordsmanship   19, 24, 42, 65, 134–135, 137,
      140–142, 173, 179–182, 189
      See also Fencing
Syon House, Middlesex   165

Talbot, Elizabeth
      See Hardwick, Elizabeth
Talbot, George, 6th Earl of Shrewsbury   63,
      124
Talbot, Gilbert, 7th earl of Shrewsbury
      (1552–1616)   41, 43, 49, 63–65, 112
Talbot, Sir Gilbert (c. 1606–1695)   254
Talbot, Mary, Countess of Shrewsbury
      See Cavendish, Mary (1557–1632)
Talbot, Lady Mary (d. 1650)   117
Temple, William   61, 317n, 322
Theatre   26, 57, 69–81, 111–128, 253
      See also Masques
Theobalds, Hertfordshire   44n, 47, 50, 152
Thibault, Girard   187–188
Thirty Years' War   86
Thomas, Keith   6
Tobey, Elizabeth   336, 345
Trease, Geoffrey   60n, 63, 64, 198n
Tremamondo, Angelo   331
Tuck, Richard   175–176
Tucker, Treva   151n, 262n
Tyndale, Thomas   168
Tynemouth Castle   225

Underdown, David   245
Urry, Sir John   234

Valenciennes   239
van Diepenbeke, Abraham   27, 56, 59, 100,
      102–103, 106, 168–169, 171, 313
Van Dyck, Anthony   12, 19, 100, 117
Veaux, Monsieur de   310
Vere, Aubrey de, 20th Earl of Oxford   250
Vernon, John   262
vertu   18, 151n, 310
Vesey, Richard   161
Villiers, George, 1st Duke of Buckingham
      11n, 42, 47, 48, 49, 51, 52, 78, 320
Villiers, George, 2nd Duke of Buckingham
      243, 246, 248, 255
Virtuosity   4n, 16–19, 151, 292, 348–349
Voltaire   5n
von Gottstein, Count Johan Arndt   247

Walker, Elaine   130, 210, 291
Walton, Colonel Valentine   85n
Wanklyn, Malcolm   217, 229

Wars
   See Bishops' Wars, Civil Wars, Thirty Years'
     War
Warburton, Eliot   234
Ware, Isaac   159–162
Warren, Robin   123
Warner, Walter   173, 193
Warwick House
   See Alington House
Warwick, Sir Philip   88, 91, 217, 219, 231
Watson, Ned   250
Watts, John   249
Weapons
   See Armour and weaponry
Webbe, Joseph   184–186, 192
Webster, John (*The Duchess of Malfi*)   121
Welbeck Abbey, Nottinghamshire   11, 12,
     16, 27, 36, 41–49, 51–59, 60, 67–69, 71,
     75–81, 93, 99, 103, 107, 112–113, 127, 140n,
     164, 165–172, 173, 175, 177–178, 183–185,
     189–194, 198, 202, 303, 344
   building history   36, 41, 51–53, 165–171
   scientific venue   173, 175, 177–178, 183–185,
     189–194
   theatrical entertainments   36, 43n,
     48–49, 54–55, 58, 71, 75–79, 122–123,
     164, 198, 303
Wentworth, Thomas, 1st Earl of Strafford   11
Whately, William   134
Whitmore Hall, Staffordshire   155

White, Peggy   50
Whitecoats, the
   See Newcastle's Lambs
Whimsy   60–61, 66–69, 73, 77–79, 81
Widdrington, William, 1st Baron
   Widdrington   222
Wilmot, Henry, 1st Earl of Rochester
     243–249, 255
Wilton House   127
Wimborne St Giles   166n
Wolfeton
   See Riding Houses
Wollaton Hall, Nottinghamshire   36, 43, 152
Woodhouse, Adrian   166, 173n
Wood, Sir Henry   243
Worcester, Battle of
   See Battles
Worksop Manor, Nottinghamshire   41–42,
     49, 51, 52n, 54, 60n, 63–64
Worsley, Giles   152, 159
Worsley, Lucy   26, 62, 68, 77n, 93, 166, 171,
     174n, 314
Wotton, Sir Henry   9, 64, 67, 171
Wroth, Lady Mary   12n, 126
Wynne-Davies, Marion   112n, 116–117

York   85, 219–222, 225–226, 232, 234, 303, 319
Yorkshire Engagement, The   220
York, Duke of
   See James II